JACK

What I've learned leading a
great company and great people

Jack Welch

with John A. Byrne

HEADLINE

First published in 2001 by Warner Books Inc

First published in Great Britain in 2001
by HEADLINE BOOK PUBLISHING

10 9 8 7 6 5 4 3 2 1

British Library Cataloguing in Publication Data

Welch, Jack (John Francis), 1935–
    Jack: what I've learned leading a great
    company and great people
    1. Welch, Jack (John Francis), 1935–
    2. General Electric Company
    3. Chief executive officers – United States –
    Biography
    I. Title
    338.7′62138′0933′092

ISBN 0 7472 4935 0 (hb)
ISBN 0 7553 1043 8 (tpb)

Printed and bound in Great Britain by
Clays Ltd, St Ives plc

HEADLINE BOOK PUBLISHING
A division of Hodder Headline
338 Euston Road
London NW1 3BH

www.headline.co.uk
www.hodderheadline.com

To the hundreds of
thousands of GE employees
whose ideas and efforts
made this book possible

The author's profits from this book are being donated to charity.

Contents

Author's Note

This may seem a strange way to begin an autobiography. A confession: I hate having to use the first person. Nearly everything I've done in my life has been accomplished with other people. Yet when you write a book like this, you're forced to use the narrative "I" when it's really the "we" that counts.

I wanted to mention the names of all the people who took this journey with me. My editors kept beating me up, trying to get the names out. We finally struck a compromise. That's why the acknowledgments in the back of the book are somewhat long. Please remember that every time you see the word *I* in these pages, it refers to all those colleagues and friends and some I might have missed.

Prologue

I spent most of the Saturday morning after Thanksgiving 2000 waiting for the "New Guy." That was the secret code for my successor, the future chairman and CEO of General Electric.

On Friday night, the board had unanimously approved Jeff Immelt to succeed me. I called him right away.

"I have some good news. Can you and your family come to Florida tomorrow and spend the weekend?"

Obviously, he knew what was going on. But we left it at that and went quickly to the arrangements to get him to Florida.

On Saturday morning, I could hardly wait to see him. The long CEO succession process was over. I was already outside when Jeff pulled into my driveway. He had a big smile on his face and was barely out of the car before I had my arms around him, saying exactly what Reg Jones said to me 20 years earlier:

"Congratulations, Mr. Chairman!"

As we hugged, I felt we were closing the loop.

In that moment, my memories took me straight back to the day when Reg walked into my Fairfield, Connecticut, office and embraced me, in just the same way.

Bear hugs, or any hugs, were not natural gestures for Reg. Yet here he was with a smile on his face and his arms wrapped tightly around me. On that December day in 1980, I was the happiest man in America and certainly the luckiest. If I could pick a job in business, this one would be it. It gave me an unbelievable array of businesses, from aircraft engines and power generators to plastics, medical, and financial services. What GE makes and does touches virtually everyone.

Most important, it is a job that's close to 75 percent about people and 25 percent about other stuff. I worked with some of the smartest, most creative, and competitive people in the world—many a lot smarter than I was.

When I joined GE in 1960, my horizons were modest. As a 24-year-old junior engineer fresh from a Ph.D. program, I was getting paid $10,500 a year and wanted to make $30,000 by the time I was 30. That was my objective, if I had one. I was pouring everything I had into what I was doing and having a helluva good time doing it. The promotions started coming, enough of them to raise my sights so that by the mid-1970s I began to think that maybe I could run the place one day.

The odds were against me. Many of my peers regarded me as the round peg in a square hole, too different for GE. I was brutally honest and outspoken. I was impatient and, to many, abrasive. My behavior wasn't the norm, especially the frequent parties at local bars to celebrate business victories, large or small.

Fortunately, a lot of people at GE had the guts to like me. Reg Jones was one of them.

On the surface, we could not have been more different. Trim and dignified, he was born in Britain and had the bearing of a statesman. I had grown up just 16 miles north of Boston, in Salem, Massachusetts, the only son of an Irish American railroad conductor. Reg was reserved and formal. I was earthy, loud, and excitable, with a heavy Boston accent and an awkward stutter. At the time, Reg was the most admired businessman in America, an influential figure in Washington. I was unknown outside of GE, and inexperienced in policy issues.

Still, I always felt a vibration with Reg. He rarely revealed his feelings, never providing even a hint. Yet I had a feeling that he understood me. In some ways, we were kindred spirits. We respected each other's differences and shared some important things. We both liked analysis and numbers and did our homework. We both loved GE. He knew it had to change, and he thought I had the passion and the smarts to do it.

I'm not sure he knew how much I wanted GE to change—but his support for all I did over 20 years never wavered.

The competition to succeed Reg had been brutal, complicated by heavy politics and big egos, my own included. It was awful. At first, there were seven of us from various parts of the company who were put in the spotlight by the very public contest for Reg's job. He hadn't intended it to be the divisive and highly politicized process that it turned out to be.

I made a few mistakes in those years, none fatal. When Reg got the board to approve me as his successor on December 19, 1980, I still wasn't the most obvious choice. Not long after the announcement was made, one of my GE friends walked into the Hi-Ho, the local watering hole near headquarters, and overheard one of the oldtime staffers repeating glumly into a martini, "I'll give him two years—then it's Bellevue."

He missed by more than 20!

Over all the years that I was chairman, I received widespread attention in the media—both good and bad. But a lengthy cover story in *Business Week* magazine in early June 1998 prompted a flood of mail that inspired me to write this book.

Why? Because of the magazine article, literally hundreds of total strangers wrote me moving and inspirational letters about their careers. They described the organizational pressures they felt to change as individuals, to conform to something or become someone they weren't, in order to be successful. They liked the story's contention that I never changed who I was. The story implied that I was able to get one of the world's largest companies to come closer to acting like the crowd I grew up with.

Together with thousands of others, I tried to create the informality of a corner neighborhood grocery store in the soul of a big company.

The truth, of course, is more complex. In my early years, I tried desperately to be honest with myself, to fight the bureaucratic pomposity, even if it meant that I wouldn't succeed at GE. I also remember the tremendous pressure to be someone I wasn't. I sometimes played the game.

At one of my earliest board meetings in San Francisco shortly after being named vice chairman, I showed up in a perfectly pressed blue suit, with a starched white shirt and a crisp red tie. I chose my words carefully. I wanted to show the board members that I was older and more mature than either my 43 years or my reputation. I guess I wanted to look and act like a typical GE vice chairman.

Paul Austin, a longtime GE director and chairman of the Coca-Cola Co., came up to me at the cocktail party after the meeting.

"Jack," he said, touching my suit, "this isn't you. You looked a lot better when you were just being yourself."

Thank God Austin realized I was playing a role—and cared enough to tell me. Trying to be somebody I wasn't could have been a disaster for me.

Throughout my 41 years at GE, I've had many ups and downs. In the media, I've gone from prince to pig and back again. And I've been called many things.

In the early days, when I worked in our fledging plastics group, some called me a crazy, wild man. When I became CEO two decades ago, Wall Street asked, "Jack who?"

When I tried to make GE more competitive by cutting back our workforce in the early 1980s, the media dubbed me "Neutron Jack." When they learned we were focused on values and culture at GE, people asked if "Jack has gone soft." I've been No. 1 or No. 2 Jack, Services Jack, Global Jack, and, in more recent years, Six Sigma Jack and e-Business Jack.

When we made an effort to acquire Honeywell in October 2000, and I agreed to stay on through the transition, some thought of me as the Long-in-the-Tooth Jack hanging on by his fingertips to his CEO job.

Those characterizations said less about me and a lot more about the phases our company went through. Truth is, down deep, I've never really changed much from the boy my mother raised in Salem, Massachusetts.

When I started on this journey in 1981, standing before Wall Street analysts for the first time at New York's Pierre Hotel, I said I wanted GE to become "the most competitive enterprise on earth." My objective was to put a small-company spirit in a big-company body, to build an organization out of an old-line industrial company that would be more high-spirited, more adaptable, and more agile than companies that are one-fiftieth our size. I said then that I wanted to create a company "where people dare to try new things—where people feel assured in knowing that only the limits of their creativity and drive, their own standards of personal excellence, will be the ceiling on how far and how fast they move."

I've put my mind, my heart, and my gut into that journey every day of the 40-plus years I've been lucky enough to be a part of GE. This book is an effort to bring you along on that trip. In the end, I believe we created the greatest people factory in the world, a learning enterprise, with a boundaryless culture.

But you judge for yourself whether we ever reached the destination I described in my "vision" speech at the Pierre in 1981.

This is no perfect business story. I believe that business is a lot like a world-class restaurant. When you peek behind the kitchen doors, the food never looks as good as when it comes to your table on fine china perfectly garnished. Business is messy and chaotic. In our kitchen, I hope you'll find something that might be helpful to you in reaching your own dreams.

There's no gospel or management handbook here. There is a philosophy that came out of my journey. I stuck to some pretty basic ideas that worked for me, integrity being the biggest one. I've always believed in a simple and direct approach. This book attempts to show what an organization, and each of us, can learn from opening the mind to ideas from anywhere.

I've learned that mistakes can often be as good a teacher as success.

There is no straight line to anyone's vision or dream. I'm living proof of that. This is the story of a lucky man, an unscripted, uncorporate type who managed to stumble and still move forward, to survive and even thrive in one of the world's most celebrated corporations. Yet it's also a small-town American story. I've never stopped being aware of my roots even as my eyes opened to see a world I never knew existed.

Mostly, though, this is a story of what others have done—thousands of smart, self-confident, and energized employees who taught each other how to break the molds of the old industrial world and work toward a new hybrid of manufacturing, services, and technology.

Their efforts and their success are what have made my journey so rewarding. I was lucky to play a part because Reg Jones came into my office 21 years ago and gave me the hug of a lifetime.

EARLY YEARS

1

Building Self-Confidence

It was the final hockey game of a lousy season. We had won the first three games in my senior year at Salem High School, beating Danvers, Revere, and Marblehead, but had then lost the next half dozen games, five of them by a single goal. So we badly wanted to win this last one at the Lynn Arena against our archrival Beverly High. As co-captain of the team, the Salem Witches, I had scored a couple of goals, and we were feeling pretty good about our chances.

It was a good game, pushed into overtime at 2–2.

But very quickly, the other team scored and we lost again, for the seventh time in a row. In a fit of frustration, I flung my hockey stick across the ice of the arena, skated after it, and headed back to the locker room. The team was already there, taking off their skates and uniforms. All of a sudden, the door opened and my Irish mother strode in.

The place fell silent. Every eye was glued on this middle-aged woman in a floral-patterned dress as she walked across the floor, past the wooden benches where some of the guys were already changing. She went right for me, grabbing the top of my uniform.

"You punk!" she shouted in my face. "If you don't know how

to lose, you'll never know how to win. If you don't know this, you shouldn't be playing."

I was mortified—in front of my friends—but what she said never left me. The passion, the energy, the disappointment, and the love she demonstrated by pushing her way into that locker room was my mom. She was the most influential person in my life. Grace Welch taught me the value of competition, just as she taught me the pleasure of winning and the need to take defeat in stride.

If I have any leadership style, a way of getting the best out of people, I owe it to her. Tough and aggressive, warm and generous, she was a great judge of character. She always had opinions of the people she met. She could "smell a phony a mile away."

She was extremely compassionate and generous to friends. If a relative or neighbor visited the house and complimented her on the water glasses in the breakfront, she wouldn't hesitate to give them away.

On the other hand, if you crossed her, watch out. She could hold a grudge against anyone who betrayed her trust. I could just as easily be describing myself.

And many of my basic management beliefs—things like competing hard to win, facing reality, motivating people by alternately hugging and kicking them, setting stretch goals, and relentlessly following up on people to make sure things get done—can be traced to her as well. The insights she drilled into me never faded. She always insisted on facing the facts of a situation. One of her favorite expressions was "Don't kid yourself. That's the way it is."

"If you don't study," she often warned, "you'll be nothing. Absolutely nothing. There are no shortcuts. Don't kid yourself!"

Those are blunt, unyielding admonitions that ring in my head every day. Whenever I try to delude myself that a deal or business problem will miraculously improve, her words set me straight.

From my earliest years in school, she taught me the need to excel. She knew how to be tough with me, but also how to hug and kiss. She made sure I knew how wanted and loved I was. I'd come home with four As and a B on my report card, and my mother would want to know why I got the B. But she would always end the conversation congratulating and hugging me for the As.

She checked constantly to see if I did my homework, in much the same way that I continually follow up at work today. I can remember sitting in my upstairs bedroom, working away on the day's homework, only to hear her voice rising from the living room: "Have you done it yet? You better not come down until you've finished!"

But it was over the kitchen table, playing gin rummy with her, that I learned the fun and joy of competition. I remember racing across the street from the schoolyard for lunch when I was in the first grade, itching for the chance to play gin rummy with her. When she beat me, which was often, she'd put the winning cards on the table and shout, *"Gin!"* I'd get so mad, but I couldn't wait to come home again and get the chance to beat her.

That was probably the start of my competitiveness, on the baseball diamond, the hockey rink, the golf course, and business.

Perhaps the greatest single gift she gave me was self-confidence. It's what I've looked for and tried to build in every executive who has ever worked with me. Confidence gives you courage and extends your reach. It lets you take greater risks and achieve far more than you ever thought possible. Building self-confidence in others is a huge part of leadership. It comes from providing opportunities and challenges for people to do things they never imagined they could do—rewarding them after each success in every way possible.

My mother never managed people, but she knew all about building self-esteem. I grew up with a speech impediment, a stammer that wouldn't go away. Sometimes it led to comical, if not embarrassing, incidents. In college, I often ordered a tuna fish on white toast on Fridays when Catholics in those days couldn't eat meat. Inevitably, the waitress would return with not one but a pair of sandwiches, having heard my order as "tu-tuna sandwiches."

My mother served up the perfect excuse for my stuttering. "It's because you're so smart," she would tell me. "No one's tongue could keep up with a brain like yours." For years, in fact, I never worried about my stammer. I believed what she told me: that my mind worked faster than my mouth.

I didn't understand for many years just how much confidence she poured into me. Decades later, when looking at early pictures of me on my sports teams, I was amazed to see that almost always I was the shortest and smallest kid in the picture. In grade school, where I played guard on the basketball squad, I was almost three-quarters the size of several of the other players.

Yet I never knew it or felt it. Today, I look at those pictures and laugh at what a little shrimp I was. It's just ridiculous that I wasn't more conscious of my size. That tells you what a mother can do for you. She gave me *that* much confidence. She convinced me that I could be anyone I wanted to be. It was really up to me. "You just have to go for it," she would say.

My relationship with my mother was powerful and unique, warm and reinforcing. She was my confidante, my best friend. I think it was that way partly because I was an only child, born to her late in life (for those days), when she was 36 and my dad was 41. My parents had tried unsuccessfully to have children for many years. So when I finally arrived in Peabody, Massachusetts, on November 19, 1935, my mother poured her love into me as if I were a found treasure.

I wasn't born with a silver spoon. I had something better—tons of love. My grandparents on both sides were Irish immigrants, and neither they nor my parents graduated from high school. I was nine when my parents bought our first house, a modest two-story masonry home on 15 Lovett Street, in an Irish working-class section of Salem, Massachusetts.

The house was across the street from a small factory. My father would often remind me that was a real plus. "You always want a factory for a neighbor. They're not around on the weekends. They don't bother you. They're quiet." I believed him, never recognizing that he was engaging in some confidence building himself.

My dad worked hard as a railroad conductor on the Boston & Maine commuter line between Boston and Newburyport. When "Big Jack" went off in the early morning at five in his pressed dark blue uniform, his white shirt starched to perfection by my mother, he looked like he could salute God himself. Nearly every day was the same, a ticket-punching journey through the same ten depots, over and over again: Newburyport, Ipswich, Hamilton/Wenham, North Beverly, Beverly, Salem, Swampscott, Lynn, the General Electric Works, Boston. And then back again, over some 40 miles of track. Later, I would get a kick out of knowing that one of his regular stops was at GE's aircraft engines' complex in Lynn, just outside Boston.

Every workday, he looked forward to climbing back on the B&M train that he always thought of as his own. My father loved greeting the public and meeting interesting people. He moved through the center aisles of those passenger cars like an ambassador, with good humor, punching tickets and welcoming the familiar faces in the bench seats as if they were close friends.

During every rush hour, he traded smiles and hellos with passengers and spread a good bit of Irish blarney. His cheerful disposition on the train would often contrast with his quiet and withdrawn behavior at home. This would annoy my mother, who would complain, "Why don't you bring some of that baloney you pass out on the train home?" He seldom did.

My father was a diligent worker who put in long hours and never missed a day of work. If he got a bad weather report, he'd ask my mother to drive him to the station the night before. He would sleep in one of the cars on his train, so he'd be ready to go in the morning.

Rarely would he get home before seven at night, always picked up at the station in the family car by my mother. He'd come home with a bundle of newspapers under his arm, all of them left by his passengers on the train. From the age of six, I got my daily dose of current events and sports, thanks to the leftover *Boston Globe*s, *Herald*s, and *Record*s. Reading the papers every night became a lifelong addiction. I'm a news junkie to this day.

My father not only got me started on knowing what was going on outside Salem, he also taught me, through example, the value of hard work. And he did something else that would last a lifetime— he introduced me to golf. My father told me that the big shots on his train were always talking about their golf games. He thought I ought to learn about this instead of the baseball, football, and hockey I was playing. Caddying was something the older kids in the neighborhood were doing. So with his push, I started early, caddying at the age of nine at the nearby Kernwood Country Club.

I was incredibly dependent on my parents. Many times, when my mother left the house to pick up my dad, the train would be late. When I was 12 or 13, the delays would drive me crazy. I'd run out of the house and down Lovett Street, my heart racing, to see if they were around the corner on the way home, out of fear that something had happened to them. I just couldn't lose them. They were my world.

It was a fear I shouldn't have had, because my mother raised me to be strong, tough, and independent. She always feared she would die young, a victim of the heart disease that struck down everyone in her family. So in my early teens, my mother encouraged me to be independent. She'd push me to take trips to Boston on my own to see a ball game or catch a movie. I thought I was cool in those days until my mother left the house to pick up my dad at the train depot and they were late coming home.

Salem was a great place for a boy to grow up. It was a town with a strong work ethic and good values. In those days, no one locked their doors. On Saturdays, parents didn't worry when their kids walked downtown to the Paramount, where a quarter bought you two movies and a box of popcorn, and you still had enough left for an ice cream on the way home. On Sundays, the churches were filled.

Salem was a scrappy and competitive place. I was competitive, and my friends were, too. All of us were jocks, living to play one sport or another. We'd organize our own neighborhood baseball, basketball, football, and hockey games, playing at the Pit, a dusty piece of flat land surrounded by trees and backyards off North Street. We'd sweep the gravel flat in the spring and summer, choose up sides and teams, even schedule our own tournaments. We'd play from early in the morning until the town whistle blew at quarter to nine. The whistle was the signal to get home.

In those days, the city was broken up into neighborhood schools, which led to intense rivalries in every sport—even at the primary school level. I was the quarterback on the six-man Pickering Grammar School football team. I was pathetically slow, but I had a pretty good arm and a pair of teammates who could really run. We won the championship at Pickering. I also was the pitcher on our baseball team and learned to throw a sweeping curveball and a sharp drop.

At Salem High School, however, I found out that I peaked very early in both football and baseball. I was too slow to play football, and my devastating curve and drop at 12 didn't come with any more break at 16. My fastball couldn't crack a pane of glass. Hitters would just sit there and wait for it. I went from being a starting pitcher as a freshman to the bench as a senior. I was lucky to be an okay jock in hockey, as captain and leading scorer of the high school team, but in college my lack of speed got me again. I had to give it up.

Thank goodness for golf, a sport that doesn't demand speed. It was my father's early encouragement that led me to Kernwood Country Club, where I began to caddy. On Saturday mornings, my friends and I would sit on the curb outside the gate to Green Lawn Cemetery, waiting for a member of the golf club to pick us up in his car and bring us a few miles to the course. On the hottest summer days, we'd sneak off to a secluded spot we called "Black Rock," strip naked, and cool off with a swim in the Danvers River.

Mostly, though, we'd sit on the grassy hill by the caddy shack and wait for "Swank" Sweeney, the caddy master, to shout our names. A tall, thin man with curly hair and glasses, Sweeney would take the bags out of the caddy shack, put them on a half door, and yell, "Welch!" I'd rush off from a game of cards or a wrestling match for my assignment.

Nearly everyone hoped to carry Ray Brady's clubs because he was the big tipper on the course, where tips were generally scarce. Otherwise, the $1.50 fee for a single 18 holes was about all you saw. We really worked for Monday mornings, when the grounds crew fixed the course. That was caddies' morning, when we would take the lost balls we found and use our taped-up clubs to play 18 holes. We'd get there at the crack of dawn because they threw us off promptly at noon.

Caddying gave me the chance to make some money and, more important, learn the game. I also got early exposure to people who had achieved some level of success. I got a very early look at how attractive or how big a jackass someone can be by watching their behavior on a golf course.

Besides caddying, I worked a number of jobs. For a while, I delivered the *Salem Evening News*. I worked at the local post office during the holiday season. For about three years, I sold shoes on commission at the Thom McCan store on Essex Street. We got seven cents a pair for selling regular shoes. If you sold the "turkeys," the 11E wingtips with the purple toes and the white trim, you'd get a quarter or fifty cents. I'd always bring them out, fit them to a pair of stinky feet, and say, "These look good on you." What I'd say for an extra quarter in those days!

One summer job really taught me a lesson. It convinced me what I didn't want to do. I was operating a drill press at the Parker Brothers game plant in Salem. My job was to take a small piece of cork, drill a hole through it by pushing down a pedal with my foot, and then toss the cork into a big round cardboard drum. Every day, I did thousands of them.

To pass the time, I'd play a game by trying to cover the bottom of the barrel with corks I drilled before the foreman came along to empty it out. I rarely made it. Talk about frustration. I'd go home with headaches. I hated it. I didn't last three weeks, but it taught me a lot.

My early years were spent with my nose pressed up against the glass. Every summer before I was old enough to work, the kids from the Salem playground took a special train to Old Orchard Beach, an amusement park in Maine. This was our summer highlight. We'd board the train at six-thirty A.M. and arrive there two hours later. Within a couple of hours, by running from ride to ride, most of us had used up the five bucks or so that we brought.

We still had a full day ahead of us and were broke. My friends and I would them comb the beach for returnable bottles, going from blanket to blanket asking sunbathers for their empties. At two cents a bottle, that got us enough money for a hot dog and a few more rides before returning home.

On the other hand, I never felt deprived. I didn't want for much of anything. My parents made many sacrifices for me, making sure I had a great baseball glove or a good bicycle. And my father allowed my mother to spoil me, without ever taking any of the credit. And she did.

She took me to the bleachers in Fenway Park to watch Ted Williams play left field for the Boston Red Sox. She'd pick me up at school in the early afternoon and drive me over to the country club so I could get a head start on the other caddies. A devout Catholic, she'd drive me to St. Thomas the Apostle Church so I could serve the six A.M. mass as an altar boy, with her praying in the first row of the right pew.

She became my most enthusiastic cheerleader, calling up the local newspapers and asking them to carry items about my small triumphs, from graduating from the University of Massachusetts to earning my Ph.D. Then she'd paste each clipping into a big scrapbook. She was shameless that way.

My mother was clearly the disciplinarian in the family. When my father once caught me on his train headed home after I'd skipped school to celebrate St. Patrick's Day in South Boston, he didn't say anything in front of my friends—even though all of us were juiced on some cheap 50-cents-a-bottle muscatel.

Instead he simply told my mother, who confronted me and doled out the punishment. Another time, I cut altar boy practice to play hockey on the frozen pond at Mack Park near my home. During the game, I fell through the ice and got completely soaked. To try to cover up what happened, I stripped off my wet clothes and hung them on a tree over a fire we built. We shivered in the January cold, waiting for our clothes to dry.

It was, I thought, a rather clever cover-up—until I walked through the front door.

It took a second for my mother to smell the smoke on my clothes. Ducking altar boy practice was a big deal to someone who hung a crucifix on the wall, prayed the rosary, and considered Father James Cronin, the longtime pastor of our church, a saint. So she sat me down, forced out a confession, and then delivered her own penance: whacking me with a damp shoe she'd just taken off my foot.

While she could be strict, she could also be a real "softie." Once, when I was not much more than 11 years old, I stole a ball from a carnival that came through town. You know, the type of lousy ball you throw to knock metal milk bottles off a pedestal to win a Kewpie doll.

It didn't take long before my mother found the ball and asked me where I got it. When I admitted that I had stolen it, she insisted that I go to Father Cronin, return the ball to him, and then confess what I did. Since all the priests knew me as an altar boy, I was convinced that they'd recognize me in the confessional the second I opened my mouth. I was scared of them.

I asked my mother if I could take the ball down to the North Canal, a murky river that ran through town, and toss it away. After negotiating with her, she let me have my way. She drove down to the bridge on North Street and watched as I threw the ball into the water.

Another time, when I was a senior in high school, I was caddying for one of the stingiest members of the Kernwood Country Club. By that time, I had been a caddy there for eight years—which was probably a little too long for my own good. We got to the sixth hole, a tee where the drive had to go only about a hundred yards to carry the pond. This day, my guy topped his ball straight into the water. It landed at least ten feet into the muddy pond. He asked me to take my shoes and socks off and wade into the pond after his ball.

I refused, and when he insisted I told him to go to hell. I tossed his clubs into the water, told him to get his ball and clubs himself, and ran off the course.

It was a stupid thing to do, even worse than flinging my hockey stick across the ice. Even though my mother was disappointed, because this incident cost me the club's caddy scholarship, she seemed to understand what I felt and didn't make as much of a big deal out of it as she might have.

An even greater disappointment was losing an opportunity to go to four years of college for free on a naval ROTC scholarship program. Three of us at Salem High passed the naval exam: me and two of my best friends, George Ryan and Mike Tivnan. My dad got state representatives to send letters of recommendation on my behalf, and I went through a battery of interviews for the program. My friends made it. George got a free ride to Tufts. Mike went to Columbia. I was hoping to go to Dartmouth or Columbia, but the navy turned me down.

I never found out why.

Ironically, the rejection turned out to be a great break. At Salem High, I was a good student who worked hard for his grades, but no one would have accused me of being brilliant. So I applied to the University of Massachusetts at Amherst, the state school, where the tuition was fifty bucks a semester. For less than $1,000, including room and board, I could get a degree.

Except for a cousin, I was the first in my family to go to college. I had no family role models to follow, other than my uncle Bill Andrews, who worked as an "engineer" at the power station in Salem. Being an engineer sounded good to me. I found out early that I liked chemistry, so I took up chemical engineering.

I knew so little about college that I almost didn't get there. I didn't take the SATs, assuming instead that the scores on my ROTC naval exams were enough. I didn't get my acceptance letter from UMass until June, just a few days before I graduated from high school. I must have been on the wait list—but I never realized it. Getting into a less competitive school, rather than the Columbia or Dartmouth I wanted, would in the end give me a tremendous advantage. The caliber of the competition I faced at UMass in those days made it easier to shine.

And though I was never short on confidence, my first week at college in the fall of 1953 was a tough one. I was so homesick that my mother had to drive three hours to the Amherst campus to see me. She tried to pump me up.

"Look at these kids around here. They're not thinking about coming home. You're just as good as they are, even better."

She was right. Back in Salem, I had been playing ball, doing a little bit of everything, from being treasurer of my senior class to captain of the hockey and golf teams, but I had never really been away from home, not even to an overnight camp. Here I thought I was this macho guy, supposedly street smart and independent, and I was totally wiped out by the experience of going away to school. I wasn't anywhere near as prepared for college as some of the other students. There were kids from New England prep schools and prestigious Boston Latin who were way ahead of me in math. I also found physics very hard.

My mother would have none of it. The pep talk worked. My anxieties went away within a week.

I struggled through my freshman year but did well on my exams, posting something like a 3.7 grade-point average, and made the dean's list every one of my four years. In my sophomore year, I pledged Phi Sigma Kappa and moved into their fraternity house by the campus pond. Our fraternity, ranked at or near the top in beer consumption, had more late night poker games and better parties than most.

It was a great crowd of guys, and although we were on probation once or twice, I was able to play hard and still get the work done. I loved the atmosphere there.

I also had my professors at UMass, especially Ernie Lindsey, head of the Chemical Engineering Department, making me something of a pet project. He liked me and pushed me through the program, as if I were his son. As with my mother, his support gave me a lot of confidence. I got summer jobs in chemical engineering at Sun Oil near Swarthmore, Pennsylvania, and at Columbia Southern, now PPG Industries, in Ohio. In 1957, I was one of the university's two best students graduating with a degree in chemical engineering. If I'd gone to MIT, I might have been in the middle of the pile. My proud parents bought me a brand-new Volkswagen Beetle as a graduation present.

During my senior year, I was being courted by many different companies. I had lots of good offers. But my professors convinced me to go to graduate school. I turned down the corporate offers and decided to go to the University of Illinois at Champaign, where I was offered a fellowship. The school was consistently ranked among the top five graduate programs in chemical engineering. It was a great school for my major.

I had been on campus no more than two weeks when I met a

pretty girl and asked her out. Our Saturday night date went so well that we ended up just off a campus parking lot in the woods. The windows in my VW had gotten foggy when all of a sudden a light flashed through. It was the campus police, and we were caught in an awkward position. I froze, terrified of the consequences.

In those days, things were quite different. The 1950s were conservative times, and we were in the conservative Midwest. The police took us both down to the campus station and kept us there until four or five in the morning before sending us home.

My life flashed before me. I thought I was about to lose everything: my fellowship, my chance to get a graduate degree, my career. But most of all, I thought about my mother's reaction when she found out what I had done. My fate would be decided after a Monday meeting with the university provost, who would determine the disciplinary action.

On Sunday morning, I gathered up the nerve to call the chairman of the Chemical Engineering Department, Dr. Harry Drickamer. I knew him only by his gruff reputation. Scared as I was, I thought he was my only hope.

"Dr. Drickamer," I said, "I have a real problem. The campus police caught me messing around. I'm devastated by it, and I need help."

I was practically wetting my pants telling him what had happened.

"Damn," he responded. "Of all the graduate students I've had here, you are the first guy to do something like that. I'll take care of this, but you better keep your pants on from now on!"

Whatever Drickamer did saved my butt. I still had to go through a difficult meeting with the provost, but I wasn't thrown out of the school. Yet that frightening incident got me much closer to Harry. We formed a wonderful relationship. He, too, treated me like a son. We bet on football games. We argued over things in the news. In the hallways, Harry would tease me mercilessly, always ragging me about the Red Sox or my already thinning hair.

He became an important influence in my life, a mentor throughout my graduate years. I needed the help. At Illinois, I wasn't as well prepared as the kids from Brooklyn Polytechnic, Columbia, or Minnesota. So in my first year, I struggled there as well. I had to really fight for my grades. I wasn't by any stretch of the imagination a star.

After my first year at Illinois in 1958, when I was to graduate with my master's degree, the country was in a recession. Instead of having twenty job offers, I got two: one from an Oklahoma oil refinery near Tulsa and another from the Ethyl Corp. in Baton Rouge, Louisiana. On the airplane for my Ethyl interview, I was traveling with one of my associates from the University of Illinois when something odd happened. The stewardess came back and said, "Mr. Welch, would you like a drink?" She then turned to my colleague and said, "Dr. Gaertner, would you like a drink?"

I thought that "Dr." Gaertner sounded a lot better than "Mr." Welch. All I had to do was stay a couple of more years. So with not much more foresight than that, I stayed at the university and went for my Ph.D. It helped that the job market wasn't very good. It also helped that I really liked my Illinois professors, especially Drickamer and my thesis adviser, Dr. Jim Westwater.

In graduate school, especially in a Ph.D. program, you live in the lab. You come in at eight in the morning and go home at eleven at night. Sometimes you felt like you were judged on the number of hours your lights were on. My thesis was on condensation in steam-supply systems. So I spent hours vaporizing water and watching it condense on a copper plate.

Day after day, I snapped high-speed photographs of the geometry of the condensing drops on the surface. I developed heat-transfer equations from these experiments. The funny thing about a graduate thesis is that you get so hooked on it, you think you're doing Nobel Prize work.

With Jim Westwater's strong support, I got my Ph.D. in three years, faster than almost anyone. It took the typical grad student four to five years to get a Ph.D. I was hardly the program's resident genius. To pass the program's two-language requirement, one summer I studied French and German day and night for three straight months. I went into an exam room and tipped my head. Everything I had put in my brain poured out the other side. I managed to pass the exams, but if you asked me one word in French or German a week later, I was done. My "knowledge" emptied the moment I handed in those exams.

Despite not being the smartest, I did have the focus to get the work done. Some of the more intelligent people in the program had trouble finishing their theses. They couldn't bring them to a conclusion. My impatience helped me.

I have always felt that chemical engineering was one of the best backgrounds for a business career, because both the classwork and required thesis teach you one very important lesson: There are no finite answers to many questions. What really counted was your thought process. A typical exam question went something like this: An ice-skater weighs 150 pounds and is doing figure-eights on ice an inch thick. The temperature is rising a degree every ten minutes to 40 degrees, and the wind is blowing 20 miles an hour. When will the skater fall through the ice?

There was no formulaic answer to that question.

The same is true for most business problems. The process helps you get closer to the darker shade of gray. There are rarely black-or-white answers. More often than not, business is smell, feel, and touch as much as or more than numbers. If we wait for the perfect answer, the world will pass us by.

By the time I left Illinois in 1960, I had decided what I liked and wanted to do and, just as important, what I wasn't so good at. My technical skills were pretty good, but I wasn't the best scientist by any means. Compared to many of my classmates, I was outgoing, someone who loved people more than books, and sports more than scientific developments. I figured those skills and interests were best suited for a job that bridged the laboratory and the commercial world.

Knowing that was a little bit like knowing I was a pretty good athlete—but far from a very good one. What I wanted to do made me something different from most Ph.D.s. They usually went into university classrooms to teach or corporate laboratories to do research. I toyed with the idea of teaching, and even interviewed at Syracuse and West Virginia Universities, but in the end I decided against that option.

Besides a degree, long-term friendships, and a way of thinking through problems, Illinois gave me something else: a great wife. I first spotted Carolyn Osburn at the Catholic church on-campus doing the Stations of the Cross during Lent. She attended mass, just as I did. I didn't meet her, however, until a mutual friend introduced us in a bar in downtown Champaign.

Carolyn was tall, pretty, sophisticated, and intelligent. She had graduated with honors from Marietta College and was on a $1,500-a-year fellowship at Illinois, getting her master's in English literature. After our first date at a basketball game in January 1959, we were always together. Five months later, we were engaged, and on November 21, two days after my 24th birthday, we were married in her hometown of Arlington Heights, Illinois.

We spent the bulk of our honeymoon driving my Volkswagen across the country and into Canada, with me interviewing for jobs. I was lucky enough to have several offers, but two fit: one from Exxon, to work in a development laboratory in Baytown, Texas, and one from GE, to work in a new chemical development operation in Pittsfield, Massachusetts.

GE invited me to Pittsfield, where I met with Dr. Dan Fox, a scientist in charge of the company's new chemical concepts. That job appealed to me most. The development group was small. It was working on new plastics, and I liked the idea of going back to Massachusetts. Like my earlier professors, Fox struck me as someone who was smart and whom I could trust. In Fox, I saw a coach and a role model who brought the best out of everyone who worked with him.

He was already something of a hero inside GE because he had discovered Lexan plastic for the company. GE began selling Lexan in 1957. A potential replacement for glass and metal, it was used for everything from electric coffeemakers to the light covers on the wings of supersonic aircraft.

Fox, like most inventors, was already on to the next project, becoming champion for a new thermoplastic called PPO (polyphenylene oxide). He convinced me that PPO was going to be the next great thing. He described its unique ability to withstand high temperatures. It had the potential to replace hot-water copper piping and stainless-steel medical instruments. He capped off the selling job by telling me that I would be the first employee in charge of getting the plastic out of the lab and into production. I accepted within a week.

What I didn't know when I showed up for work my first day on October 17, 1960, was how quickly I would become frustrated.

In just one year, GE's bureaucracy would nearly drive me out of the company.

2

Getting Out of the Pile

In 1961, I had been working at GE for a year as an engineer making $10,500 when my first boss handed me a $1,000 raise. I was okay with it—until I found out later that day that I got exactly what all four of us sharing an office received. I thought I deserved more than the "standard" increase.

I talked to my boss, and the discussion went nowhere.

Frustrated, I started looking for another job. I began scanning the "Help Wanted" ads in *Chemical Week* magazine and *The Wall Street Journal,* hoping to find a quick escape. I felt trapped in the "pile" near the bottom of a big organization. I wanted out. I got a nice offer from International Minerals & Chemicals in Chicago, not far from where my wife's mother lived. It seemed like a chance to escape.

The standard predetermined raise was just a part of my irritation at what I saw as the company's stingy behavior. When GE recruited me, the company had laid out a cushy red carpet. They convinced me I was just what they were looking for to help develop a new plastic—PPO.

When Carolyn and I arrived in Pittsfield, Massachusetts, I was expecting at least a little of the seductive treatment to continue. We came to GE with little more than change in our pockets. We had driven 950 miles from Illinois in my fading black Volkswagen. When I joined GE in October 1960, the local union was on strike. In order to avoid the picket line, I reported for work with the title of "process development specialist" in a local warehouse.

Quickly, my new boss, Burt Coplan, made it clear that the wooing process was over. Coplan, a thin, forty-something development manager, asked me if my wife and I had already found an apartment in town. When I told him we were staying at the local hotel, he said, "Well, we don't cover that, you know."

I couldn't believe it. If it hadn't been my first week in the job, I would have let him have it. But I wasn't about to blow it. Coplan could not have been more charming during the interview process. In fact, he was a decent guy. He just saw it as his job to try to scrimp on everything.

He acted as if GE were on the verge of bankruptcy.

The romance that brought me to GE was evaporating. We moved out of the hotel. I checked into a cheaper motel, while Carolyn went to live with my parents in Salem for a couple of weeks until we could find an apartment. We eventually moved into a small, first-floor flat in a two-story wood-frame house on First Street, where the landlady was so chintzy with the heat that we had to knock on the walls to get her to put the thermostat up. Even then, she'd often shout through the paper-thin walls for Carolyn or me to "wear a sweater!" To help furnish the place, my parents gave us $1,000 to buy a couch and a bed.

Everything that first year wasn't awful. There were things I liked: the autonomy to design and build a new pilot plant for PPO and the sense of being part of a team in what felt like a small company.

I worked closely with Dr. Al Gowan, who joined GE the same month as I did. He ran the earliest experiments on the new plastic in beakers. I designed the kettles to test the bigger batches and built them at a local machine shop. We constructed a pilot plant from scratch in a small outbuilding in the back of our offices. Each day, we'd run several experiments, testing different processes.

For someone just off a college campus, it was a real adventure.

Working with a new plastic like PPO, we needed all the scientific help we could get. So at least twice a month, I'd jump into my car and drive 55 miles to GE's central research and development lab in Schenectady, New York, where the plastic was invented. I'd spend the day working with researchers and scientists, always trying to excite them about the product's potential.

In those days, the central lab was funded entirely by corporate, so there was no direct incentive for the lab's scientists to focus their efforts on any one business or, for that matter, any commercialization. The scientists liked doing advanced research. The game was to get them to put time into the development of your project after the invention phase. I had no authority. It was all persuasion. It was easy to get attention from Al Hay, the inventor of the plastic, and several of his associates. But some weren't interested in commercializing products.

I looked forward to those trips to the R&D lab because it was fun "selling" my project—and the lab was a real help. These trips turned out to be relatively lucrative. I could make the trip in my VW for a buck of gas—four gallons at 25 cents a gallon—and GE would pay me seven cents a mile to use my own car. So I'd pocket something like seven bucks on every trip I made to Schenectady. It seems crazy now, but all of us would drive somewhere at the drop of a hat to get a little extra cash.

In spite of the good stuff, I was getting more frustrated every day. The penny-wise behavior that started that first week continued. In a redbrick building on Plastics Avenue, four of us shared a small, cramped office. We had to make do with only two phones, scrambling to pass them around the desks. On business trips, Burt asked us to double up in hotel rooms.

For me, the "standard" $1,000 raise was the proverbial last straw.

So I went to Coplan and quit. Just as I was about to drive my car back across the country again, Coplan's boss called me. Reuben Gutoff, a young executive based in Connecticut, invited Carolyn and me out to a long dinner at the Yellow Aster in Pittsfield.

Gutoff was no stranger. We had met in several business reviews. We had made a connection because I would always give him more than he expected. As a junior development engineer, I had given him a complete cost and physical property analysis of our new plastic versus every major competing product offered by the DuPonts, Dows, and Celaneses of the world. It projected the long-range product costs of nylon, polypropylene, acrylic, and acetel against our products.

It was by no means an earth-shattering analysis, but it was more than the usual from a guy in a white lab coat.

What I was trying to do was "get out of the pile." If I had just answered his questions, it would have been tough to get noticed. Bosses usually have answers in mind when they hand out questions. They're just looking for confirmation. To set myself apart from the crowd, I thought I had to think bigger than the questions posed. I wanted to provide not only the answer, but an unexpected fresh perspective.

Gutoff obviously noticed. Over dinner, for four straight hours, he was hell-bent on keeping me at GE. He made his pitch, promising to get me a bigger raise and, more important, vowing to keep the bureaucracy of the company out of my way. I was surprised to learn that he shared my frustration with the bureaucracy.

This time I was lucky, because many GE bosses would have been happy to let me go. I undoubtedly was a pain in the ass to Coplan. Fortunately, Gutoff didn't see it that way (but he didn't have to deal with me every day). The dinner with him went on without an answer. During his two-hour drive back home to Westport, Connecticut, he stopped at a pay phone next to the highway to continue selling. It was one A.M., Carolyn and I were already in bed, and Reuben was still making his case.

By putting more money on the table (adding $2,000 to the $1,000 raise Coplan gave me), by promising an increase in responsibility and air cover from the bureaucracy, Gutoff showed me he really cared.

A few hours after daybreak, on the morning before my going-away party, I decided to stay. That night, surrounded by a pile of gifts at what was supposed to be my farewell celebration at Coplan's house, I told my colleagues that I was not leaving after all. Most of them seemed happy, although I saw massive anxiety from Burt at the thought of having me back. I don't remember if I kept the gifts, but I think I did.

Gutoff's recognition—that he considered me different and special—made a powerful impression. Ever since that time, differentiation has been a basic part of how I manage. That standard raise I got over four decades ago has probably driven my behavior to an extreme. But differentiation is all about being extreme, rewarding the best and weeding out the ineffective. Rigorous differentiation delivers real stars—and stars build great businesses.

Some contend that differentiation is nuts—bad for morale.

They say that differential treatment erodes the very idea of teamwork. Not in my world. You build strong teams by treating individuals differently. Just look at the way baseball teams pay 20-game winning pitchers and 40-plus home run hitters. The relative contributions of those players are easy to measure—their stats jump out at you—yet they are still part of a team.

Everybody's got to feel they have a stake in the game. But that doesn't mean everyone on the team has to be treated the same way.

From my days in the Pit, I learned that the game is all about fielding the best athletes. Whoever fielded the best team there won. Reuben Gutoff reinforced that it was no different in business. Winning teams come from differentiation, rewarding the best and removing the weakest, always fighting to raise the bar.

I was lucky to get out of the pile and learn this my very first year at GE—the hard way, by nearly quitting the company.

3

Blowing the Roof Off

Years before I was given the nickname Neutron Jack, I had actually blown up a factory—for real.

It was 1963, early in my GE career. I was 28 years old and had been with the company for all of three years. I can remember that spring day as if it were yesterday. It was one of the most frightening experiences of my life.

I was sitting in my office in Pittsfield, just across the street from the pilot plant, when the explosion occurred. It was a huge blast that blew the roof off the building and knocked out all the windows on the top floor. It shook everyone, especially me, to their very toes.

With the sound of the explosion still ringing in my ears, I raced out of my office and toward the redbrick plant 100 yards away on Plastics Avenue. Oh, my God, I thought, I hope no one got hurt. Roof shingles and shards of glass were scattered everywhere. Clouds of smoke and dust hung over the building.

I ran up the stairs to the third floor. I was scared as hell. My heart was pounding, and I was bathed in sweat. The wreckage the explosion caused was worse than I expected. A big chunk of roof and ceiling had collapsed onto the floor.

Miraculously, no one was seriously injured.

We were experimenting with a chemical process. We were bubbling oxygen through a highly volatile solution in a large tank. An unexplainable spark set off the explosion. We were lucky because the safety bolts let go as designed and allowed the top to shoot straight up through the ceiling.

As the boss, I was clearly at fault.

The next day, I had to drive 100 miles to Bridgeport, Connecticut, to explain to a corporate group executive, Charlie Reed, why the accident occurred. He was over my direct boss, Reuben Gutoff, the guy who had persuaded me not to leave GE. Gutoff would also attend the meeting, but I was the guy on the line, and I was prepared for the worst.

GE's bosses had all sorts of expectations of their managers. They expected them to come up with new ideas for products. They expected them to enter new markets and increase revenues. They did not expect someone to blow up a plant.

I knew I could explain why the blast went off, and I had some ideas on how to fix the problem. But I was a nervous wreck. My confidence was shaken almost as much as the building I had destroyed.

I didn't know Charlie Reed that well. Yet from the first minute I walked into his office in Bridgeport, Reed made me feel completely at ease. A Ph.D. in chemical engineering from MIT, Charlie was a brilliant scientist with a professorial bent. In fact, he had been on the MIT faculty as a teacher of applied mathematics for five years before joining GE in 1942. He was a balding fellow of medium height and build, with an ever-present glitter in his eye.

He also had a passion for technology. A bachelor married to the corporation, he was the highest-ranking GE executive with hands-on experience in chemicals. Charlie understood what could happen when you were working at high temperatures with volatile materials.

That day, he was incredibly understanding. He took an

almost Socratic approach in dealing with the accident. His concern was what I had learned from the explosion and if I thought I could fix the reactor process. He questioned whether we should continue to move forward on the project. It was all intellect, no emotion or anger.

"It's better that we learned about this problem now rather than later when we had a large-scale operation going," he said. "Thank God no one was hurt."

Charlie's reaction made a huge impression on me.

When people make mistakes, the last thing they need is discipline. It's time for encouragement and confidence building. The job at this point is to restore self-confidence. I think "piling on" when someone is down is one of the worst things any of us can do. It's a standard joke during GE operating reviews that if one of the business CEOs is getting heat and someone in the room jumps on the bandwagon, the staff team will typically pull out the white handkerchief, toss it in the air, and flag the person for piling on.

Piling on during a weak moment can force people into what I call the "GE Vortex." It can happen anywhere. You see the "Vortex" when leaders lose their confidence, begin to panic, and spiral downward into a hole of self-doubt.

I've seen it happen to strong, bright, and self-confident general managers of billion-dollar businesses. They were doing just fine in good times but then missed an operating plan or made a bad deal—not for the first time—and self-doubt began to creep in. They became willing to agree to anything just to get out of the room and make it through another day.

It's a terrible thing to see. Few ever recover from the "Vortex." I've tried to do everything to help people through it—or better yet, avoid it.

Don't get me wrong. I enjoy challenging a person's ideas. No one loves a good and passionately fought argument more than I do. This isn't about being tough-minded and straightforward. That's the job. But so is sensing when to hug and when to kick. Of course, arrogant people who refuse to learn from their mistakes have to go. If we're managing good people who are clearly eating themselves up over an error, our job is to help them through it.

That doesn't mean you have to take it easy on your top performers. A perfect example involves one of our real A players, an executive with global R&D responsibility for a major GE business. Just last year, he and I were chatting casually over cocktails the night before our annual officers meeting. I had recently returned from a tour of our R&D operations in India and was excited by what I had seen. As I described my impression of his operations, this guy told me I was given a load of BS on my trip.

"They aren't doing anywhere near the quality of work in India you think," he said.

His comment irritated me. I couldn't believe him. The engineers and scientists in India were on *his* payroll, yet he was making a distinction between his people "here" in the United States, where he was located, and "there" in India. I always knew we had a problem getting the whole organization's mind-set around the idea of global intellect, tapping every great mind in the world no matter where it was located. When I got that reaction from one of my best, I knew it was a helluva lot bigger problem than I'd thought.

Without naming him, I launched into that story the next morning in front of 170 of GE's top executives. I used it as an example of how our company wasn't getting what maximizing global intellect is all about. I challenged everyone in the room to look at themselves in the mirror to make sure they weren't in the same boat. We could not have the R&D teams in the United States doing all of the advanced, fun work while farming out the lower-value projects to places like India. My visits to India convinced me that their research labs were filled with scientists equal to or better than those in the United States—and in a lot more disciplines than software.

Understandably, the guy felt I had clobbered him in public, and in front of his peers. I wouldn't have done that if he weren't one of the brightest and most confident executives in the company. He was a GE all-star, not a turkey.

Within a day or two of the meeting, he sent me a note explaining that he had inadvertently "diminished the significant progress made by his team in India" and had left me with the wrong impression. I immediately called to thank him for his note and assured him that he had not screwed up.

Obviously, this negative role-model act doesn't work with everyone. You can do it with your very best—as long as they know they're your best. Using role models always helped me make the point to a larger group.

The same applies to people who take what I call a "big swing" at something and miss. One of the real advantages of a big company is the ability to take on big projects with huge potential. The quickest way to neutralize that advantage is to go after the scalps of those who dare to dream and reach—but fail. That just reinforces a risk-averse culture.

The best way to support dreams and stretch is to set apart small ideas with big potential, then give people positive role models and the resources to turn small projects into big businesses. A good example of this was our early attempt in the late 1970s to develop a revolutionary new light bulb called Halarc. It was an ambitious effort to create a light bulb that lasted ten times longer than the typical product at a fraction of the energy. It appeared to be a perfect environmental solution.

This was a big $50 million swing.

Problem was, no one wanted to pay $10.95 for a single light bulb, no matter how "green" or revolutionary, and our project failed. Instead of "punishing" those involved in the Halarc effort, we celebrated their great try. We handed out cash management awards and promoted several Halarc players to new jobs. While no one was happy with the results, we made a big point of rewarding the people on the team. We wanted everyone in the company to know that taking a big swing and missing was okay.

By 1964, our project to make a new plastic had come a long way. We were getting close to a product we could sell. Gutoff assigned a general manager named Bob Finholt to run it. He was a dreamer and big thinker who quickly sold his bosses on the idea that we had something going in Pittsfield. Charlie Reed got the board to approve our new plastics plant in 1964.

The $10 million factory would produce the PPO product that brought me to GE in the first place, the same product that led to the disaster in the pilot plant. We got the money on the basis that we had a breakthrough plastic that was a step beyond GE's first engineered plastic, Lexan, which had just set a new performance standard.

It was a hard sell, in part because we didn't want to move to Mount Vernon, Indiana, where our first Lexan plastics plant had been built. Instead, we picked a 450-acre site in Selkirk, New York. I found it on a Sunday afternoon drive over from Pittsfield with my wife and three kids in the car. The five of us got out and walked all over the site. It was a beautiful piece of land, a former marshaling yard for the New York Central Railroad with a right-of-way on the Hudson River. I loved the site and wouldn't leave until the kids gave out.

Some GE executives were skeptical of the location because it was only 30 miles away from Schenectady, where GE already had one of our largest and oldest manufacturing plants. There was a lot of selfishness in our request, too. We wanted to run our own show and stay where we were. To justify it, we argued that we were creating a highly technical product and needed access to the chemists and scientists in GE's R&D center in Schenectady as well as our own research lab in Pittsfield, some 50 miles away.

We won the argument and the money. By this time, Bob

Finholt's more creative bent earned him a promotion to strategic planning at headquarters.

With the general manager's slot open, I went after it.

After a dinner in Selkirk with Gutoff and the rest of our team, I followed Gutoff to his car behind the Stone Ends restaurant and jumped into the front seat of his Volkswagen convertible.

"Why not me for Bob's job?" I said.

"Are you kidding?" Gutoff asked. "Jack, you don't know anything about marketing. That's what this new product introduction is all about."

I wouldn't take no for an answer. I stayed in Gutoff's car on that dark and cold evening for well over an hour, pounding him with my qualifications for the job—thin as they might be.

It was my turn to sell Gutoff and sell him hard. I reminded him of the time when he sold me on staying at GE. He didn't give me an answer that night, but when we drove out of that parking lot, Gutoff knew how badly I wanted the job.

Over the next seven days or so, I called him with additional arguments to bolster my case. Within a week, he called and asked me to come down to his office in Bridgeport.

"You SOB," he said. "You convinced me to give you the job, and I'm going to do it. You better deliver."

I went back to Pittsfield that day as the new general manager of the polymer products operation.

I didn't have long to celebrate.

Just after getting the new job and breaking ground on the site, we found out that our PPO product had a serious flaw. Aging tests began to show that over time it became brittle and cracked under the high temperatures it was designed to withstand. There was just no way that it would make it as a replacement for hot-water copper pipes—one of its biggest potential markets.

I had lobbied myself into a potentially career-killing challenge. There is a moment forever frozen into my memory. I was standing at the Selkirk site on a cold winter day in 1965 with

Gutoff and Allan Hay, the bow-tied GE corporate research lab scientist who invented PPO. In our overcoats and gloves, we stood at the top of a massive hole in the ground that must have been 30 feet deep, enough to bury all of us.

With the product's newly found technical flaws and the gaping hole in front of us, my GE career flashed before me.

"Al, you've got to help us fix this thing or we're all dead," I said.

Hay turned to us and replied calmly, "Hey, guys, don't worry about it. I have a couple of new plastics coming along."

I felt like throwing him in the hole. I wondered what I had gotten myself into. We were way ahead of ourselves. This was a $10 million investment in a business that the company didn't really understand. Now it became clear we didn't have a working product for the plant to produce. Even worse, the scientist who invented the product had no idea how to fix it.

It took six frantic months before we worked our way out of the problem. I practically lived in the lab during that time. We tried everything. We were sticking every compound we could think of into PPO to see if it would stop the cracking. Dan Fox, the chemist who convinced me to join GE, led a team of chemists in Pittsfield who eventually found the solution by blending PPO with low-cost polystyrene and some rubber.

We had to juggle the plant design to take care of the blending process, but it worked.

The story had a happy ending. The blended plastic was called Noryl and eventually became a winning product that today does more than $1 billion in worldwide sales.

What made it work was a crazy band of people who believed we could do almost anything. We were scared to death but filled with dreams—and just nuts enough to try anything to get the plastic to work. We may have been in one of the world's largest corporations, but in Pittsfield or Selkirk we saw ourselves as a very small, family business, with a "bank" behind us.

Talk about luck. This whole experience in the plastics business was like God coming down and saying, "Jack, this is your moment. Take it."

I was still pretty new at this. I can remember the first time a salesman took Carolyn and me to dinner. I thought that was big stuff. I was a project manager and bought raw materials from his company, Pittsburgh Consolidated Coal. He took us out for drinks and dinner at the Mill on the Floss, the best restaurant in the area, and it was free!

It might seem naive today, but everything was a new experience. I loved every minute of it, and I found pleasure in the smallest things. We used to fly a two-engine United Caravelle jet from Hartford, Connecticut, to Chicago on our way to the plastics plant that made Lexan in Mount Vernon, Indiana. On every trip, the stewardess would hand each of us a can of macademia nuts and two tiny bottles of Scotch. We'd look forward to that treat all the way to the airport.

At times, I couldn't believe that I was being paid to do all these things. Neither could my mother. When I traveled to Europe for the first time in 1964 on a business trip, she was petrified that GE might not reimburse me.

"Are you sure they are going to pay you for it?" she asked.

All these new experiences were part of growing a business from scratch, and we made just about every one of them an excuse for celebration. When we landed an order of $500 for plastic pellets, we'd stop off for beers on the way home to celebrate. We posted the names of every customer who bought $500 or more on the wall in what we called our "500 Club." Whenever we'd add ten new customers to the club—it was time for another party.

Beer kegs and pizza parties were standard practice in Silicon Valley, but they were also standard for Selkirk and Pittsfield in the mid-1960s!

Every early promotion, every bonus, and every raise were also cause for celebration. When I got a $3,000 bonus in 1964, I threw a party for all the employees at the new house we had just purchased on Cambridge Avenue, a working-class area of Pittsfield. The very next Monday, I treated myself to my first convertible, a greenish Pontiac LeMans. Boy, was I feeling on top of the world—but I'd quickly get a reminder of how things can change.

Besides the car, I also bought a new suit. I liked to differentiate myself from the rest of the pack in those early days. In the summer I would often wear tan poplin suits made by Haspel with blue button-down shirts and striped ties. Silly as it now seems, I even liked the ring of hearing someone address me as "Dr. Welch."

After work on one beautiful spring day, I went to the parking lot and got into my shiny new car. I pushed the lever to put the top down for the first time. All of a sudden, the hydraulic hose sprang a leak. Dark, grungy oil shot up onto my suit and ruined the paint job on the front of my beautiful new car.

I couldn't believe it. There I was, thinking I was bigger than life, and smack came the reminder that brought me back to reality. It was a great lesson. Just when you think you're a big shot, something happens to wake you up. It would by no means be the last time this would happen.

Even so, the family business continued to grow, and so did I. Once we had the Selkirk plant up and began selling Noryl, sales took off. We grew rapidly from 1965 to 1968 and then I got the next big break. In early June of 1968, nearly eight years after joining GE, I was promoted to general manager of the $26 million plastics business. This was a big deal, making me, at 32, the company's youngest general manager.

The move put me into the big leagues with all the trimmings—an annual invitation to the company's top management meeting every January in Florida and my first stock options.

I was on my way.

4

Flying Below the Radar

L ife appeared to be perfect. There was only one regret.

I could no longer share my success with my parents.

My mother had died on January 25, 1965, which was the saddest day of my life. She was only 66 years old but had been suffering from heart trouble for many years. I had been an undergraduate at UMass in Amherst when she had her first heart attack.

I was so upset then that after my aunt called with the news, I literally rushed out of the dorm and began running down the highway to Salem, about 110 miles away. I was too filled with emotion to stand and wait by the side of the road as I was thumbing a ride back home.

After a three-week stay in the hospital, she went home, rested, and recovered. This was all before beta-blockers and bypass surgery. (They would save my own life years later.) She suffered another heart attack three years later and went through the same routine. Three years after that, she had her third and final one. She and my father were in Florida on vacation at the time. I had given them $1,000 out of my bonus that year to help them escape a tough New England winter.

That money meant a lot to both of us. When I handed it to her, she burst with pride. She had always provided me with everything I had from the day I was born. My modest $1,000 gift was a chance to finally give her something in return. To her, it reflected the success "her product" was enjoying. She was so proud of me. Thank God I did it. One of my life's great regrets is not being able to give her all the things I could if she were alive today.

When my father told me that my mother was in a Fort Lauderdale hospital, I immediately flew down from Pittsfield and went straight to her room. She was in bad shape, weak and frail. The night she died, I remember sitting with her when she asked me to wash her back. I sponged her back clean with warm water and soap, and she was so happy I would do that. Afterward, my dad and I returned to the one-bedroom efficiency motel where they had been staying.

We never saw her alive again.

I was devastated. My father and aunt returned to Salem by train with my mother's body, while I drove my dad's car back home. I drove north all night long. I stopped for some rest at a highway motel in North Carolina but stayed there for only four hours, tossing and turning. I was so restless and so angry. I cried and kicked the car the whole way. I felt cheated, angry, and mad at God for taking my mother from me.

By the time I got home, I had cried myself out. The wake and funeral at St. Thomas the Apostle Church were really a celebration of her life. At a funeral parlor in Salem, all our relatives, neighbors, and hundreds of friends I didn't know showed up, each with a story my mother told about her son, Jackie.

Inevitably, every story she bored her friends with spoke of her pride in me.

My father also took her death hard. He was a good and generous man. He had bought me a new car when he couldn't afford it. His job and my mother's overwhelming personality kept him from having much of an impact on my life. But I loved him. Now it was so sad to see him refuse to adjust to life without her.

Without my mother, he was a lost soldier. She had kept him on a strict salt-free diet because he was suffering from edema. Now he became indifferent about what he ate; soon the water retention made his face puffy, and he began to gain weight.

He just ate himself to death with the wrong foods. He retained so much water that he was put in the hospital. I rushed back from a business trip in Europe. He was alive when I walked into the hospital elevator to get to his floor. By the time I reached his bedside, he had died. Just 15 months after my mother's death, on April 22, 1966, my father passed away. He was 71 years old.

I was thrown for a loop. My mother and father were gone, and I was feeling awfully sorry for myself. I was lucky to have my wife, Carolyn, there to pick up the pieces. She was strong, quick-witted, and always supportive. She reminded me how lucky I was to have a great family, with three healthy kids, Kathy, John, and Anne. (Mark would come later in April of 1968.) She was a real rock for me, not only then but on many other occasions.

When I worried about the consequences of rocking the boat at work, Carolyn would encourage me to do exactly what I thought was right—regardless of what others at GE might think. After each promotion, she and the kids would celebrate by decorating the house and driveway with colorful streamers.

Following my promotion to general manager of plastics, I had a 1969 interview with the *Monogram*, the company magazine. When the writer came out to Pittsfield for our interview, he referred to me as "Dr. Welch." I shot back, "I don't make house calls, so call me Jack!"—a quote he included in the article.

I was now ready to act as a businessman and not an engineer, so I was anxious to bag the Dr. Welch moniker. I bragged that my employees were "a turned-on bunch" who generated their own "electricity." I boasted that we grew the plastics business more in my first year as general manager than in the previous ten years. "There's gold here, and we were lucky enough to come along and dig the mine."

What an ass I was—so completely full of myself. Without regard for any of the previous leaders of the business, I claimed we would break all the sales and profit records. Those who read the article must have damn near choked. Fortunately, I was below the radar, insulated from the GE bureaucracy.

When I got the entire plastics operation, which included Lexan, I really believed I had inherited gold. Compared to Noryl, Lexan was a thoroughbred. It was clear as glass and tough as steel. It was flame resistant and lightweight. Boeing put 4,000 pounds of Lexan into every 747 jumbo jet it made in those days. Half of its applications replaced metal.

For years, we had been selling a blended product in Noryl, and we were always trying to get it to work. We were the second-class citizens with the second-class product. With a lower selling price, we managed to get it into business machine housings, lawn sprinklers, hair dryers, disposable razor cartridges, and color televisions. But we had to fight for every 500-pound order. When we finally got Lexan, I thought we could take on the world and was cocky enough to say so.

The statement was even more outrageous since the company's view of plastics was a lot less flattering. The guy who had been running the business was promoted to general manager of silicones, then about 50 percent larger than plastics. Silicones was very profitable, while plastics was just getting to breakeven.

Nevertheless, the future looked very bright. This was a time when forecasters believed that plastics would be the fastest-growing industry over the next decade—faster than computers and electronics. Even the movies were getting into it. In *The Graduate,* Dustin Hoffman was encouraged to get a career in "plastics!"

We added marketing people and began promoting the plastics business as if it were Tide detergent.

We hired St. Louis Cardinal pitcher Bob Gibson to be in our ads. We filmed a TV commercial with a bull in a china shop, except all the china made from Lexan plastic didn't break when the bull wreaked havoc on the set. We hired radio comedians Bob and Ray to plug our plastics in Detroit during prime time. We'd air the radio spots between seven-thirty and eight A.M., when our target customers, the automotive engineers, were stuck in traffic jams on their way to their General Motors, Ford, and Chrysler offices. We had billboards promoting Lexan on all the roads leading to work.

Denny McLain, at that time a thirty-game winner with the Detroit Tigers, hurled fastballs at me while I was holding up a Lexan plastic sheet in the parking lot of our Detroit office. The local press covered the event. All this promotion got a lot of attention because it was really different marketing for an industrial plastic.

We wanted to replace every metal part in a car with Lexan, from the trim on the dashboard to the crank handles on the windows. Because our five-person office in Detroit was competing against DuPont's 40-person office, we had to be faster and more creative. We took on the big chemical companies and did well because we could outrun them. We were using the strength of a big company and trying to run with the speed of a small company.

We were flying. By 1970, we had beaten my boastful prediction by more than doubling the plastics business in less than three years. Despite the obvious success, I was clearly ruffling the feathers of some powerful people at corporate headquarters.

One of them was Roy Johnson, the head of GE's human resources department. Johnson was the keeper of the keys, reporting directly to Chairman Fred Borch at the time and eventually to Reg Jones, and he had a big impact on hiring decisions.

Years later, I found a memo that Johnson wrote in July 1971 to Vice Chairman Herm Weiss. At the time, I was being considered for another promotion to vice president of the chemical and metallurgical division, a $400 million (sales) group of businesses. In the memo, Johnson concluded that I deserved the promotion but that the appointment "carries with it more than the usual degree of risk. Despite his many strengths, Jack has a number of significant limitations. On the plus side, he has a driving motivation to grow a business, natural entrepreneurial instincts, creativeness and aggressiveness, is a natural leader and organizer, and has a high degree of technical competence.

"On the other hand," continued Johnson, "he is somewhat arrogant, reacts (or overreacts) emotionally—particularly to criticism—gets too personally involved in the details of his business, tends to overrely on his quick mind and intuition rather than on solid homework and staff assistance in getting into and out of complex situations, and has something of an 'anti-establishment' attitude toward General Electric activities outside his own sphere."

I'm glad I found this evaluation later or I might have done something stupid—even if he had some pretty good points. At the time, I probably wouldn't have accepted the criticism. Johnson chalked up my "limitations" to "youthfulness and lack of maturity" but fortunately didn't block me for the division job. Thank goodness Herm Weiss supported me.

Looking back, there were enough reasons for Johnson and others to have reservations. Obviously, I wasn't a natural fit for the corporation. I had little respect or tolerance for protocol. I was an impatient manager, especially with people who didn't perform.

I was blunt and candid and, some thought, rude. My language could be coarse and impolitic. I didn't like sitting and listening to canned presentations or reading reports, preferring one-on-one conversations where I expected managers to know their businesses and to have the answers.

I loved "constructive conflict" and thought open and honest debates about business issues brought out the best decisions. If an idea couldn't survive a no-holds-barred discussion, the marketplace would kill it. Larry Bossidy, a good friend and former GE vice chairman, would later liken our staff meetings to Miller Lite commercials. They were loud, raucous, and animated.

And I never hid my thoughts or feelings. During a business discussion, I could get so emotionally involved that I'd stammer out what others might consider outrageous things. A couple of favorites were "My six-year-old kid could do better than that!" or "Don't Walter Cronkite me!" (That was understood by everyone to mean: "You report the bad news, but you don't tell me how you're going to fix it.")

People who couldn't fit into this informal and entrepreneurial environment left or were asked to leave. I cut my losses quickly on bad hires that didn't perform. People who were arrogant or pompous didn't last very long. Those who delivered took home outsize salary increases and bonuses, just as I now did.

I "kicked," but I also "hugged."

These differences cast me as a rebel of sorts and led to all kinds of ridiculous scuttlebutt. Most of the rumors about me were just that—rumors. They made for some fun conversations around the water cooler but had little basis in reality. The gossips claimed that I'd jump on top of desks or conference tables like some kind of temperamental bully.

That was a crock.

Yet I kept moving higher. Despite Johnson's reservations, I got the job as head of the chemical and metallurgical division in 1971, and it brought a bunch of new challenges. I had spent 11 years in GE working in the plastics arena. Now I had to figure out how to run a whole portfolio of materials businesses, including carbide cutting tools, industrial diamonds, insulating materials, and electro-materials products—and do it all with very different people.

My first job was to get a close look at my team. With a couple of exceptions, I found them wanting. I'm the first to admit I could be impulsive in removing people during those early days. But over the years, I learned a lot about how to do it. It's the toughest and most difficult thing we ever do. It's never easy, and it doesn't ever become easier.

If I learned anything about making this easier, it's seeing to it that no one should ever be surprised when they are asked to leave. By the time I met with managers I was about to replace, I would have had at least two or three conversations to express my disappointment and to give them the chance to turn things around. I would follow up every business review with a handwritten note.

Some may not have appreciated my candor, but they always knew exactly where they stood.

That first talk is when the surprise and disappointment, if any, should occur—not when the person is asked to leave. I can't remember a single instance where someone felt shocked or blindsided when our final conversation took place.

"Look," I'd say, "we gave this thing a good run. We both know it's not working out. It's time to wrap it up."

Inevitably, there's some disappointment. More often than not, there's relief. When it's time for the final conversation, the subject quickly gets to "What's my deal?" I've been lucky enough all my life to work for a company with the financial resources to be able to soften the blow.

At that point, the biggest challenge is to get everyone focused on the future. Assure them that this is another transition in their life when they can make a new start—just like the transition from high school to college, or from college to the first job. They can move on to another environment where all past warts are forgotten.

I've seen many people go on to better and happier lives after leaving jobs that just weren't working. All of us have a responsibility to try to make that happen.

I eventually had to deliver the bad news to three of the executives who reported to me in the new job in 1971. I also had a few keepers. I replaced myself in plastics with Tom Fitzgerald, a wild Irishman. Most of us in plastics were engineers. Tom was the only true peddler.

He and I were great friends as well as business soul mates. I took out the manager of our silicones business and found someone from my past: Walt Robb, the Ph.D. research engineer who recruited me at Illinois. Walt had already moved out of the lab and into an operating role as head of a small medical development business.

Into our laminating business, where I replaced the manager, I put Chuck Carson, an associate from plastics who had been my finance chief and later head of our Lexan sheet business. Laminates was a difficult business. Our major competitor, American Cyanamid's Formica brand, dominated the market and overwhelmed our brand, Textolite. We had the weakest distributors. Chuck was as strong as they make them. He was so tough we called him "Frank Nitti," after the rough guy on *The Untouchables,* a popular TV show at the time. Chuck always made the numbers in the budget but couldn't do much to improve the business's low margins or weak competitive position.

He and I tried everything to make a silk purse out of this sow's ear. It was the first time I saw the sadness in people grinding it out in a lousy business, going head-to-head with a nearly invincible competitor, with little hope of making it better.

Until then, I thought all businesses could be exciting. I believed that if you poured research and money into things, new products came, and with them future growth and success. It was my first look at the real world of bad businesses, a lesson that over my career would come to have an enormous impact. Luckily, though, our other businesses had pretty good margins, especially plastics—the real driver of growth.

I dove in to understand the people in these new businesses. In our metallurgical business in Detroit, for example, I asked to see the sales management team during an early human resources review. I could not believe the quality of the team. They came in with dull, formal presentations. They had no passion for their jobs and couldn't answer the most routine questions. I considered them the ultimate "milk run" sales force—salesmen who couldn't find new accounts to save their lives.

After the review, two managers were removed, but I met one special guy, John Opie, then market development manager. He was 35 years old and had been in the business for a dozen years. I gave him the first of many "battlefield promotions," making him national sales manager the day I met him. After having seen all his "new" regional sales managers, I told Opie that if I were him, I'd ask all six of them to leave over the next year. Eventually, five did.

That was obviously out of the ordinary—far out of the ordinary. But it jolted the team, and Opie used it to energize the business. Hardworking and totally unselfish, Opie would go on to become one of GE's best operating executives, ending up as one of my vice chairmen.

I didn't go out of my way to thumb my nose at the bureaucracy, but I was different and threatening to some of the headquarters people. Roy Johnson's comments reflected my own conflict with the corporate staff in New York. Whenever I wanted to hire a key person, corporate would serve up their slate of candidates for the "corporate dotted-line positions" in finance, human resources, and legal. In those functions, I had to fight for every person I wanted to hire.

I didn't always get to pick the ones I wanted. On several occasions, I had to settle for someone on the corporate slate. A couple of finance managers I was forced to take weren't even close to capable, and I eventually had to remove them. A big fight I lost was the time I tried to promote a young lawyer, Bob Wright, as general counsel for the plastics business.

I thought he was a lot more than a lawyer. Bob was 27 years old and had just come from private practice. When I was promoted to the division job, I brought Art Puccini with me as general counsel. Bob was the perfect candidate to succeed Art in the plastics business. GE's general counsel had a different view. He felt that Bob's age and experience made him unqualified, so he stuffed me with a slate of his cronies.

I took one of them. I solved the problem of promoting Bob Wright by asking him to take on strategy development for plastics in 1973. I could fill that position without corporate interference. Although it was an unlikely job for a lawyer, Bob was sensational in it. He had a million ideas and brought new life to the position. In 18 months, we made him the national sales manager for plastics. His quick wit and extroverted personality made him a natural fit for the job and gave him experience he would use forever. Bob eventually became president of NBC. Today he is a vice chairman of GE—a long road from being a "corporate reject" for the legal job in a business doing less than $100 million a year in sales.

Tension between the headquarters and the field is common in every organization. In Bob Wright's case, I found a way to beat the system without openly defying it. For the past 20 years, I hoped every day that GE people were making the case for the people they wanted—even if my staff and I were trying to stuff our own candidates down their throats.

While the bureaucracy often frustrated me, I tried hard not to be a very visible critic of it—especially not to the higher-ups. By the early 1970s, I had started to think about the possibility of running GE. I actually said it in 1973 when I presumptuously wrote in my performance review that my long-range career objective was to become CEO. I was determined not to blow my dream by tilting at windmills. If I bitched and moaned about the system, the system would get me.

I was fortunate. The system bent. The company gave me an incredible number of different experiences. For the most part, it let me be myself.

5

Getting Closer
to the Big Leagues

During June of 1973, I got my next big break. Reuben Gutoff was promoted to head of strategic planning for the entire company, and I got his job as group executive. The promotion meant that I had to move to corporate headquarters. Besides the chemical and metallurgical division I already managed from Pittsfield, I was now responsible for a number of other businesses: medical systems in Milwaukee, appliance components in Fort Wayne, electronic components in Syracuse.

It was a diverse portfolio of products with over $2 billion in annual sales. The group employed 46,000 people and had 44 factories in the United States, plus operations in Belgium, Ireland, Italy, Japan, the Netherlands, Singapore, and Turkey.

The promotion was a big deal. Only 16 months earlier, I was named a GE vice president at the age of 36. This new job put me on the radar screen. I was becoming a real player. I went to the New York headquarters to look at sample offices that had been set up similar to those in the company's planned new offices in Fairfield. GE would move there in August 1974. I picked out the furniture for my office, with a set number of ceiling tiles signifying one's status in the corporation.

There was only one problem—a very big one. I didn't want to move to the new headquarters in Fairfield.

Over the 13 years I had lived in Pittsfield, I had constructed the ideal life for my family and me. I loved the Berkshires. From our cramped apartment in 1960, Carolyn and I had moved into a succession of homes until we owned what I thought was one of the best houses in town.

We had a network of good friends. Our four children were still young and in local public schools. Pittsfield was a great place to bring up kids, with mountains and lakes just minutes away. I had a spectacular group of friends at the Pittsfield Country Club, where we played "life and death" games of golf and paddle tennis. I played hockey in a town pickup league well into my thirties. I knew just about everybody.

I really felt like the big fish in a little pond. I didn't want to give it up. Pittsfield had another advantage: It kept me out of the rat race at headquarters.

I flew to New York that summer to see Herm Weiss, then a vice chairman. As a group executive, I would report to Herm. He was a large and imposing man, tall with broad shoulders. An unassuming guy, Herm had been a star college athlete in football and baseball and was honored by *Sports Illustrated* as one of its Silver Anniversary Award winners.

I really liked him. We both loved golf, wisecracking, and betting on Sunday football games. First a boss, then an ally and friend, Herm took me under his wing. It seemed everywhere I went I found a mentor. I wasn't searching for a surrogate father, but good people always seemed to crop up and give me their support.

I usually looked forward to every meeting with Herm. This time I arrived in his office scared stiff. I went there to ask him to let me stay in Pittsfield. I argued that most of my time would be spent in the field with the businesses. I promised I would never be late for the monthly meetings at headquarters.

In a moment of weakness or charity, or both, Herm finally said yes. I practically jumped up and kissed him. I got out of his office in a hurry, before he could change his mind or report his decision to Reg, who I was sure wanted me at headquarters. When Reg found out, he couldn't believe Herm had let me stay in the field.

I moved out of my old office on Plastics Avenue and set up shop with a five-person staff in a suite of offices on the second floor of the Berkshire Hilton in Pittsfield. Over the next five years, I kept my promise to Herm never to miss a meeting. When Pittsfield's weather threatened to close down the airport, I would go down the night before. If we got a weather surprise, I'd jump in the car at 5 A.M. and drive like a maniac to New York in time for the start of a business review.

This group executive job was my best to date. The new $2 billion business mix gave me a large playpen to practice what I had learned. The chemical and metallurgical division, which included plastics, was growing. The appliance components business was a set of motors and widgets with good profits, but half of the sales were internal to GE. The electronic components business was a real mixed bag, from semiconductors to TV tubes and capacitors. Several of these electronic products were doing well, while others just bled red ink. The medical business, selling primarily X-ray equipment, had great potential but in 1973 was losing money.

This new job gave me the chance to put together a new team. I found a staff of bright, savvy, street-smart people with complementary skills in finance, human resources, strategy, and law. After being stuffed for years by corporate with candidates who were less than the best, I was lucky to finally get two strong GE executives from "the system": Tom Thorsen and Ralph Hubregsen.

Tom, my finance guy, was exceptionally smart, handsome, tough, and fun loving. Ralph, my human resources person, was an unmade bed. Craggy faced, he smoked cigars until their very end, scattering ashes everywhere. He was an administrative nightmare, often staying up all night long to finish the books for our presentations at headquarters. But you couldn't find anyone with a better nose for people.

I went outside for my strategic planner and found Greg Liemandt from Booz • Allen & Hamilton. He was the first of many smart people I hired from the consulting industry, which was ironic because I disliked consulting. Greg lived far outside the box, always challenging conventional thinking.

Last, I again promoted Art Puccini, my former general counsel, to the top legal job in the group. Born in Brooklyn, with degrees in pharmacy and law, Art had joined GE just a few years before. He brought a good mix of smarts and street savvy.

You couldn't have found a more diverse band of characters— some GE insiders and a pair from the outside world. All of us were earthy, without pretense or formality—always blunt.

Along with half a dozen support staff, we moved into a 3,600-square-foot group office suite at the Hilton. Without a corporate boss in sight, we wore sweaters and jeans to work. We shouted back and forth through the open doors. The place had the feel of a college dorm.

On Friday nights, we'd often go to the hotel's rooftop lounge to rehash the week over a few beers. We'd get up there about 6:30 P.M., and our wives would show up two hours later. By then, we had nearly exhausted all our exaggerated tales from the week. Listening to our war stories wasn't the biggest treat for any of them, but they were great sports. They liked one another as much as we did. Often, we'd get together on the weekends for Saturday night dinner or Sunday afternoon parties, many times with our kids.

We were having the time of our lives—and getting paid for it.

We spent most of our time in the field doing people and strategy reviews. We chartered a Citation jet that got us around easily. I was so excited to have a plane.

Carolyn saw it another way. "Jack, you're such a fool," she said. "They let you have the plane so you can work yourself to death."

She had a point, but I loved it, anyway. Often, we'd leave on a Monday morning and wouldn't return until Friday night. We'd visit Fort Wayne, Indiana, Milwaukee, Wisconsin, and Columbus, Ohio, as if they were towns next door. I'm sure some of the managers must have thought, Damn, here they come again. We'd spend hours locked in a room, peeling back the onion until all the issues were exposed. While some enjoyed the sessions and called them great intellectual combat, I'm sure others looked forward to them like they would to a root canal.

We had the best of both worlds. We had the resources of a big company, but with the same family atmosphere of my earlier years in the plastics business. Trying to oversee these diverse businesses in remote locations, I realized—more than ever before—how much my success would depend on the people I hired. From my first days in plastics, I understood the importance of getting the right people. It was clear that when I found someone great, it made all the difference in the world.

I learned a lot of this the hard way—by making some big mistakes. The inconsistency of my first hires was laughable. One of my most common errors was to hire on appearances. In marketing, I'd sometimes recruit good-looking, slick-talking packages. Some of those were good, and some were just empty suits.

I made other "beauties." I was 30 when I began hiring in Asia. Obviously, I couldn't speak Japanese. I had little feel for the culture. So I did the obvious. If a Japanese candidate spoke English well, I usually hired him. It took me a while to find out that using language as a "hiring screen" was a marginal idea at best.

Many of my hiring mistakes reflected my own silly prejudices. Probably because I went to UMass—a former agricultural school that was just emerging in engineering—academic pedigrees impressed me. For engineering talent, I'd try to hire MIT, Princeton, and Cal Tech graduates. I should have reminded myself where I had come from. Often, I found out that where they came from wouldn't determine how good they'd be.

In the early days, I fell in love with great résumés filled with degrees in different disciplines. They could be bright and intellectually curious, but they often turned out to be unfocused dabblers, unwilling to commit, lacking intensity and passion for any one thing.

In the hands of the inexperienced, résumés are dangerous weapons.

Eventually, I learned that I was really looking for people who were filled with passion and a desire to get things done. A résumé didn't tell me much about that inner hunger. I had to "feel" it.

In this new group job, I discovered that the only business I would ever know in my blood was plastics. This was a big transition in my thinking. I could no longer have fingertip control of all the details. That made my obsession about people even more intense.

My HR partner, Ralph Hubregsen, and I began going out to the businesses, spending a full day in a room first with the general manager and his HR executive and then with all his direct reports. After 10 or 12 hours of heated discussion, I'd come away with a pretty good sense of the talent we had at the top two or three levels of the business.

The reaction was total shock. No one was used to these intense personal discussions about the strengths and weaknesses of every individual on their team.

The leaders in the field who bore the brunt of these exchanges were the four divisional vice presidents who reported to me: Julian Charlier in medical, Walt Robb in chemical and metallurgical, George Farnsworth in electronic components, Fred Holt in appliance components.

Farnsworth was a real savvy GE insider who was truly his own man. He flew open-cockpit planes, was cynical yet funny, and was someone I got to like very much. Holt was another wise GE veteran. He played every corporate game there was and had been doing so for years. More often than not, he pretty much got what he wanted. Fred was probably 20 years older than me and had seen and heard it all. He saw me like a stomachache that would soon pass.

George and Fred were the first two mainstream GE corporate officers I ever managed. They often thought I was off the wall but seemed to respect my enthusiasm, if nothing else. Fred clearly was in his final job, and George was not obsessed with career advancement, although he would later get a big promotion to run our aerospace business.

Charlier, a Belgian who came from a small medical acquisition in Liège, Belgium, now ran the medical business. I had watched him for a couple of years when we both reported to Gutoff. Charlier was an urbane European who had a grandiose idea every minute but wasn't much into following up on them. He had built a beautiful new headquarters building for medical outside Milwaukee that gave the business new panache. There was a part of his bon vivant and creativity that I liked, but his inability to deliver results, which had bothered me as a peer, really drove me nuts when he began reporting to me.

I tried to stay with Charlier because I enjoyed him, but his 50,000-foot-high view of everything didn't work. We had several discussions about this and the lousy performance of the business until we finally decided that he would be better back in Europe at another company.

To replace him, I made a phone call on a Sunday night to Walt Robb. During my early days in plastics, he often called me on Sunday nights, offering support, gossip, and advice. This time I made the Sunday phone call to Walt and asked him to take over the medical business. My offer damn near knocked him on the floor. "You love technology, and you're curious," I said. "You're the perfect guy to run the medical business."

Walt thought I was crazy. In 20 months, he had gone from being head of a small $7.5 million (sales) medical development business to manager of the chemical and metallurgical division, one of GE's biggest and most profitable businesses, with $500 million in sales.

He had been in that job only four months and liked it. Now I was asking him to take over our medical business with half the revenue—and it was losing money. Walt had trouble seeing my offer to run an unprofitable business making X-ray equipment, pacemakers, and heart monitors in the middle of Wisconsin as "the opportunity of a lifetime." He took the job, intrigued by the technology and some of my own BS.

Walt inherited a business that primarily sold X-ray equipment to both radiologists and dentists. Shortly after Walt got there, EMI, the English electronics company (now the music company), had a major breakthrough, the CT (computed tomography) scanner. The advance posed a major threat to our existing X-ray business, but it was a huge challenge and really got our competitive juices flowing.

Walt, who had gotten his start at GE's research lab, went right back to his scientist friends in Schenectady for help. It was easy to excite the lab about the opportunity, since the EMI invention had captured the attention of the scientific world. My only contribution was to follow the team's progress weekly, serving at times as a cattle prod and on other occasions a cheerleader. About 80 people worked round-the-clock to create a product that would give us faster and better images than the EMI model. Everything about this had "start-up" written over it. Researchers practically lived in the lab, eating out of pizza boxes, and we made our first scanners out of a rented grocery store in Milwaukee.

By early 1976, they were taking orders for the $650,000 machine.

Once again I saw the benefits of acting like a small company. Giving the project visibility, putting great people on it, and giving them plenty of money continues to be the best formula for success.

The CT changed the medical business forever. An unprofitable operation with $215 million in sales when Walt took it over is now, in 2000, one of GE's jewels, with operating profit of $1.7 billion on over $7 billion of sales.

I broke up the chemical and metallurgical division that Walt had been running and spun out the high-growth plastics business. I put Chuck Carson, who had run our laminates business, over the slower-growing but highly profitable remaining materials businesses.

The plastics business posed something of a dilemma. My friend Tom Fitzgerald was now running silicones and was the obvious internal choice for the plastics job. But he was my closest business friend, and as a result I saw both his strengths and his weaknesses more than anyone else. I decided to compare Tom with the best I could find on the outside.

I've said that I've made my share of hiring mistakes. None would be bigger than the one I was about to make.

I passed over Tom for the job and brought in an outsider who had once run GE's silicone operations. As a young manager in the plastics business in the early 1960s, I was blown away by the presentations he gave at divisionwide meetings. He was the most articulate of all the leadership. His speaking skills were particularly impressive to me because I couldn't deliver a speech to save my life. Before reading my first speech in front of a few hundred GE executives in Cooperstown, New York, I twice had to leave the front row of the auditorium to run to the bathroom.

I was really pleased with myself for enticing him back. He seemed the perfect package: well dressed, articulate, someone who made a great first impression. He had left GE for a bigger opportunity in the chemical industry, which only impressed me more. Bringing him back as a corporate vice president was a big deal. To do this, I had to get approval from our corporate human resources people in Fairfield as well as from Herm and Reg.

It didn't take very long to realize that my new man wasn't up to the job. I had hired someone from an image I'd had 15 years ago. I knew I had to make a change. It was a real dilemma. I thought I was a candidate in the succession race for Reg's job. By hiring this outsider, I had gone against Roy Johnson, the HR head, who always favored the inside candidates. This could have been a disaster for me.

Within six months, I had to go to headquarters and tell Roy Johnson, Herm Weiss, and Reg Jones that I had screwed up and needed to remove him. Talk about a tough day. I had gone against the system. I hadn't hired one of my friends who expected and, in retrospect, deserved the promotion. I was embarrassed for the person I had recruited because it was so obvious this was the wrong job for him.

Herm's reaction was supportive. "You made a mistake. I'm glad you moved fast to correct it." Reg simply said, "Okay," but was otherwise guarded with his thoughts. Johnson used it as another example of my immaturity.

Holt and Farnsworth were not only good guys, they were savvy, and they knew how the GE system worked. This was my first real look inside the "traditional GE." Their insights opened my eyes to this other world.

There are a thousand Holt stories, but the one I liked best involves people evaluations. In Fort Wayne, one day during an HR review, Fred was giving a glowing appraisal of a guy I knew.

"Fred, how the hell could you write this? He's not that good. We both know this guy is a turkey. This appraisal is ridiculous."

To my surprise, Fred agreed.

"Do you want to see the real one?" he asked. "I can't send this to headquarters. They'd want me to kill this guy."

Fred wasn't alone in those days. He thought he was being a nice guy, protecting people who weren't up to their jobs. That's just the way it was. No one wanted to deliver bad news. In those days it was standard to fill out your appraisal form by writing that your career objective was at least your boss's job. The boss's response usually was "fully qualified to assume next position"—even if they both knew it wasn't true.

Many of these "kind" performance appraisals would come back to haunt me in the early 1980s when we had to downsize the company. That "false kindness" only misled people and made their layoff an even greater shock than it should have been.

From George Farnsworth and his electronic components business, I got two things: One was my first hard look at semiconductors, a business I disliked immediately. Yes, it had high growth, but it was too cyclical for me and ate up enormous amounts of capital. It took me close to a decade to get out of it.

The other thing I got from George would stay with me for the next 25 years: the controversy over PCBs (polychlorinated biphenyls). George managed the capacitor business in Hudson Falls, New York, which used PCBs as electrical insulators. It was my first experience dealing with the government.

From 1971 to 1977, my responsibility broadened continually, from running a $100 million business to a $400 million division and soon a $2 billion group. I learned the importance of people, supporting the best and removing the weakest. I learned to support high-growth businesses like medical and plastics and how to squeeze everything out of slow-growth operations. It was a great set of experiences.

Toward the end of 1977, I got a phone call in Pittsfield. It was from Reg in Fairfield. He wanted to see me, and it was urgent. I was there the next morning.

"I think highly of you," Reg said, "but Jack, you don't understand General Electric. You've only seen 10 percent of the company. GE's a lot more than that. I have a new job for you—sector executive for the consumer products businesses. But Jack, this job is in Fairfield. You can't be a big fish in a small pond anymore. If you want to be considered for bigger things, you're going to have to come here."

I was thrilled to get another promotion—even if it meant that I would finally have to leave Pittsfield. Carolyn was eager to move on. She was looking forward to a fresh start in a new place and felt the move would help our four kids grow.

By now, two of our four kids, Kathy and John, were in high

school, Anne was in the ninth grade, and Mark was in the fifth. Despite my crazy work habits, we were a close family. We always took a week off to ski in the winter during spring break and never missed renting a house on the Cape for a two-week vacation in the summer.

I admit I had a tough time taking a complete vacation from the job. When we were on the Cape, I'd often sneak off the beach to a pay phone to check into the office a couple of times a day. When we skied, I'd pop into the lodge to do the same.

Nonetheless, these vacations gave us lots of time to hang out together. We spent hours playing board games and sports. I'd tried to put as much fun and competition as possible into the games by egging all of them on. When we returned home, I always made up wooden plaques for the "Best Sport," "Best Miniature Golfer," or "Best Krypto Player" and handed them out to the kids. I guess I was trying to duplicate my mother's gin rummy games. Some of my kids were like me—they didn't take losing all that well.

Like most teenagers, they weren't excited to pick up and leave. Things had been good for them there. They all did well in school, and they had plenty of friends.

But it wasn't always easy for them. One morning, my son John was sitting on the school bus when it stopped to make its next pickup. A classmate climbed aboard and went straight at John, taking an unexpected swing at him. The fight broke up quickly, but poor John, then not much more than eight or nine years old, had no idea why it happened.

It wasn't until he told the story at the dinner table that night that I explained that I had asked the boy's dad to leave GE. We all felt awful for John—especially me, who still remembers that story as if it occurred yesterday.

Excited as I was about the new job, I was as sad as the kids about leaving Pittsfield. To keep a tie to the place, just before moving out, I bought five acres of inexpensive land on a mountaintop in nearby Lenox. In fact, the day we left town with our Buick station wagon packed to the gills, with our four kids in the back, we stopped off at the real estate agent's office to complete the purchase. For some reason, it made me feel better.

My promotion to Fairfield brought me to a new organizational layer as a "sector executive." There was a hierarchy at GE, like any other large company, and I had been lucky to climb through it. Sometimes it felt like the civil service, with all its 29 levels and dozens of titles and promotions, from a lab to a unit to a subsection to a section to a department, then a division and a group. The sector jobs were rated level 27, just two small steps from the 29th level attached to Reg's own job.

This was a big move. It put me in the race for Reg's job. I was excited by the possibilities, but apprehensive about whether the Pittsfield act would play in the Fairfield bureaucracy.

6

Swimming in a Bigger Pond

Early one December morning in 1977, I drove past the security guard at the front gate of GE's headquarters in Fairfield and up the winding driveway. All the trees were bare and the grounds were covered with snow that day. I turned into the concrete underground garage, parked my car in an empty slot, got in the elevator, and went to the third floor of the west building. I walked down the wide hallway to a corner office with a glass door, the farthest office away from Chairman Reg Jones.

The place was very quiet and formal—cold and unwelcoming. I had no secretary and no staff, other than three managers who had worked for one of my chief rivals for Reg's job. I didn't know many of the hundreds of people who worked in Fairfield headquarters. Reuben Gutoff, the man who had once convinced me to stay at GE, had himself left the company two years earlier in late 1975.

There were only a couple of friendly and familiar faces. Charlie Reed, the executive who had been so supportive when I blew up the Pittsfield plant, was now in Fairfield as the company's chief technologist. Mike Allen, a former McKinsey & Co. consultant whom I had first met in my plastics days, had moved to headquarters to work in strategic planning. Both men were far away from my office and busy with other things.

What really made me feel alone was the loss of my good friend and supporter in Fairfield. Herm Weiss, one of GE's vice chairmen, had died a year earlier from lung cancer. He had been my only real link to the top brass of the corporation. In a final show of support, Herm walked three holes with me during the board of directors' July golf outing. Six weeks later, in September 1976, he died at New York Hospital. I subsequently discovered that in his final days he had told Reg to keep his eye on me because I was "the person who was going places."

Talk about lonely. Forget about all that "small fish in big pond" stuff. I felt like a minnow in an ocean. Of course, I had been here many times doing various dog-and-pony routines. Even then, by the end of the day, after presenting a business plan or asking for the cash to build a new plant, I was always happy to return to Pittsfield.

This time, of course, it would be different. This was permanent.

What a difference from going to the office every day in a sweater and blue jeans, working with five of my close friends. By hiring people who became my friends and actively socializing with them and their families, I had probably broken the rules of corporate behavior.

But we got the job done, and we enjoyed doing it. We felt like a "family" instead of a business. Now all that was gone. To add to my "out there" feeling, for the next four months, I lived out of a suitcase at the Stamford Marriott, until Carolyn and our four kids could move to our new home in Connecticut. There was one positive side effect. It allowed me to bury myself in my new job.

The move to Fairfield came with a big promotion to a newly created layer of management. I was now one of five sector executives, who had all been publicly identified as candidates in a horse race for Reg's job, along with two corporate staffers, Al Way, GE's chief financial officer, and Bob Frederick, the senior vice president for corporate planning.

The four other sector heads were John Burlingame, a physicist who ran GE's international businesses; Ed Hood, a nuclear engineer who ran the technical products and services sector; Stan Gault, a longtime veteran of the appliance business who had the industrial sector; and finally, Tom Vanderslice, a former Fulbright scholar who ran power systems.

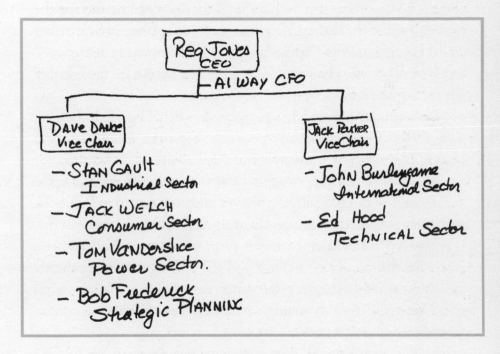

Reg put in this new layer as part of his succession process to test our skills and abilities in running multibillion-dollar portfolios that we weren't familiar with. I drew consumer products and services, the only existing sector that had been created a year earlier by Reg to try out the idea. The job put me in charge of a group of businesses with $4.2 billion in revenues, about 20 percent of the company's total sales. The businesses included major appliances, air conditioners, lighting products, housewares and audio products, television receivers, radio and TV stations, and GE Credit Corp.

The structure was a great idea to help Reg choose his successor, but there was one problem for me. My new direct boss, Vice

Chairman Walter "Dave" Dance, favored another candidate in the race—his longtime protégé, Stan Gault, who, like Dance, had invested virtually his entire career in our appliance businesses.

Dance's support for Gault was obvious and visible. He was certainly entitled to his opinion, but it made my life difficult. It was the first time in my 17 years at GE that I had a boss who was not rooting for me. Nor did it help that Gault had run my sector the previous year. So I was in a position where every move I made could appear to second-guess him or Dance.

The other vice chairman, Jack Parker, also had his favorites in the race. I was not one of them. Parker was one of the aircraft engine pioneers at GE who always supported that business and the people in it. He favored his two direct reports: Burlingame and Hood. This left Tom Vanderslice and me as the odd men out.

What gave me hope was that the two vice chairmen, Dance and Parker, didn't have much of a relationship with each other or with Reg, who hadn't chosen them in the first place. Reg had inherited both vice chairmen from his predecessor. Both had been rivals for the job. They weren't bad guys—but they were disappointed that they didn't get Reg's job.

There is probably nothing worse in business than to work for a boss who doesn't want you to win. This can happen anywhere, at any level—and probably occurs more often than we think. Until I came to work for Dance, I had never had it happen to me. I survived the experience only by doing what I thought was right. I trusted Reg and the system to be fair.

Had it been a "forever" assignment, I would have dumped it. I wouldn't have ruined my career or my sanity by sticking around. In my case, it was easier than it might be for others. I knew what I wanted, and it wasn't going to take long to find out if I was going to get it.

From day one, the succession process was thick with politics. You could feel the tension in the building every day. The five sector heads were all located in what was known as the west building of the two-building Fairfield complex. Each of us had a corner office, a conference room, and space for several support staff. Whenever we were in town, we'd usually end up in an uncomfortable situation in the corporate dining room for lunch. We'd munch on sandwiches, always being careful about what we said.

It was awful.

The field became my refuge from the politics. Fortunately, to do the job right, I needed to spend as little time in Fairfield as possible. The team behind me was talented—and mobile. David Orselet, my human resources executive, had a perfect nose for sniffing out talent and was someone everyone trusted—a priceless trait in an HR person.

I didn't know it at the time, but Dave's support of me in the final selection would be very important. Dick Schlegel, a warm man and very savvy finance guy, was also in place.

Dick helped me find two people who would play critical roles in my career: Dennis Dammerman from GE Credit, and Bob Nelson, a financial analyst who had spent years in appliances.

Dennis grew up on a farm in Grand Mound, Iowa. As a kid, he was lifted and dumped into burlap bags so he could tamp down the newly shorn wool from the family's herd of sheep. As a teen, he began working for another electric company—as an electrician's apprentice at his father's company, Dammerman Electric: "Everything Electrical."

After graduating from the University of Dubuque in 1967, Dennis found himself visiting friends in Bloomington, Illinois, where a GE factory made electrical parts. He approached the security guard at the plant's gate and asked about a job. Luckily, he was referred to a manager inside who hired Dennis for GE's financial management program. He was brilliant, tough, and as dependable a person as anyone could ever count on. Dennis had enormous capacity and loved to take on any difficult assignment.

Bob Nelson was the intellectual in the crowd. A graduate of Carleton College, he is a political science and history buff with a fabulous analytical mind. Bob seemed headed for a life as a college professor. He got a master's degree in general studies and humanities at the University of Chicago and began work on a Ph.D. in American studies. He took a detour into business, joining GE's financial management program in 1966.

Together, Dennis and Bob would become my financial tutors, and I would rely on their good judgments until the day I retired from GE. Dennis would become my chief financial officer, CEO of GE Capital Services, and a vice chairman of the company. Bob would become vice president for financial analysis.

I also brought in a friend from Pittsfield, Norm Blake, as my manager of business development. Norm was a bright, tenacious, and hyperactive entrepreneur who had held the same job with me in plastics. He would become an executive vice president at GE Capital and in 1984 left the company to become chairman of Heller International.

I went after this new job just as I always had in Pittsfield. Only now we'd fly out from Fairfield to get to know the new businesses and the people in them. We'd typically start a review at 7:30 A.M. and then spend hours peeling back the onion again. Rarely would we finish before 8 or 9 at night, when we'd go out to dinner together to review the day's session and size up the talent in each business.

Because of the lack of support from my boss, I went at my job as if he weren't there. The most difficult issues to deal with would be in the appliance business. Changes in direction could be perceived as shots at my predecessors Dance and Gault. They had run the appliance operations for more than a decade. For years, it had been a sweetheart business of GE. Dance and Gault had plans for massive expansion of our Appliance Park in Louisville, Kentucky. They had started by building an Appliance Park East in Columbia, Maryland, and there was talk of an Appliance Park West in Salt Lake City, Utah.

Their ambitious plans reflected the company's conventional view of the business's potential. It had been driven by the glow of the postwar era, when a rising middle class filled its new kitchens with new appliances. There was no question that the business would continue to grow. The real questions, however, were how fast that growth would be and how well positioned we were against our major U.S. and global competitors. My new associates Bob Nelson and Dennis Dammerman, who had both spent time in the appliance business, tore apart the numbers and the conventional assumptions.

Our look said that growth would slow. The big expansion plans needed to be reexamined. In fairness, I think Dance and Gault were coming to the same conclusion. Even more important than the expansion was our situation in Louisville. We had to improve it. While sales and profits were okay, productivity was steadily declining.

For years, headquarters had been hearing a fairly optimistic view of appliances. In Louisville, an army of economists, strategic planners, and finance people were believers in and advocates for the business. They didn't want to admit that the days of postwar growth were rapidly changing. They weren't alone. Their expansive view was shared by much of American industry.

In Louisville, the leadership team in appliances had moved out of our manufacturing and engineering center to an office suite on the top floor of a 15-story high rise five miles away. This was symbolic—they were sitting in an ivory tower while all the "doers" were back at Appliance Park making white appliance boxes.

Armed with my group's analysis, I went to Dance to recommend a significant cutback in the business he had managed for so many years. I was prepared for Dance to fight, but he didn't. Instead, I think he might have seen my recommendation as further proof of my impulsiveness. He approved my plan.

We moved quickly to make the business in Louisville more competitive by significantly downsizing what we had, scrapping plans for building additional Appliance Parks.

The layoffs were not popular in Louisville. I was fortunate to have an ally in Dick Donegan, a Dance and Gault appointee, who was running the appliance business. He bought into the new plans and had the courage to act on them—in spite of his prior relationships. Though the painful changes at Appliance Park still didn't solve all the cost problems, they did make us more competitive, improved our profitability, and kept us going.

In appliances, similar actions have gone on for more than 20 years. A business that employed just over 47,000 people in 1977 today employs less than half that total, some 19,800 salaried and hourly workers. These downsizings are awful, as hardworking people get hammered by competitive change. In difficult businesses these changes never end. I can't tell you how often I was asked in the early 1980s, "Is it over now?"

Unfortunately, it's never over.

A lot of the products that fueled the postwar boom simply became commodities, products with wafer-thin margins in slow-growing markets. Those changes drove many competitors out of the appliance business, from Ford Motor's Philco and GM's Frigidaire to Westinghouse. GE chose to stay and fight in a very tough industry. In order to stay alive in the business, however, we had to manufacture more of these products outside the United States. The price of a refrigerator today is $700 to $800 down from an average of $1,000 to $1,200 in 1980.

The only good thing about this fiercely competitive industry is that Asian competitors up to now have made few inroads into the U.S. market. That appliance experience contrasts with the experience of the U.S. automotive industry, where steady price increases invited all kinds of foreign competition.

Of all the businesses I was given as a sector executive in 1977, none seemed more promising to me than GE Credit Corp. Like plastics, it was well out of the mainstream, and like plastics, I sensed it was filled with growth potential.

No one paid much attention to GE Credit. It was the orphan child in a manufacturing company. We entered the business in 1933 almost by default, helping our appliance dealers move their inventories of refrigerators and stoves in the midst of the Depression by providing consumers with credit. We also financed furniture sales because most of our dealers carried those lines as well. But that's about all we did for the first 20 years, from the 1930s until the 1950s.

Then we branched out and financed Caterpillar construction equipment, what we called Yellow Iron. It wasn't until the late 1960s that we started leasing other equipment. By the late 1970s, GE Credit had become diversified but was still small. By then, we were financing manufactured houses, second mortgages, commercial real estate, industrial loans and leases, and private-label credit cards.

In those early days, I didn't understand the intricacies of finance. I had the staff prepare a book that translated all the jargon into layman's terms. I called it "finance for little folks," but it was just what I needed. I studied it like I was back in grad school, so I could be conversant with the people in the business.

My gut told me that compared to the industrial operations I did know, this business seemed an easy way to make money. You didn't have to invest heavily in R&D, build factories, and bend metal day after day. You didn't have to build scale to be competitive. The business was all about intellectual capital—finding smart and creative people and then using GE's strong balance sheet. This thing looked like a "gold mine" to me.

Leveraging brainpower is easier than grinding out products. Nowhere was the finance/manufacturing comparison more obvious than in profits per employee. With fewer than 7,000 employees, GE Credit's net income in 1977 was $67 million. In contrast, it took a payroll of more than 47,000 employees in appliances to make $100 million.

I'm sure this is obvious to almost everyone today—but to me it was a big insight in 1977. After all, I was a chemical engineer who had known only about "making things."

GE Credit wasn't doing badly in the late 1970s. Its profits and business grew every year. I just didn't think it was growing fast enough given its vast opportunity. In my early meetings with the leaders of the business in the spring of 1978, I was underwhelmed by the people in the organization. I'd gather them together in a room—several layers' worth of management—and grill them about the ins and outs of their business. "Let's pretend we're in high school," I said. "Take me through the basics."

During one of the more memorable instances, I recall asking a pretty simple question of one of our insurance leaders. During his presentation, he had been using a couple of terms that I was unfamiliar with. So I interrupted him to ask: "What's the difference between 'facultative' and 'treaty' insurance?" After fumbling through a long answer for several minutes, an answer I wasn't getting, he finally blurted out in exasperation, "How do you expect me to teach you in five minutes what it has taken me 25 years to learn!"

Needless to say, he didn't last long.

The insurance anecdote wasn't an isolated incident. It was par for the course. If GE Credit could make as much money as it did with the existing people, I wondered how much more potential the business would have if it were filled with nothing but A players.

We didn't have enough stars to capitalize on what looked to me like easy pickings. John Stanger, who was then leading the business, was a shrewd deal maker. He was a product of the system and didn't want to rock the boat. John had a tendency to take what he was given in people, and he hadn't been exposed to the talent pool in many other parts of the company.

During the Session C human resources reviews in the spring of 1978, I challenged all of the GE Credit managers. We had a rough first day. After the review, we invited everyone to the nearby Landmark Club in Stamford to get a better feel for them in a social atmosphere. In general, most didn't look any better after hours than they did during the day.

Stanger was plenty smart. All we had to do was get him exposed to better people. Once he got them, he flourished. Over the next couple of years, we changed more than half the leadership team in GE Credit. Many of the newcomers were recruited from other parts of GE. Many came from deep down in the organization. They made a big difference.

There was one executive in place at GE Credit who stood out like no other. He was a brusque, smart, funny, quick-talking guy who ran the commercial and industrial financing operation. His name was Larry Bossidy, and when I first met him, I thought, Where the hell did you come from?

I met him in early 1978 in Hawaii at a management meeting for GE Credit. Somehow we found ourselves playing a game of Ping-Pong at an outside table. We were playing as if our lives depended on it, diving into hedges and sweating bullets. It was intense, with each of us whacking the heck out of this little white ball. Carolyn was calling from the balcony of our hotel room to remind me we had to catch a plane. I didn't want to leave. I was excited by this guy who was so full of life and so competitive.

After the game, I couldn't let go of him. He impressed me with his quick wit and sharp observations that reinforced my instincts about the lackluster quality of middle management at GE Credit. After thinking I had found a star—Larry dropped a bomb. He confided that he was ready to leave the company for a job at Lone Star Cement. He was just as frustrated with the bureaucracy as I was years before.

I asked him to hang on.

"What the hell do you want to go to a cement company for?"

"This place is driving me nuts!" he replied.

"Give me a chance," I said. "You're just what we need. This is going to be a different place."

Bossidy stayed. A year later, in 1979, with Reg's support, I made him chief operating officer of GE Credit. He and Stanger set the stage for what would become our most important growth business. After I became chairman, Larry moved to Fairfield as a sector executive in 1981 and three years later became one of my vice chairmen. He would be a great partner for the next seven years before leaving to run his own show as CEO of AlliedSignal.

Larry's early role at GE Capital was essential. From that small base in 1977, a business earning $67 million with fewer than 7,000 employees, GE Capital has grown explosively. In 2000, the business had $5.2 billion in earnings, with more than 89,000 employees—thanks to an incredible succession of leaders.

Not everything I touched turned out so well. In the middle of the succession race, I pursued a major acquisition to increase our exposure in the broadcast business. I negotiated, with my business development head Norm Blake, the purchase of the Cox Communications cable and broadcasting operations.

In the spring of 1978, I sold the board of directors on the deal, confident that the acquisition was a very good one for GE. We already owned a few TV stations, and GE was, in fact, one of the pioneers in cable. The company had decided to exit the cable business in the 1970s because it believed the industry was too regulated. Norm and I felt differently. We believed cable had a great future and was on the verge of breaking out. Reg agreed.

Over the next 14 months, as we worked to get all the necessary approvals at the Federal Communications Commission (FCC), cable TV began to explode. I wanted to get a head start on Cox, so I transferred Bob Wright from plastics down to Cox's Atlanta headquarters to head up the cable interests in anticipation of our taking control of Cox Broadcasting. Having seen Bob's leadership in plastics sales, I thought his outgoing personality and legal background would be perfect for the rapidly expanding cable industry. The Cox management loved Bob, but as time for FCC approval dragged on, the Cox family began to raise the price tag on the deal. It was becoming increasingly clear to me that they regretted signing the contract with us.

The Cox team had done some clever lawyering. Our agreement turned out to be less a contract to buy the business and more an option for Cox to sell at their discretion. The contract allowed Cox an out. Perhaps I should have caught this, but I didn't.

I had gone out on a limb to convince Reg and the board that this deal, at several hundred million dollars, was a good one. Now, with the price escalating every time Norm and I met with the Cox people, I was coming to the conclusion the deal couldn't get done at any price. The Cox family had changed their mind about selling and was using the price as a way to end it. Losing this big deal in the politically charged atmosphere of a succession race was a potential disaster.

With all that was riding on it—the acquisition and my own future at GE—we wanted the deal badly. Norm and I spent hours agonizing over whether they would ever close. We didn't want to give up. Norm had been with me in the plastics business, and our families were close. For about ten days, we never stopped debating it, in the office or at each other's homes. After all that soul-searching, I finally decided we had to walk.

I informed Reg about my decision during the summer of 1979. He agreed but asked me to explain the rationale to the full board at its next meeting, which was in St. Louis. Now I not only had to bare my soul to Reg, I also had to face all of the company's directors. The upcoming board meeting was the time of an annual golf outing of senior executives and board members. This only added to the drama of having to go in and eat crow on a deal I had been touting so hard for over a year. I didn't know what to expect. But I put my best face on what was a difficult situation.

In an early morning board session, I made the case for not chasing the deal. The directors asked lots of questions, including "Why not keep raising the price?" Having dealt with the Cox negotiators for the last six weeks, I felt down to my toes that the Cox family wasn't going to sell to us, no matter what, but I couldn't prove it. Continuing to chase it wasn't right for GE.

I thought the meeting went well. I was hoping the directors would overlook my inability to close the deal and appreciate that I faced a tough call. I had little idea what they really thought. I got a somewhat positive reaction that afternoon when I was playing golf with three of them. As I was teeing up my ball on a short par three, one of the board members, Dick Baker, former head of Ernst & Whinney and a man with a great sense of humor, quipped, "I hope the fact that you screwed up today won't bother you on this shot!"

My seven iron fell out of my hands, and I yelled, "Foul!" The other two directors in the foursome broke out in laughter. I took it as a positive sign, because it was the first time I had seen this crowd of generally serious people joking around. I didn't think they'd be doing it at my expense if I weren't in good shape. Later I found out that some directors, concerned about my competitiveness, liked the fact that I could walk away from a deal.

In the background of all these changes was Reg's succession. Everyone in the race was trying to outshine everyone else. We were all working our butts off trying to differentiate ourselves. I didn't get any feedback from my boss, Dance. The changes I pushed at GE Credit, for example, didn't receive support or opposition from him. And I really wasn't sure where Reg stood. In my gut, I always felt he was with me, but I never knew for sure.

This was a horse race, but all the jockeys and horses were blind. No one, other than Reg, knew who was ahead or behind in the race. And Reg wasn't about to tell any candidate where he stood in the game.

The hall gossip made everyone think that his favorite was Al Way, who shared Reg's roots in finance and as CFO worked closely with him every day. Al helped engineer Reg's largest acquisition, Utah International, and also helped him dispose of our losing computer business to Honeywell Inc. Meanwhile, Dance's support of Gault, who was running the industrial sector, never wavered, nor did Parker's support of Burlingame and Hood.

My nose and my gut sensed that Reg approved of what I was doing, but I was still nagged by doubts. Those uncertainties caused me to consider leaving GE in the midst of the race. Like everyone at GE, I was always getting contacted by headhunters. This time, with the self-doubts swirling in me, I reacted positively to a telephone call from Gerry Roche of Heidrick & Struggles, the search firm, and looked at the CEO job at Allied Chemical.

In retrospect, I was testing the waters, not really wanting to leave GE but not sure where I stood in the race. That lack of self-confidence was rearing its ugly head.

At the time, there was much I didn't know about the succession process. I had no idea then that the initial list of 19 candidates put together in late 1974, when I was still in Pittsfield, failed to include my name. I didn't know that when the list was narrowed to ten names by early 1975, I still wasn't on it. I didn't know that Roy Johnson, the human resources executive, had kept me off the lists. One official HR view of me stated at the time: "Not on best candidate list despite past operating success. Emerging issue is overwhelming results focus. Intimidating subordinate relationships. Seeds of company stewardship concerns. Present business adversity will severely test. Watching closely."

The translation was simple. Johnson thought I was too young and too brash and didn't have the GE monogram stamped on my forehead. He thought I drove too hard for the results I got and had little respect for the company's rituals and traditions. Despite Johnson's reservations, Reg insisted on tossing me into the mix. He thought my results earned me at least the chance to compete for his job. I was identified as a person targeted for "intensive development—in other words, bigger jobs.

Fortunately, by 1976, Ted LeVino had succeeded Johnson as senior vice president of human resources. He had a major hand in the process, putting the first lists together for Reg and watching over the succession race on a daily basis. Ted revolutionized the human resources function at GE. He challenged the "old boys" status quo and began pushing a meritocracy. Reg had come to count on Ted as a sounding board.

In late January 1979, Reg asked me inside his office and closed the door for what I later understood to be one of the first of his famous "airplane interviews" with all the candidates. The previous chairman, Fred Borch, had used a similar interview to pick Reg.

"Jack, you and I are flying in one of the company planes, and the plane crashes," said Reg. "Who should be the next chairman of General Electric?"

Most candidates, including me, immediately and instinctively tried to crawl out of the wreckage and take control of the company. Reg politely explained that wasn't possible. We were both on the plane.

I tried to argue that I had survived the crash.

"No, no," he said, "you and I are killed. Who should be the chairman?"

I fumbled around, struggling with the answer. I told him I was so confident that I was the best candidate for the job that it was hard for me to give him another name.

"Wait a minute," Reg said. "You're done. Who should get the job?"

I finally told Reg my vote would go to Ed Hood, who ran the technical products and services business. "He's thoughtful and smart, and I'd make Tom Vanderslice the number two guy. Tom's decisive, and tough as nails. They would complement each other well." Tom ran the power systems sector and, like me, lacked support from either vice chairman.

Then Reg asked my views of each of the other contenders, drawing out my assessment of their strengths and weaknesses. He wanted to know how I rated each guy on intelligence, leadership, integrity, and public image. He was trying to find out who could work with whom. He wasn't about to saddle his successor—as he had been—with a couple of unhappy vice chairmen. In these interviews, repeated over several months, Reg gathered the opinions of all the top executives, including senior officers who weren't in the race.

When Reg compiled the results of these sessions with nine different executives, no one gave the top job to me. Seven of those interviewed favored Stan Gault. Two named Ed Hood.

Another time, in June, Reg asked me to come in again.

"Remember our airplane conversations?" he asked.

"Yeah," I replied. "You killed me."

Reg laughed. "Well, this time, we're out there together, we're flying in a plane, and the plane crashes."

"Not again," I complained.

"Jack, this time I'm done, but you live. Now who should be the chairman of General Electric?"

"That's better. I'm the guy," I said without hesitation.

Reg asked who should be on my leadership team. I told him that among all the candidates in the race, I would most want to work with Hood and Burlingame. Once again, I emphasized that the best fit with me would be Hood. I added Burlingame because I genuinely respected his intelligence, his analytical abilities, and his comfort with himself.

"Okay, if you're the man, what do you see ahead as the major challenges facing the company?"

I told Reg exactly what I thought, as I'm sure every candidate did. Reg shared our views and thoughts with the Management Development and Compensation Committee of the board, then chaired by Ralph Lazarus, chairman of Federated Department Stores. Apparently, when Reg tallied up the results of these sessions in which he had asked each person to name three executives for the top leadership team, I fared much better. Gault still got the most votes (seven), while Hood and I were tied with six each.

Through these interviews, Reg kept his usual poker face. He never gave any of us a hint if we were in good shape or not. At times, he could appear remote and hard to connect with. He showed no bias or preference, at least to me, and because of our many surface differences, I wasn't at all sure that he would eventually pick me. He was, it appeared, an English statesman, and I was an Irish street kid.

On the surface, at least, he appeared to be the opposite of me.

Yet few people, including me, knew that Reg had grown up on the outside looking in.

He was portrayed as a courtly statesman. He was written up as an adviser to three presidents and their cabinets, a man who one reporter said looked like "an industrious church deacon." He was and is all those things. But what many people missed was that Reg was not privileged. He was a self-made man from working-class roots who worked and fought hard for what he achieved. Borrowing the Bob Hope line, Reg put it best: "I'm English. I'm too damn poor to be British."

Reg grew up in a row house in Stoke-on-Trent. His dad worked as a foreman in a steel mill, and his mother itched for a better life in the United States. Reg finally arrived in America at the age of 8½ years, in an English boy's school uniform, and moved just outside Trenton, New Jersey. Whatever accent he brought was quickly knocked out of him in the schoolyard by kids who felt threatened by a smart outsider. Both his parents got jobs in a local factory, the Acme Rubber Manufacturing Co. His mother was a piece worker, sorting and packing rubber jar rings meant for the lids of Mason jars. His dad was an electrician's helper.

Reg excelled at school, working his way through the University of Pennsylvania's Wharton School by tutoring other students and shelving books in the university library. When he graduated in 1939, he went straight to GE and climbed up the ranks through the company's powerful finance function. Reg did an eight-year tour on the audit staff that took him to nearly every plant in every business of the company. He was an operating manager in several businesses before being named chief financial officer in 1968, a post that set him up for the chairman's job four years later.

Reg and I were clearly very different people. But we also had a lot of hidden similarities. Both of us were hardworking people from modest backgrounds. Like me, he was an only child whose parents were remarkably similar to my own. Our success in the only company either of us ever worked for was a tribute to the organization's meritocracy.

We both loved numbers and analyses. We both did our homework and showed little tolerance for anyone who didn't. Outsiders who for years have scratched their heads over how Reg could have chosen someone so different from himself never realized the links we shared.

Neither did I until writing this book. We were considerably more alike than anyone imagined.

The first big break in the race came in early August 1979—18 months after I first came to Fairfield. On Thursday night, August 2, after a board outing at the Blind Brook Country Club near Rye, New York, Reg sat down with his two vice chairmen and told them he was going to narrow the race down to three candidates: myself, Burlingame, and Hood.

The remaining candidates would keep their current jobs or leave the company. He said he would ask the board the next morning for approval to name the three of us as vice chairmen. Both Parker and Dance would have to retire by the end of the year.

The next morning, Parker and Dance gave their opinions to the full board—essentially opposing Reg's position that I be the third candidate. At least one of the board's most powerful directors strongly supported Gault, and there was some additional backing for Al Way because of his financial expertise. However, the board swung Reg's way, including Parker and Dance, who backed off and made the vote unanimous.

To his credit, a clearly disappointed Parker summoned me to

his office. "I want you to hear this from me and not anyone else," he said. "I didn't support you, and I don't think you're the right guy to run GE. I don't want you to screw this company up." I admired his candor, even though I disagreed with his assessment.

What I wouldn't know for many years was that Reg had already made up his mind. He wanted me to be the next CEO of the company. But a few directors still favored other candidates. By putting the three of us on the board as vice chairmen, Reg was betting that a longer look would sway the other directors in my favor.

Over the next few months, Gault, Vanderslice, Way, Parker, and Dance left the company. For the next two years, Burlingame, Hood, and I reported directly to Reg. The atmosphere cleared and the politics disappeared. Reg's airplane interviews had assured him that the three of us could work well together as a team—and we did.

Toward the end, Reg made one final request of all the candidates. He asked each of us to write a detailed memo that assessed our own performance as a vice chairman, a director, and a company representative. He also asked us to write about our personal growth and how we met what Reg called the test of "stewardship"—what the corporation should bring to society.

I was still worried about a more basic concern: that Reg and the board might pass me over because of my age. At 44, I was the youngest of the three final candidates. John Burlingame was 58. Ed Hood was 50. I considered including in my memo a promise not to hold the office for more than ten years—if I got it. I thought a pledge would offset some concern about my age and the possibility I would be in the job too long.

When I told my close friend Anthony "Lofie" LoFrisco about this, he thought I was out of my mind. Lofie is a New York lawyer I met at Silver Spring Country Club shortly after coming to Fairfield. One Sunday afternoon by the pool at my home in New Canaan, we got into a fierce argument over my idea of proposing a "term limit." He insisted I would forever regret doing it.

"Once you get in that office you'll never leave," he said. "The only way they'll get you out of there is if they entomb you in your office with cinder blocks."

"Get out of here!" I said. "You're crazy."

Larry Bossidy and his family were there, and Larry ended up on LoFrisco's side. Ultimately, I agreed with them and dropped it. (Lofie hasn't failed to remind me about his great contribution to my career for at least the past ten years.)

I later discovered that my concern was real—although not terribly serious. A couple of directors had been suggesting that Reg should name Burlingame the next chairman for a short period of time as a bridge before naming me. Reg apparently defused the issue by telling the board that I would in all likelihood leave the company if I didn't get the job.

He was right.

I spent a lot of time crafting an eight-page memo and sent it to Reg, noting, "It may be more about Welch than we both need or want to know." The letter is more stiff and formal than what I would write today. However, it was something that at 44 I felt I needed to overcome my immature image. Still, it contained many of the ideas I would in fact implement over the next 20 years.

In it, I dealt head-on with the concerns some colleagues may have had with me, including my perceived lack of maturity and sensitivity. I argued that all of my experiences at GE over 20 years, coupled with my personal growth, had given me the necessary maturity for the job and the sensitivity needed in the CEO's "stewardship" role.

I attempted to deal with my demanding nature by writing: "While I have and will continue to demand that people attain high performance standards, I have at the same time provided numerous 'leapfrog' opportunities to promising employees and have helped create an atmosphere which attracts talented and ambitious men and women."

One line I liked summed up what I thought about leadership: "The people with whom I have been associated have worked harder, enjoyed it more, although not always initially, and in the end, gained increased self-respect and self-confidence from accomplishing more than they previously thought possible."

I explained that I learned something valuable by my failure to complete the Cox acquisition. I had discovered that Wall Street's reaction to both the proposed deal and its cancellation was "general disinterest," even though its cost was in the hundreds of millions of dollars and it was in a highly attractive and visible industry. Because GE was so large, the deal's impact was not considered significant.

"It reinforces my view that what we have to sell as an enterprise to the equity investor is consistent, above-average earnings growth throughout the economic cycle," I wrote. "Our size may dictate that as the only option. The discipline to balance both short and long term is the absolute of such a strategy." Little did I know when writing this letter how true this fundamental belief would turn out to be.

Finally, I also put in a strong pitch for the job. "There is a great distance today," I wrote Reg, "between where you are and all three of us [stand]. However, I feel I have the intellectual capacity, breadth, discipline, and most of all the leadership to get there. General Electric has been my business life and its importance to me has grown with each succeeding year. Whether I can properly assemble and discharge the multiple responsibility is for others to judge—but obviously I would like the chance."

I was selling "runway"—the capacity to grow, something I've always looked for in every appointment I have made. I *always* bet on runway. I felt it was a good bet to put people in stretch jobs early in their careers. Far more often than not, they brought a lot more excitement and passion to the job and achieved greater personal growth for themselves.

As for where I stood, I started getting positive vibes in the summer of 1980. Dave Orselet, my human resources staffer and a real friend, was picking up tidbits from Ted LeVino, the corporate HR head. While Dave reported directly to Ted and was loyal to him, he couldn't withstand my relentless pumping for information.

I remember one time during a party at my house, I had poor Dave pinned against the refrigerator in my kitchen, drilling him on how he thought the race would play out. That was probably my worst transgression. Bless his heart, Dave would never tell me I was the front-runner, but he reluctantly divulged just enough information to make me feel upbeat about the eventual outcome.

The first board indication that I might be the front-runner came in September 1980, when one of GE's board members called with an unusual invitation. Ed Littlefield, a major shareholder from his sale of Utah International to GE in the late 1970s, asked me to be his partner at the Cypress Point Member Guest tournament in California. Littlefield was on our board as chairman of Utah International. When he sold Utah to Reg, he became one of GE's largest shareholders. I thought that he wouldn't be inviting me if I wasn't Reg's choice.

It was my first time at Cypress Point and a huge treat for me. Ed wanted to introduce me to all his West Coast friends. My Irish luck struck again. The first day of the tournament, we had a shot-gun start and began on the sixth hole. On the seventh, a par three, I stepped up to the tee and hit a four iron into the hole. It was my first hole in one after 30 years of golf, and it came at Cypress Point on the second hole I ever played there. That sure made it easy to meet everyone.

Littlefield was one of many directors whose outspoken boardroom support made a big difference. He was an enthusiastic advocate for me, along with Si Cathcart, G.G. Michelson, Henry Hillman, Walter Wriston, and John Lawrence. Five of these six directors would play very important roles for me in years to come.

Si, then the chairman of Illinois Tool Works, was the easiest and most natural guy in the world to be with. I liked him the first time we met. He had remarkable common sense and a unique feel for every situation. Si has helped me every year I had the job as CEO, even agreeing to come out of retirement to run Kidder, Peabody when it got into trouble.

I was impressed with G.G., then a relatively new board member from R. H. Macy & Co., though I didn't appreciate how incredibly smart, savvy, and creative she was until later. She has been an insightful confidante and played a major role in every big decision I made at GE. Henry Hillman was an exciting entrepreneur, a risk taker, someone I loved to talk with. He was bright, rich, and funny, and he never took himself too seriously. He abhorred pomposity as much as I did. He was always asking, "Are we going fast enough?" John Lawrence, a Boston Brahmin and global cotton trader who rode the very same commuter train my father worked on as a conductor, had been on the GE board for 23 years. He loved golf and always played a round with me at GE events. We always had fun together. John had seen it all and was a close confidant of Reg's. He reached mandatory retirement age just after my appointment.

As chairman of Citicorp, Wriston was one of the most influential directors on the board and was America's leading banker in the 1970s and 1980s. My first encounter with him was at a board outing at Disney World in 1979. He was trying to recruit Dennis Dammerman, then a vice president and controller at GE Capital, to a big job at Citicorp. I went after him, teasing him about being a board member and trying to steal one of my best executives.

I think he got a kick out of my "attack." That candor could have been the kiss of death or the beginning of an enduring friendship. It turned out to be the latter. Walter was as tough and smart as they made them, with a wry sense of humor—but when he liked someone he was really supportive. He was with me from day one.

They were among the directors who backed Reg in the boardroom and allowed him to come into my office on that December

15, 1980, to embrace me. On that wintry Monday, Reg told me that he had recommended me for the job and the board unanimously supported it at a dinner meeting on November 20. Reg had given the board a month's time to reflect on its conclusion and to raise any issues they wanted after the vote. There were none. Reg told me I would be formally elected chairman at the upcoming board session on Friday, December 19. He explained that Hood and Burlingame would stay as my vice chairmen and that he would spend the next three months to help me through the transition until I officially took over on April 1.

This all happened because Reg had the courage to pick someone who was 180 degrees from what was then the "model GE executive."

It had been a difficult struggle to get here. I now had the job, but some silly politics remained. To give you a sense of how thick the politics were at the time, Paolo Fresco, then a vice president, recalls being nearly physically confronted in a Fairfield hallway by an overzealous executive who reported to Burlingame yet supported me. Fresco remembers being called a "jackass" simply because he was loyal to his own boss. Shortly after I was named chairman-elect, Paolo came to me.

"Jack," he said in true Italian political style, "I give you my resignation. I want you to know I was supporting Burlingame, and my candidate lost."

I told him to stuff his resignation. I wasn't thinking about who did or didn't support me. The Italian-born Fresco, the most global guy I have ever met, later became one of my closest friends. As vice chairman, he played a major role in making GE a truly global corporation.

But this was mostly a time for celebration. In its story announcing the decision, *The Wall Street Journal* reported that GE decided to replace "a legend with a live wire." To introduce me to the corporate elite, Reg planned a coming-out party for me at the Helmsley Palace in New York City on February 24—just before I officially took over on April 1. Reg wanted to introduce me to his friends and transfer his relationships to me. It was a big affair, attended by the CEOs of the country's biggest corporations at the time.

It was a terrific bash. I had a ball. Everyone was relaxed, and nearly everyone drank a little too much, except Reg, who wanted to make sure I was introduced to every one of the 50 or 60 guests. He wanted to get me off to a perfect start. But when Reg asked me to make a few remarks late in the evening, unknown to me, he apparently felt I slurred a few of my words.

First thing next morning, he came into my office as mad as I have ever seen him.

"I've never been so humiliated in my life," Reg told me. "You embarrassed me and the company."

I was stunned. I'd had a fantastic time and thought it was a great party. For the next four hours, I think I felt every emotion known to man. I felt keenly disappointed that I had let Reg down. I was mad as hell at him because I thought he was being a stiff. I felt sorry for myself because maybe I hadn't made the great impression I thought I had. I couldn't believe our guests didn't have a great time. They just couldn't have faked it that much. I'd been to enough parties to know a good one.

Just before noon, however, things changed.

Reg came back to my office.

"I want to talk," he said. "Look, I've gotten over 20 calls in the last three hours, and everyone is saying it was the best party they've been to in New York in ten years. I'm sorry. I was too damn tough on you. Everyone had a good time. All I'm hearing are good reports about you and the party. They liked you. I just misread the evening."

God, was I relieved. I could hardly wait to get going.

BUILDING
A PHILOSOPHY

7

Dealing with Reality and "Superficial Congeniality"

On April 1, 1981, I was like the dog who caught the bus. I finally had the job.

Despite all the experiences that had gotten me this far, I wasn't nearly as sure of myself as I pretended to be. Outwardly, I had a pretty good dose of self-confidence, and those who knew me would have described me as self-assured, cocky, decisive, quick, and tough. Inwardly, I still had plenty of insecurities. Whenever I had to get up in front of people, I struggled with my speech impediment. I fussed with a comb-over to disguise my receding hairline. And when someone asked me how tall I was, I had myself believing I was at least an inch and a half taller than the five feet eight I really was.

I came to the job without many of the external CEO skills. I had rarely dealt with anyone in Washington, even though the government was more into business than ever. I had little experience dealing with the media. My only press conference was the scripted session with Reg on the day GE announced I would be the next chairman. I had only one or two brief outings before the Wall Street analysts who followed GE. And our 500,000-plus shareholders had no idea who Jack Welch was and whether he would be able to fill the shoes of the most admired businessman in America.

But I did know what I wanted the company to "feel" like. I wasn't calling it "culture" in those days, but that's what it was.

I knew it had to change.

The company had many strengths. It was a $25 billion corporation, earning $1.5 billion a year, with 404,000 employees. It had a triple-A balance sheet, and its products and services permeated almost every part of the GNP, from toasters to power plants. Some employees proudly described the company as a "super-tanker"—strong and steady in the water. I respected that but wanted the company to be more like a speedboat, fast and agile, able to turn on a dime.

I wanted GE to run more like the informal plastics business I came from—a company filled with self-confident entrepreneurs who would face reality every day. Every milestone could trigger a celebration that would make business fun. With a few notable exceptions, fun was not the norm at the time.

I knew the benefits of staying small even as GE was getting bigger. The good businesses had to be sorted out from the bad ones. I wanted GE to stay only in businesses that were No. 1 or No. 2 in their markets. We had to act faster and get the damn bureaucracy out of the way.

The reality was that at the end of 1980, GE was, like much of American industry, a formal and massive bureaucracy, with too many layers of management. It was ruled by more than 25,000 managers who each averaged seven direct reports in a hierarchy with as many as a dozen levels between the factory floor and my office. More than 130 executives held the rank of vice president or above, with all kinds of titles and support staffs behind each one: "vice president of corporate financial administration," "vice president of corporate consulting," and "vice president of corporate operating services."

There were eight regional or "consumer relations" vice

presidents located around the country without direct sales responsibility. The bureaucracy this structure created was huge. (Today, in a company six times as large, we have roughly 25 percent more vice presidents. We have fewer managers, and most now average over 15 direct reports, not seven, with in most cases fewer than six layers between the shop floor and the CEO.)

It didn't take very long to bump up against some of the worst practices.

A couple of months into the job, Art Bueche, the head of our R&D operations, stopped by my office. He wanted to give me a series of cards with written questions for our upcoming planning sessions with GE business leaders. The centerpiece of these meetings, held every July, were thick planning books that contained detailed forecasts of sales, profits, capital expenditures, and myriad other numbers for the next five years. These books were the lifeblood of the bureaucracy. Some GE staffers in Fairfield actually graded them, even assigning points to the pizzazz of each cover. It was nuts.

I looked through the cards Art handed me, surprised to see corporate crib sheets filled with "I gotcha" questions.

"What the hell am I supposed to do with these?"

"I always give the corporate executive office these questions. That lets them show the operating people that they studied the planning books," he replied.

"Art, this is crazy," I said. "These meetings have got to be spontaneous. I want to see their stuff for the first time and react to it. The planning books get the conversation going."

The last thing I wanted was a series of tough technical questions to score a few points. What was the purpose of being CEO if I couldn't ask my own questions? The corporate staff had its rear end to the field—and it was too busy "kissing up" to the bosses.

The corporate executive office, including my vice chairmen, wasn't the only group at headquarters getting crib sheets. For every business review, headquarters people loaded up their own staff heads with questions.

We had dozens of people routinely going through what I considered "dead books." All my career, I never wanted to see a planning book before the person presented it. To me, the value of these sessions wasn't in the books. It was in the heads and hearts of the people who were coming into Fairfield. I wanted to drill down, to get beyond the binders and into the thinking that went into them. I needed to see the business leaders' body language and the passion they poured into their arguments.

There were too many passive reviews. One annual ritual was the spring trip to the appliance product review in Louisville. A team of designers and engineers hauled out cardboard and plastic mock-ups. Here we were from Fairfield, being asked for our opinions on futuristic refrigerators, stoves, and dishwasher models.

I'll never know how many of these models ever made it to the dealer's selling floor. I did know that some of the mock-ups had to have the dust brushed off them because they had been paraded out in prior reviews for years. I also knew that the comments from the Fairfield contingent, including myself, were of little value. This ritual was a waste of everyone's time.

I wanted to break the cycle of these dog-and-pony shows. Hierarchy's role to passively "review and approve" had to go.

After the planning sessions my first summer, I tried to create the environment I was looking for with my own staff. I thought a good way to break the ice was to take everyone off site for a couple of days. In my earlier jobs, we always found a way to make sure we got a dose of golf mixed with the business at first-class golf courses (places like Harbor Town at Hilton Head and the Cascades at the Homestead).

I had just become a member of Laurel Valley, a wonderful golf club just outside Pittsburgh. So in the fall of 1981, I invited about 14 executives to Laurel for the two-day retreat. The group included all the functional staff heads and our seven sector executives. It was my first real attempt at creating a collegial group at the top, what we would later call the CEC, or Corporate Executive Council.

Among the 14 executives, a core group of at least seven or eight advocates signed up for the new agenda. Reg was right when he picked John Burlingame and Ed Hood as vice chairs. They were supportive and never undermined my efforts, despite the fact that they may have had some reservations about the pace of change.

Together, in fact, they served as a moderating force. Larry Bossidy, the guy I had discovered over a Ping-Pong table, had come to Fairfield as a sector executive in 1981 and had become a business soul mate. We both shared a hatred of bureaucracy. I had strong support from two of my most senior staff guys, chief financial officer Tom Thorsen and human resources chief Ted LeVino.

Tom was an old associate from Pittsfield. He had been tapped a few years earlier by Reg to come to Fairfield as CFO. He understood what we wanted to do. While he thought it was a sport to take shots at me, I still loved him for his candor and his smarts. LeVino represented the bridge between the old and the new GE. His support for many of the early initiatives was vital.

If I didn't have all 14 of our top executives completely behind me at this moment, I knew I had enough to start the process. The first morning at Laurel Valley, I filled a conference room with blank easels, anxious to capture everyone's thoughts. I got up in front of the crowd and started asking what they thought about our No. 1 or No. 2 strategy, what they liked and disliked about GE, and what things we ought to change quickly. We spent time discussing the just-concluded planning sessions and how they could be improved. Creating an open dialogue was difficult. Only those I worked closely with were willing to let it rip. Most of the guys didn't want to stick their necks out.

We got through the morning with only half the group engaged.

After a fun afternoon of golf and a few drinks over dinner, things loosened up a little bit and a few more got involved. The second day was more of the same. Perhaps it was too early. Many of them weren't sure where they stood or what they were dealing with. The two-day outing failed to build any kind of consensus for change.

I thought we needed a revolution. It was obvious we weren't going to get one with this team.

GE's culture had been built for a different time, when a command-and-control structure made sense. Having been in the field, I had a strong prejudice against most of the headquarters staff. I felt they practiced what could be called "superficial congeniality"—pleasant on the surface, with distrust and savagery roiling beneath it. The phrase seems to sum up how bureaucrats typically behave, smiling in front of you but always looking for a "gotcha" behind your back.

Organizational layers were another residue of size. I used the analogy of putting on too many sweaters. Sweaters are like layers. They are insulators. When you go outside and you wear four sweaters, it's difficult to know how cold it is.

On one early plant tour in a Lynn, Massachusetts, jet engine factory, I ended up in the boiler room with a group of employees who knew many of the guys I grew up with in Salem. During a casual conversation about old times, I happened to learn that they had four layers of management supervising the boiler operation. I couldn't believe it. It was a funny way to find out about layers. I used that story at every opportunity.

Another effective analogy was comparing an organization to a house. Floors represent layers and the walls functional barriers. To get the best out of an organization, these floors and walls must be blown away, creating an open space where ideas flow freely, independent of rank or function.

In the 1970s and 1980s, big business had too many layers—too many sweaters, too many floors and walls. The impact of these layers was seen most easily in the capital appropriations request process. When I first became CEO, almost every request for a significant capital expenditure would come to me for approval. A package of paper would arrive on my desk for a signature to buy something like a $50 million mainframe computer. In some cases, 16 other people had already signed it, and my signature was the last one required. What value was I adding?

I did away with that process and haven't signed an appropriations approval in at least 18 years. Each business leader has the same delegation of authority that the board gave me. At the beginning of every year, the business made the case for the capital it needed. We allocated the dollars, ranging from $50 million to several hundred million. They own it and decide how far to delegate the spending authority. The people closest to the work know the work best. They become more accountable. They take their recommendations more seriously if they know a bunch of signatures aren't piled on top of them.

In those days, I was throwing hand grenades, trying to blow up traditions and rituals that I felt held us back. In the fall of 1981, I tossed one in the middle of the Elfun Society, an internal management club at GE. (Elfun was short for Electrical Funds, a mutual fund that its members could invest in.) It was a networking group for white-collar types. Being an Elfun was considered a "rite of passage" into management.

I didn't have a lot of respect for what Elfun was doing—I thought it represented the height of "superficial congeniality."

It evolved into an elitist group for those who wanted to be seen by their bosses or their bosses' bosses at dinner meetings. I remember paying dues and going to a few of these dinners early in my career. If a corporate vice president who oversaw a business in the town showed up, he'd get a packed house. Everyone would go to win points and get face time. If the speaker had no real impact on their careers, Elfun would have trouble filling a small conference room.

As the new CEO, I was invited to speak before the group's annual leadership conference in the fall of 1981. It was supposed to be a nice meeting, one of those pat-on-the-back speeches from the new guy. I showed up at the Longshore Country Club in Westport, Connecticut, where some 100 Elfun leaders from all the local chapters in the United States gathered. After dinner, I got up and delivered what one member still remembers as a classic "stick-in-the-eye" speech.

"Thank you for asking me to speak. Tonight I'd like to be candid, and I'll start by letting you reflect on the fact that I have serious reservations about your organization."

I described Elfun as an institution pursuing yesterday's agenda. I told them I never could identify with their recent activities.

"I can't find any value to what you're doing," I said. "You're a hierarchical social and political club. I'm not going to tell you what you should do or be. It's your job to figure out a role that makes sense for you and GE."

There was stunned silence when I ended the speech. I tried to soften the blow by milling around the bar for an hour. However, no one was in the mood for cheering up.

The next morning, one of our senior officers, Frank Doyle, went as he always did to meet with the group at its opening business session. This time he had a real job. He had to pick up the pieces from my speech the evening before. Frank just about walked into a wake. They felt as if they had been run over by a train. Like me the night before, he challenged them to change.

A month later, Elfun president Cal Neithamer called me and asked for a meeting. I invited Cal, an engineer in our transportation business in Erie, Pennsylvania, to Fairfield for lunch. He came armed with charts, but more important, he was excited about a new idea for Elfun. His dream was to turn the organization into an army of GE community volunteers. The idea came at a time when President Reagan was urging people to volunteer their time—to step in where government was reducing its role.

God, was I excited by Cal's vision! I've never forgotten that lunch. Although Cal retired a few years ago, I still hear from him more or less once a year. What a job he and his successors did.

Today, Elfun has more than 42,000 members, including retirees. They volunteer their time and energy in communities where GE has plants or offices. They have mentoring programs for high school students that have achieved remarkable results.

At Aiken High School, an inner-city school in Cincinnati, coaching by GE volunteers raised the percentage of graduating students going on to college to more than 50 percent from less than 10 percent in the past ten years. Similar programs are going on in schools in every significant GE community, including Albuquerque, Cleveland, Durham, Erie, Houston, Richmond, Schenectady, Jakarta, Bangalore, and Budapest.

They've also done everything from building parks, playgrounds, and libraries to repairing tape players for the blind. Today, no one is excluded from the organization, whether the person is a factory worker or a senior executive. Membership is determined solely by the desire to give back. Some 20 years later, the organization I almost turned my back on has become one of the best things about GE. I love the organization, the people in it, what it stands for, and what it has done.

Elfun's self-engineered turnaround became a very important symbol. It was just what I was looking for.

Not everything I wanted to change was at headquarters. Some of the real eye-openers were far from my office. I spent most of 1981 with a team in the field reviewing businesses—just as I had done for ten years. I had a good feel for about a third of the company and wanted to dig into the rest.

I quickly found that the bureaucracy I saw when managing appliances and lighting was nothing compared to what I would see in some of GE's other operations. The bigger the business, the less engaged people seemed to be. From the forklift drivers in a factory to the engineers packed in cubicles, too many people were just going through the motions.

Passion was hard to find. Schenectady, the home of our power turbine business, was particularly frustrating. It had been our flagship business for GE for a long time, replacing lighting, our first business, as the core of the company. It had great technology, and its gas turbines were the envy of the world. With $2 billion in sales and 26,000 employees, more than 20,000 in Schenectady, it was important—and it "acted" important, despite only making $61 million of net income.

Power represented much of what had to change, not the technology and products, but the attitudes. Too many managers considered their positions as rewards for service to the company, a career capstone rather than a fresh opportunity. There was an attitude that customers were "fortunate" to place orders for their "wonderful" machines. The long-cycle nature of the business, with product life cycles and order backlogs measured in years, only compounded the lack of pace, excitement, and energy.

Little did I know that out of all of these field visits, I'd stumble upon a relatively small and troubled business that would prove to be a big help. It was our nuclear reactor business in San Jose, California. Nuclear power was one of GE's three big 1960s ventures, along with computers and aircraft engines. Our engine business was going strong, but computers had already been sold, and our nuclear business was filled primarily with "hope."

No business was undergoing more change than the nuclear power industry at that moment. Only two years earlier, in 1979, the Three Mile Island reactor accident in Pennsylvania put an end to what little public support remained for nuclear energy. Utilities and governments were reevaluating their investment plans for a nuclear future. Ironically, this once promising GE business would become the perfect role model for my "reality" theme.

The people who worked in San Jose were among the best and brightest of their time. Coming out of graduate school in the 1950s and 1960s, they had invested their lives in the promise of nuclear energy. They were the Bill Gateses of their generation, expecting to change the way we live and work.

In the spring of 1981, I visited this billion-dollar business. During my two-day review, the leadership team presented a rosy plan, assuming three new orders for nuclear reactors a year. They had a terrific track record in the early 1970s, selling three to four reactors each year. The business saw the Three Mile Island disaster as little more than a blip.

Their view was completely at odds with reality. They had received no new orders in the last two years and had suffered a $13 million loss in 1980. Though they would turn a small profit in 1981, the reactor side of the business by itself was on its way to a $27 million loss.

I listened for a while before interrupting with what they saw as a bombshell.

"Guys, you're not going to get three orders a year," I said. "In my opinion, you'll never get another order for a nuclear reactor in the U.S."

They were shocked. They argued, with the not-so-subtle implication being, "Jack, you really don't understand this business."

That was probably true, but I had the benefit of a pair of fresh eyes. I hadn't invested my life in this business. I loved their passion, even though I felt it was misdirected.

Their arguments contained a lot of emotion but few facts. I asked them to redo the plan on the assumption they'd never get another U.S. order for a reactor.

"You figure out how to make a business out of selling just fuel and nuclear services to the installed base," I said.

At the time, GE had 72 active reactors in service. Safety was the principal preoccupation of both utility managers and government regulators. We had an obligation and an opportunity to keep those reactors up and running safely.

Obviously, our review didn't go well. I had thrown a bucket of cold water on their dreams. Toward the end of our meeting, they resorted in frustration to one of the favorite "when all else fails" arguments heard in business.

"If we take the orders out of the plan, you'll kill morale and you'll never be able to mobilize the business when the orders come back."

That wasn't the first or the last time I heard desperate business teams use the argument. That reasoning falls into the same category as the other plea I often heard during tough times: "You've cut all the fat out. Now you're into bone and you'll ruin the business if we cut more."

Both arguments don't make it. They're both weak. Management always has a tendency to take the smallest bite of the cost apple. Inevitably, managers have to keep going back, again and again, to cut more as markets deteriorate. All this does is create more uncertainty for employees. I've never seen a business ruined because it reduced its costs too much, too fast.

When good times come again, I've always seen business teams mobilize quickly and take advantage of the situation.

Fortunately, the leader of this business, Dr. Roy Beaton, was the most realistic GE trooper in the room. He reluctantly accepted the challenge. I left not knowing what I'd get. During the summer, we had a few more heated exchanges when the team pleaded its case to put one or two reactors in the plan instead of three. I remained stubbornly committed to zero and the full development of a fuel and services business.

To their credit, by the fall of 1981, the team—now headed by Warren Bruggeman, who succeeded the retiring Beaton—had a plan and was prepared to implement it. They reduced the size of the salaried employees in the reactor business from 2,410 in 1980 to 160 by 1985. They eliminated most of the reactor infrastructure and focused only on research for advanced reactors in the event the day would come when the world's view of nuclear changed. The service business became very successful and was an early indicator that service could play a huge role in GE's future. With its success, nuclear's overall net earnings grew from $14 million in 1981 to $78 million in 1982, and to $116 million in 1983.

Some 20 years after that first meeting, the business has gotten orders for only four of their technologically advanced reactors. Not one of them has come from the United States. The team built a profitable fuel and services business that has made money every year. The nuclear business kept GE's obligations to the utilities' installed base and invested consistently to support advanced reactor research.

Their story of success was one of the thrills of my early days as CEO. It had little to do with economics but a lot to do with the company "feel" I was looking for. The people who engineered the transformation at our nuclear business were not "typical Jack Welch types." They weren't young, loud, or confrontational. They didn't see the bureaucracy as the enemy. They were GE careerists and mainstreamers.

The opportunity to make heroes out of people who were not obvious Welch disciples was a breakthrough. It sent a clear message: You didn't have to fit a certain stereotype to be successful in the new GE. You could be a hero no matter what you looked like or how you acted. All you had to do was face reality and perform. That message was a big deal at a time when some GE people were unsure where they stood or whether or not they had some kind of "nut" running the company.

I used this nuclear story over and over again in the first few years as CEO to pound home the need for a reality check. I shouted it out from every rooftop. Facing reality sounds simple—but it isn't. I found it hard to get people to see a situation for what it is and not for what it was, or what they hoped it would be.

"Don't kid yourself. It is the way it is." My mother's admonition to me many years ago was just as important for GE.

In a business plan, there's little percentage in betting on hope. Self-delusion can grip an entire organization and lead the people in it to ridiculous conclusions. Whether it was appliances in the late 1970s, nuclear in the early 1980s, or dot.coms at the turn of the century, getting people to face reality was the first step toward an eventual solution.

When I became CEO, I inherited a lot of great things, but facing reality was not one of the company's strong points. Its "superficial congeniality" made candor extremely difficult to come by. I got lucky. The changes at our nuclear reactor business and at Elfun gave me important weapons to demonstrate what I wanted GE to "feel" like.

I told their stories again and again to every GE audience at every opportunity. For the next 20 years, I used that same storytelling technique to get ideas transferred across the company.

Slowly, people started listening.

8

The Vision Thing

My first time in front of Wall Street's analysts as chairman was a bomb.

I had been in the job for eight months when I went to New York City on December 8, 1981, to deliver my big message on the "New GE." I had worked on the speech, rewriting it, rehearsing it, and desperately wanting it to be a smash hit.

It was, after all, my first public statement on where I wanted to take GE. You know, the vision thing.

However, the analysts arrived that day expecting to hear the financial results and the successes achieved by the company during the year. They expected a detailed breakdown of the financial numbers. They could then plug those numbers into their models and crank out estimates of our earnings by business segment. They loved this exercise. Over a 20-minute speech, I gave them little of what they wanted and quickly launched into a qualitative discussion around my vision for the company.

The setting for this event was the ornate ballroom of the Pierre Hotel on Fifth Avenue. The GE stagehands had been there for a full day of advance work. I rehearsed my remarks behind a podium hours before the analysts arrived. Today it's hard to imagine the formality of it all.

My "big" message (see appendix) that day was intended to describe the winners of the future. They would be companies that "search out and participate in the real growth industries and insist upon being number one or number two in every business they are in—the number one or number two leanest, lowest-cost, worldwide producers of quality goods and services. . . . The managements and companies in the eighties that don't do this, that hang on to losers for whatever reason—tradition, sentiment, their own management weaknesses—won't be around in 1990."

Being No. 1 or No. 2 wasn't merely an objective. It was a requirement. If we met it, we were certain that by the end of the decade, this central idea would give us a set of businesses unique in the world. That was the "hard" message of the day.

As I moved into "soft" issues like reality, quality, excellence, and (would you believe?) the "human element," I could tell I was losing them. To be a winner, we had to couple the "hard" central idea of being No. 1 or No. 2 in growth markets with intangible "soft" values to get the "feel" that would define our new culture. About halfway through, I had the impression I would have gotten as much interest if I'd talked about my Ph.D. thesis on drop-wise condensation.

I pressed on, not letting their blank stares discourage me. Today, some of this might sound like corporate cliché. In fact, looking back on that speech years later, I can't believe how formal it was.

"We have to permeate every mind in this company with an attitude, with an atmosphere that allows people—in fact, encourages people—to see things as they are, to deal with the way it is, not the way they wished it would be," I said. "Establishing throughout the organization this concept of reality is a prerequisite to executing the central idea—the necessity of being number one or number two in everything we do—or do something about it."

I went on to say that quality and excellence would create an atmosphere where all our employees would feel comfortable stretching beyond their limits, to be better than we ever thought we could be. This "human element" would foster an environment where people would dare to try new things, where they would feel assured in knowing that "only the limits of their creativity and drive would be the ceiling on how far and how fast they would move."

By doing all that, melding these hard and soft messages, GE would become a place that was "more high-spirited, more adaptable, and more agile" than other companies a fraction of our size. We wouldn't merely grow with the GNP (gross national product), an objective of many big companies at that time. Instead, GE would be "the locomotive pulling the GNP, not the caboose following it."

At the end, the reaction in the room made it clear that this crowd thought they were getting more hot air than substance. One of our staffers overheard one analyst moan, "We don't know what the hell he's talking about." I left the hotel ballroom knowing there had to be a better way to tell our story. Wall Street had listened, and Wall Street yawned. The stock went up all of 12 cents. I was probably lucky it didn't drop.

I was sure the ideas were right. I just hadn't brought them to life. They were just words read on stage by a new face.

The highly structured formality of GE's analyst meetings didn't help my cause. Every detail was planned, even the seating arrangements. The analysts sat politely in their seats. GE staffers strolled up and down the aisles, collecting cards that the analysts had scribbled questions on. The cards were brought to three other GE people, including the chief financial officer, who sat behind a long table at the side of the room. Their job was to weed out the potentially embarrassing, controversial, or tough questions they felt the chairman wouldn't or couldn't answer.

The "lay-ups" were delivered to me.

What a difference between that day and GE analyst meetings now. Today there are no scripts. Charts are used, and you can't get through two of them without a question or a challenge. We have intellectual food fights now, just like the reviews inside GE. We come away a lot smarter about what's on the minds of investors— and the analysts are better informed about GE's outlook and strategic direction.

My first meeting was a flop, but everything we did over the next 20 years, stumbling two steps forward, one back, was toward the vision that I laid out that day. We lived that hard reality of No. 1 or No. 2 and fought like mad to get that soft "feel" into the company.

The central idea came from my earlier experiences with good and bad businesses and was supported by the thinking of Peter Drucker. I began reading Peter's work in the late 1970s, and Reg introduced us during my transition to CEO. If there was ever a genuine management sage, it is Peter. He always dropped a few unique pearls into his many management books.

The clarity of No. 1 or No. 2 came from a pair of very tough questions Drucker posed: "If you weren't already in the business, would you enter it today?" And if the answer is no, "What are you going to do about it?"

Simple questions—but like much that is simple, they were also profound. Those were especially good questions to ask at GE. We were in so many different businesses. In those days, if you were in a business that was profitable, that was enough reason to stay in it. Changing the game, getting out of low-margin, low-growth businesses and moving into high-margin, high-growth global businesses, was not a priority.

At that time, no one in or outside the company perceived a crisis. GE was an American icon, the tenth largest corporation by size and market capitalization. The Asian assault had been coming for many years, swamping one industry after another; radios, cameras, televisions, steel, ships, and finally autos. We saw it in our television manufacturing business as global competition—particularly from the Japanese—began eating up profits. We had several vulnerable businesses, including housewares and consumer electronics.

Yet if you were in our housewares business back then, plugging along making toasters and irons, and if that's all you knew and it was profitable, that was enough. Even today, we'll have these crazy conversations where people will say, "Well, you're making a profit. What's wrong?"

Well, in some cases, there's a lot wrong. If it's a business without a long-range competitive solution, it's just a matter of time before it's over.

The No. 1 or No. 2, "fix, sell, or close" strategy passed the simplicity test. People discussed it and understood it, and most agreed to it intellectually. When it came time to implement it, the emotional connection was more difficult for people to make. Those working in a clear No. 1 business had no trouble. In businesses that weren't leaders, people felt tremendous pressure. They had to face the reality that their business had to do something fast—or that new guy in Fairfield might sell it on them.

Like every goal and initiative we've ever launched, I repeated the No. 1 or No. 2 message over and over again until I nearly gagged on the words. I tried to sell both the intellectual and emotional cases for doing it. The organization had to see every management action aligned with the vision.

Like most visions, the No. 1 and No. 2 strategy had limits.

Obviously, some businesses have become so commoditized that leadership positions give you little or no competitive advantage. It made little difference if we were No. 1 in electric toasters or irons, for instance, where we had no pricing power and were facing low-cost imports.

There are other multitrillion-dollar markets like financial services that cover the ocean. In those cases, not being No. 1 or No. 2 is less critical as long as you are strong in your niche—product or region.

The vision was simple, but I was still having a helluva time communicating it across GE's 42 strategic business units. I had been thinking about how to do it better for a long time. Oddly enough, I found an answer on a cocktail napkin in January of 1983.

I often drive people crazy by sketching my thoughts out on paper anytime, anyplace. This time, while trying to explain the vision to my wife, Carolyn, at Gates restaurant in New Canaan, I pulled out a black felt-tip pen and began drawing on the napkin that had been under my drink. I drew three circles and divided our businesses into one of three categories: core manufacturing, technology, and services. Inside the core circle, for example, I put lighting, major appliances, motors, turbines, transportation, and contractor equipment.

Any business outside the circles, I told Carolyn, we would fix, sell, or close. These businesses were the marginal performers, or were in low-growth markets, or just had a poor strategic fit. I liked the three-circle concept. Over the next couple of weeks, I expanded it, filling in more details with my team (see opposite page).

The chart really hit home. It was the simple conceptual tool I needed to communicate and implement the No. 1 or No. 2 vision. I began using it everywhere, and *Forbes* magazine eventually featured it in a cover story on GE in March of 1984.

For people who worked in businesses inside the circles, it created a certain sense of security and pride. But it raised all kinds of hell within organizations placed outside the circles, particularly in operations that were the heart of the old GE, including central air-conditioning, housewares, television manufacturing, audio products, and semiconductors. The people in these "fix, sell, or close" businesses were naturally upset.

They felt angry and betrayed. Some asked, "Am I in a leper colony? That's not what I joined GE to become." Union leaders and city fathers complained. This turned out to be a bigger issue than I anticipated. I knew it was something I had to come to grips with.

In the first two years, the No. 1 or No. 2 strategy generated a lot of action—most of it small. We sold 71 businesses and product lines,

1 or # 2
"Fix, Sell or Close"

- Microelectronics
- LADD Petroleum

Services
- FINANCIAL
- Information
- Construction & Engineering
- Nuclear

High Technology
- MEDICAL
- MATERIALS
- INDUSTRIAL ELECTRONICS
- AEROSPACE
- AIRCRAFT ENGINES

Core
- MAJOR APPLIANCES
- LIGHTING
- TURBINES
- TRANSPORTATION
- MOTORS
- Contractor Equipment

- Central Air Conditioning
- LARGE Transformers
- TV & Audio
- Mobile RADIO

- Small Appliances
- Switchgear
- Wire & Cable
- TV Stations

receiving a little over $500 million for them. We completed 118 other deals, including acquisitions, joint ventures, and minority investments, spending over $1 billion. These were peanuts, but the cultural significance of this churning was felt throughout the company, especially the sale of our central air-conditioning business.

With three plants and 2,300 employees, it was not one of GE's larger businesses, and it wasn't very profitable. Its sale to Trane Co. in mid-1982 for $135 million in cash raised eyebrows, because air-conditioning was right in the belly of our company. It was a division in our major appliance operations in Louisville. Yet its market share of 10 percent paled in comparison with the other GE appliance businesses.

I disliked the business the first time I was exposed to it as a sector executive. I felt it had no control of its destiny. You sold the GE-branded product to a local distributor like "Ace Plumbing." They installed it with their hammers and screwdrivers and drove away, leaving the GE-branded air conditioners behind. How Ace installed our products and how it serviced its customers reflected directly back on GE. We were frequently getting customer complaints that had nothing to do with us. We were being tarred by something we had no control over.

Because of our low market share, our competitors had the best distributors and independent contractors. For GE, this was a flawed business. You never would have known it by the reaction we got when it was sold. It really shook up Louisville.

The air-conditioning sale to Trane reinforced my thinking that putting a weak operation into a stronger business was a true win-win for everyone. Trane was a market leader. With the sale, our air-conditioning people became part of a winning team. A month after the sale, a phone call confirmed my thinking. I called the general manager of our former business, Stan Gorski, who had joined Trane with the divestiture.

"Stan, how's it going?" I asked.

"Jack, I love it here," he said. "When I get up in the morning and come to work, my boss is thinking about air-conditioning all day. He loves air-conditioning. He thinks it's wonderful. Every time I talked to you on the phone, it was about some customer complaint or my margins. You hated air-conditioning. Jack, today we're all winners and we all feel it. In Louisville, I was the orphan."

"Stan, you've made my day," I said, before hanging up.

Through the onslaught of criticism to come, Stan's comments helped to fortify my resolve to carry out the No. 1 or No. 2 strategy, no matter what. The air-conditioning deal also established another basic principle. We used the $135 million from its sale to help pay to restructure other businesses.

Every business we sold was treated the same way. We never put those gains into net income. Instead, we used them to improve the company's competitiveness. In 20 years we never permitted ourselves or any of our businesses to use one-time restructuring charges as an excuse for missing an earnings commitment. We paid our own way.

From the day I wrote Reg about my qualifications for the CEO job, I adopted "consistent earnings growth" as a theme of mine. Fortunately, we had a number of strong and diverse businesses that could deliver on that pledge. We managed businesses—not earnings.

When we sold a business like air-conditioning and realized an accounting gain as well as cash, this gave us the flexibility to reinvest in or fix up another business. That's what shareowners expected from us and paid us to do.

I liken our treatment of these gains to fixing up a house. When you don't have the money to repair the ceiling, you put a bucket underneath the leak to catch the drips. When you find money in the budget, you fix the leak. That's what we did at GE with much of the cash from a divestiture. We took actions to strengthen our businesses for the long haul.

Every now and then we'd get a critic, challenging how we achieved "our consistent earnings growth." One reporter even suggested that if we took a charge to close a business in one quarter and took a gain to sell another business in the following quarter, our earnings would not have been consistent.

Duh!!! Our job is to fix the leak when we get the cash.

If you didn't do that you'd be managing nothing. If you follow the cash, and in this case GE's cash, you see what's really happening in a company. Accounting doesn't generate cash, managing businesses does.

Getting out of the air-conditioning business sparked a firestorm, but it was principally contained in Louisville. The next sale, of Utah International, was a much more difficult situation for me. Reg Jones had purchased the business for $2.3 billion in 1977. At the time, it was the largest acquisition ever—for Reg, for GE, and for all of Corporate America.

Utah was a highly profitable, first-class company that derived its income largely from selling metallurgical coal to the Japanese steel industry. It also had a small U.S. oil and gas company and large proven but undeveloped copper reserves in Chile. Reg purchased the company as a hedge against the wild inflation of the 1970s.

To me, with inflation abating, it didn't fit the objective of consistent income growth. Its lumpy earnings clashed with my goal to have everyone feel their individual contribution counted.

GE makes its money every quarter by bringing in cash from every corner of the world, nickel by nickel. Every day, everyone's contribution counts. As a sector executive and vice chairman, I had sat in meetings with my peers, listening as we all told how valiantly we had worked to make the quarter's or the year's numbers. Then, the executive in charge of Utah would stand up and unknowingly overwhelm those contributions one way or another.

"We had a strike at the coal mine," he'd say, "so we're going to miss our profit projection by $50 million." All of us would stare in disbelief at the size of the number. Or he could just as easily come to the meeting and say, "The price of coal went up ten bucks, so I have an extra $50 million to toss into the pot." Either way, Utah tended to make our nickel-by-nickel contributions seem fruitless.

I felt the cyclical nature of Utah's business made our goal of consistent earnings impossible. I didn't like the natural resource business, where I felt events were often beyond your control or, in the case of oil, the behavior of a cartel diminished the ingenuity of the individual.

As an aside, I believe DuPont's acquisition of Conoco in 1981 had some of the same impact. Conoco was also purchased as a hedge against natural resource inflation—oil. But it too was large enough to make the individual efforts of many of DuPont's business units less meaningful. Some of my Illinois graduate student friends had joined DuPont. I heard from them and others I had known in DuPont's plastics business how personally enervating the swings in Conoco earnings could be to them. DuPont eventually spun off Conoco in 1998.

Natural resource businesses belong with natural resource companies.

Despite my feelings about Utah, I was hesitant to undo Reg's biggest deal, which he had concluded only four years earlier. I owed everything to him. I didn't want to appear disrespectful by selling it immediately. Before making the decision, I sent Reg a presentation laying out the rationale for the sale. I followed up with a telephone call, asking him to think about it.

Over the years, I called Reg a lot. I never did a major thing without letting him know—even though he left the board the day I became chairman.

A few days after our phone conversation about Utah, Reg called back and after grilling me for a while gave me his support. In fact, for more than 20 years, he never second-guessed me inside or outside the company.

Within a year of becoming CEO, I had privately met in New York's Waldorf Towers with Hugh Liedtke, CEO of Pennzoil. I offered to sell him Utah. He looked at it for a while but decided it didn't fit. He had bigger fish to fry—and he ultimately went after Getty Oil in a highly publicized takeover battle with Texaco.

I talked with other potential U.S. buyers, but found little interest.

Fortunately, my vice chairman John Burlingame had a better idea. John found what he considered the best strategic buyer for Utah, the Broken Hill Proprietary (BHP) Co. This Australian-based natural resources concern seemed the perfect fit. John contacted BHP and the company showed initial interest. He then pulled together a team with himself, Frank Doyle, and his old friend Paolo Fresco. John and Frank would strategize the discussions in the back room, while Paolo, brought back from Europe for this special assignment, would do the face-to-face negotiations.

The discussions with BHP went on for several months, complicated by size and geography. Utah's headquarters were in San Francisco, while its assets were all over the world. BHP was based in Melbourne. After the usual ups and downs of any big deal, the teams reached a definitive letter of intent by mid-December 1982.

We were ecstatic. This was a massive property with a big price tag, and there weren't all that many buyers for it. The sale was a huge hit for us and fit our strategy perfectly. The purchase had the same impact for BHP. The plan was to take the deal to the directors for final approval at the regular December board meeting.

The Thursday evening before that session, all the senior officers of the company and our directors were gathered in New York at the Park Lane Hotel for what had become an annual Christmas dinner and dance party. I began these social get-togethers the year before to bring management and the board closer. This time everyone at the party was pumped because of the deal. About 11 P.M., however, I noticed a staff person hurriedly escort John Burlingame off the dance floor. When the normally poker-faced John returned a half hour later, I could see he was visibly shaken—but still pretty cool.

Certainly cooler than I turned out to be after he came over to my table to report the bad news.

"Jack," he said, "the deal's off. I got a call from Paolo. He said that BHP just called him to say its board couldn't go through with it. They can't swing it financially."

I was devastated. I was really counting on this one. The sale would have been the first big step on the strategic path I had outlined. Now, as the band continued to play, I saw all this blowing up in my face. Carolyn and I stayed till the end of the party, before returning to a suite at the Waldorf that we were sharing with Si Cathcart and his wife, Corky.

Si had quickly become a close confidant on the board. He and I stayed up until 3 A.M., talking through all the alternatives. We were somewhat in the dark, without the benefit of many details on what had gone wrong. That night, I was lower than whale manure, and poor Si had to listen to me ramble on into the wee hours.

The next morning, Burlingame and I filled in all the directors on the news. They were obviously disappointed but encouraged us to try to get the deal back on track. When I returned to my hotel room on Friday evening, I found on my bed a stuffed teddy bear with its thumb stuck in its mouth. Si had attached a note to the bear, which his wife had gone out that morning to buy. "Don't let it get you down," Si had written. "You'll find a solution."

Having been in the job just 21 months, I wasn't sure if I had blown a big one. Si's note hit the spot. This was the first of many times that he would prove a great help to me. He was not alone—I had enjoyed incredible board support from the first day in the job, and it would turn out to be needed on more than this occasion.

After Christmas, the Burlingame-Doyle-Fresco team went back to work on the deal. They dealt with BHP's financial constraints by offering to take businesses out of Utah, including U.S. oil and gas producer Ladd Petroleum. This made the deal acceptable to Broken Hill, and the company bought the remainder of our Utah subsidiary for $2.4 billion in cash before the end of the second quarter of 1984. It took another year to get all the necessary government approvals. Six years later, in 1990, we sold the last piece, Ladd, for $515 million.

With the divestiture of air-conditioning and now Utah, I was feeling pretty good about our strategy and its implementation—

probably a bit too good. The air-conditioning deal had upset only people in the major appliance business, where it resided. Utah didn't cause even the slightest blip. We had held the company only a short time, and it had never really become part of GE.

The next move—our sale of GE housewares—would prove to be a lot different.

I had overseen our housewares operations for almost six years and thought it was a terrible business. Steam irons, toasters, hair dryers, and blenders aren't very exciting products. I recall a "breakthrough" being the electric peeling wand, a device to make potato peeling a lot easier.

Not the type of "hot technology" we needed.

These products weren't for the new GE, and we were sitting ducks for Asian imports. The industry's manufacturers were primarily U.S. players, and all were plagued with high-cost factories. The business had low barriers to entry, and retail consolidation was diminishing any brand loyalty that existed.

I had put it outside the three circles. For me, selling this business was a no-brainer. I thought we would be losing nothing, and this would put another stake in the ground for our No. 1 or No. 2 strategy. Black & Decker had apparently heard of our view of housewares and decided it fit with their business. The company boasted a strong consumer brand in power tools and had a strong position in Europe, where we didn't participate. Its leadership wanted to aggressively expand into a new area of business and targeted housewares.

In November of 1983, I received a telephone call from Pete Peterson, a B&D director and investment banker whom I had met on several occasions.

"Would you be interested in selling your appliance business?" asked Peterson.

"What kind of a question is that?" I said.

We played a little cat-and-mouse game for a few minutes, until Peterson said he was calling on behalf of Black & Decker's chairman and CEO, Larry Farley.

"Okay, if you're serious," I said, "what can I do for you?"

"On a scale of one to five, one being you'll never sell it, two being you'll sell it only for a big check, and three being you'll sell it for a fair price, where do you stand?" asked Pete.

"My major appliance business is somewhere between a one and a two," I replied. "My small appliance business is a three."

"Well, that's what we're interested in," Pete said.

Within a couple of days, on November 18, Pete, Larry, and I were sitting in GE's New York offices at 570 Lexington Avenue. Larry went through a long list of questions, and I answered most of them. Pete then asked straight out what I needed for the business.

"Not a penny less than $300 million, and the general manager of the business, Bob Wright, doesn't go with the deal."

By this time, I had enticed Bob back to GE from his Cox Cable post and put him in a holding pattern in charge of housewares. I didn't want to lose him again. I saw Bob the next day and brought him up to date on my conversation, telling him, "Don't worry. I'll have a better job for you very quickly."

It didn't take long to hear back from Larry and Pete, who both agreed to go to the next step. While the due diligence was proceeding, an internal argument broke out over the pending sale. GE traditionalists claimed that the company benefited greatly by having our name and logo on these household products. We commissioned a quick study that showed just the opposite. The consumers' perception of a GE hair curler or iron was okay but in no way valuable to the company. On the other hand, major appliances at that time and even today continue to rate highly with consumers.

The negotiations proceeded easily. We all trusted one another and wanted to get the deal done. Every time an issue came up during the negotiations, we resolved it easily. That would not be the last time Pete's straightforward style and high integrity would be important to me. Within a few weeks of my first phone call, we sold the housewares business.

The ease of the business negotiation to sell housewares masked the turmoil going on inside much of GE. Employees in many of the traditional businesses were upset. The $2 billion divestiture of Utah didn't raise an eyebrow, but selling this $300 million low-tech, tin-bending housewares business brought out unbelievable cries. I got my first blast of angry letters from employees.

If e-mail had existed, every server in the company would have been clogged up. The letters were all along the lines of "How could we be GE and not make irons and toasters?" or "What kind of a person are you? If you'll do this, it's clear you'll do anything!"

The buzz around the water cooler was not good.

And there was a lot more to come, a helluva lot more.

9

The Neutron Years

In the early 1980s, you didn't have to be in a GE business that was up for sale to wonder if Jack Welch knew what he was doing or where he was going. The turmoil, angst, and confusion were everywhere. The causes were the goal to be No. 1 or No. 2, the three circles, the outright sale of businesses, and the cutbacks now occurring in many parts of GE.

Within five years, one of every four people would leave the GE payroll, 118,000 people in all, including 37,000 employees in businesses that were sold. Throughout the company, people were struggling to come to grips with the uncertainty.

I was adding fuel to the fire by investing millions of dollars in what some might call "nonproductive" things. I was building a fitness center, guesthouse, and conference center at headquarters and laying plans for a major upgrade of Crotonville, our management development center. My take on this was that all these investments, at a cost of nearly $75 million, were consistent with the "soft" values of excellence I had outlined at the Pierre Hotel.

But people weren't buying it. For them, it was a total disconnect.

It didn't matter that the money I was investing in treadmills, conference halls, and bedrooms was pocket change to a company that was spending $12 billion over the same period on new plants and equipment. That $12 billion, spread across factories around the world, was invisible and considered routine.

The symbolism of the $75 million was too much for people to handle. I could understand why it was difficult for many GE employees to get it.

But I was sure in my gut it was the right thing to do.

A key supporter during this period—of spending while downsizing—was human resources chief Ted LeVino. He was the rock, a link to the past, an up-from-the-ranks GE veteran who had the respect of everyone in the system. His motives and integrity were unquestionable. I know many shaken executives sat on Ted's couch fresh from one of their early encounters with me. Ted counseled many of the senior people who had to go. He had backed me during the selection process and, more important, knew what he was getting and believed GE needed it.

Ted's support was important because people were out of their minds over these investments. Nothing I could say or do would ever completely satisfy the detractors or fully calm the organization's jitters. I wasn't going to hide. I used every opportunity to reach out. In early 1982, I began holding roundtable discussions every other week with groups of 25 or so employees over coffee. Whether administrative assistants or managers were in the room, the questions never varied.

One question inevitably dominated those sessions: "How can you justify spending money on treadmills, bedrooms, and conference centers when you're closing down plants and laying off staff?"

I enjoyed the debates. I wasn't necessarily winning the argument, but I knew I had to try to win people over, one by one. I'd argue that the spending and the cutting were consistent with where we needed to go.

I wanted to change the rules of engagement, asking for more—from fewer. I was insisting that we had to have only the best people. I'd argue that our best couldn't be asked to spend four weeks away for training in cinder-block cells at a worn-out development center. Guests shouldn't have to come to headquarters and stay at a third-class motel. If you wanted excellence, at a minimum, the ambience had to reflect excellence.

At these roundtables, I'd explain the fitness center was as much about getting people together as it was about health. A headquarters building is filled with specialists who make nothing and sell nothing. Working there is so different from working in the field, where everyone in a business can focus on and be excited by landing a new order or launching a new product. At GE headquarters, you'd park your car in an underground garage, take an elevator to your floor, and generally work in a corner of the building until the end of the day. The cafeteria was a common meeting place, but most tables were occupied by the people who worked together.

I thought a gym would provide an informal place to bring together all shapes, sizes, layers, and functions. If you will, it could be that back room of a store where people took their breaks. If investing a little over $1 million could make that happen, it was worth it. Despite my good intentions with the fitness center, people had trouble seeing the benefits in the face of layoffs.

Some of the same logic went into the decision to put up a $25 million guesthouse and conference center at headquarters, which was an island unto itself. It was in the country, some sixty miles north of New York City, off the Merritt Parkway. There was no natural place to congregate after work. Fairfield and the surrounding area lacked a decent hotel to put up employees and guests who came from all over the world. I wanted to create a first-class place where people could stay, work, and interact. The facility featured fireplaces in the lounges and a stand-up bar in the pub where everyone could mingle.

The traditionalists were shocked. I persevered because I wanted to create a first-rate informal family atmosphere and needed this ambience to get it. Everywhere I went, I was preaching the need for excellence in everything we did. My actions had to demonstrate it.

The story of Crotonville is no different. Our corporate

education center was already a quarter of a century old—and unfortunately looked it. Managers were being housed in barren quarters four to a suite. The bedrooms had the feel of a roadside motel. We needed to make our own people and our customers, who came to Crotonville, feel that they were working for and dealing with a world-class company. Nonetheless, some critics began calling it "Jack's Cathedral."

My answers to the complaints during the early 1980s was that business is, in fact, a series of paradoxes:

- **Spending millions on buildings that made nothing, while closing down uncompetitive factories that produced goods.**

These goals were consistent with becoming a world-class competitor. You couldn't hire and retain the best people, and at the same time become the lowest-cost provider of goods and services, without doing both.

- **Paying the highest wages, while having the lowest wage costs.**

We had to get the best people in the world and had to pay them that way. But we couldn't carry along people we didn't need. We needed to have better people if we were to get more productivity from fewer of them.

- **Managing long-term, while "eating" short-term.**

I always thought any fool could do one or the other. Squeezing costs out at the expense of the future could deliver a quarter, a year, maybe even two years, and it's not hard to do. Dreaming about the future and not delivering in the short term is the easiest of all. The test of a leader is balancing the two. A favorite retort for at least the first ten years was, "GE and you are too focused on the short term." That's just another clichéd excuse to do nothing.

- **Needing to be "hard" in order to be "soft."**

Making tough-minded decisions about people and plants is a prerequisite to earning the right to talk about soft values, like "excellence" or "the learning organization." Soft stuff won't work if it doesn't follow demonstrated toughness. It works only in a performance-based culture.

Think of those dichotomies, those paradoxes, I was trying to get across. We needed to produce more output with less input. We needed to expand some businesses while shrinking or selling others. We needed to function as one company, but our diversity demanded different styles. And yes, we needed to treat people in a first-class way if we wanted to attract and keep the best.

The logic behind these paradoxes didn't go far in an environment overcome with so much uncertainty. In fact, the internal upheaval was so great, it began spilling outside the company. By mid-1982, *Newsweek* magazine was the first publication to pick up the moniker "Neutron Jack," the guy who removed the people but left the buildings standing.

I hated it, and it hurt. But I hated bureaucracy and waste even more. The data-obsessed headquarters and the low margins in turbines were equally offensive to me.

Soon, Neutron began cropping up almost everywhere in the media. It was as if reporters couldn't write a GE story without using the tag. It was a painful new image twist for me. For years, people thought I was too wild, that I was too growth focused, hired too many people, and built too many facilities—in plastics, medical, and GE Credit. Now I was Neutron.

I guess that was a paradox, too. I didn't like it, but I came to understand it.

Truth was, we were the first big healthy and profitable company in the mainstream that took the actions to get more competitive. Chrysler did it a few years earlier, but the stage was set for their actions by a government bailout and their widely publicized struggle to avoid bankruptcy.

There was no stage set for us. We looked too good, too strong, too profitable, to be restructuring. Our $1.5 billion in net income and $25 billion of sales in 1980 made GE the ninth most profitable company in the Fortune 500 and the tenth largest.

However, we were facing our own reality. In 1980, the U.S. economy was in a recession. Inflation was rampant. Oil sold for $30 a barrel, and some predicted it would go to $100 if we could even get it. And the Japanese, benefiting from a weak yen and good technology, were increasing their exports into many of our mainstream businesses from cars to consumer electronics.

I wanted to face these realities by getting more cost competitive, and that's what we were doing.

I also saw firsthand the impact of this changing environment on many of the CEOs in the New York/New Jersey/Connecticut tri-state area. I served as a corporate chairman for the United Way campaign in the early 1980s. Time after time, as I visited with CEOs to strong-arm them for contributions, I'd hear them say, "We'd like to give it to you, but we can't," or, "We can't give as much as we did in the past. Things are too tough." This experience bolstered my notion that only healthy, growing, vibrant companies can carry out their responsibilities to people and their communities.

The costs of fixing a troubled company after the fact are enormous—and even more painful. We were fortunate. Our predecessors left us a good balance sheet. We could be humane and generous to the people we had to let go—although most probably didn't feel we were at the time. We gave our employees significant notice and good severance pay, and our good reputation helped many find new jobs. By moving early, more jobs were available for them. It's still true in 2001. If you were the first dot.com to cut the payroll, each of your employees had many job offers. If you were the last, your people could be in the unemployment line.

But that's not what some thought when a "healthy" old-line company like ours was closing a steam iron plant in Ontario, California, in 1982. We learned that *60 Minutes* was sending Mike Wallace and a film crew to cover it. Having *60 Minutes* call to talk about a plant closing is not likely to be a pleasant event, and it ended up not being a pretty sight. Wallace reported that we laid off 825 people simply because we weren't making enough profit and wanted to move those jobs outside the United States to Mexico, Singapore, and Brazil. He interviewed former employees who said they felt betrayed and a religious leader who condemned the plant's closure as "immoral."

That view was understandable then—but the facts were somewhat different. The plant made metal irons when consumers already overwhelmingly favored plastic models. We had four plants, including one in North Carolina, making plastic irons. Ontario's product line had to be discontinued. Closing the plant was uncomfortable for everyone, but it was the highest-cost plant in our system, and we were going to be competitive.

In fairness to *60 Minutes,* the program did point out that we had given our employees six months' advance notice when the average then was only one week. Wallace also reported that we helped to fund a state-run job center on GE property to teach job-interview and other skills.

We did a lot more because our balance sheet let us. We extended life and medical insurance coverage for a year and placed 120 workers in other jobs by the time the plant closed. Nearly 600 employees would be eligible for GE pensions, and we also found a buyer for the factory that would eventually rehire many former GE employees. Despite all that, losing your job stank.

I had been in the CEO job less than a year when, in late February 1982, *60 Minutes* accused us of "putting profits ahead of people." Some critics used us as a counterpoint to such companies as IBM, which at that time still promoted the concept of lifetime employment. In fact, IBM itself launched an advertising campaign touting its nonlayoff policies in 1985. IBM's tagline: ". . . jobs may come and go. But people shouldn't." Several GE managers brought the ads to our Crotonville classes and pointedly asked, "What's your reaction to this?"

At a time when I was being routinely assaulted with the Neutron tag, those ads really pissed me off.

Sadly for the IBM people, their day would come as the company lost competitiveness.

Any organization that thinks it can guarantee job security is going down a dead end. Only satisfied customers can give people job security. Not companies. That reality put an end to the implicit contracts that corporations once had with their employees. Those "contracts" were based on perceived lifetime employment and produced a paternal, feudal, fuzzy kind of loyalty. If you put in your time and worked hard, the perception was that the company took care of you for life.

As the game changed, people had to be focused on the competitive world, where no business was a safe haven for employment unless it was winning in the marketplace.

The psychological contract had to change. I wanted to create a new contract, making GE jobs the best in the world for people willing to compete. If they signed up, we'd give them the best training and development and an environment that provided plenty of opportunities for personal and professional growth. We'd do everything to give them the skills to have "lifetime employability," even if we couldn't guarantee them "lifetime employment."

Removing people will always be the hardest decision a leader faces. Anyone who "enjoys doing it" shouldn't be on the payroll, and neither should anyone who "can't do it." I never underestimated the human cost of those layoffs or the hardship they might cause people and communities. To me, every action had to pass a simple screen: "Would we like to be treated that way? Were we fair and equitable? Can you look at yourself in the mirror every day and say yes to those questions?"

As a company, we could look at ourselves in the mirror when it came to softening the rough edges of radical change. The speech I had to give 1,000 times was, "We didn't fire the people. We fired the positions, and the people had to go."

We never resorted to "across the board" cutbacks or pay freezes, two old management favorites to reduce costs. Carried out under the guise of "sharing the pain," both actions are examples of people not wanting to face reality and differentiation.

That's not managing or leading. Edicts to impose a uniform 10 percent layoff policy or a wage freeze undermine the need to take care of the best. In the spring of 2001, several economy-impacted GE businesses, such as plastics, lighting, and appliances, were downsizing. Meanwhile, some businesses, such as power turbines and medical, couldn't add people fast enough.

Unfortunately, in the 1980s most of GE's employment levels were headed downward. We went from 411,000 employees at the end of 1980 to 299,000 by the end of 1985. Of the 112,000 people who left the GE payroll, about 37,000 were in businesses we sold, but 81,000 people—or 1 in every 5 in our industrial businesses— lost their jobs for productivity reasons.

From the numbers, you could make the case that there was either a Neutron Jack or a company with too many positions. I naturally took comfort in the latter, but the Neutron tag still got me down. I was fortunate to find remarkable support that got me through it—at home, in the office, and in the boardroom. I'd come home obviously a little down from the experience. Carolyn would always be supportive, no matter how tough the press. She always ended a conversation with, "Jack, you have to do what you think is right for everyone."

In the 1980s, the massive nature of the changes at GE would have been impossible without a core of strong supporters inside the company. Once rivals and now partners, my two vice chairmen John Burlingame and Ed Hood backed all the moves. So did two of the most powerful staff players at headquarters, HR chief Ted LeVino and chief financial officer Tom Thorsen. Tom and I were thick as brothers in Pittsfield and happy to be reunited in bigger jobs at headquarters. Larry Bossidy, whom I brought to Fairfield in 1981 to take over a newly created materials and service sector, had become my sounding board, confidant, and close friend.

Without strong backing from the board, these changes couldn't have happened. Board members heard all the complaints, sometimes from angry employees who wrote critical letters directly to them, and they read all the negative press. From day one, however, the board never wavered.

When I first became CEO, Walter Wriston went around New York telling everyone he met that I was the best CEO in the history of the company—even before I did anything. It sure felt good to hear that, especially during my Neutron days. He was a stand-up, gutsy guy who kept telling me to do what I had to do to change the company.

Still, the pressure to avoid some of these tough decisions was considerable. The lobbying wasn't only internal—the calls came in from mayors, governors, state and federal legislators.

Once, on a scheduled visit to the Massachusetts state house in 1988, I met with Governor Michael Dukakis.

"It's a great thing that you're in the state," said Dukakis. "We'd really like to see you put more work here."

The day before my meeting, our aircraft engine and industrial turbine plant in Lynn, Massachusetts, had distinguished themselves once again by being the only GE union in the chain to reject our new national labor agreement.

"Governor," I said, "I have to tell you. Lynn is the last place on earth I would ever put any more work."

Dukakis's aides were shocked. There was a long silence in the room. Everyone was expecting me to make some reassuring comment about our commitment to employment and possible expansion in Massachusetts.

"You're a politician and you know how to count votes. You don't put new roads in districts that don't vote for you."

"What do you mean?" he asked.

"Lynn is the only local in all of GE that has rejected our national union contract. They seem to do this as a ritual over the years. Why should I put work and money where there is trouble, when I can put up plants where people want them and deserve them?"

Governor Dukakis chuckled. He instantly understood the point and sent his labor representative to Lynn to improve things. Progress has been slow to say the least, but Lynn did vote for the national contract in 2000.

I took another solid hit in early August of 1984 when *Fortune* magazine put me at the top of its list of "The Ten Toughest Bosses in America." This was a case where being No. 1 or No. 2 wasn't something you were looking for. Fortunately, the article had some good things to say as well. One former employee told the magazine that he had never met someone "with so many creative business ideas. I've never felt that anybody was tapping my brain so well." Another actually credited me "with bringing to GE the passion and dedication that characterize the best Silicon Valley start-ups."

I liked all that, but the positive reactions were overshadowed by comments from "anonymous" former employees who said I was very abrasive and didn't tolerate "I think" answers. "Working for him is like a war," claimed another unidentified person. "A lot of people get shot up; the survivors go on to the next battle." The article claimed that I attacked people almost physically with questions, in the words of the writer, "criticizing, demeaning, ridiculing, humiliating."

In truth, the meetings *were different* from what people were used to. They were candid, challenging, and demanding. If former managers wanted a reason why they didn't cut it, there were plenty of ways to spin the story.

I got the article as I was leaving the office for California to spend a weekend at the Bohemian Grove as the guest of director Ed Littlefield. I shared the story with Ed, who shrugged it off.

I couldn't get it out of my mind. The story made it a long

weekend. The net effect of all this publicity was that the "Neutron Jack" and "Toughest Boss in America" labels would stick for some time.

The ironic thing was that I didn't go far enough or move fast enough. When MBAs at the Harvard Business School in the mid-1980s asked me what I regretted most in my first years as CEO, I said, "I took too long to act."

The class burst out laughing, but it was true.

The facts were that I was just too hesitant to break the glass. I waited too long to close uncompetitive facilities. I took too long to take apart the corporate staff, keeping on economists, marketing consultants, strategic planners, and outright bureaucrats much longer than I needed to. I didn't blow up our sector structure until 1986. It was just another insulating layer of management and should have been cut the moment the succession race was decided.

The seven executives in these sector jobs were the best people we had. They should have been running our businesses. I was wasting them in these oversight positions. We promoted our best executives to those jobs, and in turn those jobs made some of our best people look bad. Once we blew it up, we quickly discovered something else. Without the sector layer, we got a much better look at the people really running the businesses.

It changed the game. Within months, we could see clearly who had it and who didn't. Four senior vice presidents left the company in mid-1986. It was a huge breakthrough.

While the media focused on the layoffs, we focused on the "keepers." I could talk my face blue about facing reality, or being No. 1 or No. 2 in every business, or creating an organization that thrived on change, but until we got the right horses in place, we didn't get the traction we needed to truly change the company. I shouldn't have wasted so much time on the resisters, hoping they'd "buy in."

When we finally got the right people in all the key places, the game changed quickly. Let me illustrate what putting the right person at the top can do. I can't think of a better example than our appointment of Dennis Dammerman as chief financial officer in March of 1984.

If you had asked thousands of employees at that time to come up with a list of five folks who would succeed Tom Thorsen as CFO, none would have named Dennis because he was so far down in the financial hierarchy.

Tom and I always had a complex relationship. I loved his brains, his cockiness, and his companionship. In spite of his outwardly flamboyant manner and his great support for where we were going, he saw himself as the protector of the strongest functional organization in the company.

Ironically, he was also the sharpest critic in the company, tough and decisive about everything and everyone, including me. Yet, when it came to finance, he couldn't bring himself to step on the function's sacred turf. We had many conversations about this but could never agree. Tom moved on to become CFO of Travelers.

With 12,000 people strong, finance had become too large and too entrenched a part of the bureaucracy. Most of the "nice to know" studies originated in the finance function, which at that time spent $65 million to $75 million a year on operations analysis alone.

Finance had become an institution of its own. It had the company's best training program. Their smartest graduates went on to the audit staff, where they rotated from business to business for several years. The result was, we had a strong, capable, but set-in-its-ways financial institution that was controlling the hell out of the place but didn't want to change either the company or itself.

By appointing Dennis to the job, I wanted him to lead his own revolution. When I asked him to become chief financial officer, he was general manager of GE Capital's real estate division. He had never made a presentation to the board of directors. He was only 38 years old, which made him the youngest CFO in the company's history.

Dennis had worked for me for two years when I was a sector

executive. During that period, he demonstrated incredible smarts, courage, and versatility. He could slice and dice the smallest details of the appliance business on one day, then analyze the most complex deal at GE Capital the next. During the Session C people reviews, he instantly knew the difference between the A and the B players.

Just as important, he didn't carry any of the bureaucratic baggage that the players on the more typical list of candidates would have had. I gave him the ultimate stretch assignment. Though Dennis wasn't sure he was qualified for the job, I knew he could do it and I was completely committed to help him.

Dennis was as shocked as the finance organization over his appointment. He was sitting in his office at GE Capital when I called at 7:15 A.M. one day in March of 1984 and asked him to meet me at 6 P.M. at Gates, the same restaurant where I had written the three-circle strategy on a cocktail napkin.

I told Dennis to keep our meeting a secret from everyone. I have no idea what went through his mind during those ten hours before our session. I'm sure he figured this was something that was going to be good for him. One thing he never imagined was that I would ask him to take the top finance job.

When I arrived at Gates, Dennis was already sitting at the bar. I sat next to him, ordered a drink for myself, and got right to the point.

"Dennis," I said, "I'd like to go to the board this week and appoint you senior vice president and chief financial officer. Are you okay with this?"

Completely surprised, he managed to mutter, "Yes . . . okay."

Once over the excitement, Dennis started asking dozens of questions about the job, so many that I finally called home and invited Carolyn down to join us. We all celebrated Dennis's good news together.

When his appointment became public, shock waves ran through the company and really rocked the finance function. This was just what I wanted. Dennis's appointment created the crisis we needed. I added more heat to the situation by writing Dennis a three-page critique of his new function. Dennis shared it with his team.

In a May 1984 letter, I wrote, "The first thing I'd like to do is make it clear that I don't 'hate' the function. I think its strengths . . . have made it the best single functional organization in the company. It has been 'some of the glue' that's kept the company together. But that is the past. What worked before—control—is not enough for tomorrow. . . .

"Everything done in the past is open for question—question, not criticism—from the financial management program, its input, size, and the training it provides to the headquarters and field organization's size and role."

Change doesn't come from a slogan or a speech. It happens because you put the right people in place to make it happen. People first. Strategy and everything else next. Dennis was in many ways the perfect inside "outsider" we needed to break the bureaucratic hold finance had on our company.

Over time, Dennis dramatically changed the face of finance. Two years into the job, he was still battling the financial bureaucracy. Headquarters loved data, and it took years to stop the financial people from overanalyzing it. In 1986, a detailed analysis of international sales came across my desk, projecting GE's total revenues for the next five years in every country, including, of all places, Mauritius, the tiny island off the coast of Africa.

I went bonkers. The name at the bottom of the report was Dave Cote, a financial analyst, at headquarters, two levels below Dennis. I asked my assistant to call Cote and get him over to my office.

"Dave," I said, "you look like a smart guy. What are you doing bothering people in the field to get this stuff? Sales? Five years out? In Mauritius? I doubt you even know where it is!"

Dave didn't know what to say. Unbeknownst to me, he had tried to shut the report down two months earlier. We got rid of that report for good that day. Dave got visibility and a series of promotions within the company, the last as CEO of appliances. He left in 1998 and is now CEO of TRW in Cleveland.

Dennis Dammerman persevered against incidents like this and a hundred more like it. Over his first four years in the job, he cut the finance staff in half. He led the consolidation of the 150 different payroll systems we had in the United States alone. He changed the financial management program, which used to be 90 percent finance and 10 percent general management, so that nearly half of its content was on management and leadership. And he changed our audit staff so that our auditors became business supporters, not corporate policemen.

Changing the role of the audit staff would be a huge win for us—a very big deal. Getting auditors into this business partner role and out of the green eyeshade "gotcha" role changed not only what they did, but ultimately who they would become. Three of our key initiatives—in services, Six Sigma, and e-business—wouldn't be where they are today without the passionate leadership and support of this young group of stars. They relentlessly transferred best practices from one GE business to another around the globe.

Today the CFOs of all of GE's businesses see their jobs as COOs—and not controllers. In the 14 years that Dennis served as chief financial officer, until becoming a vice chairman of GE in 1998, he transformed an audit-driven finance organization into the best school for business leadership. Three of his former audit staff heads have become huge stars at GE: John Rice at power and Dave Calhoun at aircraft engines are now CEOs of our two largest single businesses. Jay Ireland became CEO of the NBC station group. Charlene Begley, a 36-year-old mother of three, ran GE's 180-person audit staff and then went on to become CFO of GE's specialty materials business in mid-2001. Charlene was replaced by 37-year-old Lynn Calpeter. She had been chief financial officer of NBC's station group.

There's a similar success story in the legal arena. We had a legal organization that was on the wrong end of the Rolodex. If a problem came up, our lawyers basically knew whom to dial up. The outside counsel would then run the case, and our legal staff would serve as backup. Unlike finance, there was no internal candidate to make the transformation we needed. I talked to all kinds of outside lawyers to get help in my search for the best.

Just as Dennis seemed an unlikely hire as chief financial officer, so was my new general counsel, Ben Heineman. He was a constitutional lawyer in Washington, D.C., whose practice was appellate Supreme Court litigation. Ben had been a Rhodes scholar, a reporter for the *Chicago Sun-Times*, the editor of the *Yale Law Journal*, a Supreme Court law clerk, and a public interest lawyer in Washington. His first job after clerking for Justice Potter Stewart was defending the mentally handicapped. He worked in government as undersecretary of the Department of Health, Education and Welfare and in private practice as managing partner of Sidley and Austin's Washington office when I met him in 1987.

To some, Ben seemed a bizarre choice to head our legal staff. I didn't think so—but even he had some doubts. Before our final interview, he said, "Remember, I'm a constitutional lawyer. I'm not a corporate lawyer. I'm not a New York lawyer."

"I don't care," I shot back. "You'll hire good lawyers. That's what I want you to do."

Ben didn't have the same stable of talent Dennis inherited in finance. He had to go outside, and he did. I gave him carte blanche to pay as well as the best law firms and then added options into the mix as the upside kicker. He was able to pry out some of their smartest partners.

This was the classic case of As hiring As.

Ben was "over the top" about résumés. He couldn't talk about people without getting into a line-by-line description of their credentials, from their school and position on the *Law Review* to which federal judge they clerked for. We all kidded him about it.

I'll concede that in this case résumés counted, and Ben found stars. He brought in John Samuels, a former partner at Dewey

Ballantine, to head our tax department; Brackett Denniston, the former chief legal counsel for Massachusetts governor Bill Weld, to run litigation; Pamela Daley, a partner at Morgan, Becker & Lewis in Philadelphia, to head up M&A; Steve Ramsey, a former Department of Justice (DOJ) environmental litigation head, to run environmental health and safety; and Ron Stern, an antitrust partner at Arnold & Porter, to head up our antitrust practice based in Washington. (In 2001, Ron spent most of his time in Brussels, having an experience no one should go through.)

Ben put the same caliber of talent into the general counsel jobs at almost every GE business.

We got more than great legal advice.

Three of Ben's associates left the law and played significant roles in GE operations: Henry Hubschman, former general counsel at aircraft engines, in now CEO of GE Capital Aviation Services. Frank Blake, general counsel at power systems, became head of business development for the company. Jay Lapin, former general counsel at appliances, went on to become president of GE Japan.

Ben turned the place upside down. Today, I believe GE has the best legal firm in the world (almost everyone agrees it is the best corporate legal team). Our lawyers design the work and plot the strategy, with the advantage of having an intimate knowledge of our company and its people. The outside law firms work much more closely with us. They are partners in our firm.

Ironically, I shouldn't have agonized as long as I did on so many people who weren't going to cut it. The consistent lesson I've learned over the years is that I have been in many cases too cautious. I should have torn down the structures sooner, sold off weak businesses faster than I did. Almost everything should and could have been done faster.

This so-called Toughest Boss in America honestly wasn't tough-minded enough.

10

The RCA Deal

I 'll never forget the time I walked through a Japanese manufacturing plant. It was in the mid-1970s, after putting together a
joint venture with Yokogawa Medical Systems. On a tour of a
Yokogawa plant outside Tokyo, I watched in total amazement as
ultrasound units were being assembled.

The process was like nothing I had seen in the United States.
When the machines were finished, a worker unbuttoned his shirt,
dabbed some gel on his chest, and ran the ultrasound probes over
his body for a quick quality test. The same guy then wrapped up
the product, put it in a box, attached a shipping label, and got it on
the loading dock.

It would have taken a lot more people to get this done in
Milwaukee—one of GE's best plants.

The incredible efficiency of the Japanese was both awesome
and frightening. What I saw in Japan was occurring in many of
our markets. The Japanese were tearing apart the cost structure in
industry after industry. Television sets, automobiles, and copying
machines were being hammered.

I was looking for a business that would give us a place to hide.
In the early 1980s, three businesses seemed to ring the bell: food,

pharmaceuticals, and television broadcasting. Everyone needed to eat, and the United States had a strong agricultural position in the world. We evaluated several food companies, including General Foods, but couldn't make the numbers work. At the time their price-earnings ratios were much higher than GE's. As for pharmaceuticals, the numbers weren't even close.

The government's foreign ownership restrictions made TV attractive. Like the food industry, it had strong cash flow that could strengthen and expand our businesses.

The Japanese threat would lead to a deal that would really change GE—the $6.3 billion acquisition of RCA in 1985. At the time, it was the biggest non-oil deal in history. We bought RCA primarily to get NBC. What came with it would transform us.

The network business had always fascinated me.

Before RCA, we came close to getting CBS. In the spring of 1985, Ted Turner was trying a hostile takeover of the network. CBS chairman Tom Wyman and I met over dinner at our headquarters in Fairfield to discuss the possibility of our being a white knight. But Wyman fended off Ted's threat, and we weren't needed. The CBS deal evaporated. But my "secret" meeting with Wyman hadn't escaped attention.

There are no secrets on Wall Street. As a Lazard Frères partner, Felix Rohatyn put together many of the biggest deals in those days. Though I hadn't done an acquisition with him, I was a big admirer of Felix. He heard about my interest in CBS and knew of my earlier effort to get Cox Broadcasting. Meanwhile, Felix and Thornton "Brad" Bradshaw, chairman of RCA, were friends and had been discussing RCA's strategic options.

Brad had been brought in to fix RCA in mid-1981 after a successful run as the president of ARCO. He was quiet, self-effacing, and incredibly wise. I felt very good about him right away. Brad had done a good job and was particularly successful with NBC by enticing TV producer Grant Tinker to head up the network.

From the start, Brad had no intention of staying all that long.

Ironically, he found his replacement in Bob Frederick, who had been one of the GE executives in the race for Reg's job. Bob had joined RCA three years earlier as chief operating officer and president. He was made CEO in 1985. Brad remained as chairman but was having all kinds of second thoughts about whether RCA could make it on its own.

Out of the blue, I got a call from Felix, who asked me if I'd like to meet with Brad. A few days later, on November 6 of 1985, we got together in Felix's New York apartment for drinks. Brad showed up dressed in a tux so he could skip out for a formal dinner. It was quickly clear that, like me, Bradshaw was worried about Asian competition. He was as focused on being No. 1 or No. 2 as I was.

We never talked about a specific deal that night, but we found out we liked each other. Felix had been a good matchmaker. Brad and I were comfortable with each other and shared a common understanding for the strategic rationale behind a combination. Ours was a short meeting—a little less than an hour. When I left Felix's apartment, we hadn't scheduled a second meeting.

At this point, we were just dating. But I felt that there was a real shot at marriage.

The next day, I put together a team, including Dennis Dammerman, our chief financial officer, and Mike Carpenter, our head of business development, to dig through RCA. We worked on the project under the code name "Island."

The day before Thanksgiving, our team got together to decide whether to take the next step. For more than four hours, Larry Bossidy, the Island team, and I wallowed through all the pros and cons of the acquisition. For me, "wallowing" has always been a key part of how we ran GE. Get a group of people around a table, regardless of their rank, to wrestle with a particularly tough issue. Stew on it from every angle—flush out everyone's thinking—but don't come to an immediate conclusion.

With RCA, we wallowed to the point of seeing that there was a lot more than just a broadcast network. We had a small semiconductor business. So did RCA. We had an aerospace division. So did RCA. We both were in the TV set business. Combining operations in these businesses would make each one of them a lot stronger.

We had been in the TV station business for years, and our short courtship with CBS gave us enough understanding to become reasonably comfortable with the network. We put a $3.5 billion valuation on the broadcast business. If we could stomach paying about $2.5 billion for everything else, then the deal could be a home run.

Our major concern was the valuation of NBC. Though its ratings were strong in 1985, cable television had started to eat into its network audience. We made some very aggressive assumptions on cable penetration and still decided that the deal was right.

I kept asking, "Ten years from now, would you rather be in appliances or in network television?"

We all agreed to go away and think it over during the long Thanksgiving Day weekend. We met again first thing Monday morning. All of us had come to the same conclusion: The numbers worked, and beyond the network we saw that most of RCA's other businesses were a great fit with ours.

It was a go.

I let Felix know that at the right price, we were interested. He set up another meeting between Brad and me on Thursday, December 5, in Brad's duplex at the Dorset Hotel in midtown Manhattan.

After some small talk, we quickly got to the point.

"I'd like to buy your company," I told him. "Our companies are a perfect fit."

The fit was obvious to him as well.

I tried a price in the $61-a-share range, more than $13 higher than RCA's stock was trading at that time. He paused and, in his professorial way, let me know it wasn't quite enough. By the time I left, we agreed to pursue the deal and to disagree on a final price.

The next day, things got a little hairy. It turned out that Brad hadn't discussed our meetings with Bob Frederick. When Bob found out, he became angry, to say the least. He felt the company was being sold out from under him. Bob and Brad had a brief falling-out over this, and Bob tried to marshal some of the directors on RCA's board against the deal. When the board met on Sunday, December 8, Brad was able to get a majority of the board to approve the deal.

Afterward, he called me to report the good news but said the price still wasn't right. He had retained Felix to represent him. I needed an investment banker, so I signed up my good friend John Weinberg, who was running Goldman, Sachs.

Over the next few days, meeting at a suite in a New York hotel, Brad, Bob, and Felix negotiated with John and me. At the end, as usual, we got down to nickels and dimes. Brad was at $67 a share, and I was at $65. The deal closed when I gave Brad $66.50— probably 50 cents more than he expected.

I always tried to leave some goodwill on the table when the seller's ongoing involvement was important to the company's success.

By Wednesday evening, December 11, we had a deal to buy RCA for a total of $6.3 billion in cash.

There was an odd footnote to the deal. Only months before, in August, a lower-level lawyer at RCA had called one of our attorneys and said he would like to get rid of an old GE-RCA consent decree. During World War I, the U.S. government asked GE, AT&T, and Westinghouse to form the Radio Corporation of America for defense purposes.

In 1933, the Justice Department decided that we should spin it off as a separate company. We did that and took over their headquarters building at 570 Lexington Avenue as compensation. However, the consent decree resulting from that transaction restricted GE from buying RCA common stock. The Justice Department eliminated the 50-plus-year restriction by October, clearing the way for the deal two months later.

Talk about dumb luck! None of us had a clue the consent decree existed.

After wrapping up the deal that Wednesday night, I left RCA's lawyers' offices and went back to the GE building on Lexington Avenue to celebrate. It was the same building the company had gotten for its part of RCA in 1933.

What a night!

We broke out the champagne. We were laughing and giving each other high-fives. All of us—Larry Bossidy, Mike Carpenter, Dennis Dammerman, and the others—were like kids. I'll never forget the kick we got looking out the windows through the fog and seeing the RCA sign illuminated on top of their building at Rockefeller Center. It was just three blocks away from ours. We could hardly wait to get the GE logo up there. We felt like hot stuff at the moment.

From my first meeting with Bradshaw to final board approval, it had taken 36 days to nail down the largest non-oil merger at the time. The deal, announced December 12, was a turning point for GE. The critics, and there were many, focused on GE getting into the network business. They asked, "What in the world was a light bulb company doing buying a TV network?" Broadcasting gave us pizzazz and great cash flow—and the hideaway I wanted from foreign competition. The hidden value would come in the less glamorous assets that got little attention.

The RCA acquisition gave us a great network and a lot more strategic chips at the table. It also sparked a new, energized GE. We had been going through lots of turmoil with our restructuring and downsizing. The deal changed the atmosphere. I remember walking up to the stage for the opening session of our operating managers meeting in Boca that January, a few weeks after the acquisition was announced.

All of a sudden, some 500 people in the room stood up in a spontaneous ovation. RCA became the kick-start to a new era.

Once the deal closed, we sold RCA's nonstrategic assets,

including records, carpeting, and insurance. We didn't like the culture in the record business. The carpet business didn't fit with anything we did, and neither did a small insurance company. Within a year of the deal, we had $1.3 billion of our $6.3 billion back.

I tried hard to keep Grant Tinker as head of NBC. With Brandon Tartikoff as his partner, the two of them had turned around the network with lots of great hits, from *The Cosby Show* to *Cheers*. Tinker had signed on for a five-year stay that would be up in July. He had been commuting weekly between New York and California and was tired of it. Although Tinker told Brad before the acquisition that he intended to leave, I tried to convince him to stay with us. We had dinner in New York where I offered him, what was for me, an ocean of money. There was nothing I could do to get him to reconsider.

Fortunately, I had a backup plan from day one. Bob Wright was now running GE Capital after the sale of housewares. He had been sent by us to Cox Broadcasting when I tried to buy it and stayed there three years as president of Cox Cable.

Bob was the perfect fit. He had a feel for the business, was familiar with GE, and was a close ally as we moved into strange territory. I appointed Bob head of NBC in August 1986. The media asked, "How could this GE guy run a network?"

The long and short of it is that 15 years later, Bob is still there with a great track record.

While we left NBC as a separate business, we immediately began to integrate the RCA and GE operations that complemented each other. We reduced overhead by putting joint teams together that met with me every week. The teams' objective was $1 + 1 = 1$: one GE and one RCA staff professional would equal one in the merged company. The integration teams agreed that the best from each company would get the jobs.

This wasn't idle BS. GE got the top staff jobs, but in the complementary businesses, RCA won most of the big jobs. We ended up the No. 1 U.S. TV set producer and put in an RCA executive to run it. We did the same with our combined aerospace and semiconductor businesses, with RCA leaders selected. Heading up a fourth business in government services and satellite communications was Gene Murphy from RCA, later to become head of GE's aerospace and aircraft engine business and eventually a GE vice chairman. Gene had a military bearing. He always delivered on his commitments. I considered him Mr. Integrity—as high a compliment as you could pay anyone.

These assets, or chips, gave us strategic options that weren't possible before. Over the next decade, each of these chips would create real value for GE.

Unfortunately, while I was doing the biggest deal of my professional career, the biggest merger in my personal life was ending.

Carolyn and I had been having difficulty in our marriage for many years. Through all my GE years, I was the ultimate workaholic, while she did a great job raising our four kids. All of them were on their way and doing well. Katherine, our oldest, had graduated from Duke University and was in her first year at Harvard Business School. After getting an undergraduate degree from the University of Virginia, my oldest son, John, was getting his master's degree in chemical engineering at Illinois. Our other daughter, Anne, graduated from Brown University and was going to the Harvard School of Architecture for her master's degree. Our youngest son, Mark, was in his freshman year at the University of Vermont.

Carolyn and I simply found ourselves on different paths. Other than our friendship and mutual respect, we had little in common. It was difficult and painful, but we divorced amicably after 28 years of marriage in April 1987. Carolyn went to law school, got her law degree, and eventually married her undergraduate sweetheart, who is also a lawyer.

Suddenly, I found myself single again. Being single and having money was like standing six feet four with a full head of hair.

Everyone is trying to fix you up, and you get lots of dates with interesting and attractive women.

Nothing really clicked until Walter Wriston and his wife, Kathy, arranged a blind date with Jane Beasley, an attractive attorney who worked for Kathy's brother at the New York law firm Shearman & Sterling. When Jane's boss called her to ask if she would go out with Jack Welch, she thought he was talking about another lawyer at the law firm.

"I can't go out with him," she said. "He's a colleague."

"Not him," he said. "This Jack Welch is the chairman of General Electric, and he's a little bit older than you."

"That doesn't matter. I'm not going to marry the guy."

At the time, Jane was in London on an extended assignment with the firm. Six months later she returned, and in October 1987, we went out to dinner with the Wristons at Tino's, an Italian restaurant in New York.

With Walter sitting there, the date was a little stiff. I had to be on my best behavior. But Jane and I left at 10 P.M. and went on to close the bar at Café Luxembourg. It took a second date over burgers at Smith & Wollensky, both of us arriving in leather jackets and blue jeans, to really make the match.

Jane is bright, tough, witty, and 17 years younger than I am. She is down-to-earth in every way. Jane is from a small town in Alabama. As a kid, she picked butter beans at 5:30 A.M. on her father's farm until her back ached. Her mother was a teacher, and she was a tomboy in a family with three brothers. She went to law school at the University of Kentucky and then came to New York to become a mergers and acquisitions lawyer.

I wasn't always the ideal date. In the summer of 1988, I invited her to Nantucket for the weekend. She had to go through a major negotiation with her boss to get the time off. On Friday night, we went out to dinner.

The next morning, I woke up, got dressed, and started to walk out the door.

"Where the hell are you going?" she asked.

"I'm going to play golf."

"You're kidding," she said. "I had to practically sign away my birthright to get this weekend off and you're going *golfing?*"

I honestly didn't know any better. This is what I did when I was married. I worked hard all week and then on Saturday morning I got dressed and went out the door to play golf with the guys.

This time, I knew this routine was over.

When we started to get serious, we had the "why it won't work" talk. I told her it bothered me that she didn't ski or play golf. She told me it bothered her that I didn't go to the opera. We made a deal: I agreed to go to the opera if she agreed to ski and golf. I really wanted a full-time partner, someone who would be willing to put up with my schedule and travel with me on business trips. Jane would have to give up her career. She took a leave of absence to try it out and, luckily for me, decided to make this her full-time occupation.

We got married in April 1989 at our house in Nantucket, with my four kids present. For the next few years, I went to the opera, calling it "husband duty" until Jane later relieved me of the obligation.

While my appreciation for opera didn't grow, teaching her golf took me to a whole new level.

I had been trying to win club championships for years and had never gotten anywhere. We got better together. Even though she had never played golf before meeting me, Jane won the club championship at Sankaty Head in Nantucket four years in a row—and I won it twice. She's become the perfect partner.

Back at work, the first chip that we played in the RCA deal was the TV manufacturing business.

In June 1987, Paolo Fresco and I were in Paris at the French Open, entertaining customers at this NBC telecast event. Alain Gomez, the chairman of Thomson, France's government-owned electronics company, stopped by our hospitality suite. He was a fun and gutsy guy.

We already had planned to see him at his office the following day. When we got together, it was not unlike my first meeting with Bradshaw. Both our companies had businesses that needed help. Thomson had a very weak No. 4 or No. 5 medical imaging business called CGR that I wanted. We had a No. 1 U.S. position in medical equipment, from X-ray devices, CT scanners, and magnetic resonance imaging machines. We had no meaningful position in France because the government's ownership of Thomson essentially closed the country to us.

Alain Gomez made it clear he had no interest in selling his medical business outright. Paolo and I decided to see if he might be interested in a trade. We always knew what businesses in our portfolio we didn't like. I jumped up and went to an easel in Thomson's conference room, grabbed a Magic Marker, and began to write down businesses we could swap for their medical operations.

My first try was our semiconductor business. That didn't fly. Then I tried the TV manufacturing business. He liked that idea immediately. His TV business was subscale and strictly European based. Alain saw the trade as a way to unload his losing medical business and overnight become the No. 1 producer of television sets in the world.

The three of us got excited about this deal. We decided that Paolo Fresco would meet with one of Alain's people to get the discussions started within a week. Alain took us down the elevator to our car waiting outside his office. As the car pulled away from the sidewalk, I grabbed Paolo by the arm.

"Holy s——," I said, "I think he really wants to do this." We were both giddy.

I'm sure Alain went back upstairs feeling the exact same way. Alain knew that his TV set business was too small to compete against the Japanese. The deal gave him the economies of scale and market position to mount a strong challenge. Our domestic consumer electronics business had $3 billion in annual sales and 31,000 employees. Thomson's medical equipment business had $750 million in annual revenues.

The trade would triple our market share in Europe to over 15 percent, giving us a presence against our biggest competitor, Siemens. Within six weeks, the deal was done and announced in July. Besides the swap, Thomson gave us $1 billion in cash and a patent portfolio that for 15 years threw off $100 million annually in after-tax dollars. Meanwhile, Thomson became the largest TV set producer in the world.

Our move out of TVs, however, was a tough nut for many to swallow. Media critics claimed we were bowing to Japanese competition by selling out. Some attacked the deal as un-American. I even got called a chicken for running away from a fight.

The criticism was media nonsense at its best. We ended up with a more global, high-tech medical business—and a lot of cash. One year of the patent stream income was more than we had made in the previous decade in the TV set business.

We both struggled in the short term. We lost money in medical in Europe for almost a decade. Thomson did the same with the consumer electronics business. We both stayed with it and ultimately made each business successful.

Within two years, we found the solution for our semiconductor business. Harris Corp., like us, had a subscale chip business. In July, I got a call from Harris chairman Jack Hartley, who wanted to come to Fairfield to feel me out on buying the business. Harris was primarily a defense electronics contractor with a small semiconductor operation that mainly supported its military sales. Hartley didn't think the company could survive in semiconductors if it didn't bulk up and gain volume from the industrial side.

I never liked semiconductors. The chart I drew for our board captured my feelings (see opposite page). The business was capital

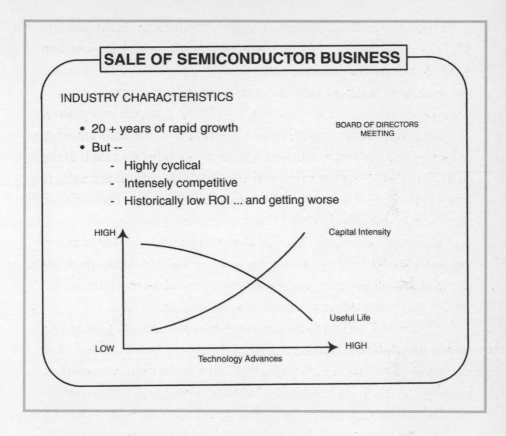

SALE OF SEMICONDUCTOR BUSINESS

INDUSTRY CHARACTERISTICS

BOARD OF DIRECTORS MEETING

- 20 + years of rapid growth
- But --
  - Highly cyclical
  - Intensely competitive
  - Historically low ROI ... and getting worse

HIGH

Capital Intensity

Useful Life

LOW — HIGH

Technology Advances

intensive and cyclical, it had short product life cycles, and the returns for most players were historically low. Getting out of it would let us use our capital for other things, like jet engines, medical equipment, and power turbines that had better returns.

Fortunately, our major global competitors stayed with semiconductors. That business used large amounts of their capital and diverted a lot of their management attention.

My desire to get out made a deal with Harris pretty easy. I wasn't asking for much, just a graceful exit. Over lunch, Hartley and I outlined the deal. We put on a piece of paper the six major deal points and gave them to our financial teams.

Two months later, by mid-September 1988, the deal was done. Harris got the GE people, the facilities, and the business, and we received $206 million in cash.

It took much longer, five years later, to move out of aerospace.
The cold war was over. There was too much capacity chasing too
little business. We concluded we had to get out. The one company
that seemed to be a good fit was Martin Marietta, a pure aerospace
business.

In late October of 1992, I went to a Business Council meeting,
looking for Martin Marietta CEO Norm Augustine. Norm is a guy
with enormous integrity. He's bright, thoughtful, and literate, a
great storyteller. We had barely known each other when we met
that fall in the lobby of The Homestead resort. I suggested to him
that we ought to get together to talk about what each of us was going to do with our aerospace businesses. He had been thinking
along the same lines but had been reluctant to approach us, partly
fearful that we might want to buy his company.

"We treasure our independence," Norm said. "While I'd love
to talk to you, I don't want to do anything that would jeopardize
that independence."

"I promise you it won't be that kind of discussion," I replied,
and suggested a private dinner soon.

Within a few days, Norm came up to Fairfield. By then, our
team had the deal rationale all laid out on charts. Norm sat and ate
his fish while I pitched. A deal was clearly in both our interests. Martin Marietta had to get bigger. For us, a deal could give us another
graceful exit, this time from a military business I didn't like. Complex, almost Byzantine government procurement rules made GE a
juicy target for attorneys general looking for a corporate scalp.

Over dinner, we agreed to put aside the usual tactics and lay
down the non-negotiable positions of what a reasonable deal
might look like. By getting right down to business and agreeing to
place reasonable offers on the table, we were hoping to minimize
the chances of a leak that could put Martin Marietta in play. Before Norm left, we were close enough to think a deal could be put
together.

We agreed to close the gap without investment bankers or outside law firms. During negotiations, Norm made three secret overnight trips to our offices. Martin Marietta's top 100 executives were in the middle of an off-site meeting on Captiva Island in Florida at the time. Augustine would spend his day in Captiva, grab a quick dinner, and then fly to New York to negotiate with me and Dennis Dammerman for half the night. Then he would fly back down, sleep on the airplane, and shave and shower before turning up for his company's meeting. For three nights straight, until 2 or 3 A.M., that was the routine.

After the third night, we had the deal's essentials sketched out on a cocktail napkin and shook hands on it. Our mutual trust accelerated the negotiation. We also agreed to control the egos of lawyers and bankers. Those outside teams often engage in food fights to prove who's smartest. I told Norm, "Whenever that starts, let's get on the phone and resolve it quickly."

We did. Over the next three weeks, the deal got done.

When the sale was announced on November 23, 1992, the market capitalization of each company jumped by $2 billion in the first four hours. From our first dinner in Fairfield to the announcement of what was then the largest deal in the history of the aerospace industry took all of 27 days.

Martin Marietta couldn't raise much more than $2 billion for the $3 billion deal. So Dennis Dammerman came up with a convertible preferred stock structure that helped to fund the deal and made us owners of 25 percent of Martin Marietta.

Now we had a continued interest in the success of the transaction. The deal doubled the size of Martin Marietta and sparked a massive aerospace industry consolidation. Two years later, Martin itself would merge with Lockheed. By the time we sold our Martin position in 1994, our convertible note had doubled the value of the original $3 billion deal.

The Martin Marietta and Harris transactions and the Thomson

trade were possible because of the chips acquired with RCA. The scale created by combining businesses in aerospace, semiconductors, and TV set manufacturing was the key.

Our last RCA-related transaction didn't occur until 2001. We had put RCA's satellite business into GE Capital, where its appetite for cash could be more easily satisfied. We built a strong satellite communications company, expanding RCA's original business. We had 20 satellites and access to every cable system in the United States, reaching 48 million households. While we were the largest fixed satellite provider in the United States, the business wasn't global enough.

At our long-range planning review in July 2000, GE Capital CEO Denis Nayden and his team decided we had to either expand the business by making a big acquisition or sell to or merge with an existing player. Denis mapped out a strategy to find a partner and ultimately negotiated a deal with SES, a Luxembourg company with 22 satellites that reach 88 million households. We sold our satellite holdings to them for $5 billion, split almost equally in cash and stock. The pending deal would give us a 27 percent stake in the new SES Group and make the entity a true global player.

RCA ended up giving us a great network and station lineup with strong cable assets, a truly global medical business, a significant position in a global satellite company, and tens of billions of dollars in cash—all for an initial investment of $6.3 billion in 1985.

RCA was a strategic win for GE. The emotional lift from the transaction was every bit as important.

11

The People Factory

After I became chairman, Joyce Hergenhan was the first officer I hired from outside the company, one of a handful of officers ever brought in from the outside. She was outspoken and tough as nails, a very smart MBA who was well schooled in hard knocks. She had been Con Edison's senior vice president for public affairs at a time when the utility was suffering power outages and generating more heat than light.

Before we met, I had done a little background check and learned she was a sports trivia nut. Over dinner, for fun, I decided to throw her a high, hard one for my first question.

"Who played second base for the 1946 Red Sox?"

"Bobby Doerr," she said without any hesitation.

I was impressed. I was a lifelong Red Sox fan and remembered the 1946 World Series as if I were 11 years old again.

I decided to press further. "Right so far, but who held the ball too long?"

"Oh," she came right back, "you mean when Enos Slaughter scored from first base on a single?"

"That's right."

"Johnny Pesky!"

Of course, I didn't hire Joyce for her baseball knowledge. She offered a lot more. Over 16 years, she helped shape GE's reputation as V.P. of Public Relations.

She wasn't the first to get hired in an offbeat way. Almost 20 years earlier, I was in my VW on the New Jersey Turnpike when the engine blew. I got towed to a local garage, where I met a German mechanic, Horst Oburst. Over the course of the next two days, while he was scrambling to get parts, we struck up a relationship. Impressed with his gutsy determination, I offered him a job. A week later, he was in Pittsfield on the payroll at GE Plastics.

Horst worked there for 35 years, getting several promotions along the way.

Finding great people happens in all kinds of ways, and I've always believed "Everyone you meet is another interview."

In fact, GE's all about finding and building great people, no matter where they come from. I'm over the top on lots of issues, but none comes as close to the passion I have for making people GE's core competency. In this case, while it may seem contradictory, the system plays a very important role in making it all happen. For a guy who hates bureaucracy and rails against it, the rigor of our people system is what brings this whole thing to life.

In a company with over 300,000 employees and 4,000 senior managers, we need more than just touchy-feely good intentions. There has to be a structure and logic so that every employee knows the rules of the game. The heart of this process is the human resource cycle: the April full-day Session C, held at every major business location; the July two-hour videoconference Session C follow-up; and the November Session C-IIs, which confirm and finalize the actions committed to in April.

That's the formal stuff.

In GE every day, there's an informal, unspoken personnel review—in the lunchroom, the hallways, and in every business meeting. That intense people focus—testing everyone in a myriad of environments—defines managing at GE. In the end, that's what GE is.

We build great people, who then build great products and services.

While we have a system, with its binders and clear-cut agendas, it is by no means static. Other than the agendas, carefully prepared in advance, there's nothing neat and pretty about the way the people review process plays out.

No matter what we put in our books—and we put everything in them—it's not simply the binders that count. What counts is the passion and intensity everyone brings to the table. When managers put their necks on the line for their direct reports, you learn as much about them as the people you're discussing.

Sometimes we can debate for an hour over one page.

Why are these sessions so intense?

One word: differentiation.

In manufacturing, we try to stamp out variance. With people, variance is everything.

Differentiation isn't easy. Finding a way to differentiate people across a large company has been one of the hardest things to do. Over the years, we've used all kinds of bell curves and block charts to differentiate talent. These are all grids that attempt to rank performance and potential (high, medium, low).

We've also led the charge into "360-degree evaluations," which take into account the views of peers and subordinates.

We loved that idea—for the first few years it helped us locate the "horses' asses" who "kissed up and kicked down." Like anything driven by peer input, the system is capable of being "gamed" over the long haul. People began saying nice things about one another so they all would come out with good ratings.

The "360s" are now only used in special situations.

We were always groping for a better way to evaluate the organization. We eventually found one we really liked. We called it the vitality curve (opposite). Every year, we'd ask each of GE's businesses to rank all of their top executives. The basic concept was we forced our business leaders to differentiate their leadership. They had to identify the people in their organizations that they consider in the top 20 percent, the vital middle 70, and finally the bottom 10 percent. If there were 20 people on the management staff, we wanted to know the four in the top 20 and the two in the bottom 10—by name, position, and compensation. The underperformers generally had to go.

Making these judgments is not easy, and they are not always precise. Yes, you'll miss a few stars and a few late bloomers—but your chances of building an all-star team are improved dramatically. This is how great organizations are built. Year after year, differentiation raises the bar higher and higher and increases the overall caliber of the organization. This is a dynamic process and no one is assured of staying in the top group forever. They have to constantly demonstrate that they deserve to be there.

Differentiation comes down to sorting out the A, B, and C players.

The As are people who are filled with passion, committed to making things happen, open to ideas from anywhere, and blessed with lots of runway ahead of them. They have the ability to energize not only themselves, but everyone who comes in contact with them. They make business productive and fun at the same time.

They have what we call "the four Es of GE leadership": very high *energy* levels, the ability to *energize* others around common goals, the *edge* to make tough yes-and-no decisions, and finally, the ability to consistently *execute* and deliver on their promises.

We actually started with three Es: energy, energize, and edge. When we did our first Session Cs appraising people based on these Es, we saw several managers with plenty of energy, the ability to energize their teams, and a lot of edge. As we went from business

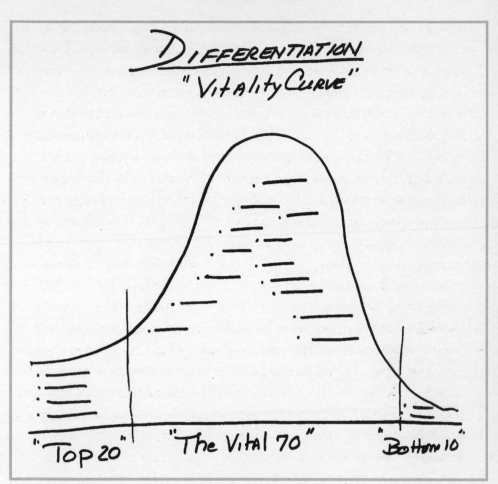

to business, we kept running into one or two who met the three E criteria but didn't look very good to us. Before we got home, we decided we were missing something. What these managers were lacking was the ability to deliver the numbers. So we added the fourth E—execute. That did it.

In my mind, the four Es are connected by one P—passion.

It's this passion, probably more than anything else, that separates the As from the Bs. The Bs are the heart of the company and are critical to its operational success. We devote lots of energy toward improving Bs. We want them to search every day for what they're missing to become As. The manager's job is to help them get there.

The C player is someone who can't get the job done. Cs are likely to enervate rather than energize. They procrastinate rather than deliver. You can't waste time on them, although we do spend resources on their redeployment elsewhere.

The vitality curve is the dynamic way we sort out As, Bs, and Cs, the most important tool of the Session C. Ranking employees on a 20-70-10 grid forces managers to make tough decisions.

The vitality curve doesn't perfectly translate to my A-B-C evaluation of talent. It's possible—even likely—for A players to be in the vital 70. That's because not every A player has the ambition to go further in the organization. Yet, they still want to be the best at what they do.

Managers who can't differentiate soon find *themselves* in the C category.

The vitality curve must be supported by the reward system: salary increases, stock options, and promotions.

The As should be getting raises that are two to three times the size given to the Bs. Bs should get solid increases recognizing their contributions every year. Cs must get nothing. We give As large numbers of stock options at every grant. About 60 percent to 70 percent of the Bs also get options, although the same people might not receive them at every grant.

Every time we hand out a raise, give an option, or make a promotion, the vitality curve is our guide. Attached to every recommendation for a reward is the person's position on the curve.

Losing an A is a sin. Love 'em, hug 'em, kiss 'em, don't lose them! We conduct postmortems on every A we lose and hold management accountable for those losses.

It works. We lose less than 1 percent of our As a year.

This system—like any other—has its flaws. Identifying the As is one of the treats of managing. Everyone enjoys doing that. Developing and rewarding the valuable keepers in the middle 70 percent poses little difficulty.

Dealing with the bottom 10 is tougher.

The first time new managers name their weakest players, they do it readily. The second year, it's more difficult.

By the third year, it's war.

By then, the most obvious weak performers have left the team, and many managers can't bring themselves to put anyone in the C column. They've grown to love everyone on their team. By that third year, if they have 30 people in their management group, they often can't identify a single bottom 10 percent player, much less three of them.

Managers will play every game in the book to avoid identifying their bottom 10. Sometimes they'll sneak in people who were planning to retire that year or others who already have been told to leave the organization. Some have stuck on these lists the names of employees who are already gone.

One business even went to the extreme of putting into the bottom 10 category the name of a man who had died two months before their review.

This is hard stuff. No leader enjoys making the tough decisions. We constantly faced severe resistance from even the best people in our organization. I've struggled with this problem myself and have often been guilty of not being rigorous enough. Every impulse is to look the other way. I've fought it. If a GE leader submitted bonus or stock option recommendations without identifying the bottom 10, I'd send them all back until they made differentiation real.

The problem with not dealing with Cs in a candid, straightforward manner really hits home later when a new manager shows up. With no emotional attachment to the team, he or she has no difficulty identifying the weakest players.

The bottom 10 percent is quickly identified.

Some think it's cruel or brutal to remove the bottom 10 percent of our people. It isn't. It's just the opposite. What I think is brutal and "false kindness" is keeping people around who aren't going to grow and prosper. There's no cruelty like waiting and telling people late in their careers that they don't belong—just when their job options are limited and they're putting their children through college or paying off big mortgages.

The characterization of a vitality curve as cruel stems from false logic and is an outgrowth of a culture that practices false kindness. Why should anyone stop measuring performance when people leave college?

Performance management has been a part of everyone's life from the first grade. It starts in grade school with advanced placement. Differentiation applies to football teams, cheerleading squads, and honor societies. It applies to the college admissions process when you're accepted by some schools and rejected by others. It applies at graduation when honors like summa cum laude or cum laude are added to your diploma.

There's differentiation for all of us in our first 20 years. Why should it stop in the workplace, where most of our waking hours are spent?

Our vitality curve works because we spent over a decade building a performance culture with candid feedback at every level. Candor and openness are the foundations of such a culture. I wouldn't want to inject a vitality curve cold turkey into an organization without a performance culture already in place.

W̲hat's a typical Session C like?

A month before we go out into the field, the corporate executive office and Bill Conaty, our head of human resources, put together an agenda for all the major businesses to follow. (See the 2001 agenda for our Session Cs in the appendix.)

The action then shifts to the units, which now have to prepare the elaborate information requested. The underlying purpose is not to win a paper war. The key objective is to show how our human resources strategy is being applied to all the major initiatives of the business.

The binders, the charts, the grids, may seem formidable, but the meetings themselves are built around informality, trust, emotion, and humor.

Nonetheless, there is a lot at stake. This review is our most important meeting of the year. A review breaks down this way:

In the morning, we talk about the organization and the people in it.

At lunch, we focus on diversity.

In the afternoon, we review the game-changing initiatives and the people who are leading them.

The morning is where most of the heat is generated. We're talking about careers, promotions, vitality curves, the strengths and weaknesses of individuals. It's a rule of the game that every person has pluses and minuses, strengths and development needs. We spend most of our time on those needs and whether in fact these managers are fixable.

The strengths of a manufacturing leader we recently reviewed were in delivering the results (great productivity, terrific yield improvement, strong Six Sigma). But there were glaring weaknesses—too tough on people and not open to ideas from others. After a long debate over these pluses and minuses, we all concluded that this guy ought to get a warning notice. He had to change.

He was running the risk of becoming a C. Not being an open thinker would be a killer.

Of course, we had our lighter moments.

I challenged nearly everyone, and often in outrageous ways. The Session C binders include photographs and miniature biographies of every executive. When a photo might reveal slumping shoulders, drooping eyelids, or a hanging head, I wouldn't hesitate to point him out and say, "This guy looks half-dead! He can't be any good. He's in the job for six or seven years and he hasn't gone anywhere. What the hell is going on? Why haven't you moved on him?"

Obviously, every picture of an expressionless person doesn't tell the story. What I wanted was a lively discussion. I expected to hear a business leader fight for his or her people. Everyone had to come out of a Session C knowing that people were the whole ball game: the players, the national anthem, the hot dogs, the seventh-inning stretch, the whole game.

In March of 2001, I was in Pittsfield again for a Session C review, accompanied by our new CEO, Jeff Immelt. Going through a binder, I spotted a funny picture of one of GE plastics' high-potential managers.

"If this guy is that good, you better get him a new picture," I joked. "Someone will get the wrong impression."

Later that day, I met the employee and teased him.

"Geez," I said, "you don't act anything like your picture. The great job you're doing doesn't go with that photo."

I think he got a kick out of it (and probably a new picture).

Each of these pictures is always accompanied by a nine-square grid, like a tick-tack-toe box in which one "X" has been filled in to show the manager's potential and performance (opposite). The best rating is the upper-left-hand square. The criteria used to place that "X" rely heavily on our corporate objectives—the four Es as well as our critical initiatives: customer focus, e-business, and Six Sigma.

Under each picture, some quick capsule comments highlight a manager's pluses and minuses. Most of these capsules are pluses, but our rules of engagement require that there be at least one negative that requires improvement. We don't allow a total white-wash. One executive has pluses such as "financial pit bull," "7,000-foot runway," "gets e-business." The negative: "Wears ambition on sleeve." We never liked people more focused on the next job than the one they were doing. This could be a career killer. Another is called "bright, driven, and ramping up." On the minus side: "Execution is still a question." Failure to deliver on commitments is, in the end, unacceptable.

Behind these summaries are the backup details of accomplishments and development needs. Each employee also does his or her

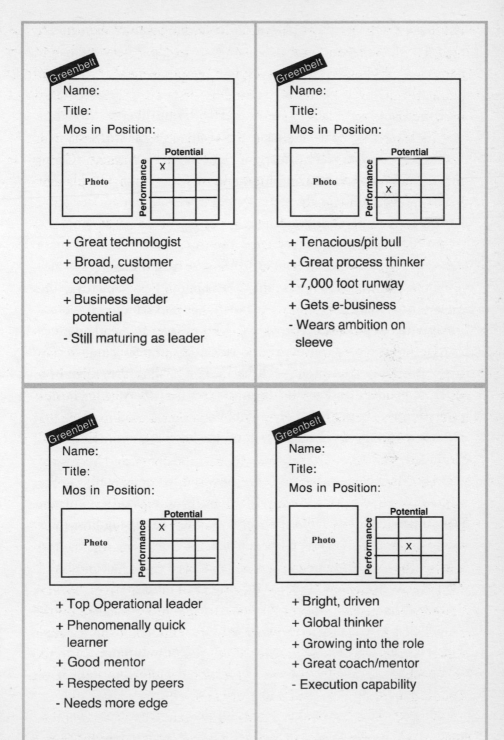

Greenbelt

Name:

Title:

Mos in Position:

Photo

Performance | Potential
X

+ Great technologist

+ Broad, customer connected

+ Business leader potential

- Still maturing as leader

Greenbelt

Name:

Title:

Mos in Position:

Photo

Performance | Potential
X

+ Tenacious/pit bull

+ Great process thinker

+ 7,000 foot runway

+ Gets e-business

- Wears ambition on sleeve

Greenbelt

Name:

Title:

Mos in Position:

Photo

Performance | Potential
X

+ Top Operational leader

+ Phenomenally quick learner

+ Good mentor

+ Respected by peers

- Needs more edge

Greenbelt

Name:

Title:

Mos in Position:

Photo

Performance | Potential
X

+ Bright, driven

+ Global thinker

+ Growing into the role

+ Great coach/mentor

- Execution capability

own assessment, which is placed on the same page as their boss's analysis.

For the last several years, we've met with our diverse "high potentials" at lunch. Each one has been assigned a mentor from the business leadership team. I made it clear over the years that these mentoring programs had nothing to do with explaining the benefit plans. We were talking about personnel development and used the discipline of product development.

In this case, the mentees were the "products." The business leadership staff—their mentors—had the responsibility to develop these products. That meant either taking their mentees to the A level or finding new ones. At lunch, we had candid conversations about the program's progress. Both the mentors and mentees bought into the very tough ground rules. In our performance culture, both understood that each had a responsibility to deliver a superior product and would be measured that way. The senior leadership was being held accountable.

It's working. Over 80 percent of the 1999 mentees have been promoted.

After lunch, the sessions were devoted to the initiatives. We wanted to see who was leading them and who was on each team. We got presentations from the teams on their results against their yearly targets. We picked up best practices from each business to take to the next. And most important, we got a great assessment of just how much horsepower was driving each initiative.

We'd leave each meeting with a clear-cut to-do list, which we'd share with the businesses. Two months later, in July, we'd revisit these priorities with a two-hour videoconference to check the progress. That same list would serve as the agenda for the Session II meeting in November to close the loop.

Despite the rigor of this process, I was surprised by what employees told us in our annual attitude surveys. Out of 42 questions, we always got the lowest marks on this statement: "This company deals decisively with people who don't perform satisfactorily."

In 2001, only 75 percent of GE professionals agreed with the statement—and that response was an improvement over 1999, when just over 66 percent agreed. The level of satisfaction on that issue contrasts sharply with exceptionally good scores across the rest of the survey. (When asked if an employee's career with GE has had a "favorable impact on me and my family," more than 90 percent of the responses were favorable.)The results vividly illustrate how important differentiation is at all levels of the company and how much our employees want an even more aggressive and candid approach.

During Session C, at major locations, we spent at least an hour meeting with local union leaders. We wanted the local union leaders to know us, and we wanted to know them and their concerns.

Our mutual respect for union leadership at every level was real and ran deep. At the national level, we fought like hell with Bill Bywater for 15 years and his successor, Ed Fire, presidents of the International Union of Electrical Workers (IUE). Once or twice a year, first Frank Doyle and for the last seven years Bill Conaty, our HR heads, and I would sit down with them over dinner and argue over pay, benefits, and the other typical issues. The biggest philosophical difference between us was my feeling that if we were doing our job right, our employees didn't need an organization to represent their interests. My position always drew a heated response from Bill and Ed, who objected to our resistance to their organizing efforts. Our differences were always in the open. There were no hidden agendas between us, and GE never had a major strike in more than 20 years.

On the broader labor front, my predecessor, Reg Jones, had led a labor-management group of about ten labor leaders and ten CEOs that was active with George Meany and Lane Kirkland of the AFL-CIO in the 1970s. I liked the idea a lot and shared the leadership of this group first with Lane Kirkland and then John Sweeney. John and I can both be thick-headed Irishmen, but I always felt we shared a genuine respect for each other. We've tried to get agreement on subjects like health care, trade, and education. While the group has been only marginally successful on policy, over our many meetings, we've benefited from a better understanding of one another's positions.

Our approach to dealing with labor unions was no different from the way we felt about all our employees. Many outsiders often asked me, "How can the GE culture possibly work in various cultures across the world?" The answer to that question was always the same: Treat people with dignity and give them voice. That's a message that translates around the globe.

There weren't enough hours in a day or a year to spend on people. This meant everything to me. I'd always try to remind managers at every level that they had to share my passion. While I might be the "big shot" standing in front of them today, they were in fact the "big shots" to the people in their businesses. They had to transmit the same energy, commitment, and accountability to their people, to whom Jack Welch didn't mean a thing. My ex-wife, Carolyn, always reminded me that I worked in the company ten years before I ever knew who was chairman. The important thing I urged every GE manager to remember was that "they were the CEO" as far as their people were concerned.

Even our biggest and best stars know the rules. As Andy Lack, president of NBC, says, "Jack and I have been friends for eight years, and our wives see each other all the time. If I started down a path where I made four incredibly bad decisions, I know he would fire me. He'd hug me, say he's sorry and maybe you won't want to go to dinner with me anymore, but he wouldn't hesitate to get rid of me."

It's all about performance.

12

Remaking Crotonville to Remake GE

C hange has no constituency—and a perceived revolution has even less.

In early January 1981, just two weeks after being named chairman-elect, I was in Florida for GE's annual general management meeting. I had been going to this event at the Belleview Biltmore in Clearwater since 1968. It was during a cocktail reception before dinner one evening that I searched out Jim Baughman. Jim was a bearded academic, a former Harvard Business School professor, who had consulted for GE over the years. He had been named the head of Crotonville, our management development center, a year earlier.

I found Jim mingling in a small crowd.

"You're just the guy I'm looking for," I said.

I grabbed Jim by the arm, introduced myself, and quickly got past the small talk. I told him to get ready for the ride of his life.

"We're going to be making all kinds of changes in this company, and I need Crotonville to be a big part of it."

Without Crotonville, I didn't think we had a prayer. I needed to communicate the rationale for change to as big an audience as I could. Crotonville was the place to do it.

Crotonville, a 52-acre campus in Ossining, New York, had been at the heart of an earlier management makeover. Former CEO Ralph Cordiner built the facility in the mid- to late-1950s to push his decentralization idea down into the ranks.

Thousands of GE managers were taught to take control of their own operations with profit-and-loss responsibility. For many years, the center's instructors taught a useful menu of training courses based on the "Blue Books," nearly 3,500 pages of management dos and don'ts. Thousands of general managers were raised on this gospel. Back in those days, the POIM (Plan-Organize-Integrate-Measure) principles spelled out in the Blue Books were like commandments.

Once decentralization took hold, Crotonville was used less as a training ground for leadership development than as a forum to deliver technical training or important messages in times of crisis. During the 1970s, when escalating oil prices fueled rampant inflation, Reg sent hundreds of managers through seminars on managing in inflationary times.

By 1980, the facilities had aged. Crotonville gradually became more a consolation prize than a place where the company's best gathered. The programs used open enrollment, and the quality of the attendees varied widely. Much of the company's future leadership wasn't bothering to attend. Only two of the seven contenders for Reg's job had taken the multiweek general management course. I wasn't one of them, although I remember taking a one-week marketing class in the late 1960s. I liked the course but didn't particularly like the accommodations.

By 1981, Crotonville was tired. Real tired.

I wanted to bring the place to life and needed this former Harvard professor to lead the effort. I saw Crotonville as a place to spread ideas in an open give-and-take environment. It could be the perfect place to break through the hierarchy. I needed to connect with managers deep in the organization, without my message being interpreted by layers of bosses.

But if Crotonville was to do all this, it would have to change. Within a few weeks of meeting Jim Baughman in Florida, we were sitting together in Fairfield over a three-hour lunch, wrestling with the center's future. I wanted to change everything: the students, the faculty, the content, and the physical appearance of the facilities. I wanted it focused on leadership development, not specific functional training. I wanted it to be the place to reach the hearts and minds of the company's best people—the inspirational glue that held things together as we changed.

"I don't want anyone to go there who doesn't have great potential," I told Jim. "I want the good ones coming up, not the tired ones looking for a last reward."

If we were going to ask only the best to go, we had to make Crotonville a world-class center. We had to reinvest in facilities when we were in the middle of gut-wrenching change—the restructuring of our portfolio and downsizing. We renovated the Pit, the main multilevel classroom, right away and began building a helipad so our leadership team could get there and back faster. (It was an hour's drive each way by car from Fairfield.) I asked Jim to pitch our case to the board. He did that in June 1983 and included a request for $46 million to build a new residence center there. Jim recalls that when I reviewed his presentation, I crossed out the payback analysis on his last chart. I drew an "X" over the transparency and scrawled the word *Infinite* to make the point that the returns on our investment would last forever.

I meant it.

It was slow going. My first session with a class of GE managers went over like so many of my early meetings. We weren't set up yet at Crotonville. The executives in a four-week management course were bussed to Fairfield for what was billed "An Evening with the Chairman." In June 1981, I was up in front of fifty managers in our headquarters auditorium. All of us were dressed in suits and ties. The class sat in front, and the company's human resources staff sat in the back. My off-the-cuff remarks that night were based on my favorite themes: our No. 1 and No. 2 strategy and my desire to change the "feel" of the company.

After discussing where I wanted to take GE, I opened it up for questions.

There were a few, but no one in the room wanted to challenge any of my thoughts. At least 70 percent of the people in the auditorium had that skeptical look (you know the look I mean—when people aren't with you).

To be fair, I'm sure I intimidated the hell out of them. Here I was, pacing back and forth in front of the class, threatening to fix, close, or sell the very businesses they worked in, while all the people in charge of their careers sat in the back row. It had to be pretty nerve-racking. Only the few managers frustrated with the bureaucracy liked it.

I understood the confusion and fear in the room. Hell, those managers signed up for a different, more traditional GE. I was struggling to find the right words and was blurring the impact of my message. The themes of excellence, quality, entrepreneurship, ownership, facing reality, and No. 1 and No. 2 were overwhelming these people, who were worried about whether they would still have a GE job.

I continued holding the classes at the Fairfield auditorium, bussing managers to headquarters for an evening session followed by a reception over drinks. Things gradually got better. But it was tough sledding.

The company's mood fluctuated on the bullishness of our press clippings and the price of our stock. Every positive story seemed to make the organization perk up. Every downbeat article gave the whimpering cynics hope.

Fortune magazine weighed in early with an upbeat assessment in January of 1982, "Trying to Bring GE to Life." Less than six months later, I got whacked with the Neutron tag. A strong endorsement followed in *Forbes* magazine in March of 1984, "Extraordinary Designs for a Whole New Future." I remember flying in a helicopter from Fairfield to New York with Henry Kissinger when the cover story came out. He thought the story was sensational. Coming from media-savvy Henry, that was a big deal. Any good feeling from that was gone quickly. Five months later, *Fortune* was calling me "the Toughest Boss in America."

In the media, at least, I went from prince to pig—and pig to prince—very quickly.

Fortunately, the equity market was on my side. After years of being stuck, GE stock and the market began to take off, reinforcing the idea that we were on the right track. For many years, stock options weren't worth all that much. In 1981, when I became chairman, option gains for everyone at GE totaled only $6 million. The next year, they jumped to $38 million, and then $52 million in 1985.

For the first time, people at GE were starting to feel good times in their pocketbooks.

The buy-in had begun.

In 1984, I started going to Crotonville for every one of our top three management classes. We overhauled all of them. They had been based on case studies at other companies. We changed that to tackle real GE issues. Jim Baughman recruited an innovative University of Michigan management professor, Noel Tichy, who helped to remake the coursework. Tichy, who became head of Crotonville from 1985 to 1987, brought great passion to the job and introduced "action learning."

Many courses ran at Crotonville, ranging from new employee orientation to specific functional programs. There were three courses that focused on leadership: the EDC (executive development course) for the highest potential managers; the BMC (business management course) for midlevel managers; and the MDC (management development course) for fast-trackers early in their careers.

The first level of these was the three-week MDC, which ran six to eight times a year. These courses, attended by 400 to 500 managers annually, were held exclusively at Crotonville in a class-room atmosphere.

Tichy's "action learning" concept of working on real business issues became the heart of the more advanced BMC and EDC classes. Projects were focused on a key country, a major GE business, or the progress the company was making on an initiative like quality or globalization. Interestingly enough, we had BMC classes in Berlin the same day the Wall came down and in Beijing the very day of the Tiananmen Square protest. The students watched both events, but all came out safe and sound and smarter for the experience.

We held three BMCs a year, with about 60 in each class, and one EDC a year for 35 to 50 of our most high-potential managers. Both these courses were three weeks long and were scheduled so that each class could present their recommendations in a two-hour session at the quarterly meetings of our Corporate Executive Council (CEC). The CEC meetings bring together 35 GE executives—the CEOs of the major businesses and the top corporate staff.

These classes became so action-oriented, they turned students into in-house consultants to top management. The classes looked at our opportunities for growth and how other successful companies were going after it in just about every developed and developing country in the world. They evaluated how fast and effective our four initiatives were taking hold. In every case, there were real take-aways that led to action in a GE business. Not only did we get great consulting by our best insiders who really cared, but the classes built cross-business friendships that could last a lifetime.

The courses became an important recognition of achievement. No one could go to BMC without business leader approval. No one could go to EDC without approval from HR head Bill Conaty, the vice chairmen, and me. All nominations for the classes were reviewed at our Session Cs.

By the mid-1980s, the faces and the dialogue in the classrooms were improving. The makeup of these classes had changed dramatically. After we began handing out stock options to a larger number of managers in 1989, I began the entry class asking, "How many of you have received grants?"

At first, less than half would usually raise their hands.

"Well, I have good news for everybody. For those who got options, congratulations. You wouldn't have them if you weren't A players. The stock has been strong, and with continued strong performance, you should look forward to making real money on those options."

By this time, the rest of the crowd, none of whom had ever seen a stock option, were wondering what was going to come next.

"And it's good news for those of you who haven't received a grant," I said. "Now you know that your boss isn't leveling with you. If your boss told you that you're a star, something's wrong—because all our stars are getting options. You should go back and talk to your manager and ask why you're not getting them." Surprisingly, many didn't—because they knew in their gut where they stood.

In 1991, we decided that no one could attend Crotonville's top programs if they didn't receive a grant. All the A players should get stock options, and all should gain the experience of going to Crotonville.

In 1995, I read a piece in *Fortune* magazine on how PepsiCo executive Roger Enrico and his team were teaching leadership to Pepsi executives. I liked the Pepsi model and decided that every member of our leadership team should teach a session. Before, our senior staff and business leaders had done it only on a sporadic basis. The Pepsi model gave the classes a close look at our most successful role models, and it gave our leadership a broader pulse of the company. Today some 85 percent of the Crotonville faculty are GE leaders.

By 1986, the physical overhaul of Crotonville had been completed. We had a new residence hall to go with our new classrooms. And most important, the people in the classrooms had really changed. They were more energetic and much more likely to ask challenging questions.

In all, it took perhaps ten years for most of our people to really get it. In the past decade, the Pit has been filled with excited and engaged people. The faces are young and diverse. The questions are smart and challenging—for me and for them.

Crotonville is now an energy center, powering the exchange of ideas.

When all is said and done, teaching is what I try to do for a living. Truth is, I've always liked teaching. After getting my Ph.D., I even interviewed at a few universities. In my first days at GE, I regularly taught math to one of my technicians, Pete Jones. During lunch hour, we'd get together in my Pittsfield office. I knew he was smart, and I wanted him to go back to school.

Pete would tell you I was an impatient teacher. Sometimes I'd throw chalk at him when he failed to understand the formulas I wrote on my office blackboard. Somehow it all worked. Pete left GE and got his degree and later taught for thirty years in the Pittsfield school system.

It was easy for me to get hooked on Crotonville. I spent an extraordinary amount of my time there. I was in the Pit once or twice a month, for up to four hours at a time. Over the course of 21 years, I had the chance to connect directly with nearly 18,000 GE leaders. Going there always rejuvenated me. It was one of the favorite parts of my job.

Whenever I went to Crotonville, I never lectured. I loved the wide-open exchanges. The students taught me as much as I taught them. I became a facilitator, helping everyone learn from one another. I had ideas that I brought to every class, and our exchanges enriched them. I wanted everyone to push back and challenge. For the last ten years, they have.

Before I showed up, I would sometimes send ahead a handwritten memo of what I expected to cover during a session. For our MDC, I typically asked them to think as a group about some issues (see next page).

"I'll be talking about A, B, and C players. I'll be asking your thoughts about the differing characteristics of each . . . and want to engage you in a discussion about them."

"What are the major frustrations you deal with . . . that I can help with?"

"What don't you like about a career in GE that you would like to see changed?"

"Are you experiencing the quality initiative? How would you accelerate it in your area, your business, and the company?"

For our EDC program, I had a different set of issues. I asked them what they'd do if they were appointed CEO of GE tomorrow.

"What would you do in your first 30 days? Do you have a current 'vision' of what to do? How would you go about developing one? Present your best shot at a vision. How would you go about 'selling' the vision? What foundations would you build on? What current practices would you jettison?"

I'd also ask each person to be prepared to describe a leadership dilemma they faced in the past 12 months, such as a plant closing, a work transfer, a difficult firing, or the sale or purchase of a business. I'd bring my own experiences into the classroom to tee up these discussions. One favorite story involved a November meeting in 1997 I had with Boeing Co. chairman Phil Condit. At the time, we were trying to win a billion-dollar-plus contract to supply aircraft engines for Boeing's new long-range 777 jet.

I had been the after-dinner speaker at Bill Gates's annual summit in Seattle. That night, I sought out Phil and asked him for a private lunch the next day. The GE and Boeing teams had been working long and hard on the engine selection for the long-range

10/22/96

MDC Class.

I look forward to seeing you on what appears to be a full Monday for you. I know you will enjoy interacting with the BOD.

I have a few thoughts for you to think about prior to our session.

As a class (perhaps in three sections)

Ⓐ What are the major frustrations you deal with on a daily basis that
- You or your immediate leader can confront
- I can help with

Ⓑ What are the three best things about a GE career.

Ⓒ What don't you like about a career in GE that you would like to see changed.

Individually —

Ⓐ Are you experiencing the Quality initiative.... How would you accelerate it in your area? your business? the Company.

Jack

version of the 777. Phil was well briefed on the subject. I made a pitch on why our engine was right for the plane and why GE was the right partner.

Phil listened carefully, asked a few questions, and ended the conversation with some great news.

"Let's leave this luncheon by saying you've got the deal," he said. "But you've got to make a promise to me. You won't tell your people they've got it. They will have to continue to negotiate in good faith."

I agreed. Over the next 60 to 90 days, those negotiating the deal were calling me up, saying we had to give Boeing more price concessions and more help with the development. I was dying each time my guys called to tell me about their latest concessions. Yet there was no way I could let them know of my conversation with Phil.

So they kept giving and giving.

Finally, it came down to the last day, and we were getting one more squeeze from Boeing. I couldn't take it anymore. I picked up the phone and called Phil.

"Phil, I'm choking. I can't sit here any longer. I've got to break this commitment."

"You've gone far enough," he replied. "Tell your team to say no. They've got the deal."

Another dilemma I'd share was the decision to move the production of our refrigerators from Louisville, Kentucky, to Mexico in the late 1990s. The economics clearly favored the decision. On the other hand, the union had been incredibly helpful at the local and national levels in trying to make our U.S. facilities more competitive.

From a pure business case, the numbers dictated the move. We had other operations in Louisville and a national union leadership that was trying hard to work with us. In the end, we made the call to keep manufacturing a line of refrigerators there, saving roughly 900 jobs in Louisville. I told the class that the goodwill we gained from this decision would help us become more competitive in Louisville. Still, it was a real dilemma to go against the numbers.

I'd tell those stories and others like them, involving everyone in the class in my ethical and leadership quandaries. Then I'd call on someone I knew had just been in a tight spot to discuss their dilemma. The floodgates would open. These personal discussions were some of the richest moments we had at Crotonville. Everyone in the room left knowing they weren't alone in facing a tough call.

In the first-level courses, I'd start off by asking each student to introduce him- or herself. I'd spend the first of four hours just doing this. I tried to strike a personal connection and get them talking for a minute. Then I'd listen to presentations on their likes and dislikes about the company and what they would change if they were in my shoes.

Crotonville also became an invaluable place to clarify any confusion our initiatives were creating in the organization. During our early globalization efforts, people were asking, "Do I have to have a global assignment to get ahead in GE?"

"Of course not," I'd say, "but your chances are better if you have one. It's a growth experience for you and your family."

When I was trying to drive our shift toward services, class participants inevitably asked, "Are we getting out of products?"

"You can't have services if you don't have great products."

During the early phase of our Six Sigma quality program, people began asking, "Does everybody have to have Six Sigma black belt training to get ahead in GE?"

"It would sure help," I replied. "It's another way to get out of the pile."

And when we launched our e-business initiative in 1999, people asked whether they needed to have black belts anymore. Some of them were so eager to get into our digitization efforts that they didn't want to invest two years in Six Sigma training. I'd reply: "Six Sigma is fundamental education, another differentiator for you, like getting your undergraduate or graduate degrees. Digitization is just one tool, like reading or writing. Everyone will have it."

After every class, I usually joined the group for a drink in our recreation center before taking off for headquarters. Three days later, I'd get a response on what the class thought on three questions:

"What did you find about the presentation that was constructive and clarifying?"

"What did you find confusing and troublesome?"

"What do you regard as your most important take-away?"

The comments were helpful. In the early 1980s, many managers left confused and troubled. I took all the reviews seriously, trying to bring what I learned from their responses into the next class. I read every comment religiously. If someone signed their name to the comments, I'd sometimes drop them a quick note, especially if I'd created a misunderstanding.

By the mid-1980s, the responses were showing more buy-in. After hearing the strategy and the vision, they said they understood it better. What they heard me say, however, often didn't jibe with what their bosses told them back home. Some of their managers had been prepping them for the session by saying that what they would hear was nonsense. Deep in the organization, pockets of resistance were still alive and well.

By 1988, some 5,000 GE employees were going to Crotonville for various courses every year. Yet I was still getting the same questions and comments over and over again. People were saying that the message and vision made sense. But they often added, "That's not the way it is back home." Damn it, after all this effort, the message still wasn't getting all the way through.

One afternoon in September of 1988, I left Crotonville frustrated as hell. I had just about had it. That day had produced a particularly good session. The people in class poured out their frustrations about trying to change their businesses. I knew we had to get the candor and passion out of the classroom and back into the workplace.

On the helicopter ride back to Fairfield, Jim Baughman had to listen to me vent my frustrations. "Why can't we get the Crotonville openness everywhere?"

I didn't let him answer the question. I knew what we had to do.

"We have to re-create the Crotonville Pit all over the company."

By the time we landed in Fairfield, we had the answer. We had sketched out an idea that when fully developed over the next few weeks would become a GE game-changer called Work-Out.

The Crotonville Pit was working because people felt free to speak. While I was technically their "boss," I had little or no impact on their personal careers—especially in the lower-level classes. We had to create an atmosphere like this in all the businesses. Obviously, we couldn't have the business leaders run these sessions because they would know everyone in the room. The dynamics would change, and openness would be more difficult.

We came up with the idea of bringing in trained facilitators from the outside, mainly university professors who had no ax to grind. Work-Out was patterned after the traditional New England town meeting. Groups of 40 to 100 employees were invited to share their views on the business and the bureaucracy that got in their way, particularly approvals, reports, meetings, and measurements.

Work-Out meant just what the words implied: taking unnecessary work out of the system. Toward this end, we expected every business to hold hundreds of Work-Outs. This was going to be a massive program.

A typical Work-Out lasted two to three days. It started with a presentation by the manager who might issue a challenge or outline a broad agenda and then leave. Without the boss present and with a facilitator to grease the discussions, employees were asked to list problems, debate solutions, and be prepared to sell their ideas when the boss returned. The neutral outside facilitator, one of two dozen academics drafted by Jim Baughman, made the exchanges between the employees and the manager go a lot easier.

The real novelty here was that we insisted managers make

on-the-spot decisions on each proposal. They were expected to give a yes-or-no decision on at least 75 percent of the ideas. If a decision couldn't be made on the spot, there was an agreed-upon date for a decision. No one could bury the proposals. As people saw their ideas getting instantly implemented, it became a true bureaucracy buster.

I'll never forget attending one of the Work-Out sessions in April 1990 in our appliance business. Together with 30 employees, we were sitting in a conference room in Lexington, Kentucky, at a Holiday Inn. A union production worker was in the middle of a presentation on how to improve the manufacturing of refrigerator doors. He was describing a part of the process that occurred on the second floor of the assembly line.

Suddenly, the chief steward of the plant jumped up to interrupt him.

"That's BS," he said. "You don't know what the hell you're talking about. You've never been up there."

He grabbed a Magic Marker and began scribbling on the easel in the front of the room. Before you knew it, he had taken over the presentation and had the answer. His solution was accepted immediately.

It was absolutely mind-blowing to see two union guys arguing over a manufacturing process improvement. Imagine kids just out of college with shiny new degrees trying to fix this manufacturing process. They wouldn't have a chance. Here were the guys with experience, helping us fix things.

Small wonder that people began to forget their roles. They started speaking up everywhere.

Hundreds of stories like this one spread throughout the organization. By mid-1992, more than 200,000 GE employees had been involved in Work-Outs. The rationale for the program could be summed up by the comment made by a middle-aged appliance worker: "For 25 years," he said, "you've paid for my hands when you could have had my brain as well—for nothing."

Work-Out confirmed what we already knew, that the people

closest to the work know it best. Almost every good thing that has happened in the company can be traced to the liberation of some business, some team, or an individual. Work-Out liberated many of them. From a simple idea hatched at Crotonville, Work-Out helped us to create a culture where everyone began playing a part, where everyone's ideas began to count, and where leaders led rather than controlled. They coached—rather than preached— and they got better results.

Ultimately, Crotonville became a boiling pot for learning. Our most valuable teachers there became the students themselves. Through their classwork and field studies, they taught the company's leaders and one another that there often was a better way.

Crotonville became, in fact, our most important factory. And soon we would make it even more productive with an idea that would change the organization forever.

13

Boundaryless:
Taking Ideas to the Bottom Line

I was sitting on the beach under an umbrella in Barbados in December 1989 on a belated honeymoon with my second wife, Jane. My year-in-advance schedule had kept us from having a typical honeymoon when we were married in April. Now we were having our "romantic vacation" at last, but as usual I ended up talking about work—not what you'd call pillow talk.

Fortunately, Jane loved business.

Work-Out had become a huge success. We were kicking bureaucracy's butt with it. Ideas were flowing faster all over the company. I was groping for a way to describe this, something that might capture the whole organization—and take idea sharing to the next level.

I was testing out on Jane my idea of focusing the brainpower of 300,000-plus people into every person's head. It would be like having a great dinner party with eight bright guests all knowing something different. Think how much better everyone at the table would be if there was a way to transfer the best of their ideas into each guest. That's really what I was after.

Sandy Lane in Barbados was a great place. I'd never experienced a Caribbean Christmas—it was different. Seeing Santa Claus pop out of a submarine while I was lying on the beach may have been just the jolt I needed. That day, I got the idea that would obsess me for the next decade.

Poor Jane. I was on a roll. I kept talking about all the boundaries that Work-Out was breaking down. Suddenly, the word *boundaryless* popped into my head. It really summed up my dream for the company. I couldn't get the word out of my mind.

Silly as it sounds, it felt like a scientific breakthrough.

A week later, all wound up with my newest obsession, I went directly from Barbados to our operating managers meeting in Boca Raton. Boca is the two-day session that I always closed by outlining our challenges for the coming year. This time, the last five pages of scribbles were all about boundaryless behavior. (I think the remarks sounded better than they were jotted down [see opposite page].) As usual, I was a bit over the top. I had learned that for any big idea, you had to sell, sell, and sell to move the needle at all.

In my closing remarks, I called boundaryless the idea that "will make the difference between GE and the rest of world business in the 1990s." (I was not bashful about this vision.) The boundaryless company I saw would remove all the barriers among the functions: engineering, manufacturing, marketing, and the rest. It would recognize no distinctions between "domestic" and "foreign" operations. It meant we'd be as comfortable doing business in Budapest and Seoul as we were in Louisville and Schenectady.

A boundaryless company would knock down external walls, making suppliers and customers part of a single process. It would eliminate the less visible walls of race and gender. It would put the team ahead of individual ego.

For our entire history, we had rewarded the inventor or the person who came up with a good idea. Boundaryless would make heroes out of people who recognized and developed a good idea, not just those who came up with one. As a result, leaders were

> *Finally the thing that* **believe will make the difference** *between /GE & the Rest of world business in the 90's That is what one could call the creation of "Boundryless Organization" We'll have "no inside barriers" between Functions — (Mfg/Eng/MKTG) → Projects PF — (Country Mgrs/Bus) → Globalize BWH — (Company owned Bus) → Environ Staff on Plants ("Job to be done" "Work") will dictate Grouping*

encouraged to share the credit for ideas with their teams rather than take full credit themselves. It made a huge difference in how we all related to one another.

Boundaryless would also open us up to the best ideas and practices from other companies. We had already made a dent in killing NIH (Not-Invented-Here) by using ideas like kanban manufacturing from Japan, a precursor to just-in-time inventory. Boundaryless was much broader. It would make each of us wake up with the goal of "Finding a Better Way Every Day." It was a phrase that became a slogan, put up on the walls of GE factories and offices around the world.

The idea gave new momentum to the learning culture

Work-Out had started. By 1990, we were already getting some sharing across businesses. Boundaryless just gave us a word to express it and make it part of our everyday life. We ranted about it at every meeting. We'd use it to lightheartedly embarrass someone who wasn't sharing an idea or a manager who wouldn't give up a good employee to another business. Someone would joke, "That's real boundaryless behavior!"

They got the message.

By 1991, in our Session C human resources reviews, we began grading managers on their degree of boundaryless behavior. Every manager in the company was rated high, medium, or low based on their peers' evaluations and later the views of their supervisors. An empty circle next to a person's name meant they had to change fast or leave. Everyone got feedback on where they stood on this value—and soon everyone knew how important this value had become.

In 1992, at Boca again, I did something that made our values, including being boundaryless, really come to life. We discussed the different kinds of managers based on their ability to deliver numbers, while maintaining GE values. I described four types of managers.

The Type 1 manager delivers on commitments—financial or otherwise—and shares the values. His or her future is an easy call.

Type 2 is one who doesn't meet commitments and doesn't share our values. Not as pleasant a call, but just as easy as Type 1.

Type 3 misses commitments but shares all our values. We believed in giving them a second or perhaps third chance, preferably in a different environment. I've seen some real comebacks.

Type 4 is the most difficult for all of us to deal with. That's the person who delivers on all the commitments, makes the numbers, but doesn't share the values—the manager who typically forces performance out of people, rather than inspires it. The autocrat, the tyrant. Too often, we've all looked the other way at these bullies. I know I have.

Maybe in other times this was okay. But in an organization where boundaryless behavior was to become a defining value, we could not afford the Type 4 manager.

In front of 500 people at Boca, without using names, I explained why four corporate officers were asked to leave during the prior year—even though they delivered good financial performance. When I wanted to make a point, I'd never use the traditional "left for personal reasons" excuse.

"Look around you," I said. "There are five fewer officers here than there were last year. One was removed for the numbers, and four were asked to go because they didn't practice our values."

I explained that one officer was removed because he wasn't a believer in Work-Out or idea sharing—he didn't get what boundaryless meant. Another couldn't build a strong team, while a third officer wouldn't empower the team he had, and the fourth never got the idea of globalization.

"The reason for taking so much time on this is that it's important. We can't be talking about reality, candor, globalization, boundaryless, speed, and empowerment and have people who don't embrace these values. Every one of us must walk the talk."

You could hear a pin drop. When I used the lack of boundaryless behavior as one of the principal reasons for a manager's leaving, the idea really hit home. You could feel the audience thinking, This is for real. They mean it.

Suddenly, "Finding a Better Way Every Day" wasn't just a slogan. It was the essence of boundaryless behavior, and it defined our expectations. After years of working on the hardware of GE—the restructuring, acquisitions, and dispositions—boundaryless was at the heart of developing what we would later call the "social architecture" of the company.

These were the core values of GE that would set us apart.

We had to insist on excellence and be intolerant of bureaucracy. We had to search for and apply the best ideas regardless of their source. We had to prize global intellectual capital and the people who provided it. We had to be passionately focused on driving customer success. At the same time, over 5,000 employees worked at Crotonville over a three-year period to hammer out a values statement. We considered those values so important that we put them on laminated cards that we all carry.

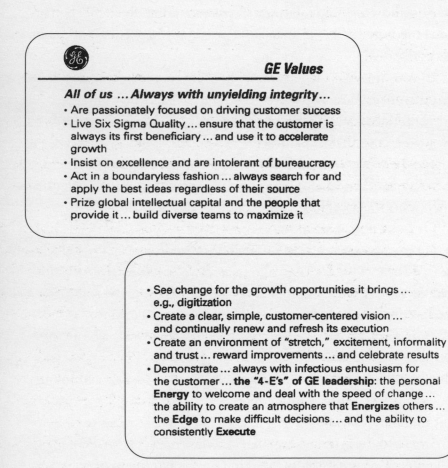

GE Values

All of us ... Always with unyielding integrity...
- Are passionately focused on driving customer success
- Live Six Sigma Quality ... ensure that the customer is always its first beneficiary ... and use it to accelerate growth
- Insist on excellence and are intolerant of bureaucracy
- Act in a boundaryless fashion ... always search for and apply the best ideas regardless of their source
- Prize global intellectual capital and the people that provide it ... build diverse teams to maximize it

- See change for the growth opportunities it brings ... e.g., digitization
- Create a clear, simple, customer-centered vision ... and continually renew and refresh its execution
- Create an environment of "stretch," excitement, informality and trust ... reward improvements ... and celebrate results
- Demonstrate ... always with infectious enthusiasm for the customer ... **the "4-E's" of GE leadership**: the personal **Energy** to welcome and deal with the speed of change ... the ability to create an atmosphere that **Energizes** others ... the **Edge** to make difficult decisions ... and the ability to consistently **Execute**

In short, we wanted to create a learning culture that would make GE much more than the sum of its parts—so much more than a conglomerate. From my first day as CEO, I knew we were more than a portfolio of disconnected businesses. Early on, I came up with a term—"integrated diversity"—in an effort to communicate the advantage GE got from sharing ideas across businesses.

That term didn't work. It was "businessese." It wasn't personal or human enough.

Amazing what a couple of words can or can't do.

Of course, a word or a phrase wasn't enough. We had to back it up with a system that would make it happen. Primarily, we had to change how we paid our best. The prior system made the annual bonus the big reward. It was based on how your individual business performed.

If you did well—even if the overall company did poorly—you got yours.

I couldn't stand the idea of the company sinking and some businesses making it to shore. The compensation system didn't support the behavior I wanted. If we wanted every business to be a laboratory for ideas, we needed to pay people in a way that would reinforce the concept.

Our compensation system was working against us. The day I was announced as chairman in 1980, I had options on 17,000 shares of GE stock and had realized gains of less than $80,000—after 12 years of getting option grants. Imagine how little the other officers had. If someone was making $200,000 in salary then and their business unit had a great year, their bonus could be 25 percent of their base pay, or $50,000. The individual bonus far outweighed the value of the stock option grants. I wanted the overall company's results and stock price to mean more to people than the results of their individual businesses.

I went to the board in September 1982 and got support to make a change. We increased the size and frequency of option grants. When the stock market cooperated in the early 1980s, people saw their gains from the company's performance overwhelm anything they ever got from their businesses. That reinforced idea sharing among the top 500 people.

I should have done more, faster. It took me until 1989 to broaden the plan. In that year, instead of just 500 people, 3,000 of our best people got options. Today, 15,000 employees get them every year—and more than twice that number already have them.

These changes in the option plan and a healthy stock market drove idea sharing. In 1981, the value of exercised options for everyone at GE was only $6 million. Four years later, that number increased to $52 million. In 1997, 10,000 GE people cashed in options worth $1 billion. In 1999, about 15,000 employees got $2.1 billion from them. In 2000, about 32,000 employees held options worth over $12 billion.

Holding stock in employee savings plans and stock options make GE employees the single largest shareholders in the company.

What a kick! Every Friday I got a printout listing all the employees who exercised stock options and the size of their gains. The options were changing their lives, helping them put their kids through college, take care of elderly parents, or buy second homes.

The most fun was spotting names I didn't know. It wasn't only fat cats. Boundaryless was paying off for everyone.

Stock ownership changes behavior—and the compensation changes gave us momentum for the 1990 launch of boundaryless. Still, it was only one piece of the puzzle. We needed more. We needed a way to surface the best ideas and move them quickly through the organization.

That's what our operating system came to be.

Like all companies, we always had a series of planned meetings and reviews throughout the year. What boundaryless did was link the meetings to create an operating system that was built on continuous idea flow.

I saw every meeting as a building block for ideas. Each one built upon the other until the ideas became bigger and better. That's what made it more than just a bunch of boring, time-consuming business sessions. New employees often comment that what makes GE different is the steady drumbeat of reinforcing core ideas, meeting, after meeting, after meeting.

Our operating system kicks off in early January with the top 500 operating leaders meeting in Boca. It's a celebration of the best people and the best ideas in the company. Over the two-day event, speakers from all levels showcase in ten-minute bursts their progress on a specific company initiative. No long, boring speeches, no travelogues—just the transfer of great ideas. (See Appendix D for 2001 agenda.)

In March, we have the first of our quarterly Corporate Executive Council (CEC) meetings in a room we call "the Cave" at Crotonville. At the CEC, the business leaders update their operations and describe their newest thinking around the initiatives. Everyone is expected to put forth one new outside-the-box idea that can apply to other units.

In April and May, the corporate executive office and our head of HR, Bill Conaty, go into the field to review every business for the Session Cs. These can be fun brawls: aggressive, gossipy, brutally honest meetings about our best people. We look at the business' progress on our initiatives and the caliber of the people down in the organization who are working on them.

That gives us a look at our best and brightest young people. I always tell students at Crotonville, "Jump on the initiatives. That's the way to get face time."

In July, we have a two-hour follow-up by videoconference to see if the personnel changes we agreed on had been implemented. If we had concluded with the business that there wasn't enough horsepower behind an initiative, it would always get fixed before the July videoconference.

In June and July, the business leaders come to Fairfield for strategy reviews of their businesses, the Session I. We focus on our competitors, trying to anticipate and leapfrog their moves. This is a chess game, and we assume our competitors are Russian masters.

In October, the company's 170 officers get together at Crotonville for their annual meeting. Here the best ideas we found in the HR and strategy sessions are highlighted in 10-minute-long role-model presentations.

In November, we have Session II, where business leaders present their operating plans for the upcoming year. Half the day is spent on the specific plans for each initiative. Here we get another batch of fresh ideas.

Then it's back to Boca. For this agenda we have a year's worth of best ideas to pick from. It gives us the chance to launch the new year and another cycle of exciting, fresh stuff that everyone can put to use.

To assist this relentless sharing of best ideas, we built a corporate initiatives group. This is the only corporate staff I allowed to grow. I hired Gary Reiner from the Boston Consulting Group in 1991 as head of business development. We changed the group's focus from acquisitions to driving ideas in support of the initiatives across the company. His group was principally made up of 20 or so MBAs who had been in consulting for three to five years and wanted to get into the real world.

They came to GE with the promise that if they delivered, the GE businesses would steal them within two years. They had to be "stolen." That made sure they were not only moving ideas, but also seen to be helping the business leaders implement them. I didn't want a corporate group squealing on the businesses. If they couldn't sell the ideas and help the businesses, they were gone. Over 10 years, the businesses hired nine out of every ten people Gary recruited into his group. About 65 of them are still with GE, including several who are now officers.

Stock options got us a start. An operating system connected the dots, creating a learning cycle out of what otherwise would have been a series of routine meetings. An HR evaluation on boundaryless got everyone focused on idea sharing. A corporate initiatives group accelerated these changes.

All of these steps contributed to the idea that started when Santa popped out of the sub in Barbados.

Only four months after my Boca speech, I was in a Session C review with Lloyd Trotter, then a VP of manufacturing for our electrical products business. Lloyd told us about a "matrix" he had created that helped to capture the best practices from each of his 40 factories. Lloyd first came up with 12 measurements and processes common to all the plants. Then he asked the managers of each factory to rate themselves on each one, from inventory turns to order fulfillment.

On one axis of the matrix was their evaluation, a score of 1–5, with 5 being best. On the other axis was the process or procedure. When he gathered his plant managers together for a staff meeting, he asked everyone who rated themselves best to explain how they got there.

When "the 5s" were giving somewhat lame explanations as to why they had rated themselves so highly, it became pretty clear to Lloyd that his first try at best practices wasn't taken very seriously. There were a lot of embarrassed people. It was during the next go-round that the real learning began. For instance, a Salisbury, North Carolina, plant had inventory turns of more than 50 per year. The average for the rest of the plants was 12. It didn't take long for everyone to go to Salisbury to find out what they were doing right.

The self-evaluations quickly gave way to quantitative measurements.

Lloyd had a habit of drawing circles around the best practices and rectangles around the worst. Quickly these marks were called "halos" and "coffins"—appropriate recognition for their status in Lloyd's mind.

Lloyd's highly visible matrix got everyone's attention. No one wants to be last. So people scrambled to visit the best plants to learn how to make theirs better. How do we know it worked?

Well, in a slow growth market, Lloyd's operating margins went from 1.2 percent in 1994 to 5.9 percent in 1996. In 2000, they hit 13.8 percent.

I talked up Lloyd's matrix everywhere we went and anywhere we had common activities. The "Trotter matrix" became a hot tool all around GE. I've never seen a case—from a comparison of sales regions to an analysis of business-by-business sourcing savings—when the matrix failed to generate a significant improvement in performance.

Sounds obvious, but I found it wasn't being done everywhere. Whenever we did an acquisition, we would often see people operating in silos. In 2001, during a Honeywell integration meeting, we met the manager of a sensor plant in Freeport, Illinois, operating at a Seven Sigma quality level.

Frankly, I was blown away. I'd never seen a plant operating with that kind of efficiency. The plant didn't have a single defect in any of the 11 million components it shipped in 2000. I asked the 20 Honeywell people in the room how many of them had visited that factory. Not one person raised a hand. In GE, that poor plant manager would have been inundated with GE visitors. Like Lloyd in 1991, he would have been on the Boca agenda.

Every time we got an idea, we flogged it. Some we paraded out too early. A couple didn't pan out. But when we saw an idea we liked, it went on stage at Boca. I sometimes fell in love too fast. But if the ideas weren't working, I could fall out of love just as fast.

In the early 1990s, the ideas were coming fast and furious from everywhere, including from outside the company. I picked up a good one in a visit with Sam Walton, the founder of Wal-Mart. In October 1991, Sam asked me to come to Bentonville, Arkansas, to share a stage with him in front of Wal-Mart's managers. I first met Sam in Nashville in 1987 during one of his regional managers' meetings, when he agreed to link his cash register data with our lighting business (a perfect example of boundaryless). That way, we could replace the light bulbs on Wal-Mart shelves rapidly, without a lot of paperwork.

In 1991, I flew down to Arkansas, and Sam met me at the plane in his truck. He was visibly ill, with an IV bag attached to him, feeding him chemotherapy drugs. Before his management group, Sam had me go through my tales on how tough it was to get bureaucracy out of a company, and then he took over. He challenged his managers to never let bureaucracy creep into and take over Wal-Mart. We spent a couple of hours having a ball, exchanging ideas with his team about the evils of bureaucracy.

On the way back to the airport, Sam took me to a Wal-Mart store. We were walking the aisles when all of a sudden Sam grabbed a microphone to announce our presence. "Jack Welch is here from GE to go through the store," he said. "If you have any trouble with their products, be sure to come and see him." Luckily, there were no takers. Sadly, only six months later, Sam died, caring to the end about the company he built.

During the visit, I learned about a Wal-Mart idea that I really liked.

Every Monday, Wal-Mart's regional managers in Bentonville would fly into their territories. They'd spend the next four days visiting their stores and those of the competition. They'd return on Thursday night for a meeting with the top officers of the company on Friday morning to deliver their intelligence from the field. If a regional manager found a store or region sold out of a hot-selling product, headquarters would shift inventory from other stores to fill the gap.

It was a weekly pulsing of the customer at the most basic level, the aisles of every store.

Wal-Mart had sophisticated computer and inventory control systems. At the Friday meetings, the sales managers would sit in the front of the room. One by one, they'd relate their experiences in the field. The high-tech team responsible for the information systems would be there to respond immediately to the needs of the regional managers.

The day I was there, managers reported that it had been warm in the Midwest and colder in the East. They had an excess of antifreeze in one region and a shortage in another. They fixed it on the spot. This match of high-touch from the field and high-tech at headquarters was one of the things that Sam and President David Glass used to keep Wal-Mart's small-company responsiveness as it grew by leaps and bounds.

I came back from Bentonville excited about how we could use this system. Sam let me send several GE business teams to his place so they could sit in on the Friday sessions.

Once our people saw it, they loved it. The business leaders grabbed the idea and adapted it to the GE culture. They began holding weekly telephone calls with their sales teams in the field. Besides the CEO, the business's top marketing, sales, and manufacturing managers would be on the call so that they could respond immediately to an issue, whether it was delivery, price, or product quality.

We called it "Quick Market Intelligence" (QMI)—and followed its progress at every quarterly CEC meeting. It was a big hit. It brought all our leadership closer to the customer. On the spot, we were solving product availability issues and finding quality problems that might not have shown up until much later.

Our business leaders also brought their own great ideas to the CEC. In 1995, Bob Nardelli, CEO of GE Transportation, described a new source of great talent. With its headquarters in Erie, Pennsylvania, the transportation business had struggled for years to attract the best people. Bob said he found an endless supply of talent in junior military officers (JMOs). Most were graduates of U.S. military academies who had put in four to five years of military time. They were hardworking, smart, and intense, had leadership experience, and were surprisingly flexible because they had served time in some of the toughest places in the world.

Nardelli's idea spread like wildfire. After we had 80 former

JMOs on staff, we asked them to come to Fairfield for a day. We were all so impressed with the quality of what we saw that we put a plan in place to hire 200 of them every year. We used our Session Cs to measure the success each business had hiring and promoting ex-JMOs.

Today we have more than 1,400 on the payroll. Bob had the idea—boundaryless helped our operating groups jump all over it.

The key to the operating system is the understanding that it's all about learning and driving results. It's used to regenerate and to re-iterate ideas. During a meeting of our sourcing leaders in 1999, for example, it came out that our power systems business was getting great savings running supplier on-line auctions. They got the auction software from an outside firm for $100,000 and a pay-by-the-drink fee. Jack Fish, the sourcing leader of our transportation business, liked the idea but didn't want to spend $100,000-plus for it.

Instead, he returned to the business and asked Pat McNamee, then transportation's IT manager, if he could come up with one on the cheap. With a couple of Penn State students and some help from our software engineers in India, McNamee built a prototype in three weeks for $17,000. Two weeks later, they held the first on-line auction—for industrial gloves. I picked up the story from Jack during a Session II operating plan review in November and put Pat on the Boca agenda in January 2000.

The other businesses picked up on it quickly—and we dumped most outside vendor auction programs for good.

The next time I saw Jack Fish was four months later at the Session C for the transportation business. Jack updated his on-line auction activity. He told us his objective was to put $50 million of the division's purchases on-line that year. By then, I had been around the circuit to Session Cs in other GE businesses where the auction goals were much higher. Power systems had a target of $1 billion. Another business was at $300 million; another one was

$500 million. They were talking real savings. For every $100 million purchases we put on-line, we cut our buy costs by $5 million to $10 million.

"Jack," I said to him half-jokingly, "I know this sounds like no good deed goes unpunished. You're the guy who got everybody started. You're the damn inventor. Now you have the lowest target."

A week later, after checking with his peers, he sent me an e-mail with a new goal of $200 million and said he should be able to beat it.

He did.

The first person with the new idea has a pretty easy time. That person's goals set the bar for the next—and the cycle begins again.

Gary Reiner's corporate initiatives group not only spread ideas, they generated their own. In Gary's wrap-up of our Session I strategy reviews in 1992, he found that our selling prices were going down 1 percent a year while our costs for purchased goods were still rising. He illustrated the trend in a simple view graph called the "monster chart." It was a monster because the gap between our selling price and purchase costs was narrowing. So were profits.

If we didn't do something about the monster, it would eat us alive.

Gary shared this analysis with the CEC in September. At the officers meeting in October and at Boca in January 1993, the company's two best sourcing leaders explained how they were getting lower purchasing costs. During the Session C reviews in 1993, we looked in depth at every sourcing organization.

For the next four years, sourcing leaders came to Fairfield for quarterly Sourcing Council meetings to share their best ideas with a vice chairman or me. Business leaders knew they had to send their very best people. If they didn't, we'd see new faces the next time.

Once we had better people, we had better ideas. This focus killed the monster—and the chart.

Of all the ideas that have been driven through the operating system over the years, however, one of the best came from a Crotonville Business Management Course (BMC). It's a great example of how we directly linked Crotonville to all the company's learning. In 1994, Bob Nelson and his financial team came up with an analysis that showed what GE had to do to become a $100 billion company with $10 billion in profits before the end of the century. At the time, GE's sales were $60 billion, with $5.4 billion in after-tax earnings.

I liked the goal and in February 1995 challenged a management class at Crotonville to give us some new ideas on how to reach the $100 billion target. Part of the class assessed what GE did well by interviewing the senior leaders at 10 of our businesses. Another group visited key customers to hear what they thought of our growth prospects. A third team visited executives of high-growth companies to see what we could learn from them.

Ironically, though, the single best idea didn't come from a company at all—it came from the U.S. Army War College in Carlisle, Pennsylvania. Tim Richards, who ran the four-week BMC class for us at Crotonville, drafted the plan to merge our class with a War College class of colonels. He read that the army was trying to radically change its mission from a cold war model to one that gave it the flexibility to mount dozens of small, remote battles around the world.

Tim thought there might be a fit. "It was one of those harebrained ideas that happened to work," he says.

During the four-day visit, an army colonel told the class that our strategy of being No. 1 or No. 2 in a marketplace might be holding us back and stifling growth opportunities. He said GE had plenty of intelligent leaders who would always be clever enough to define their markets so narrowly that they could safely remain No. 1 or No. 2.

Ordinarily, this class would have reported its findings in Crotonville to our executive council at its June 1995 meeting. I was recovering from open-heart surgery at the time, so I didn't hear the presentation until late September when seven members of the class came to Fairfield.

The colonel's insight about how to redefine market share came in one of eight charts. On it, the team recommended a "mind-set change." They said we needed to redefine all our current markets so that no business would have more than a 10 percent market share. That would force everyone to think differently about their businesses. This was the ultimate mind-expanding exercise as well as a market-expanding breakthrough.

For nearly 15 years, I had been hammering away on the need to be No. 1 or No. 2 in every market. Now this class was telling me that one of my most fundamental ideas was holding us back.

I told them, "I love your idea!" Frankly, I also loved the self-confidence they showed in shoving it in my face.

This was boundaryless behavior at its best.

Having a high share of a narrowly defined market may have felt good and looked great on a chart, but the class was right: We were getting boxed in with the existing strategy, which proved that any bureaucracy would beat anything you put in.

I took their idea and put it into my closing remarks a couple of weeks later at our annual officers meeting in early October (see opposite page).

"Doing this has to open your eyes to growth opportunities. Perhaps our stress on No. 1 and No. 2 or 'fix, sell, or close' now limits our thinking and hurts our growth mind-set."

I asked each of the businesses to redefine its markets and give us a page or two of "fresh thinking" on this during the S-II operating plans in November.

Using this wider vision of our markets changed our growth rates. It reinforced our resolve to aggressively expand into services. GE went from a "market definition" of about $115 billion in

Before. Getting to Quality I'd like you to reflect on the recent BMC Challenge to all the business leaders --- How Can you define Your MKT in such a way that your present product offering represents <<10% share of this NEWLY DEFINED MKT

-- ~~Doing~~ this just has to Open Your eyes to Growth Opportunities --- Perhaps our Stress on #1 #2 or Fix, Close or ~~Sell~~ now Limits our thinking ~~& stress on Growth~~ hurts our Growth MINDSET.

We are going to ask you and your teams in S-II to Come up with ~~Some fresh thinking~~ --- ~~on this~~ --And Give us a page or two on ~~how you can before your current~~ ~~how~~ what you would add to ~~expand~~ ~~your~~. Your MKTS to define your Market Share as Less than 10%.

1981 to well over $1 trillion today, providing plenty of room for growth. In medical systems, for example, we went from measuring our share of the diagnostic imaging market to measuring all of medical diagnostics, including all equipment services, radiological technologies, and hospital information systems.

Power systems saw its services business mainly in supplying spares and doing repairs on GE technology. Defined that way, we had a 63 percent share of a $2.7 billion market. That looked pretty good—damn good. By redefining the market to include total power plant maintenance, power systems had only a 10 percent share of a $17 billion market.

If you continued to broaden the market definition to include fuel, power, inventory, asset management, and financial services, you could play in a marketplace potentially as big as $170 billion. Our share of that was just 1 to 5 percent.

Once again, the exercise opened our eyes and fueled our ambitions.

Over the next five years, we doubled our top-line growth rate at GE with the same yet newly energized portfolio of businesses. We went from $70 billion in revenue in 1995 to $130 billion in 2000. A lot of things made this happen, but this new mind-set played a big role. I loved the fact that we gave a Crotonville class a challenge and it went out and found a great idea in the head of an army colonel in Pennsylvania.

This was boundaryless behavior at its best. Our people really were finding "a better way," and it was making the difference between GE and the rest of the business world. You could measure it by the results. Our operating margins went from 11.5 percent in 1992 to a record 18.9 percent in 2000. In our industrial businesses, our working capital turns jumped from 4.4 to a record 24 in 2000. Our revenues hit $130 billion, with nearly $13 billion of net income.

Boundaryless was helping a lot of us ordinary people do some extraordinary things.

14

Deep Dives

There are advantages to being the chairman.

One of my favorite perks was picking out an issue and doing what I called a "deep dive." It's spotting a challenge where you think you can make a difference—one that looks like it would be fun—and then throwing the weight of your position behind it. Some might justifiably call it "meddling."

I've often done this—just about everywhere in the company.

I got involved in everything my nose told me to get involved in, from the quality of our X-ray tubes to the introduction of gem-quality diamonds. I picked my shots and took the dive. I was doing this up until my last days in the job.

One of my last dives involved CNBC in May 2001.

After a two-year absence, Lou Dobbs was returning as anchor of CNN's *Moneyline*. His return was a potential threat to our *Business Center* on CNBC in the 6:30 to 7:30 P.M. time slot. Co-anchors Ron Insana and Sue Herera's ratings had blown by *Moneyline* after Dobbs's departure. I got a call from Sue in late April, asking me if I'd send an e-mail to psych up the team as it got ready to battle his return on May 14.

CNBC has always been a pet project of mine, and Sue has

been the rock of CNBC from its first day. She had always been helpful across GE and our women's network. I thought of her as a friend. With CNN doing heavy promotion on Dobbs, she canceled her family vacation to take on the challenge.

"Sue, instead of an e-mail, why don't I come over to your place and meet with the whole team?"

"Let's do it," she said.

Within a week, I was sitting over cookies and soda at CNBC's New Jersey studio, kicking around dozens of ideas with Ron, Sue, and 15 or so members of the team. To me, it felt like one of those early Work-Out sessions a decade ago. The team came up with the thought of going to a longer format, starting at 6 P.M., to gain a 30-minute jump on *Moneyline*. I loved that one and several other ideas they came up with.

By the time I left the meeting, I promised them an extra $2 million to promote the program. In the car on the way back, I called Andy Lack, who that day had been named NBC president. I asked him if he would put Sue and Ron on the *Today* show the morning of Dobbs's relaunch. Then I called NBC Sports president Dick Ebersol, and he agreed to run *Business Center* promos during the NBA playoffs over the weekend.

By the end of the week, people from all over NBC, from graphics to set design, had jumped into the fray.

Dobbs's return would get viewer sampling for sure, but we weren't going to make it easy. This was going to be a long war— we wanted to win the first battle.

When my successor, Jeff Immelt, called to shoot the breeze at the end of that day, I had to confess. I told him I had been over at CNBC playing "project manager" again. From his days in plastics and medical systems, he knew what a pest I could be.

"Jeff, I promise it was the only meddling I did today. There'll only be a couple more months of meddling and then you'll be rid of me."

Thank God for this book. It kept me out of Jeff's hair during most of the transition.

Jeff and I left together on Sunday night for Tokyo, so I couldn't watch the opening-night face-off. The CNBC team kept me posted with daily e-mail results. *Business Center* held even with Dobbs on Monday, the first night of his return. By Thursday, *Business Center*'s audience was much larger. Fortunately, I got home from Tokyo about 5:30 P.M. Friday, just in time to watch the final show of the week live.

Ron and Sue were great. The team had given the show new life. I was happy for all of them. They had won the first skirmish. What a kick!

Over the years, I did hundreds of these "deep dives." They weren't always successful, and many of my ideas were never adopted. For me, the satisfaction and fun was getting in there and mixing it up, creating excitement and debate over the direction a project should take.

Aside from my title, I think I "got away with it" because people felt I was trying to help. We always had a common goal, if not a common way, to get there. They knew that I didn't hold any hard feelings if my ideas got tossed in the basket. (*Editor's Note:* The hell you didn't!)

Another business I always had my nose in was GE Medical. One way or another, I was involved in that business for 28 years. I loved the technology, the people, and the customers. It always felt special working on medical stuff. In the 1970s and early 1980s, I was the "virtual project manager" for CT scanners and MRI machines.

Early in the 1990s, I fell in love with another project, ultrasound imaging. GE had been an also-ran in this noninvasive, nonradiation technology. I was sure we could do more.

Starting in 1992, I jokingly became its unofficial "project manager." After we decided against an expensive acquisition to improve our competitive position, we launched our own internal development effort. I asked John Trani, the CEO of medical, to bypass all the typical reporting relationships and have the project report directly to him. John loved results and got them by building loyal teams who could take any hill.

We set up the team in an old manufacturing building and totally renovated it to make them feel like winners. The corporate research lab made the project a priority. After the project manager retired, we decided to go outside GE to the ultrasound industry for a replacement. I interviewed the candidates, selling them on our commitment to ultrasound, which many industry pros questioned because of our false starts.

We found Omar Ishrak, a Bangladesh native and a guy you could feel had ultrasound running through his veins. He had worked for a major competitor. All of us thought he was just what we needed and hired him.

We were off to the races. I made sure he got lots of funding and attention. Every time I went to Milwaukee to visit our medical systems division, I'd make a big deal over Omar and ultrasound even though it was a small part of the total business.

I became his biggest cheerleader. He hired great people, many from the industry, and the rest is history. We went from nowhere in 1996 to number one in 2000, creating a highly profitable business growing 20 percent to 30 percent a year to more than $500 million in annual revenues today. Omar became a corporate officer, and I got as much fun out of his success as he did.

Another deep dive in medical had to do with the quality of the tubes that go into GE's X-ray and CT scan machines. It started in 1993. I had been on a customer swing, visiting GE customer groups in several cities. The medical customers thought we had the best CT technology but were complaining loudly about our tube life. When I got back, I found that our tubes were averaging about 25,000 scans, less than half of what competing tubes were getting.

Our CT system was so good, it obscured what could become the Achilles' heel of the business—the tube.

I went to Milwaukee and reviewed the problem with John Trani and his team. In a sexy high-tech business like medical systems, components can sometimes be second-class citizens. John took me on a tour of our tube facility. Ironically, it was in the same building as the ultrasound development where we had made all the renovations. Separated by only a dividing wall, the tube facility was being treated like an orphan.

To show we were serious, we asked the manufacturing manager for all of medical systems if he would take on the tube job, reporting directly to Trani. He thought our offer was nuts. He was a traditional manufacturing guy and already had *the* manufacturing job, with tube production reporting to him. No amount of money or "promised glory" would ever convince him this "tube job" made sense for his career.

We were lucky. We ended up with just the right guy. Trani suggested Marc Onetto, an excitable and effusive Frenchman who was general manager of service for our medical systems business in Europe.

I invited him to Fairfield to impress on him the importance of the job and the need to go from 25,000 CT scans to 100,000 between failures. I promised he'd get all the resources he needed to do it.

We gave Marc the funds to upgrade the factory and helped him recruit great talent, including Mike Idelchik, an engineer's engineer who lived to design aircraft engines. Mike left his technical base at aircraft to come to the job as engineering manager. He and his engineers were key in improving the tube. In the middle of it all, Mike got an enticing offer to leave GE. Marc asked me to intervene and I spent a Sunday night convincing Mike to stay. He did and later became vice president of engineering for lighting and has a big leadership future ahead of him.

Marc came up with the slogan "Tubes—The Heart of the System," to symbolize the importance of this previously ignored component, and he put signs all over the place to get everyone's attention.

For the next four years, he faxed weekly reports to me, detailing the team's progress. Marc recalls getting a response from me with the message: "Too slow, too French, move faster or else." Marc would stuff these replies in his desk drawer.

Other times, I'd send notes, congratulating him for making progress. Marc would post these in the plant for everyone to see (opposite page).

In five years, the team took tube life from 25,000 scans to close to 200,000. By 2000, using Six Sigma technology, they came out with a new tube that averaged 500,000 scans and is considered the industry standard. Getting that key component right allowed us to introduce the fastest-selling CT scanner ever, the GE LightSpeed.

By making the tube the heart of the system, our team changed the mind-set of the component business. Everybody got something out of this success. Marc moved on to lead our Six Sigma initiative in the medical business and is now a corporate officer heading up medical's global supply chain.

Another deep dive that's clearly a work in progress involves our industrial diamonds business. In 1998, Gary Rogers, the CEO of GE Plastics, and Bill Woodburn, the head of industrial diamonds—asked to come to Fairfield for a "secret meeting" with me.

I didn't know what to expect. GE has produced industrial diamonds since the 1950s. They're made by treating carbon at very high temperatures and pressures. These diamonds aren't gem quality and are used for cutting tools and grinding wheels in heavy industry.

Gary and Bill showed up with a bag of brown natural stones and half a dozen blue suede jewelry boxes, containing gorgeous gem-quality diamonds. These men are both soft-spoken. This time, they were practically whispering when they told me that our scientists had come up with a way to take brown natural diamonds from the earth and finish the natural conversion process to clear rare

GE

John F. Welch
Chairman of the Board

General Electric Company
3135 Easton Turnpike, Fairfield, CT 06431

9/14/97

Dear Mike & Marc,

I saw the *hide page* E-Mail. Sounds _very_ exciting. I just wanted to congratulate both of you for this great progress.

Hope we can make the improvements permanent & the Gemini *hide the* new standard!

You're going

Jan

cc: J I
LSE

gemstones. In essence, the new process would re-create the conditions that form diamonds in the core of the earth over thousands of years and finish what mother nature started.

I was stunned and excited by the huge potential opportunity this new business might create. I could hardly wait to play. Talk about a fun project—here were gemstones as large as 28 carats, the challenge of entering a new consumer business we knew nothing about, plus the chance to completely transform an industry by technology we created.

I instantly became Bill's No. 1 backer. I helped him free up resources and over the next three years sat in on countless meetings, consulting on everything from deciding what to call our product to how to price it.

Sounds easy, right?

Breaking into Fort Knox might be easier than getting into this centuries-old trade. Afraid we might undermine the pricing of gem diamonds, the old Antwerp network of traders and wholesalers did everything to freeze us out of the business. They leveled false statements, making our diamonds appear artificial and less desirable. An Antwerp boycott forced us to go from a strategy of selling them at wholesale, 50 to 100 at a time, to selling them in ones and twos to high-end jewelers at retail.

To jump-start the sales, we offered our gem diamonds at a discount to employees, who are now buying them at a rate of $100,000 a month. I even offered a similar deal to our board members, hoping the disclosure of their purchases in GE's 2000 proxy statement would generate some publicity over this "perk."

Several directors bought them at prices ranging from $26,000 to $410,000. Wouldn't you know it? With all the media hype on pay and perks, the diamond purchases completely escaped notice. The one time you wanted the press, they were sleeping.

In our second full year, we'll do about $30 million worth of business, less than a third of what we had originally planned. For a breakthrough in a multibillion-dollar industry, that's obviously not what we were looking for. Our team keeps reminding me to be patient. It's a work in progress—just another pet project I'll have to leave to my successor.

Another idea I'll leave behind is one that developed when I was visiting Japan in the fall of 2000. I had been going there for years and found it difficult to get the best male Japanese graduates to join us. We were having increasing success, but still had a long way to go.

Finally, it dawned on me. One of our best opportunities to differentiate GE from Japanese companies was to focus on women. Women were not the preferred hires for Japanese companies, and few had progressed far in their organizations.

Again, I got revved up. Fortunately, we had Anne Abaya, an ideal Japanese-speaking U.S. woman in a senior position at GE Capital. She agreed to go to Tokyo to become head of human resources for GE Japan. I gave her a million dollars for an advertising campaign to position GE as "the employer of choice for women."

What I didn't know was how much talent we already had in place. In May 2001, when Jeff and I were on a Japanese business trip, we had a private dinner with 14 of our high-potential women. They ranged from CFO of GE Plastics Japan, general manager of sales and marketing of GE Medical Systems Japan, marketing director of GE Consumer Finance Japan, to the heads of human resources for GE-Toshiba Silicones and GE Medical Systems.

Jeff and I had never been with a more impressive young crowd. It confirmed for me how big the opportunity could be.

This is a really early dive, but one I know Jeff will take to new levels.

I loved the excitement of these dives—perhaps more than the people who bore the brunt of them.

I'll bet anything that Jeff will define his own deep dives and get the same kick out of meddling that I did.

UPS AND DOWNS

15

Too Full of Myself

F or chrissakes, Jack, what are you going to do next? Buy McDonald's?"

The remark came from a foursome of guys across the seventh fairway at Augusta as I was teeing off from the third hole in April 1986. Four months after announcing the deal to buy RCA, I had just acquired Kidder, Peabody, one of Wall Street's oldest investment banking firms.

While the guys were only kidding, there were others who really didn't think much of our latest decision. At least three GE board members weren't too keen on it, including two of the most experienced directors in the financial services business, Citibank Chairman Walt Wriston and J. P. Morgan President Lew Preston. Along with Andy Sigler, then Chairman of Champion International, they warned that the business was a lot different from our others.

"The talent goes up and down the elevators every day and can go in a heartbeat," said Wriston. "All you're buying is the furniture."

At an April 1986 board meeting in Kansas City, I had argued for it—and unanimously swung the board my way.

It was a classic case of hubris. Flush from the success of our acquisitions of RCA in 1985 and Employers Reinsurance in 1984, I was on a roll. Frankly, I was just full of myself. While internally I was still searching for the right "feel" for the company, on the acquisition front I thought I could make anything work.

Soon, I'd realize that I had taken it one step too far.

Our logic for buying Kidder was simple. In the 1980s, leveraged buyouts (LBOs) were hot. GE Capital was already a big player in LBOs, helping to finance the acquisition of more than 75 companies in the prior three years, including one of the earlier successes of the LBO game—Bill Simon's and Ray Chambers's acquisition of Gibson Greeting Cards.

We were getting tired of putting up all of the money and taking all of the risk while watching the investment bankers walk away with huge up-front fees. We thought Kidder would give us first crack at more deals and access to new distribution without paying these big fees to another of Wall Street's brokerage houses.

Eight months after closing the deal, we found out we had walked into one of the most public scandals ever to hit Wall Street. Marty Siegel, a Kidder star investment banker, admitted trading insider stock tips to Ivan Boesky in exchange for suitcases full of cash. He also admitted that Kidder had made trades based on information allegedly obtained from Richard Freeman at Goldman Sachs. He pleaded guilty to two felonies and cooperated with U.S. attorney Rudy Giuliani's investigation.

As a result, armed federal deputies stormed into Kidder's offices on February 12, 1987, at 10 Hanover Square in New York. They frisked, cuffed, and removed from the building the head of arbitrage, Richard Wigton. They also arrested another ex-Kidder arbitrageur, Tim Tabor, and Goldman's Freeman for alleged insider trading. The charges against Wigton and Tabor would eventually be dismissed. Freeman would be sentenced to four months in prison and a $1 million fine.

Though the illegal trading occurred before GE acquired Kidder, as the new owners we got saddled with the legal responsibility. After the arrests, we began an investigation, cooperating fully with the SEC and Giuliani. It showed that there were lots of weaknesses in the firm's control systems. Kidder chairman Ralph DeNunzio had nothing to do with the scandal, but it was clear Siegel had been given great latitude.

Siegel had complete run of the equity trading floor, and when he asked the risk arbs to make a trade, there were few questions. He also had a strange habit that would prove to be part of his downfall. He kept file drawers full of every pink telephone message slip he had ever received. With those slips and Kidder's detailed phone records, it wasn't hard to establish a pattern to Siegel's trading.

Giuliani, who could have gotten Kidder's licenses suspended and put it out of business, wanted us to dismiss much of the senior management. Larry Bossidy, then a GE vice chairman, spent a couple of Saturday mornings with Giuliani negotiating a settlement. We ended up paying fines of $26 million, shutting down Kidder's risk arbitrage department, and agreeing to put in better controls and procedures. While all that was going on, Ralph De-Nunzio and several of his key people decided to leave.

As far as senior management was concerned, this left us with little more than the furniture Wriston warned us about. We had to go out and find someone who could build back the trust in the company. I thought Si Cathcart was the perfect choice. He was savvy, honest, and someone I trusted completely. Si had been on the GE board for 15 years and had been chairman of Illinois Tool Works.

When I called him in Chicago and told him about my idea for him to run Kidder, his first reaction was not exactly encouraging.

"Are you out of your cotton-pickin' mind?" he asked.

"Si, just listen. I'll come out there or you come to New York and we'll have a good discussion about it."

A few days later in March, Larry Bossidy and I met him in a small Italian restaurant in New York. Si showed up with a sheet of yellow legal paper with 15 reasons why it was a bad idea. He had the names of half a dozen people he thought would be better for the job. I looked over his notes and crumpled them up.

"Si, we've got a real problem and you're the only guy who can help us," I said. "We have to stabilize things and get Kidder back on a recovery path. The job won't last much more than a couple of years. You and Corky will have a great experience in New York. You're too young to retire."

I probably said a lot more. Larry and I really needed him. Si finally agreed to go home and talk it over with his wife, Corky. Fortunately, she was excited about coming to New York and Si wanted to help us. He called back in a couple of days and agreed to accept the job.

On May 14, the day after Giuliani dismissed indictments against Wigton and Tabor, Si took over as CEO and president of Kidder. Larry Bossidy announced the change on Kidder's interoffice squawk box at 10 A.M. sharp. Not everyone was ecstatic. *The Wall Street Journal* article quoted an unnamed Kidder official: "Just what we need, a good tool and die man."

One of the problems was that Marty Siegel was not simply another guy who took the money and caused the scandal. He was Kidder's star. Good-looking, smooth-talking, and the highest-paid employee in the place, he was one of the leading investment bankers on Wall Street.

The media called Siegel "the Kidder franchise." Many of Kidder's traders idolized and worshiped the guy. For pleading guilty to two counts of insider trading, Siegel paid $9 million in fines and was sentenced to two months in prison and probation. Why, with all he had going for himself, he got involved with Boesky and bags of money was beyond anyone's comprehension.

Many of Kidder's employees lived off Siegel's franchise. Losing it sank the morale in the rest of the firm. As Si dug into things, he found that it wasn't very pretty. When he asked about purchasing—a question someone from manufacturing might ask—no one knew who ran the department or where it was. The bonus system was ad hoc. Ralph would sit down with the top people in the firm and negotiate one by one their year-end bonuses.

Frankly, the bonus numbers knocked most of us off our pins when we saw them. At the time, GE's total bonus pool was just under $100 million a year for a company making $4 billion in profit. Kidder's bonus pool was actually higher—at $140 million—for a company that was earning only one-twentieth of our income.

Si remembers that on the day Kidder employees got their bonus checks, the place would clear out in an hour. "You could shoot a cannon off without hitting anyone," he told me. Most of them lived a lifestyle dependent on those annual bonuses. It was a different world from what Si or I knew.

When Si went through his first bonus exercise, he'd ask everyone at Kidder to give him a list of his or her accomplishments for the year. Inevitably, he'd have six people claiming credit for being the key player on the same deal. Every one of them believed they made the deal happen. The attitudes were symbolic of the problem: an entitlement culture where every player overvalued themselves.

Where God parachutes us is a matter of luck. Nowhere is that more true than Wall Street. There are more mediocre people making more money on Wall Street than any other place on earth. Sure, there are some stars, and some earn every nickel they make. The crowd they carry along with them is something else. Wall Street might be the only place in the world where a $100,000 raise is considered a tip.

When you handed someone a check for $10 million, they'd look you in the eye and say, "Ten? The guy down the street just got 12!" "Thank you" was a rare expression at Kidder.

The outrageous pay in a good year was bad enough. It really drove me nuts in a bad year. That's when the argument would go something like this: "Yeah, we had a tough year, but you've got to give them at least as much as they made last year or they'll go across the street."

This place had the perfect we-win, you-lose game.

Wall Street had to have been better when the companies were private and the partners were playing with their own money rather than "other people's money." The concept of idea sharing and team play was completely foreign. If you were in investment banking or trading and your group had a good year, it didn't matter what happened to the firm overall. They wanted theirs.

It's a place where the lifeboats carrying millionaires were always going to make it to shore while the *Titanic* sank.

Si's stay at Kidder was tough. He put in better controls and hired some good people. Five months into the job, in October 1987, the stock market crashed. Kidder's trading profits disappeared. Kidder losses hit $72 million that year, and we had to lay off about 1,000 of the 5,000 people on the payroll.

It was obvious to all of us that the cultural differences between Kidder and GE were so great that I should have listened to the dissenters on my board. I wanted out, but was looking for a way to do it without losing our shirt. I hoped to show some results before selling the business.

Si wanted out, too. He had a steadying influence on the place, but after two years in the job, he felt that Kidder needed a permanent leader. We hired a search firm to look for Si's replacement. We couldn't get one.

Larry and I asked an old friend, Mike Carpenter, then an executive vice president at GE Capital, if he would run Kidder. Larry, Dennis, and I had met Mike in late 1980 when we were trying to acquire TransUnion, a Chicago-based railcar lessor. We lost the deal to Bob and Jay Pritzker but got to know Mike, who was then with the Boston Consulting Group and had recently completed a strategic analysis of TransUnion.

I hired him in 1983 as business development leader for GE.

Mike was a big player in the RCA deal and was doing a great job at GE Capital, where he had responsibility for our LBO business. He wanted to run his own show and agreed in February 1989 to take on what he knew was a very tough assignment at Kidder.

Si stayed for several months, helping Mike in the transition. Mike continued Si's efforts to make integrity a key value of the place. He also developed a well-defined strategy for each of Kidder's businesses. Profits recovered, and Kidder went from losing $32 million in 1990 to making $40 million in 1991 and $170 million in 1992.

We still wanted out and started conversations with Sandy Weill of Primerica. We came very close to striking a deal that would have gotten us out whole. But it fell apart over the 1993 Memorial Day holiday. Sandy and I had a general agreement on Friday of that weekend. We all felt that on Wall Street, you had to make the deal fast, over a weekend if possible before the news leaked, or you'd quickly lose the employees and get slaughtered. Dennis Dammerman, then chief financial officer, negotiated the fine print over the weekend, staying in touch with me in Nantucket by phone.

I expected to return on Memorial Day to wrap it up with Sandy.

It didn't work out that way. By the time I returned it was obvious that we weren't going to get the deal we started with. Sandy has done one of the great jobs in American business by building an enterprise through great acquisitions. I'm one of his biggest fans. But it was a challenge negotiating with him. By Monday, the deal that was going to get us out whole had been scratched, clawed, and picked at so that it was unrecognizable.

I spent a few hours that evening trying to get it back to where it had been. After a couple of tries, I saw it was hopeless and walked down the hall and told Sandy, "This deal is not for us." He smiled. We shook hands and have remained friends.

After the Primerica deal collapsed, Mike went back to work

and we stayed out of the spotlight. Profits reached $240 million in 1993, and things appeared to have stabilized—or at least I thought they had.

I was getting ready to leave the office for a long weekend on Thursday night, April 14, 1994, when Mike called with one of those phone calls you never want to get.

"We've got a problem, Jack," he said. "We have a $350 million hole in a trader's account that we can't identify, and he's disappeared."

I didn't yet know who Joseph Jett was, but over the next few days I would learn more than I cared to about him. Carpenter told me that Jett, who ran the firm's government bond desk, had made a series of fictitious trades to inflate his own bonus. The phony trades artificially boosted Kidder's reported income. To clean up the mess, we would have to take what looked like a $350 million charge against our first quarter earnings.

The news from Mike made me sick: $350 million, I couldn't believe it.

It was overwhelming. I rushed to the bathroom, and my stomach emptied in awful spasms. I called Jane, who was already waiting for me at the airport, told her what I knew, and asked her to come home instead. That evening I called Dennis Dammerman, who was teaching at Crotonville.

When he came to the phone, I told him: "It's your worst nightmare."

Actually, it was my own worst nightmare. I had made a terrible mistake in buying Kidder in the first place. It had been nothing but a headache and an embarrassment from the start—and now this.

Dennis went down to Kidder's offices with a team of eight others and began working around the clock throughout the weekend. I couldn't do much because they were doing gritty audit work, checking account balances. I sat by the phone, waiting for updates from Dennis. If I had gone down there, I probably would have driven them nuts.

By Sunday afternoon, I had to see it for myself. When I did, Dennis and Mike said they were sure the paper entries reported as earnings were bogus. We didn't have all the facts, but with our first quarter earnings release two days away, they were convinced we had a $350 million noncash write-off to deal with.

I spent hours trying to figure out exactly how hundreds of millions of dollars could disappear overnight. It didn't seem possible. We obviously didn't know enough about the business. We'd later discover that Jett had taken advantage of a flaw in Kidder's computer systems.

That Sunday evening, I called 14 of GE's business leaders to deliver the bad news and apologize to each of them for what had happened. I felt terrible, because this surprise would hit the stock and hurt every GE employee.

I blamed myself for the disaster.

The previous year, 1993, when Jett's phantom trades accounted for nearly a quarter of the profits made by Kidder's fixed income group, Jett had been named Kidder's "Man of the Year." We had approved Mike's request to give Jett a $9 million cash bonus, a huge award even for Kidder. Normally, I would have been all over this. I would have dug into how one person could be so successful, and I would have insisted on meeting him. I didn't.

It was my fault because I didn't ask the "why" questions I normally did. It turned out that Kidder was as culturally distant from us as GE appeared to the Kidder employees.

The response of our business leaders to the crisis was typical of the GE culture. Even though the books had closed on the quarter, many immediately offered to pitch in to cover the Kidder gap. Some said they could find an extra $10 million, $20 million, and even $30 million from their businesses to offset the surprise. Though it was too late, their willingness to help was a dramatic contrast to the excuses I had been hearing from the Kidder people.

Instead of pitching in, they complained about how this disaster was going to affect their incomes. "This is going to ruin everything," one said. "Our bonus is down the toilet. How will we keep anyone?" The two cultures and their differences never stood out so clearly in my mind. All I heard was, "I didn't do it. I never saw it. I never met with him. I didn't talk to him." No one seemed to know anyone or work for anyone.

It was disgusting.

We fired Jett and reassigned six other employees that night. When I got home later, I told Jane to hunker down. We were going to go through a very long and very tough ride.

"The media's going to come after me. Just hang on."

The coverage was brutal. Again, I went from prince to pig. In the space of a year, we ended up in the right-hand column of the front page of *The Wall Street Journal* numerous times. *Time* magazine had a new moniker for me: "Jack in the Box." A *Newsweek* writer claimed that "you can hear the sound of the pedestal cracking."

A cover story in *Fortune* on the disaster jumped to the ridiculous conclusion that the scandals at Kidder were brought on by poor GE management. It was BS. The problem at Kidder was confined to Kidder. It was all about having a bad apple and insufficient controls.

The internal investigation of what went wrong at Kidder was led by Gary Lynch, a former SEC enforcement chief who was now with Davis Polk & Wardwell. With enormous help from GE's audit staff, he found that the oversight of Jett's trades was a big part of the problem. Lynch reported that time and again questions raised about the unusual trading profits were "answered incorrectly, ignored, or evaded. . . . As his profitability increased, skepticism about Jett's activities was often dismissed or unspoken."

At Kidder, the fixed income group had become the franchise, earning more than the firm earned in total. When they spoke, the firm listened, and few questioned the basis for their success. We weren't the first on Wall Street to learn this lesson. Michael Milken and Drexel Burnham was the most vivid example, but even terrific leaders like Frank Zarb and Pete Peterson struggled with the dominance of trading at Lehman Brothers. The lesson was there to be heard. We hadn't listened.

Later, an SEC administrative law judge found that Jett had acted "egregiously" in committing fraud on Kidder. Judge Carol Fox Foelak found that Jett had intentionally deceived his supervisors, auditors, and others with false denials and misleading and conflicting explanations. She barred Jett from association with any broker dealer and ordered him to pay $8.4 million in penalties.

Kidder cost us years of trouble and some of our best executive talent. By mid-June of 1994, I had to ask my friend Mike Carpenter to leave his job. That was about the hardest decision I ever had to make. Mike was a great executive, who had attacked the Jett problem—one he didn't create.

He was a bigger victim of the scandal than anyone. The media wanted his hide, and until they got it the negative coverage would never end. He and I had a long conversation, which I concluded by saying, "This isn't going away until you go." He understood and was a class act. Jett's immediate boss, Ed Cerullo, the head of the fixed income area at Kidder, left a few weeks after Mike.

In Mike's place, we temporarily moved Dennis Dammerman to Kidder as chairman and CEO and Denis Nayden, another smart GE Capital veteran, as president and chief operating officer.

Four months later, in October 1994, we finally struck a deal to sell Kidder for $670 million plus a 24 percent stake in PaineWebber. Once again, Pete Peterson played an important role. Negotiations between GE Capital and PaineWebber CEO Don Marron had broken down over a weekend in early October.

I called Don to see if we could put things back together again. Don called in Pete, a longtime friend of his, as an adviser on the deal. Don and I knew each other only vaguely, so Pete became the key player in the negotiations. Pete, Don, Dennis, and I quickly reached a general agreement and shook hands. I left for a ten-day Asian business trip, and Dennis did the final negotiation. Pete called me a couple of times, once I remember at 3 A.M. in Thailand, to work out a couple of stumbling blocks.

The deal was concluded in about ten days, and the friendship among the four of us has never wavered.

The story has a somewhat happy ending. Late on a Friday in mid-2000, Pete called me just as I was about to leave the office.

"Jack, I'm sorry to bother you," he said, "but I wanted to make your weekend for you."

Pete said that he and Don had reached an agreement to sell PaineWebber to Swiss bank UBS for $10.8 billion. "We just made over $2 billion for you, and I hope you'll go along."

"Make my frigging weekend?" I shouted. "You made my whole frigging year!"

Don, his team, and several key Kidder players made the merger a great success. That success gave us an eventual after-tax return of 10 percent a year over the 14 years from the purchase of Kidder to the sale of PaineWebber. By no means was it a financial success, but the outcome was better than a few others.

However, there's no amount of money that would make us want to go through that again.

The Kidder experience never left me. Culture does count, big time. During the dot.com craze of the late 1990s, several people in the GE Capital equity group were enjoying success—not unlike day traders in their living rooms. These folks decided they would stay with GE only if they got a piece of the equity in the deals they were investing GE money in.

I told them to take a hike. A few did, and the media gave us some heat, claiming we were "not with it." We didn't get the New Economy. "Absolutely!"

It gave me another chance at the officers meeting in October to make the point that at GE there is only one currency: GE stock (below). There are different amounts of it for different levels of performance, but everyone's life raft is tied to the same boat. One culture, one set of values, one currency, doesn't mean, however, one style—every GE business has its own personality.

For the same reason—a big culture gap—I've passed up opportunities to acquire high-tech companies in Silicon Valley that appeared to be a good strategic fit. I didn't want to pollute GE with the cultures that were developing there in the late 1990s. Culture and values count too much.

There's only a razor's edge between self-confidence and hubris. This time, hubris won and taught me a lesson I'd never forget.

On another issue... Forbes this week has an article on People leaving GE Equity/NBC for internet ~~investing~~ Investment -- because I wouldn't agree to give them a piece of the action in their investments ... It's true ... the article is Completely true ... There is only one equity Currency in GE -- AND That is GE Stock ---

16

GE Capital:
The Growth Engine

One night in June 1998, I was sitting on the couch at home, leafing through the "deal book" for the next day's GE Capital board meeting. One of the ideas up for approval struck me as one of the wackiest I had seen in my 20 years on the board.

The proposal was to buy $1.1 billion of auto loans in Thailand from a group of failed finance companies that had been seized by the government. I knew the country was in the worst recession in its history, and we were the only auto finance company still standing.

I quickly explained the deal to Jane, who was sitting across from me.

"The guy making this pitch won't even get to sit down," I told her. "We'll blow him out of the meeting in five minutes or less."

These sessions aren't your run-of-the-mill board meetings. We finance billions of enterprises yearly, and potential deals are put through a monthly torture chamber. The meetings are hands-on, no-holds-barred discussions among some 20 GE insiders with more than 400 years of diverse business experience.

This crowd has looked at and torn apart literally thousands of deals before we make a decision. Although all the proposals have been rigorously prescreened before they hit the board—and 90

percent of the proposals eventually get approved—we still send
back one in five for another look.

When I read the details on the Thai deal that night, I was convinced this one was headed for the Dumpster. The proposal, a
50/50 partnership with Goldman Sachs, would make us the owner
of one of every nine cars in Thailand. To pull it off, we'd have to
hire 1,000 extra employees in the country to underwrite the loans,
collect the payments, and manage the disposition of any repos-
sessed cars. If our bid was accepted, we'd take over the loans for 45
percent of their face value. The idea had come from Mark Nor-
bom, who headed up GE Capital's business in Thailand.

The next morning, I walked into the meeting in Fairfield with
a smile on my face.

"Thai auto loans?" I said, laughing. "I can hardly wait to get to
that one."

When I turned the page to Mark's proposal, I frowned and
shook my head.

"How could we possibly hire and train those 1,000 people
within a few months?" I asked.

Mark's answer impressed me. He said his team had already
screened 4,000 job candidates, interviewed more than 2,000, and
issued 1,000 contracts contingent on winning the bid. He told us
that a car is among the most prized possessions in Thailand. People
would give up almost everything else—would even sleep in their
cars—before losing them for nonpayment of a loan.

After a bit of banter and a passionate pitch from Mark, we
bought it. Talk about changing your mind on something because
of a good presentation and a lot of passion. That was as good an
example as I could remember.

I walked into that meeting thinking, This guy's outta here, and
I walked out thinking, Isn't this neat?

Mark was right. Over the next three years, GE has done well,
and the company built an ongoing and profitable auto business
in Thailand. The transaction led to several other troubled asset

purchases in Asia, all of which panned out well for GE and the local economies.

Mark did okay, too. He became president of GE Japan.

The small Thai deal was one of thousands that show how GE Capital, once a popcorn stand, has become one of the most valuable parts of GE. When I got my first look at the business as a sector executive in 1978, GE Capital earned $67 million on $5 billion in assets. (In 2000, GE Capital made $5.2 billion, 41 percent of GE's total income, on more than $370 billion in assets.)

The story of that phenomenal growth has been told many times and in many ways. What most people outside GE don't know is the incredible intensity, ingenuity, and entrepreneurship that goes on behind that success.

What I saw in 1978 was immense opportunity—not just the benefit you get on a balance sheet, but the additional leverage you get by putting together two raw materials: money and brains.

Since I had been involved in making things all my life, pounding and grinding it out to make a nickel, I couldn't believe how easy this "appeared" to be. The business already demonstrated there were terrific deals with good collateral that could produce remarkable returns on equity. One example: Leveraged leases on aircraft could earn 30 percent or better returns.

I fell in love with the idea of melding the discipline and the cash flows from manufacturing with financial ingenuity to build a great business. Of course, we needed the right people to make this happen.

Dennis Dammerman would always remind me of Ben Franklin's old adage, "You don't earn interest unless you collect the principal." Fortunately, GE Capital already had a culture that insisted the people making the deals stayed with them from womb to tomb. If you pitched a deal, you'd better make damn sure it was going to work. Or else you'd better be able to take over the asset and make it work yourself.

I was sure the opportunity was enormous. All we had to do was take the business from the back of the boat to the front. Better people and a greater financial commitment could lead to huge profits.

Happily, I found Larry Bossidy playing Ping-Pong. Larry, along with GE Capital CEO John Stanger, was the guy who shook the place up. From our game in Hawaii, I understood his frustration. In 1978, GE Credit was an orphan business, outside the mainstream of the company. Plastics, too, had been an orphan business during my earlier days there. Larry wanted to put GE Capital up on center stage. A former auditor, he came from deep inside GE Capital, and he knew what had to be done.

The first big move I made at GE Capital was to get Reg's approval to make Larry chief operating officer in 1979. Larry, like me, was not a picture-perfect GE executive. No model of sartorial splendor, Larry could always be recognized from the back because his shirttail flew in the wind. His idea of a summer suit was to take his winter suit and dress it up with a white belt and shiny white patent-leather shoes. (With his increasing prominence in the business world, Larry's now become *GQ* cover material.)

He has always been a remarkable family man. His wife, Nancy, did a fantastic job raising their nine kids. Larry helped but often worked late nights and weekends. Three of their children came to work for GE, including Paul, who now runs commercial equipment finance with $38 billion in assets, one of our top 20 GE businesses.

Larry and I thought along the same lines on a lot of things, nowhere more so than on the people front. Not only did we have Session Cs to look closely at people, but we had the monthly board reviews where we held their feet to the flame. We saw people under real fire, pitching deals every month—and in some cases, explaining later how they'd work their way out of trouble.

Over my 23-year involvement with GE Capital, I saw the growth develop in four distinct stages: from 1977 to 1985, CEO John Stanger and Larry Bossidy lured some of the best people we had into GE Capital. In the second half of the 1980s, Bossidy (by then a vice chairman) and CEO Gary Wendt began to aggressively grow the business by making GE Capital an acquisition machine.

Through the 1990s, Wendt and operating chief Denis Nayden created a global financial services business by leading a decade of unprecedented deal making. The current team of Denis as CEO and Mike Neal as COO is expanding that global franchise and bringing to financial services the rigor of Six Sigma and digitization.

Looking back over the years of uninterrupted double-digit growth, it almost seems surreal. I can still remember when I stewed and stewed over a $90 million GE Capital deal. Compared to those Thai auto loans and the billions of dollars we might commit in a board meeting today, this was insignificant—but not back in 1982.

That's when Larry Bossidy, Dennis Dammerman, and I were at a GE Capital management meeting in Puerto Rico, debating whether we should acquire American Mortgage Insurance from Baldwin United. We were just about dying over the deal—then GE Capital's largest ever—mulling over how much to bid and worrying about every potential complication.

It's a matter of perspective. Before we decided to buy American Mortgage in 1983, Dennis was literally signing every insurance policy we issued because his insurance business was so small that he couldn't justify the purchase of a signature machine. After the deal, we not only could buy the machine, we became a major player in the business.

A year later, in 1984, we topped the little $90 million deal with our $1.1 billion acquisition of Employers Reinsurance Corp. (ERC). John Stanger and Dennis Dammerman first looked at ERC, one of the three largest property and casualty reinsurance companies in the United States, in 1979. The insurer asked us to be a white knight to fend off an unwanted bid from Connecticut General Insurance. At the time, our insurance assets were pretty small. ERC preferred us as a parent over Connecticut General, which obviously was a big player in the industry.

But, ERC went with their definition of a perfect white knight, a company that knew absolutely nothing about insurance: Getty Oil. In one of the most notorious deals of the decade, Getty was eventually acquired by Texaco, which had little use for a reinsurance company. With the background work done years earlier, we were able to move quickly to bring ERC into the fold. I negotiated the final details of the $1.1 billion deal with Texaco CEO John McKinley.

We were still puny operators in those days. When the ERC team came to Fairfield for Sunday night dinner after the deal, they told us they were going to fall short of the annual earnings forecasts assumed in the transaction.

I immediately wanted a discount on the price. My friend John Weinberg of Goldman Sachs had represented us in the acquisition. I phoned him at Augusta, pulled him off the golf course, and ranted about the earnings shortfall. I told him to call McKinley to get an adjustment on the price.

Fortunately, McKinley was a gentleman, accepted the new numbers, and gave us a $25 million discount. We ended up paying $1.075 billion. It makes me feel a little embarrassed today to have done that, but I was relatively new in the job and probably a bit too competitive for my own good.

The ERC acquisition was a big leap forward. We had a great run in ERC, growing net income from $100 million in 1985 to a peak of $790 million in 1998, until tough pricing and a rash of storms in 1998 and 1999 derailed us. We earned only $500 million in 2000.

We made Ron Pressman CEO to get it back on track. A former auditor, Ron had built a highly profitable real estate business and had just the right mix of smarts and discipline. Pricing is better, Six Sigma is taking hold, and if the weather cooperates, Ron will make this business hum again.

Most of what we did in the 1980s, we did in small steps. One of the hallmarks of GE Capital has been a "walk before running approach" to the markets. Before diving into a specific market, we tiptoed into the water.

We never had a great strategic vision for GE Capital.

We didn't have to be No. 1 or No. 2. The markets were enormous. All we needed to do was couple GE's balance sheet with GE brains to grow.

In the 1970s, the focus was on traditional consumer lending like mortgages and auto leasing, with some transportation and real estate investments.

In the 1980s, our focus shifted to stronger growth while maintaining tight control of risk. We didn't change the conservative risk profile that existed in the seventies. What we did was hire unique people. We set them free to find the ideas, make the case to invest in their ideas, and grow.

Grow we did, as deals came from everywhere. Over the past 20 years, GE Capital exploded into a host of equipment management businesses from trucks and railcars to airplanes. We jumped on private-label credit cards. We became more aggressive in real estate. We went from half a dozen financial niches in 1977 to 28 different GE Capital businesses by 2001.

If ever there was a lesson that people made the difference, this was it. Over the years, we had a murderers row of talent—Larry Bossidy, Dennis Dammerman, Norm Blake, Bob Wright, Gary Wendt, and Denis Nayden. Every one of them would go on to become CEOs inside or outside the company.

A perfect example of homegrown success was Denis Nayden, who started right out of the University of Connecticut in 1977 as marketing administrator for air-rail financing. Over the next two decades, he moved up the ladder to become Wendt's right-hand man until being named CEO in 1998.

We used talent from our industrial businesses to turn GE Capital from a pure financial house into a business with deal making as well as operational skills. Half of the current top leadership at GE Capital Services grew up on the industrial side.

Our managers knew how to run businesses. When a deal went sour, we rarely put a line through it. We hated write-offs. Instead, we took it over and ran it ourselves. We had the operational capability that let us stick with a tough asset.

When a loan to Tiger International went bad in 1983, we stepped in and became a railcar leasing company. When some of our passenger planes came off lease into a soft market, we converted the planes to cargo carriers and launched Polar Air, an independent cargo line. Our long experience in aircraft leasing led to the purchase of Polaris and the expansion of our business with Irish-based Guinness Peat Aviation's assets in 1993 and 1994.

Today, GE Capital Aviation Services (GECAS) manages $18 billion in assets.

We built GE Capital deal by deal—big or small—with the great majority of the deals coming before our monthly board meetings. The company was always careful about the bets it made in financial services. I didn't add any new discipline to the GE Capital risk process from the 1970s—but I didn't lessen the discipline, either. Any equity deal involving more than $10 million and any commercial risk per customer over $100 million had to be brought before the board.

We never changed the approval levels as we grew.

I was in on just about every one of these transactions, so I share credit for the good decisions and blame for the bad ones. We did get into the leveraged buyout craze in the 1980s. In one LBO deal, we financed the buyout of Patrick Media, an advertising billboard company, in 1989. The business had decent cash flows and reasonable growth rates. Only one thing bothered me. Patrick was being sold by John Kluge, head of Metromedia and a famous deal maker.

I didn't know much about billboards, but I knew that when

John Kluge was selling, I shouldn't be buying. I had met John during my days negotiating the Cox deal. I liked him a lot, but I also knew he was one of the savviest investors around. I should have followed my instincts and walked away. When billboard use hit bottom in the late 1980s, we took ownership of the company to avoid a $650 million write-off. We rebuilt the business, eventually earning a modest gain on its sale in 1995.

We also did an LBO of Montgomery Ward in 1988. It was almost a home run. Our 50/50 partner, Bernie Brennan, made the Forbes 400 as one of the richest men in the world, and Wards flourished. The retailer later hit a wall. Despite the valiant efforts of a new management team, Wards went through hell and eventually went bankrupt in 2000.

However, the good deals far outweighed the bad, and their range was extraordinary. For instance, we went into auto auctions. I had liked the business and had seen it at Cox Broadcasting during the failed negotiations in 1980. Cox owned Manheim, the leader in auto auctions. It was a pure service opportunity with low investment and high margins. Ed Stewart, who then ran auto leasing, began buying little auction companies in the early 1980s. Ed eventually bought more than 20 auto auction companies and formed an 80/20 joint venture with Ford Motor.

An auction was like going to a flea market, set up on grounds with wooden bleachers. Roving vendors sold hot dogs and beans and Harley-Davidson leather belts from the stands. Auctioneers were selling off used cars one a minute. In the end, Manheim was also the reason we sold the business. They were much bigger than we were and had the opportunity to consolidate the industry. We took the gain and sold to Manheim in the early 1990s.

Many of the best deals before the board—and some of the wildest—came from Gary Wendt, who led GE Capital's strong growth as CEO from 1986 until 1998. The deals he pitched were imaginative and creative. Gary was not just a brilliant deal guy, he also had the rare ability to tell you what it would take to make a good deal out of a not-so-good deal.

Gary was a trained engineer, a Harvard MBA, and a natural negotiator. He was doing workouts at a real estate investment trust in Florida when he was recruited to GE Credit as manager of real estate financing in 1975. Later, he oversaw all commercial finance dealings, becoming chief operating officer of GE Capital in 1984. When Bob Wright left as GE Capital's CEO to run NBC in mid-1986, Larry Bossidy put Gary Wendt in charge. Gary and Larry continued to work together to build GE Capital.

By 1991, Larry wanted to run his own show. He was 55 and a vice chairman, yet he couldn't really go any higher at GE because I still had ten years in front of me as CEO. Larry wanted a chance to run a large company, and he got it through Gerry Roche, the headhunter at Heidrick & Struggles.

On a Monday morning in late June, Larry came into my office with the news.

"Jack," he said, "you know the time has come for me to move on. I don't want to sit here for the rest of my career. Something's come up, and I'm going to take it."

"When are you going to do it?" I asked.

"It will be announced tomorrow."

"So you've made up your mind?" I asked.

"Yep. I've just got to do it," he said.

It was an emotional meeting. We went way back, from the time in 1978 when we played Ping-Pong together in Hawaii and I convinced him to stay at GE. A lot of tears fell, and we hugged each other.

Then Larry told me he was going to become CEO of AlliedSignal, the industrial products company in New Jersey.

My mom,
Grace Welch, 1920.

Mom and Dad, around 1930.

The apple of my mother's eye, 1939.

In Old Orchard Beach, Maine, with my buddies Bill Cullen *(left)* and Mike Tivnan *(center)*, 1945.

At the beginning of a lifelong love affair, 1950.

Getting ready to throw the "curve" with my friendly "neighbor" across the street in Salem, 1950.

Senior portrait at Salem High, 1953.

"Big Jack" at work on the Boston & Maine commuter line, where he picked up the golf idea.

On vacation in Nantucket with Carolyn.

My children *(left to right)*: Katherine, John, Anne, and Mark.

H ON THE ART
NG SMALL

On a visit to my office in 1993, grandson Jack finds some media coverage interesting.

With grandson Jack in Nantucket, 1996.

My son John,
his wife,
Jackie, and
their five
children.

With Katherine's son Luke at
Mark and Sheila's wedding in
June 2001.

Relaxing in Nantucket with
granddaughter Carolyn.

With daughter Anne and new
granddaughter Claire.

Vacationing with Jane in Capri, 1991.

The Barbados Santa whose arrival on the beach indirectly helped me dream up the concept of "boundaryless" in 1990.

Watching the fireworks with Jane at the maharaja's palace in India, 1993.

Relaxing with the Frescos and the Fiores in Capri, 1992 *(left to right)*: Marlene Fresco, Gino Fiore, Corry Fiore, Jane Welch, Paolo Fresco.

Hitting the links in Ireland with a real golf pro, my wife, Jane, 1997.

At Augusta with my regular GE golfing buddies *(left to right)*: Dave Calhoun, Bill Meddaugh, Chuck Chadwell.

Showing the perfect form (note the location of the ball!).

Jane and I golfing in the Canadian Rockies with GE board member and good friend Si Cathcart and his wife, Corky.

At the Sankaty Head Member-Guest Tournament with partner, son John, in 1995.

Jane and I filling in for Matt and Katie on the *Today* show set in Sydney during the 2000 Olympics.

With my family at the GE annual shareowners' meeting in Richmond, April 2000 *(left to right)*: son-in-law Stephen McMillan and daughter Anne, daughter-in-law Sheila and son Mark, Jane, daughter-in-law Jackie and son John, daughter Katherine. *Photo courtesy of the State of Virginia*

"Staring into the hole" in Selkirk, future site of the Noryl plastics plant *(left to right)*: myself, Allan Hay, Reuben Gutoff. *Photo courtesy of R. Gutoff*

Having the time of our lives, and getting paid for it. "Blowing the roof off" with the plastics team in the early '70s.

GE's new sector chief, 1973.
Photo courtesy of GE

Reg Jones introduces the "new guy" to GE employees, 1981.
Photo courtesy of GE

At my first board meeting as
chairman—a rather formal gathering.
Photo courtesy of GE

My first official portrait as chairman,
with vice chairmen
Ed Hood *(left)* and
John Burlingame.
Photo courtesy of GE

Larry Bossidy, my new vice
chairman, joined Ed Hood and me
in the corporate office in 1984.
Photo courtesy of GE

Announcing the $6.3 billion
RCA deal with Bob Frederick and
Thornton "Brad" Bradshaw
in New York City, 1985.
Photo courtesy of GE

At President Bush's state dinner for Queen Elizabeth. I always regret my parents missed these amazing moments.

Meeting China's president Jaing Zemin in the early '90s. *Photo courtesy of GE*

With President Mikhail Gorbachev in Russia in the late '80s.
Photo courtesy of GE

With President Clinton on Martha's Vineyard in the summer of 1999.

Congratulating President Bush at the Inaugural in 2001.

Doing a little "deep diving" with the manufacturing guys, 1995.
Photo courtesy of GE

With K.P. Singh and Paolo Fresco on that first memorable trip to India.
Photo courtesy of GE

Pounding home an initiative.
Photo courtesy of GE

Pausing during a global trip with Paolo Fresco *(far left)*, Larry Bossidy, and Jane in 1993.

Jane and my great friends Anthony "Lofie" LoFrisco and his wife, Eleanor.

Celebrating NBC's success with Bob and Suzanne Wright.

In India with Jane *(bottom second from left)*, K.P. Singh *(top left)*, Paolo Fresco *(top right)*, and his wife, Marlene *(bottom second from right)*.

With Bill Gates and
Bob Wright at the
launch of MSNBC,1995.
*Photo courtesy
of NBC*

Learning about "quick market
intelligence" from Sam Walton
and the Wal-Mart team in
Bentonville. John Opie,
a future GE vice chairman,
is at far left.

With the smartest guy in *any* room.
Warren Buffett and I having some fun
at Frank Rooney's in Florida with our
"Most Admired" caricatures from
Fortune magazine.

In "the Pit" at Crotonville, 1998.
Photo by Mark Peterson, Saba

Posing for the 1997 Annual Report with vice chairmen Paolo Fresco *(left)*, John Opie, and Gene Murphy.
Photo by John Abbott

"*Ro!*" Rosanne Badowski and I at work.
Photo by Mark Peterson, Saba

A team meeting in my conference room with *(from bottom left)* Paolo Fresco, Gary Reiner, Dennis Dammerman, Bill Conaty, and John Opie.
Photo by Mark Peterson, Saba

A fateful day at the NYSE. A CNBC reporter asked for my thoughts on United Technologies' announcement that they would buy Honeywell. "Interesting. I'll have to look at it," I said. *Photo courtesy of NYSE*

Meet the "new guy"; with Jeff Immelt in New York City, November 2000. *Photo courtesy of GE*

The new team *(clockwise from lower left):* President and Chairman-Elect Jeff Immelt, GE vice chairmen Bob Wright and Dennis Dammerman, and one soon-to-be GE retiree. *Photo by Timothy Greenfield-Sanders*

At home with two of my eight new best friends.

Larry said AlliedSignal appealed to him because it was a turn-around situation and it was located in the Northeast so he wouldn't have to move his family.

When Roche called me later, I said, "Gerry, half my face is crying because you're taking away my best friend and my best guy. The other half is smiling because he can run any company in this country and he deserves to run his own show."

In the 1990s, Gary Wendt wanted to plant a flag everywhere he went. He told his team not to worry about a few wounds. "We're going to win the war," he said. "You've got to take ground."

While every business took on globalization, no one practiced it more effectively than GE Capital. With Europe in a slump, Gary led a massive effort there. In 1994, Gary and his team picked up $12 billion in assets, more than half offshore. In 1995, they more than doubled the pace, acquiring $25 billion in assets, with $18 billion outside the United States.

GE Capital was on a global roll, acquiring consumer loan companies, private-label credit operations, and leasing operations for truck trailers and railcars.

The stories behind many of these deals are enough to fill volumes. One summer, during his vacation in 1995, Gary and his head of business development for Europe, Christopher Mackenzie, drove a van through eastern Europe. An idea machine, Christopher was Gary's deal finder. They came back energized to do all kinds of deals in that part of the world. They also had in hand a proposal to buy a bank in Budapest. We liked Hungary and the bank fit nicely with GE Lighting, already there as a major employer in the country.

We also bought banks in Poland and the Czech Republic and used them to move into personal finance in those markets. The Czech bank deal had a funny twist because the bank's owner also had an appliance distribution company and a warehouse loaded with Russian TVs. We agreed to the deal after being assured we wouldn't get stuck with this Czech appliance business.

All three banks today are modestly profitable, throwing off about $36 million in annual net profits. Gary's road trip is still paying off.

Another funny one was the time Dave Nissen, CEO of global consumer finance, set the stage for a pitch on buying Pet Protect, the second largest British company selling life and health insurance for cats and dogs. This one fell into the Thai auto loan category, appearing to be dead on arrival.

Dave began his presentation in 1996 with the words, "This dog will hunt."

I didn't know much about the market for pet insurance. We found out the business was growing by 30 percent a year with annual premiums of $90 million. The U.K. market ranked second only to Sweden in the percentage of cats and dogs insured, 5 percent versus 17 percent, so there was plenty of upside.

Jim Bunt, a GE Capital board member and treasurer, had a lot of fun with this one. In his review of the deal, Jim joked that the principal product coverage included "kennel costs if the dog owner was suddenly hospitalized," but not "catastrophic loss due to dog bites."

We gave the okay not because we knew pet insurance, but because we trusted the guys making the pitch.

With a price tag of $23 million, this deal was also a little one. There were many other bigger ones that raised serious questions. One time, in 1997, Nissen was pitching a deal to buy Bank Aufina, the consumer finance unit of a large bank in Switzerland. I balked.

Swiss bankers owned the banking world. Why would they agree to sell anything that would actually be any good? It didn't compute. Nissen explained that Swiss bankers are real bankers who prefer the bigger deals and were more interested in global investment banking. A personal loan and auto financing business was a diversion.

We ended up buying two companies in Switzerland. In 2001, they made $78 million.

These deals were part of a grand plan by Nissen to build a global consumer finance company. The first big one, giving GE Capital a major European presence, was our acquisition in 1990 of the private-label credit card operations of the Burton Group, Britain's largest clothing retailer. The next year, Dave added Harrods and House of Fraser.

During the difficult negotiations for this deal, the head of Harrods had a demanding and unusual negotiating style. When he didn't like the way things were going, he'd leave the room and tell the guys that he'd be back in five minutes and wanted a better answer. After the tenth time he pulled the ploy, Nissen and his team made up cards with big block letters that spelled "SCREW YOU."

When the head of Harrods came back into the room, the guys held up the letters. He got a kick out of it, and the humor took a lot of the tension out of the negotiations. They soon closed the deal.

While Gary and Denis were driving global growth, a lot was going on here in the United States. Some of the more interesting deals were being brought in by Mike Gaudino, head of commercial finance. While I looked every day at companies I wanted to buy, Mike looks at companies he wants to save. He always points out that more than half the companies in the United States are non-investment grade. Mike comes into the board six to seven times every year with troubled companies already in or often headed for bankruptcy. Along with judging the company's leadership, Mike digs into our ability to recover the receivables and inventories. It's an upside-down look at a business—the opposite of what we're used to.

A good example is Eatons, a large retail chain in Canada that experienced financial difficulty in 1997. When other lenders wouldn't provide financing, Mike sought approval for $300 million in loans to help the retailer out of bankruptcy. After another downturn, however, the company ultimately had to be liquidated. Mike managed to get back every penny of our investment and all of our projected returns. By working out dilemmas, like Eatons, Mike built great credibility. He's had only one deal out of more than 200 turned down in the past six years. Mike's upside-down approach coupled with strong underwriting has taken the business from breakeven in 1993 to close to $300 million in net income in 2000.

Gary Wendt became the high priest of growth inside GE Capital. He made business development a key part of its culture. Besides the more than 200 people dedicated to looking for acquisitions, each GE Capital executive came to work every morning thinking about potential deals. It was part of the growth mindset Gary brought to the business. The *Harvard Business Review* used GE Capital as a model for successfully integrating acquisitions, giving a blow-by-blow account of how Gary and his team did them—and there were a ton.

In the 1990s, Gary and Denis Nayden closed more than 400 deals involving over $200 billion in assets.

Gary lived for the deal, and everything with Gary was a negotiation. Denis Nayden remembers the time he and Gary were in Hong Kong and Gary went into a shop to buy a radio. He haggled with the salesperson for what seemed like an hour to get the price down and left happy with his bargain. Down the street, Gary nearly died when he spotted the same radio he had just bought in the window with a price tag lower than his highly negotiated purchase.

It drove him nuts over the weekend.

Gary also loved plotting strategies to sell deals. Mike Neal tells of the time he came in for his first preboard pitch to Gary in 1989. Mike wanted to buy Contel Credit, a telecom company leasing business. Throughout Mike's entire presentation, Gary seemed bored and didn't say a word—until Neal was completely finished.

"Mike," he said, "this may be the worst acquisition we've ever had anyone pitch us, but we have another deal that's big and sporty. It's a commercial aircraft deal we really like. We're going to let you take your deal up to the board meeting first and put you right in front of the deal we like. Jack seldom turns down two in a row. You'll set us up to get the okay."

Mike came in and pitched. We bought his deal. Gary's preferred transaction got shot down.

We fought like hell over a lot of deals, but Gary had a very high batting average.

Years before Japan allowed foreign investment, Gary had sent a small business development team there to scout potential opportunities. When the Japanese economy began to sour in the mid-1990s, the country's banking and insurance sectors were overleveraged and filled with bad investments. Nonperforming loans were out of sight. They needed new capital and new ownership.

When Japan began to open to foreign investment, Gary's early groundwork gave GE Capital a head start.

The first deal in 1994 was to acquire Minebea, the $1 billion consumer finance company subsidiary of a ball-bearing company. Along with Jay Lapin, then the head of GE Japan, Gary put together several innovative deals in consumer finance, insurance, and equipment leasing. A former lawyer in our appliance business, Jay was the perfect area executive. He had worked hard to gain the trust of Japanese regulators and the business community. He loved Japan and its people. They knew it and responded. The parties he held at his home when I visited Japan brought me together with the CEOs of many of the country's largest corporations and key opinion leaders.

By 1998, we really hit stride. The GE Capital team made two more deals that year in life insurance, consumer finance, and leasing that put us on the map as a big player in financial services in Japan.

The first one in February was a $575 million joint venture with Toho Mutual Life Insurance. Mike Frazier brought the deal to the board. Mike, too, had been a GE auditor. He had worked for me in

Fairfield, searching the world for best practices and had been president of GE Japan in the early 1980s. Mike had built a strong U.S. insurance company, integrating 13 separate acquisitions into a highly successful whole. Now he was planting a flag for his business in Japan, with Gary's strong support.

I was scared stiff over this one, and I gave it a lot of pushback. Toho was a bankrupt company, and the scale and scope of the acquisition overwhelmed me. This was unfamiliar territory. I didn't know the laws, and I wanted to make sure Mike and his team had done the homework to assess all the risks. So we had a lot of back-and-forth. During December, he shuttled to Tokyo and back several times to satisfy both our and the seller's concerns. The deal closed shortly before Christmas.

The second deal, announced in July 1998, was our $6 billion acquisition of the consumer loan business of Lake, Japan's fifth largest consumer finance company. Lake was a provider of short-term consumer loans through automated teller machines. With 600 branches across Japan and nearly 1.5 million customers, it made us a big player in consumer finance in Japan. This was a highly complicated deal with a virtually bankrupt company that took nearly three years of work to complete.

The first overture in 1996 by Dave Nissen was rejected because we refused to take over the company's liabilities. A second offer a year later didn't go much further. Finally, in 1998, Nissen and his team came up with an unusual structure to pull it off. We'd buy Lake's personal loan operations and help set up a separate company that would hold the rest of Lake's assets, including some $400 million worth of art bought by the company's owner. We agreed to put extra money on the table—an earn-out—that would give Lake's shareholders some upside if we hit certain earnings targets.

To get the deal done, we had to convince 20 different banks in Japan to take a discount on the debt they had issued to Lake. Nissen's team even hired Christie's to assess the value of the Picassos and Renoirs that hung in Lake's offices. Though we weren't buy-ing all this fancy artwork, if Lake could raise more cash from the sale of these and other assets, we'd have to pay less under the earn-out provision.

Before bringing Lake to the GE Capital board, Nissen and his team hammered out the deal in eight preboard sessions with Gary, Dennis Dammerman, and CFO Jim Parke.

I liked the concept. After we acquired Lake, I was playing golf with Warren Buffett at Seminole when he told me he really loved the transaction we'd just completed in Japan. I always pictured Warren sitting in Omaha, being cagey and smart. I didn't think of him as be-ing all that global, but he has more tentacles out than anyone.

"How do you know about Lake?" I asked.

"That's one of the best deals I've seen," he said. "If you weren't there, I would have taken that one."

Warren was a bit more aggressive when in 2001 GE Capital tried to participate in a restructuring of Finova, a finance com-pany. As a major bondholder of Finova, Warren was trying to do a workout of the troubled concern. I would have liked to have worked with Warren, but he couldn't go with us because he al-ready had a partner in Leucadia. We bid for the company. Warren improved his offer and won Finova.

This time, we were on the outside, looking in.

Gary Wendt was quirky, to say the least. You never knew where he was coming from or what kind of mood he would be in. One thing he didn't like was supervision. Whether it was Larry Bossidy, Bob Wright, or me, any boss drove Gary nuts. Having a boss who said no once in a while really sent him off the wall.

Parting ways with Gary in late 1998 was an inevitable conse-quence of the CEO succession process.

Denis Nayden, president, and Mike Neal, an executive VP,

were ready. Denis, who has worked at GE for 21 years, is a remarkably driven person, a superb underwriter with the brainpower to structure big, complex deals. His best characteristic is his tenacity. He can work a deal until there's no blood left in it. While Gary was the big idea guy, Denis was always the get-it-done guy.

I always thought of Mike Neal as the soul of GE Capital. Unlike most managers there, he didn't come to business with a financial background. A former sales manager in GE Supply, he had to learn the business—and he has. Mike's greatest strength is the way he connects with people. He's well liked and witty, always ready with a quip to defuse the tension in a room.

Jim Parke has been chief financial officer since 1989 and a key part of the growth story. He has great judgment and knows the business backward and forward.

Dennis Dammerman, who had been in or out of the business three times during his career, gave us all comfort that we had the bridge of expertise to the next generation of leadership at GE Capital.

With this succession team in place, Gary and I concluded that he didn't want to work for the next CEO at GE. He had earned and deserved great treatment, and his severance package reflected that. We also got a noncompete.

In June 2000, Conseco, the insurance and financial services company, was in deep yogurt. Their stock had plunged 33 percent in 1998 and 41 percent in 1999, and they needed help fast. The principal Conseco shareholders, Irwin Jacobs and Thomas Lee & Associates, wanted Gary to bail them out. In fact, Gary was the perfect guy for this turnaround assignment.

He could finally be his own boss.

One of my more enjoyable negotiations was getting phone calls from Jacobs, telling me why I should release Gary from our noncompete contract. I got my first call from Jacobs to ask how much I would want to let Gary out.

"Irwin, you must think I have hay between my teeth. You want me to negotiate against myself?"

Irwin asked if $20 million would do it.

"Forget it. I'm not letting him out. He's too smart and too valuable."

Irwin called several times and suggested higher prices, but nothing close to what Gary was worth.

Not long afterward, I got another call from David Harkins, a Conseco board member and interim chairman and CEO. Like Irwin, David was very pleasant, trying to mollify me into a deal, each time modestly upping the ante. After several more phone calls over two days, we worked out an agreement. I agreed to cancel the noncompete in exchange for Conseco buying out all of GE's obligations to Gary and issuing 10.5 million warrants for GE to buy Conseco stock at $5.75 a share—the market price at the time of the agreement.

The nice thing about this deal is that everybody won. Gary found his ideal spot, a place where he's the boss and his brains will work wonders. Conseco got the turnaround in stock price that it wanted, and we got to sit on the sidelines and cheer for Gary again. We had skin in the game and could take the ride with him.

When Gary left, I named Dennis Dammerman the new chairman of GE Capital Services and he was elected a GE vice chairman. We promoted Denis Nayden from chief operating officer to president and CEO. I felt the two of them—both long involved in GE Capital's success—would give us the leadership we needed to take the business into the next century. They kept the team intact, and GE Capital continued to build on its great strengths. In 1999 and 2000, the business acquired $47 billion in assets, including $33 billion outside the United States. GE Capital Services's net income grew 17 percent in 2000 to $5.2 billion, another record year of double-digit earnings growth.

* * *

The numbers don't tell the entire story.

The chart I like best is one that was shown by Jim Colica, the longtime head of risk management, at a GE board meeting in June 2001 (below). It captures the growth and breadth and risk containment of GE Capital Services. While there were many blips in individual deals, the diversity of our business and our philosophy of controlled risk provided consistent growth. In 1980, GE Credit had 10 businesses and $11 billion in assets and was based only in North America. By 2001, GE Capital Services had 24 businesses and $370 billion in assets in 48 countries.

GE Capital Services is the story of melding finance and manufacturing. Combining creative people with the discipline of manufacturing and money really worked.

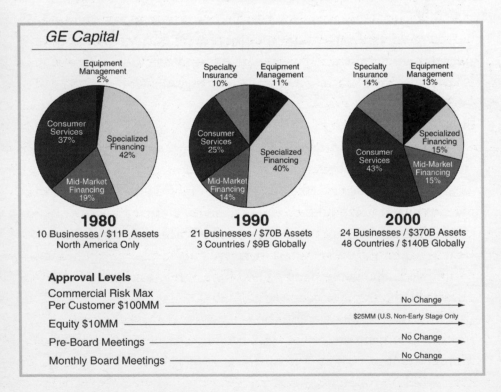

GE Capital

1980
10 Businesses / $11B Assets
North America Only

1990
21 Businesses / $70B Assets
3 Countries / $9B Globally

2000
24 Businesses / $370B Assets
48 Countries / $140B Globally

Approval Levels

Commercial Risk Max
Per Customer $100MM ———————————————— No Change

Equity $10MM ———————————————— $25MM (U.S. Non-Early Stage Only)

Pre-Board Meetings ———————————————— No Change

Monthly Board Meetings ———————————————— No Change

17

Mixing NBC with Light Bulbs

When we announced the acquisition of RCA in December 1985, NBC looked great. The network was a $3 billion business with 8,000 employees that had a lot of juice. It was on the verge of being first in prime-time ratings, first in late night programming, and first in Saturday morning children's programs. Led by *The Cosby Show,* the highest-rated series on TV, we had nine of the 20 most-watched TV programs, including *Family Ties, Cheers,* and *Night Court.*

At the top of my mind was, How do we keep it going? I spent a lot of time getting a handle on the business during the integration meetings prior to completing the acquisition in June 1986.

It didn't take a brain surgeon to realize that NBC president Grant Tinker and his entertainment division head, Brandon Tartikoff, were the two players who made NBC work. They had picked the shows that made NBC No. 1.

Grant was tired of commuting between New York and California and told me the day of the acquisition that he was not going to stay. Grant thought he had a leadership team in place that would keep NBC on top. He assured me everyone, including Brandon, was on board.

Fortunately, I had an old friend in Don Ohlmeyer, an independent TV producer, whom I had known from his association with Ross Johnson of Nabisco. We had played golf in the Nabisco/Dinah Shore Open. As a favor, Don called to tell me that Brandon was getting itchy.

At the age of 30, Brandon had been the youngest president of entertainment at a major network. He played a big role in NBC's hits, including *L.A. Law, Miami Vice, Cheers, The Cosby Show, Family Ties,* and *Seinfeld.*

I didn't want to lose him.

I called and asked Brandon to meet me for dinner at Primavera in New York on May 12. We really hit it off. He was a baseball nut like I am. I assured him things would be better than anything he had seen in the past. A month later, he signed a new four-year contract. Having Brandon heading up our entertainment team gave me confidence that GE could succeed in the network business.

During that summer, I interviewed the candidates on Grant Tinker's staff to find a potential replacement for him as CEO of NBC. They were all good guys. Grant recommended I select Larry Grossman, then head of the news division. However, Larry didn't have the business vision and edge I was looking for.

I told Grant I couldn't go with any of his candidates. I asked him to meet with Bob Wright, who I felt from day one was the ideal person for the job. I arranged to have Grant fly up to Fairfield for dinner with Bob and his wife, Suzanne, who had been a key partner in Bob's success. While Grant and Bob liked each other, nothing was going to dissuade Grant from wanting to promote one of his own guys.

Nevertheless, two months later, in August, I made Bob the CEO of NBC.

The reaction was predictable. People wondered how a "light bulb maker" could run a network. I was confident Bob was right for the job. He had been with me in Plastics, Housewares, and GE Capital, where he was CEO.

Bob had a lot going for him. His three-year stay with Cox Cable gave him the experience to help us expand beyond the traditional network business. His style radiated the management and creative skills to deal with talent. He was also a generous man, who took business friendships to deeper levels, always rushing to the side of someone with a personal crisis.

Bob and I were enjoying the success of NBC's entertainment results, but there were clear signs of trouble ahead. NBC appeared stuck in the past. Entertainment was strong, but cable was steadily eroding its audience. News had been in the red for years and in 1985 was losing about $150 million a year. Typical of the entertainment business, spending seemed extravagant.

NBC wasn't facing any of these realities.

We first tackled the losses in news. That brought us once again to NBC News president Larry Grossman. We were on different planets. He had been in advertising for NBC early in his career and later was president of PBS when Grant recruited him back in 1984.

Early in our relationship, Larry invited Bob and me along with our wives to his home with several of NBC's stars and their spouses—*Nightly News* anchor Tom Brokaw, and *Today* show cohosts Bryant Gumbel and Jane Pauley.

The Grossmans put on a nice evening.

There was only one problem: It was the night of the sixth game of the 1986 World Series, with my Red Sox playing the New York Mets. I had lived and died with the Sox since I was six years old.

This was the night they could finally win their first World Series in my lifetime. NBC was televising the game. I doubted Larry even knew it was World Series time. It turned out to be the saddest night in Red Sox history, when Bill Buckner let a ball dribble between his legs and the Red Sox eventually lost in the tenth inning.

I was shocked by Larry's insensitivity to the game's importance, but he might have felt equally upset that such a "trivial
thing" could consume me. It was an odd night, but it wouldn't be
the last awkward experience between us.

Despite our demands on NBC News to cut losses, Larry stunned
me in November when he showed up for the S-II budget review proposing an increase in spending.

Larry hated this kind of meeting. He thought it was demeaning to talk about costs with some business suits. He operated under
the theory that networks should lose money while covering news
in the name of journalistic integrity. His dismissive attitude only
added to the friction. I was ripped after the meeting.

I stewed on it overnight. In the morning, I decided to confront
the issue and asked Bob to helicopter with him up to a meeting in
Fairfield.

'"Larry, I didn't like the way the meeting went yesterday."

"What didn't you like?" he asked.

"I didn't like your lack of responsiveness to our cost challenges."

I never touched him. We were miles apart. After a couple of
hours, Larry looked at his watch and said, "Jack, I've got to get this
over with. I have to get back to New York because I have dinner
with Chief Justice Burger."

"Larry, if you like having dinners with the Justice Burgers of
the world, you better get this thing in line fast. You work for Bob
Wright. You work for GE. Get your costs in line or move on."

We put up with Larry for 18 months until he left in July 1988.

During his transition out of the company, Larry, like so many
people, ended up on the couch of Ed Scanlon. I met Ed during my
RCA integration meetings. He was RCA's head of human resources, a job that theoretically put him in charge of NBC's human
resources even though NBC thought of itself as pretty independent. I really liked him. Ed was straightforward and street smart. He
was particularly helpful in melding the RCA and GE cultures.

I wanted to keep him but didn't have a position equal to what he had at RCA. I thought he was the best HR person in RCA and felt he would help GE link with NBC. Ed lived in New Jersey, and all he had to do was move down about 40 floors at 30 Rock to take on the top HR job at NBC. The network had the visibility to make the job attractive to Ed.

He accepted.

What a lucky break for us. Ed related well with everyone, from union leaders to the on-air talent and their agents. He could bridge the gap between corporate and creative. Bob and I would work closely with him for the next 15 years.

NBC's success was making it even more difficult for many of the top managers to face the new realities. Bob asked me to share my thoughts at his March 1987 management meeting at the Sheraton Bonaventure Hotel in Fort Lauderdale. It was a little bit like the first Elfun meeting in Westport six years earlier.

Not everyone was pleased.

I spoke before dinner to Bob's top 100 executives and told them NBC had to change and adapt to a new world. "Cable is coming, and it's going to change your life. Too many people in this room are living in the past. There are too many staff people living off the entertainment gravy train, and that train is not going to run forever. You must take charge of your destiny. If you don't, Bob will."

For the A players, this could be a real opportunity.

"For the turkeys," I said, "it will be marginal at best."

Less than 20 percent liked what I had to say. The rest thought I ought to be arrested or committed.

We looked long and hard for Larry Grossman's replacement. Michael Gartner came highly recommended by Tom Brokaw, the anchor of *Nightly News* and the dean of NBC. Michael had great news credentials. He had been the front-page editor of *The Wall*

Street Journal and editor of the *Des Moines Register* and the *Louisville Courier-Journal*. Despite a somewhat quirky personality, he had a reputation for doing a top-notch job editorially and financially. He seemed the perfect fit, and in many ways he was.

Gartner joined in July 1988. His first management change would end up leading to a great NBC success story.

Tim Russert had been serving as Larry Grossman's deputy. Gartner wanted his own guy, so Bob Wright suggested that Russert get an operating job. Tim had been a staff assistant to Governor Mario Cuomo and Senator Pat Moynihan, so he'd never run anything.

Michael offered him the job of bureau chief for NBC's Washington bureau. Tim resisted, worried about leaving the center of power in New York for an outpost. I spent an hour with him, describing why he should jump at the job to manage NBC News's biggest field operation. Here was the chance to show us what he could do as a manager.

Tim's move to Washington was a win for everyone. He hired Katie Couric as a Washington correspondent in 1989. That was the start of what would be an incredible career.

Katie became co-host of the *Today* show in April 1991 and immediately caught on, establishing an easy rapport with the morning audience. The ratings began to climb. Katie has been the show's longest recognizable star. Sadly, Katie had a personal tragedy when her husband, Jay Monahan, died of colon cancer in 1998.

All of America grieved with her. To increase awareness of colon cancer, she even went on national TV to have a colonoscopy, bringing attention to the procedure. During a recent physical, my doctor told me that as a result of Katie's efforts he was booked for the next year.

Meanwhile, Tim Russert's insights from Washington impressed Michael during the daily teleconferences with bureau chiefs for the *Nightly News*. In 1990, Michael put him on *Meet the*

Press as a panelist. A year later, Tim replaced Garrick Utley as host of this show when Garrick moved to New York with the weekend *Today* show.

Tim has been special in so many ways. He's taken *Meet the Press* to first in the ratings, becoming arguably the leading political commentator on TV. His fame has not gone to his head. He's a straight shooter and extremely popular everywhere, particularly in GE. He'll go to any of our plants to give a talk and meet with employees.

I wasn't sure Tim understood our stock option program when I got a notice that his ten-year-old grant was about to expire in three months. I called him and said, "You know, this piece of paper you have in your drawer is worth a lot of money, and it runs out in 90 days."

"Jack, I've got faith," he said. Turned out he had more faith and more smarts than most of us and did very well by holding his options to the last days.

Gartner didn't put just Tim into a position to succeed. He also was responsible for making Jeff Zucker the executive producer of the *Today* show. Jeff had joined Dick Ebersol, the head of NBC Sports, straight out of Harvard as an assistant at the Seoul Olympics. Dick liked him, took him under his wing, and got him involved in the *Today* show. With Ebersol's encouragement, Gartner and Bob decided to make Jeff, at age 26, executive producer of the *Today* show. Their confidence was rewarded a thousand times over with the tremendous success of the *Today* show under Jeff's leadership. Jeff was named president of NBC's entertainment division in 2001. Now we need him to work his magic there.

Everything wasn't perfect under Michael. His unfamiliarity with TV and his management style caused some issues. His courage to attack the NBC News cost structure, while popular with us, didn't win him support there. But Michael suffered his biggest blow when a major controversy broke out over a *Dateline* news feature. On November 17, 1992, *Dateline* ran a segment on allegations about the safety of General Motors pickup trucks. "Waiting to Explode?" depicted GM trucks exploding on impact. On February 8, 1993, GM sued NBC, accusing the network of rigging the crash tests.

An internal investigation found that some of the reported facts were suspect. Although Jane Pauley wasn't involved in the GM story, she agreed to go on *Dateline* and read an on-air apology that brought the issue to closure. That was the ultimate in being a team player. Jane was great to do that, and her well-earned credibility with the audience made a huge difference.

Although Michael Gartner was not directly responsible, he never recovered from the *Dateline* incident. Before resigning on March 2, Michael was in the process of enticing Neal Shapiro from ABC to become executive producer of *Dateline*. Neal is creative, genuine in every way, and deservedly one of the most popular figures at NBC. He not only restored the show's credibility, he expanded *Dateline* into three to four prime-time hours every week. The show became a huge success for NBC, and so did Neal. In 2001 he became president of NBC News.

After the *Dateline* incident, Bob interviewed just about everybody in the news business to replace Gartner. Again, Tom Brokaw played a big role. Tom's reputation made him the public face of NBC News. He's been a mentor to many young newspeople over a 30-year career.

Tireless and very demanding of himself, Tom has been a great help to Bob, who has used his counsel on almost every major decision at NBC News. After Bob interviewed all the obvious candidates, it was Tom who suggested that Bob talk to Andy Lack, then an executive producer at CBS.

Andy and Bob had a long dinner at the Dorset Hotel, where Andy made a big impression. After this dinner, Bob wanted me to meet him, and I did a couple of days later.

I think I've told everyone that Andy was the most exciting person I ever interviewed for a job. He was totally different from any of the news leaders I had met. He was humorous, spontaneous, filled with energy, and totally comfortable with himself— traits by now you know I find appealing.

He charmed the hell out of me.

Twenty minutes into the conversation, I turned to Bob and said, "What are we waiting for?"

"Let's do it," Bob said.

I looked at Andy and asked, "Why aren't you jumping up and down? This is a huge job we're offering you."

He responded, "After all the stuff I heard about you guys, I'm wondering whether I'd get the resources to get news back on its feet."

We both assured him he'd get what he needed to turn around the news operation.

Andy called Bob on Sunday and took the job. He quit CBS on Monday morning and joined us in early April 1993.

Meanwhile, Bob was moving ahead on cable.

When we bought NBC, the network's only cable asset was a one-third financial interest in the Arts & Entertainment channel. Bob was desperate to enter the cable business in a big way. The window was closing. In early 1987, he hired Tom Rogers, who had spent several years on the Hill working on telecommunications policy as a congressional aide to Representative Tim Wirth. Bob put Tom in charge of expanding NBC's cable efforts. He had great contacts in the industry and was a terrific negotiator and a brilliant strategist.

Tom and Bob went first to Chuck Dolan, a pioneer of the cable TV business. Chuck had founded Cablevision Systems in Long Island, a company that became one of the largest U.S. cable operators. Chuck launched Bravo, was co-founder of HBO, and had developed a group of other cable properties. Bob knew Chuck and his family and had almost left Cox in the early 1980s to become president of Cablevision.

They struck a partnership in January 1989, with NBC buying half of Chuck's Rainbow Properties for $140 million. The deal gave us interests in Bravo, American Movie Classics, Sports Channel USA, and regional sports services across the United States. NBC also would buy stakes in Court TV, the Independent Film Channel, the History Channel, and Romance Classics.

Bob's deal with Chuck let either side bring to the partnership any new ideas we wanted to develop from scratch. The first big one was CNBC, the business news network. I loved the idea from the start. I thought there was an opportunity for a business channel, and unlike entertainment and sports, business programming wouldn't involve any rights fees.

The only other competitor at the time was Financial News Network (FNN), and it was losing money. Chuck agreed to go into CNBC with us on a 50/50 basis, and CNBC went on the air in April 1989.

By 1991, our cumulative losses were nearly $60 million. Business news was not taking off. FNN went into bankruptcy in January. At that time, FNN had access to 32 million homes. CNBC had 20 million subscribers. Chuck had no interest in going after FNN in bankruptcy.

He'd had enough. Chuck withdrew his 50 percent ownership of CNBC, and we went after FNN alone.

We thought we could get it for $50 million. We were all surprised when the opening bid from Westinghouse and Dow Jones was $60 million. The bidding reached $150 million when Bob and Tom Rogers came back and said they needed another $5 million. Silly as it now seems, the GE guys, including myself, agonized over our bid because it was three times our preliminary evaluation of the deal. Fortunately, we badly wanted a financial news network, and the extra $5 million closed the deal.

The deal more than doubled our distribution. We retained the best FNN talent, including Ron Insana and Sue Herera, who today co-anchor our top-rated *Business Center* news program, and Bill Griffeth, who hosts *Power Lunch*.

On the entertainment side, things weren't going as well.

From 1988 to 1992, we introduced dozens of shows that didn't click. I wasn't worth a nickel here. After acquiring NBC, I went to Hollywood once to look at the pilots for the new prime-time schedule.

You ought to hear the presentations and the wild predictions of success for each pilot. Every show has a shot: a great producer, sensational stars, an Emmy-winning this or that. Every comedy is *Seinfeld* reincarnated and every drama is *ER*.

Thank God there are so many optimists in the business.

Facts are, I've never seen anyone predict a sure thing. Most of the shows bomb. Something like one in ten that come out of development make it on the air, and you're lucky if one in five of those are successful. The odds of getting a series that really clicks, like *Seinfeld, Frasier,* or *Friends,* is something like 1 in 1,000.

People would always say to me, "How can you own NBC? You don't know anything about dramas or comedies."

That's true, but I can't build a jet engine or a turbine, either. My job at GE was to deal with resources—people and dollars. I offered as much (or as little) help to our aircraft engine design engineers as I offered to the people picking shows in Hollywood.

We weren't doing too well out there. Most of the past NBC hits had run out of gas. Brandon Tartikoff left NBC to run Paramount in 1991. Bob named Brandon's deputy, Warren Littlefield, as president of entertainment. Warren inherited a difficult situation. We didn't have any new shows, and the TV advertising market fell into its worst slump in two decades. NBC's profits fell from a peak of $603 million in 1989 to $204 million in 1992.

That year we had to make a difficult decision. We were in

Boca in 1992 at the time of the decision on who should take over *The Tonight Show* from Johnny Carson. This was a terrible dilemma because both Jay Leno and David Letterman were on our network at the time.

Close to midnight, CFO Dennis Dammerman and I walked into a conference room in the middle of a hot discussion. Most of the East Coast guys wanted Letterman. The West Coast guys, hooked up by videoconference, favored Leno. Bob wanted to keep both of them. He feared that picking one would risk a defection by the other to CBS, which had nothing going for it on late night. Dennis and I sat in the back of the room, listening to the debate, when Bob turned to us.

"What do you guys think?"

"You know I'm not qualified to pick either one," I said. "But if I were you, I would do this: I'd go for GE values. You like Leno's values. He's good for the affiliates. He's a good human being. The American public will find out that's true."

We got beat up over the Leno decision. Letterman left us for CBS and pulled ahead in the early going.

The critics were everywhere, and they were joined by Grant Tinker. I liked Grant and thought I had a good relationship with him. In 1994, he came out with a book that blamed Bob and me for the decline.

He called my decision to appoint Bob head of the network a "kamikaze assignment." He said our decision to replace Johnny Carson with Jay Leno was dead wrong. He claimed we overpaid for FNN, and he placed CNBC in the dead-air category.

"Other than its stock ticker, CNBC has failed to develop any discernible persona," wrote Tinker in his book. "I've wondered whether Jack ever watches it and what he thinks of it."

The venom in Grant's comments surprised me until I noticed that his book was co-authored by Bud Rukeyser. Bud was a former public relations head of NBC who had left on less than amicable terms in the spring of 1988.

In the middle of the slump, we added to our problems. We partnered with Chuck Dolan to do a cable Triplecast of the 1992 Summer Olympics in Barcelona. For an extra $125, cable subscribers could have three channels to watch over 1,000 hours of live and taped coverage without commercials.

It was a flop.

We had hoped to sign up as many as 3 million of the 40 million homes that could receive the offer. Instead, we drew about 250,000 viewers. We took a real beating—in the media and financially. We were looking at a $100 million loss on the Triplecast alone. While Bob was confident Chuck would honor his commitments, our accountants worried that we'd get stuck for the majority of it, even though Dolan was our 50/50 partner.

Chuck is as tough a negotiator as they come. He is also as honorable a guy as you'll meet. In November we received a check from him for $50 million to cover his share of the Triplecast losses.

Triplecast was just another problem in a troubled time.

From 1992 until 1994, we spent a lot of time struggling with all these issues and were searching for a solution. That led to talks with lots of players, including Paramount, Disney, Time Warner, Viacom, and Sony. We weren't looking for cash. We were trying to put things together to make NBC a bigger and stronger player. We came closest with Disney and Paramount.

Dennis Dammerman, our advisers, and I had a dinner meeting with Disney CEO Michael Eisner and a team from Disney one evening during the summer of 1994. We came to a tentative understanding that Disney would buy 49 percent of NBC but would have operating control while we retained majority ownership. My main condition was that Bob Wright would be the CEO of the combined Disney TV production studios and NBC's operations.

Michael liked it, and Dennis and I were thrilled.

By morning, though, Michael had changed his mind and didn't want to do the deal. We had several other serious discussions, including some with Marty Davis of Paramount, that ended up the same way. With all these discussions going on, the press naturally got hold of it. Speculation about GE's plans for NBC ran rampant throughout 1994.

Bob Nelson, Dennis, and I prepared an analysis on why we thought staying in the network business made sense long-term. The value of the property at the time was somewhere in the $4 billion to $5 billion range. We were confident we could create a far more valuable asset with very limited downside. I took the analysis to the board in October 1994, recommending that we stay in the business.

It was the only time I ever polled every board member, one by one, for a show of support for a decision. They agreed unanimously to stick with NBC, and we went public with our commitment to the network.

Meanwhile, Warren Littlefield was having success developing new shows. Bob decided to give Warren more support and hired as head of West Coast operations Don Ohlmeyer, the old friend who had tipped me off to Tartikoff's itchiness. Warren and Don were a perfect match. Warren was deep into the programming details. Don, a blunt and irreverent six-foot-three bear of a guy, had a knack for promotion. He was running his own successful production company, and we actually bought it to get him. His larger-than-life presence helped bring back a sense of pride to our Burbank Studios. *Seinfeld* and *Mad About You*—two shows begun under the earlier administration—were already catching on.

Within 18 months of their collaboration, under Don's leadership, the two of them launched *Frasier, Friends,* and *ER.* A turnaround was under way.

News was also enjoying success under Andy Lack. When he arrived in April 1993, we were a distant three out of three. None of our news programs was No. 1—*Today, Nightly News,* or *Dateline.* There were even suggestions that we give back the second hour of the *Today* show to our affiliates because the show's ratings were so weak.

Within two months of joining us as president of news, Andy was pitching at a business review what some of his colleagues believed was a crazy idea. He wanted to move the *Today* show out of its old third-floor studio in the GE building and build a new studio at street level in Rockefeller Center.

He thought this could really change the game.

"We could use Katie Couric and Bryant Gumbel in ways to get some buzz and engage the audience," said Andy. "This is not a cheap idea. It will cost $15 million. If it bombs, it will be a big bomb."

"No! No! No!" I shouted. "It's not going to bomb. It's a great idea. Let's do it!

"Dennis," I said, "you can find 15 million bucks."

After moving into the new studio 18 months later in the fall of 1994, *Today* began to take off. The massive windows that allowed people to peer into the studio and the opportunity to take the show into Rock Center made *Today* a New York City tourist attraction. On Friday mornings, *Today*'s live outdoor concerts in the plaza often attract thousands of people.

On the other hand, Bryant Gumbel—after 15 years with the *Today* show—was getting tired of the morning drill. He and his agent made it clear to Andy that they wanted to try something new. Andy and Bob started thinking about replacements. A solution was in our backyard.

Bill Bolster, the president of WNBC, NBC's New York station, had been facing the challenge of fixing the 5-to-7 morning show that preceded the *Today* show. He had watched Matt Lauer a few years earlier hosting an interview show on Channel 9 in New York.

Since then, Matt's career had been going nowhere. In fact, one morning, Matt spotted a "Help Wanted" sign on the back of a truck of a tree trimming firm. He called and left a message for the job. When Bill Bolster telephoned the next day, Matt thought the call was from the landscaper. Instead, it was Bolster with a better offer—a much better offer!

He hired Matt to co-anchor WNBC's early morning news.

Shortly after joining the station in late 1992, I watched him at 6:30 A.M. on WNBC after starting the morning on the treadmill with CNBC. Like Bill, I thought Matt filled the screen. He was unassuming yet charismatic, and he looked like a potential replacement for Bryant.

Within a year, my campaign began.

I'd call Andy endlessly, acting as Matt's best agent. Bolster had an ally.

"What do you think of Matt Lauer?"

"He's great," Andy said.

"When are you going to give him the job?"

"He needs a little more seasoning."

"Oh . . . come on! Let's go!"

Today's executive producer, Jeff Zucker, tried Matt out as a news reader in 1994, and gradually Matt began subbing when Bryant was out on vacation. Everyone liked his style.

CBS took Bryant out of the morning business with a great offer for his own prime-time show. We were all happy for Bryant.

Matt took over for him in early 1997. Katie Couric and Matt turned out to be a great match, instantly captivating the morning audience.

Today, which became the No. 1 morning show in 1996, widened the gap between itself and No. 2 ABC's *Good Morning America*. The following year, Tom Brokaw made *Nightly News* No. 1, a position it still holds. *Dateline* executive producer Neal Shapiro, with co-anchors Jane Pauley and Stone Phillips, turned around our prime-time magazine show after the GM debacle.

Andy really had things working at NBC News.

The person who got CNBC going was Roger Ailes, a former political adviser to President George Bush and executive producer of Rush Limbaugh's TV show. Bob found Roger and hired him as CEO of CNBC in August 1993. I was an instant fan. Roger was an edgy and excitable guy, full of opinions. He created a distinctive look for CNBC, plotted its prime-time programming, and promoted personalities like Chris Matthews. Chris brings energy to the coverage of Washington mishaps. Roger also created from scratch a "talking heads" network called America's Talking.

He built CNBC's operating profits from $9 million in 1993 to $50 million in 1995. The creation of MSNBC, our joint venture with Microsoft, indirectly drove Roger out of the company. He didn't like our decision to fold his baby, America's Talking, into MSNBC. I hated losing Roger when he left in January 1996 to start up Fox News Channel, which he has made into a real success.

We replaced Roger with Bill Bolster, who had built WNBC to a No. 1 position in New York. Bill put on the CNBC screen a real-time ticker for stock market prices and treated our business coverage as a fast-paced sports event. He expanded the "pregame show" for the stock market with a three-hour block of *Squawk Box*.

Squawk Box has developed an ensemble of characters: Mark Haines, Joe Kernen, and David Faber. Their spontaneous banter and sharp insights rev up the market before it opens. The show's popularity has just about every CEO in America watching.

The "game" is reported, often from the "field" or trading floor, by CNBC's first real celebrity, Maria Bartiromo, whose inside scoops earned her the reputation of being one of the best financial journalists in the country.

The "postgame" show, *Business Center,* hosted by Ron Insana and Sue Herera, is like ESPN's *Sports Center.* They've made it the most authoritative financial news program on television.

As he was shaping the day's programming, I pestered Bill constantly. I sent him clips of the same business stories out of *The Wall Street Journal* and the *New York Post*, urging him to adopt the *Post*'s more blunt and entertaining approach.

After all, business is a game. Bill and his team, led by Bruno Cohen, former news director at NBC TV in New York, have, in fact, captured the sport of it.

CNBC's profits over the next five years rose to $290 million in 2000, making it one of the most profitable assets in cable television.

By 1996, NBC had turned around. Operating profits surpassed $1 billion for the first time. *ER* had become the No. 1 drama series on TV. *Seinfeld* was the No. 1 sit-com. CNBC was profitable and growing rapidly. America agreed that Jay Leno was the best late night host as *The Tonight Show* won the late night battle with CBS's David Letterman.

Late in 1995, Bob Wright, aware that Microsoft was thinking of making an investment in CNN, started discussions with them about a possible tie-up. We had always wanted to develop a cable news channel, but it was very expensive to do from scratch. At an NBC strategy review session in October 1995, Bob described his ongoing negotiations with Microsoft.

We were having trouble figuring out the right relationship with Microsoft. One possibility was a licensing arrangement. I jumped up and went to an easel and led a discussion of all the alternatives, eventually drawing on a flip chart a partnership structure similar to that of many previous GE deals. In this structure, we'd have a couple of 50/50 joint ventures: one on the cable side with NBC in control, and another on the Internet side with Microsoft in control.

Tom Rogers and Bob then began negotiating this concept with the Microsoft team. Microsoft was primarily interested in using our news-gathering operation and developing an on-line news channel. Cable was secondary, which made the negotiations more difficult. The evening before a December 1995 press conference to announce the partnership, there were still a number of sticking points.

Tom and his team had been up all night, trying to close the deal. Bill Gates's concern about cable was the last open issue.

By 7 A.M., just two hours before a major press conference at NBC's New York studios, the deal still wasn't done.

The announcement was scheduled to be a grand affair, with Bill hooked up by satellite from Hong Kong and Tom Brokaw in Germany. To close the deal, Bob Wright asked me to intervene with Gates.

I called him. Bill was concerned that he could get stuck with major losses in cable.

"Jack," Bill asked, "do you believe the cable forecasts?"

"I think cable's a no-brainer," I replied. "You're the guy who has the tough job with the on-line part. I don't have any doubt we'll make cable work."

I gave Bill some guarantees on cable performance to protect Microsoft from major losses if we couldn't get the channel into more homes.

"That's enough for me," he replied.

About 40 minutes before the press conference, Bill Gates and I agreed. MSNBC turned into the black in 2000 and MSN became the No. 1 news Internet site.

MSNBC also gave NBC the chance to showcase Brian Williams. Brian had joined the network in 1993 and was backing up Tom Brokaw on *Nightly News* and doing weekend anchoring. Andy Lack gave him his own show, *The News with Brian Williams*.

While you don't see it much on the air, Brian can be one of the funniest guys you'd ever meet. I actually think he's so talented that, if he wasn't already committed as a news anchor, he could have his own late night show.

Bob and Tom Rogers continued looking for Internet opportunities and made a number of dot.com investments, later merging most of them into a new public company called NBCi. Like so many other dot.coms at the time, NBCi focused too much on advertising revenues. When the Internet ad market fell apart in early 2000, its business model couldn't make it. In 2001, we repurchased NBCi and began using it as a portal to promote the rest of NBC.

Toward the end of 1997, Bob and I got some bad news. Jerry Seinfeld, star of television's hottest prime-time sit-com, wanted to call it quits. Jerry wasn't only America's favorite comic, he was also mine. At a Sunday brunch in Bob's New York apartment in December 1997, we tried to convince Jerry to stay on the air for one more season.

A year earlier, we had gone through the same drill and convinced Seinfeld to stay on through the 1997 season. That time, Bob called me down to his office to see if I could help make the sale. It was a quirky meeting. To convince Jerry to stay, we had given him a package of stock options and restricted stock. Jerry asked me to take him through what they meant. It was a priceless moment as I pretended to give a finance lesson to someone who could play dumb as a fox as well as he could get a laugh.

We talked him into returning then—now he wanted out again, before the 1998 season. This time, Jerry brought along two wonderful friends, George Shapiro and Howard West, who could have come out of Central Casting as oldtime Hollywood agents. Bob made a great presentation, a typical GE pitch with charts, to show that Jerry would be the only television star who left while his series was still growing. No show in the history of TV, not even Milton Berle's, was growing its audience in its ninth year.

Jerry wanted to go out on top. Bob argued that Jerry hadn't even seen the peak. It was a great pitch—and we offered Jerry $100 million in GE stock to stay just one more year.

Bob and I thought we had made the sale. That feeling lasted about ten days. On Christmas Eve, I got a phone call in Florida from Jerry in Burbank.

"Jack," he said, "this is a very hard decision for me, and I hate to disappoint you."

I felt awful. I knew we had lost him.

"Jack, it's Christmas Eve and I'm in my cubicle. Everyone else has gone off to their families, and I'm here writing a show. I can't do it another year, Jack. I can't."

"I wish you'd made a different decision," I said.

I thanked him for all that he had done for us. I respected his choice. He wanted to go out on top, and he did.

We not only lost Jerry, we also "lost" the NFL. After televising pro football since 1965, we lost the broadcast rights to the National Football League in early 1998.

Passing on this was an easy decision. There was no one at NBC, even in sports, who wanted to touch the numbers needed to get the rights.

Of course, my favorite paper, the *New York Post*, always has great fun with things like this. They put a mug shot on the front page, showing me dropping the ball.

Yet this wasn't a fumble. We passed on that $4 billion eight-year deal because the numbers were nuts.

Losing the NFL led to our effort to launch in 2001 a new football league, the XFL (for "Extreme Football"), with Vince McMahon, head of the World Wrestling Federation. It turned out to be a bomb, and I was right in the middle of it. If you screw up in another business, you can generally hide it—but not on TV.

Everybody's always watching, especially the critics.

I was as big a supporter of the XFL as anyone in the company. We had nothing going on Saturday nights. Vince McMahon had flair and made a big success with the WWF. Minnesota governor Jesse Ventura added drama as an announcer. We launched the new league with eight teams in some key markets.

Our problem was we could never decide whether the XFL was entertainment or football. The dilemma began when they brought the Vegas bookies to the training camps. The bookies didn't want the crazy rules the XFL had proposed because that made it more difficult to put odds on the games. Our sports division thought we needed the credibility and publicity the betting lines would provide. That closed the door to doing some things that might have made the XFL far more entertaining.

The first game got off to a big ratings start, but even then we lost audience during the long game. The sportswriters tore us apart. The only coverage the league got was opinion pieces on how the XFL threatened the sanctity of professional football.

The fans didn't like either the entertainment or the football. The death watch began. Nobody watched the games. Everyone watched our failure.

After a single 12-week season, we called it quits. The XFL turned out to be a rock. It cost us $60 million, the equivalent of a couple of failed sit-coms—and eight out of ten of those don't make it. While it wasn't pleasant, it wasn't a large financial hit. Taking those swings is one of the big benefits of GE's size. You don't have to connect all the time.

Although the XFL failed, almost everything else Dick Ebersol was involved with was a success. Dick, who joined in early 1989, was the protégé of Roone Arledge, the pioneer of *Monday Night Football* and Olympics coverage. Dick succeeded Roone as the master of televised sports.

In 1995, Dick pulled off the ultimate coup in sports programming. For the first time in 20 years, the International Olympics Committee agreed to give NBC broadcast rights without competitive bidding. NBC laid the groundwork for Dick's agreement, televising the Summer Olympics in Seoul in 1988, Barcelona in 1992, and Atlanta in 1996.

Toward the end of July 1995, Bob and Dick called me with a novel proposal. Dick and his team wanted to make an unprecedented offer to the Olympics committee to acquire both the 2000 Sydney and the 2002 Salt Lake City Olympics. By going for two games instead of one, Dick believed, they could get both games and eliminate the usual bidding process.

They wanted to move quickly. To get approval, Dick arranged a conference call with Bob on a boat off the Nantucket coast, while Dennis Dammerman joined us from a cabin in Maine, and I participated from my summer house in Nantucket.

The price was steep: $1.2 billion.

"Dick, what's the worst-case scenario here?" I asked.

"We could lose $100 million," he replied.

We all agreed to go for it. Dick immediately took the GE jet to Sweden to meet with Juan Antonio Samaranch, president of the International Olympics Committee, and then flew to Montreal to meet with Dick Pound, the committee's head of TV rights.

Within 72 hours, he had locked up both Olympics.

A few days later, Dick was thinking about doing more. By early December 1995, four months later, we had gained the rights to broadcast three more Olympics—in Athens, in Torino, and for the 2008 games—for $2.3 billion.

The Olympics deal has been a home run for both the network and particularly its cable properties. Carrying the Olympics on our two major cable properties allowed David Zaslav, head of cable distribution, to significantly extend the duration of the carriage and the reach of CNBC and MSNBC into millions of homes. Today, CNBC has commitments to be in over 80 million homes, and MSNBC, which had fewer than 25 million subs in 1995, will be in over 70 million homes in 2002.

Over the years, NBC has proved an enormous benefit to GE.

We've profited from its financial results and from the glitter that makes most employees proud to wear a T-shirt with the NBC logo. Bob's vision to see NBC as more than just a network was a winner. The network audience has continued to erode, making his bets on cable television look even better. CNBC is the leader in financial news, and MSNBC is the top-rated cable news network on a 24-hour basis among 25 to 54-year-old viewers. Even though NBC has fallen to third place in household ratings as I'm writing this book, it's still the leading network among people 18 to 49, the most important demographic group for advertisers.

Through it all, Bob Wright has become one of the longest-serving network heads in TV history. He has proved that a "light bulb maker" can make it big in the TV business.

18

When to Fight, When to Fold

One of my strongest childhood memories is of climbing the stairs to my parents' second-floor flat in Salem, Massachusetts, and hearing my mother crying. I was only nine years old in 1945. I had never heard my mother cry before. When I walked through the doorway, she was standing over an ironing board in the kitchen, pressing my father's shirts. Tears were streaming down her face.

"Oh, God," she said. "Franklin Roosevelt has died."

I was stunned. I didn't know why the president's death would cause my mother such heartache. I didn't understand it at all. Yet I felt some of the same feelings when John Kennedy was assassinated 18 years later, and I was glued to the TV set.

My mother's reaction to Roosevelt's death came from her heartfelt belief that he had saved our country and our democracy. She put her faith in him and our government. So did my father. Both of them believed that the government served the will of the people, protected its citizens, and always did what was right.

For many years, I shared my parents' faith, but that faith has been severely tested on a number of occasions. I've seen government up close, both right and wrong, both good and almost evil, from honest, hardworking public servants to politically motivated, devious self-promoters.

I'd seen many small instances of bad government in action, but my first big case didn't come until 1992.

I was in the middle of a board meeting in Florence, South Carolina, when our general counsel, Ben Heineman, pulled me aside. He said that *The Wall Street Journal* was doing a story for the next day, April 22, on a lawsuit filed by Ed Russell, a vice president who had been fired in November.

This was no ordinary suit for wrongful discharge. Russell, who had run our industrial diamonds business in Ohio, accused us of conspiring with De Beers of South Africa to fix diamond prices. He claimed that he was fired because he complained about a meeting his boss, Glen Hiner, had with De Beers to supposedly fix these prices.

I left the board meeting that afternoon and huddled with Ben and Joyce Hergenhan, our vice president of public relations. I knew Russell wasn't telling the truth. For one thing, Glen Hiner, head of GE plastics, had impeccable integrity. For another, Russell had been fired for performance reasons. I knew, because at one crucial point, I had written his direct boss, telling him Russell had to go—something that even Russell didn't know.

I had met him shortly after he joined GE in 1974 as a strategic planner. He moved up through our lighting business and in 1985 became general manager of GE Superabrasives, the name of our industrial diamond business. I knew that business well because I oversaw it from Pittsfield in the early 1970s. At first, Russell did well in the job, increasing revenues and profits nicely. But in 1990, he hit a wall. Profits dropped to $57 million, from $70 million the year before.

Over the course of 1991, Russell's problems continued. His numbers didn't improve, and he had difficulty explaining the situation in a series of reviews with his boss, Glen Hiner, the head of our plastics business. I was troubled by it. I had been a supporter of Russell's for many years and approved his promotion to general manager of superabrasives in the first place.

However, in September, Hiner and I had what would be our last review with Russell in Pittsfield. He was totally unable to answer my questions. At one point, he said he wasn't prepared to discuss some straightforward issues in his business because he didn't think that was the purpose of the meeting. My financial analyst, Bob Nelson, was in the session with me and felt as surprised as I was by Russell's response.

The next day, I scribbled a note to Glen Hiner summarizing the meeting. In it, I included the observation that Russell "made a fool of himself in July and yesterday he appeared totally out of it. Bottom line, Russell has to go" (see below).

The next month, Hiner called him back to Pittsfield and on November 11 fired him.

Now, Russell had filed a lawsuit making all kinds of crazy claims, accusing Hiner of wrongdoing. Before drafting a response to it, I remembered the note I had sent Hiner and had it faxed to me in Florence. Luckily, my note made clear that Russell was fired for performance reasons and that I did it—not Hiner, who was the target of Russell's made-up charges.

Ben, Joyce, and I drafted a statement for the *Journal* and other

> Russell has to go. He made a fool of himself in July and yesterday he appeared totally out of it. Imagine a presentation to you and I and he had _no_ numbers and more importantly knew none. I don't want to fool with this fellow much longer but will respect your end of year type timing

reporters. We made it clear that Russell was removed for "performance shortcomings" and that he had many conversations with GE people, trying to get a better severance package. Russell never brought up any antitrust issues in those talks. He was a bitter employee who had been canned.

The next day's stories contained even worse news: Russell had gotten the Justice Department to open a criminal investigation into his price-fixing allegations. When a *Journal* reporter asked me about it after the meeting, I called it "pure nonsense." We began our own investigation. We called in lawyers from Arnold & Porter and Dan Webb, a litigator with Winston & Strawn, to look into the charges.

It didn't take much longer than six weeks for the outside lawyers to conclude that Russell wasn't telling the truth. Now we had to convince the Justice Department. We shared with them the results of the investigation and put together a "white paper" that documented 12 outright misrepresentations Russell had told in his depositions in the case.

It fell on deaf ears.

In February 1994, Ben Heineman and I went to Washington to meet with an assistant attorney general to make our case. She couldn't have cared less about our arguments. She was out to get an indictment, and nothing was going to get in her way. To avoid an indictment for price-fixing, she asked us to plead guilty to a felony and pay a fine.

There was no way I was going to do that. We hadn't done anything wrong. The government's case was built on a bunch of lies. We had to fight this all the way.

A grand jury indictment is usually routine when the government requests it. Three days after our meeting in Washington, she got her indictment against us and De Beers for allegedly conspiring to fix prices. She didn't trust her own lieutenants, so she hired an outside lawyer at the government's expense.

Eight months later, on October 25, the trial started in a federal court in Columbus, Ohio. Dan Webb led the litigation team, with great support from Bill Baer of Arnold & Porter and Jeff Kindler, GE's inside litigation chief.

The team did such a good job destroying the government's case that we never had to present our evidence.

On December 5, after listening to all the government's evidence, Judge George Smith threw out the entire case. "The government's conspiracy theory falls apart completely," he said. "The government's arguments are without merit. . . . Even when the evidence is viewed in the light most favorable to the government, no rational trier of fact" could find GE guilty.

The clear victory in the Russell case justified fighting for what we knew was right. The government had no case, just a knee-jerk dislike of a big company. Judges almost never dismiss a criminal antitrust case in the middle of a trial—before a defendant has even presented its side. But that's what happened here. The fight took us three years, three years of bad press every time it was mentioned. Only the facts told us we were right.

This was government at its worst. They got the FBI to wire a dismissed employee and got nothing. They spent a great amount of time chasing nothing. They hired an expensive outside gun to try the case—all so some government types could make names for themselves.

Of course, we're not perfect. In a completely different case a year earlier, the government had been right.

This one started with Ben as well, when he called me on a Saturday afternoon at home in December 1990.

"You're not going to believe this," he said, "but we have an employee who has a joint Swiss bank account with an Israeli air force general."

I couldn't believe my ears. If there was one thing I preached every day at GE, it was integrity. It was our No. 1 value. Nothing came before it. We never had a corporate meeting where I didn't emphasize integrity in my closing remarks.

When Ben called me at home that Saturday, we knew only what had been reported in the Israeli newspapers and picked up by a GE employee over there. The press reported that an employee of our aircraft engine business, Herbert Steindler, had conspired with Air Force General Rami Dotan in a scheme to divert money from major contracts to supply GE engines for Israeli F-16 warplanes.

By the time this mess was over, 19 months and many headlines later, we had to discipline 21 GE executives, managers, and employees, pay the U.S. government $69 million in criminal fines and civil penalties, and testify before a congressional committee. The head of our aircraft engine business had to stand up in federal court to plead guilty for the company, and a GE vice chairman spent a week in Washington getting our engine business off suspension.

I nearly choked when I heard Ben's news. Imagine having a crook on your payroll. Steindler was suspended immediately, and when he refused to cooperate with our internal investigation, he was fired in March. We hired a group of outside lawyers from Wilmer, Cutler and Pickering to help a GE audit team do an investigation. For most of the next year, they virtually lived in Cincinnati, the home of our aircraft engine business. Working with our audit staff, they traced every process of the contracts and talked to every participant. Over a nine-month period, they reviewed 350,000 pages of documents and interviewed more than 100 witnesses.

It turned out that Dotan, with Steindler's help, had set up a fake New Jersey subcontractor. A close friend of Steindler's owned the firm, and they used it to divert about $11 million to the joint Swiss bank accounts owned by Dotan and Steindler. Dotan was a demanding and intimidating customer. As early as 1987, some employees began raising questions about certain aspects of Dotan's transactions. But the air force general portrayed himself as a great patriot in Israel who was simply cutting through red tape, and Steindler convinced his superiors there was nothing to be concerned about.

Only one employee knowingly violated our policies for direct financial gain: Steindler. Throwing him overboard was easy. The problem was that 20 other GE employees who didn't gain a cent were not sensitive to the scheme. Those 20 people had worked for GE for a total of 325 years. Some of them had been employees their entire professional lives, as long as 37 years. Many had impressive track records and superb performance reviews. Two of them were corporate officers and good friends of Brian Rowe's, head of our aircraft engine business.

Brian was a larger-than-life figure in the aircraft industry, a pioneer who still enjoyed designing engines. Brian loved his guys. He was having a difficult time deciding what to do with them. Brian's indecision was understandable. With the exception of Steindler, who ended up going to jail, most of the other people caught up in this were guilty of omission—not commission. None of them benefited personally from the scheme. They were outsmarted, or just sloppy, or they ignored warning signals.

Beyond Steindler, everyone else's involvement was less clear. That made the disciplinary case very difficult for everyone—but especially so for Brian.

The only good thing that came out of it was that I found Bill Conaty. Bill, who would later become head of human resources for all of GE, had just taken over the HR job at aircraft engines. He bore the brunt of the disciplinary action, making sure that everyone was treated as fairly as possible under the circumstances. All the employees caught up in this mess received detailed letters outlining our "concerns" or "allegations" based on our internal investigation. They had the opportunity to give their side of the story, with the help of lawyers they hired—at our expense. Bill came back with disciplinary recommendations for each employee.

At one point during a two-month period, Bill, Brian, Ben, and I were on the phone nearly every day.

Frankly, it was easier for Ben and me sitting in Fairfield to be tough disciplinarians than for poor Brian, whose longtime friends were involved. Fortunately, all three of us had great respect for Bill, and he was able to bridge any differences that existed among us.

Ultimately we fired or asked for the resignations of 11 of the 21 people involved. Six other employees were demoted, and the remaining four were reprimanded. One officer had to be demoted, and the other one resigned.

It sent a clear message through the company: Sergeants weren't going to be shot while generals and colonels could continue on as if nothing happened. We wanted our managers to know that if an integrity violation occurred on their watch, it was their responsibility. That chiefs got shot for being indifferent to integrity was a huge event in GE.

In many ways, it was a big learning experience for me—both internally in terms of discipline and externally with Washington and the media. Outside GE, the idea began to surface that it was the pressure of competition and the drive for profits that made people cheat. Some didn't want to see it for what it was—an isolated violation in a company with hot lines, ombudsmen, voluntary disclosure policies, and constant leadership emphasis on integrity.

I went to Washington in July 1992 to testify before a House subcommittee chaired by U.S. Representative John Dingle. I found Dingle tough, but honest and fair. It was all I could ask for. We had settled with the Justice Department, agreeing to pay $69 million, a week before my appearance on the Hill.

Testifying was not the most pleasant thing I ever did. But I felt strongly about my message—and I wanted to deliver it in person. I told the committee, "Excellence and competitiveness aren't incompatible with honesty and integrity."

I added, "Mr. Chairman, we have an employee population that would rank with St. Paul or Tampa if it were an American city. We have no police force, no jails. We must rely on the integrity of our people as our first defense. Unfortunately, that system wasn't good enough in this case. But I take great pride that 99.99 percent of our 275,000 people get up every morning all over the world and compete like hell with absolute integrity. They don't need a policeman, or a judge. They only need their conscience as they face the mirror each morning.

"They see no conflict between taking on the world's best, every day, all over the globe, giving 110 percent and more—to compete and win and grow—and at the same time maintaining an instinctive, unbendable commitment to absolute integrity in everything we do."

I got a fair hearing that day. Despite the ugliness of why I was there, I felt very good about making the point, and I feel even more strongly today that integrity must be the foundation for competitiveness.

One of the most frustrating issues I've had to deal with for 25 years—20 as CEO—was PCBs (polychlorinated biphenyls).

PCBs, a liquid chemical, were used prior to 1977 as an insulating fluid for electrical products to prevent fires. They became the focal point of a massive Hudson River dredging proposal by the Environmental Protection Agency (EPA) in December 2000.

The agency came up with this plan in the final days of the Clinton administration. It's really a case where good science and common sense have become drowned out by loud voices and extreme views—to prod the government to punish a large global corporation.

Over the years, this debate has gone from PCBs to a more fundamental crusade. Extremists have latched on to issues like PCBs to challenge the basic role of the corporation. These people often see companies as inanimate objects, incapable of values and feelings.

GE isn't made up of bricks and buildings. It's nothing more than the flesh and blood of the people who make it come alive. It's made up of people who live in the same communities, whose children go to the same schools, as the critics. They have the same hopes and dreams, the same hurts and pains.

Corporations are human.

When they're big, they're an easy target. And when they're winners, they're an even bigger target.

Facts are, GE has one of the best environmental and safety records of any company in the world. It has more than 300 manufacturing and assembly locations and virtually no disputes with governments over compliance issues. Nearly 60 facilities in the United States have been given special "STAR" recognition by federal regulators for health and safety compliance.

In the last decade, we've reduced emissions of 17 ozone-depleting chemicals by more than 90 percent and our total emissions, which the EPA measures, by over 60 percent.

This didn't happen by accident. All our plant managers go through rigorous training programs and report annually on their performance to their business CEOs and a VP for environmental programs. Every three months, I got an update on each business's environmental and safety performance.

In short, we've approached the environment and worker safety the way we did everything else: We set the bar high, we measure, and we expect outstanding results.

We're not perfect, nobody is, but we were always striving to be the best.

Money is never the issue. GE has the resources to do the right thing, and we know that doing the right thing is always better for our bottom line over the long run. Only in this context can you appreciate why we've been so adamant about the PCB issue.

For me, the PCB story started accidentally a couple of weeks before Christmas 1975, when I was a group executive in Pittsfield. I was visiting a semiconductor plant in Syracuse one day when the division manager happened to mention casually that New York's Department of Environmental Conservation (DEC) was going to hold a hearing soon. He said it would focus on a possible violation by two of his capacitor plants in upstate New York that were discharging PCBs into the Hudson River.

I had never dealt with PCBs before, but being a chemical engineer, I was familiar with plant discharges, and I was curious about this hearing.

A couple of days later, I was in my Pittsfield office and had a slow day. I decided to drive over the mountain to Albany to find out what was going on. I sat in the back of the hearing room, and no one knew I was there.

That day, GE's expert witness was testifying. A biologist and vice president of a laboratory hired by us, he claimed his tests showed negligible levels of PCBs in fish from the Hudson. Our expert didn't look or sound like one. He seemed unsure of his own work. He had trouble giving a straight answer. The more I listened, the more uncomfortable I got.

I knew if he couldn't convince me, he couldn't convince the hearing officer.

After the hearing, I called Art Puccini, my general counsel, and asked him to come over from Pittsfield. This now seemed important enough that I should stay overnight. Art and I asked the "GE expert" to come to my motel room. We asked him to walk us through all the details of his handwritten control sheets for the study. After questioning him until 2:30 A.M., we were convinced that he hadn't done a thorough job. We felt we could not use his data or allow the hearing officer to use it, either.

I could have strangled him.

The next day, I told our outside defense lawyers not to rely on his data and to tell the hearing officer the same thing. Two months later, the DEC hearing officer issued an interim ruling that in his words claimed "PCB contamination" was a result "of both corporate abuse and regulatory failure," because our PCB usage had been legal and we had state permits to discharge them.

Now I was into it. Art and I negotiated a settlement with DEC commissioner Peter Berle, who later became president of the National Audubon Society. The DEC hearing officer, a Columbia University law professor named Abe Sofaer, helped to mediate the settlement. We agreed to pay $3.5 million to a river cleanup fund, support research on PCBs, and stop using the chemical. New York's DEC agreed to match our contribution and release us from any further liability on the Hudson.

Berle and I eventually signed the settlement. *The New York Times* ran a picture of both of us above the headline, "GE-State Pact on PCB Is Praised As Guide in Other Pollution Cases" (opposite page). The *Times* quoted Sofaer, who called the settlement "an effective precedent for dealing with situations of joint culpability." Governor Hugh Carey later offered to drink a glass of water from the Hudson River to demonstrate his confidence that the river water was not harmful.

The September 8, 1976, agreement even required the state to turn to the federal government for money if any further action to protect public health and resources were needed. That's as clear as can be on page three of the agreement: *"In the event that the funds herein provided for implementing remedial action concerning PCBs present in the Hudson River shall be inadequate to assure protection of public health and resources, then the Department will use its best efforts to obtain additional funds, from sources other than General Electric, that are necessary to assure such protection. These best efforts will include preparation by the Department of a plan of action to obtain such funds including specifying applications will be made to federal agencies and/or other sources of funds in as expeditious a manner as possible."*

But it didn't end there.

The settlement had been made on the basis of animal studies. I wanted to know if PCBs caused cancer in humans and whether our workers were at risk. I knew that if a company-funded study was going to have any credibility, I had to get the most widely respected scientist I could find. So I went down to see Dr. Irwin Selikoff, then

THE NEW YORK TIMES, THURSDAY, SEPTEMBER 9, 1976

Associated Press

Peter A. A. Berle, left, Commissioner of Environmental Conservation, and John F. Welch, a vice president of the General Electric Company, sign an agreement in Albany settling the case of the PCB's dumped into the Hudson.

G.E.-State Pact on PCB Is Praised As Guide in Other Pollution Cases

Special to The New York Times

ALBANY, Sept. 8—The Columbia University law professor who conducted hearings on state pollution charges against the General Electric Company said here today that yesterday's agreement to stop the company's chemical contamination of the Hudson River was "an effective precedent for dealing with situations of joint culpability."

The comment, by Prof. Abraham T. Sofaer, came after Commissioner Peter A. A. Berle of the State Department of Environmental Conservation and John F. Welch, a G.E. vice president, signed a quasi-legal agreement under which the company pledged to stop dumping toxic PCB's (polychlorinated biphenyls) by July 1, 1977.

G.E. uses PCB's to make capacitors—an electronic device for storing a charge—at plants employing about 1,200 workers in Hudson Falls and Fort Edward, north of Albany. After the manufacturing process, the PCB's have been routinely discharged into the Hudson for about 25 years.

In recommending the agreement, Professor Sofaer, whose hearings earlier this year covered 11 days of testimony, noted that G.E. had "requested and obtained" Federal and state permits to dump PCB's into the Hudson.

Until exactly a year ago, Professor Sofaer noted, when former State Environmental Commissioner Ogden R. Reid began an action against the company, "no one had ever claimed that G.E.'s PCB discharges violated state water quality standards." Governor Carey joined Commissioner Berle in saying that the agreement emphasized the "shared responsibility of the state and G.E. in PCB pollution of the Hudson."

That is why, Mr. Berle said, both the state and G.E. will cooperate in attempts to cleanse a 50-mile stretch of the Hudson, from Fort Edward to Albany, of PCB's now encrusted in the earth as sludge beneath the river.

From what is described as "reclamation" of the river, G.E. and the state will each pay $3 million. The company has agreed to put up $1 million more for state-directed research into toxic chemicals.

head of Mount Sinai's Environmental School of Medicine. Selikoff had become something of an environmental icon after finding that exposure to asbestos could cause lung cancer. He listened carefully to my request. I asked him if he would go to our plants to study GE employees who had the greatest exposure to PCBs. For years, those employees had worked in it up to their elbows.

I gave Selikoff total access to our employees. He put a research team together and set up a lab at our Fort Edward plant. Selikoff first examined over 300 volunteers from the two GE factories. His study, finally published in 1982, is what convinced me more than anything else that PCBs didn't cause cancer.

Selikoff's mortality study found there were no cancer deaths or other serious side effects among workers 30 years after they were first exposed. Normally, in a population of the size he studied— without any major PCB exposure—at least eight cancer deaths would have been expected.

Other scientists studied utility workers and Westinghouse employees who had been heavily exposed to PCBs. Alexander Smith, of the government's National Institute for Occupational Safety and Health (NIOSH), gave the most succinct summary of this work in 1982. He wrote: "One would expect that adverse human health effects from exposure to PCBs, if they exist, would most readily be identified in groups with the greatest exposures. None of the published occupational or epidemiological studies (including ours), however, have shown that occupational exposure to PCBs is associated with any adverse health outcome."

The PCB issue had been raised much earlier when two major false alarms were sounded. The first was in the 1930s, when a chemical mixture containing PCBs known as Halowax led to a serious acnelike condition and, in a few cases, deaths due to liver disease. A Harvard scientist studying the incident first reported that PCBs were the most toxic component of the mixture.

After studying this further, however, he corrected himself in 1939, by stating that PCBs were "almost non-toxic." Unfortunately, his correction got little or no recognition. Almost 40 years later, in 1977, a government report by NIOSH stated that the Halowax experiences "have continued to be erroneously cited."

Even today, it's not unusual to get a call from a reporter thinking he has discovered some new "explosive evidence" in these old Halowax incidents discredited by both scientists and the government.

Another false alarm, the Yusho incident, was sounded in Japan in 1968. About 1,000 people using a type of vegetable oil from rice hulls in cooking developed severe acne and other symptoms. When PCBs were detected in the oil, the incident became known as the "PCB oil disease."

However, later analysis by Japanese scientists found that the oil also contained high levels of two other chlorinated chemicals, both high-temperature by-products of PCBs. They also examined Japanese electrical workers and found they had higher levels of PCBs in their blood than the Yusho patients. But the workers weren't sick. When scientists dosed monkeys with PCBs and these different chemicals, they concluded that it was these other chemicals—and not PCBs—that caused the Yusho incident.

It was those false alarms that prompted an American researcher, Dr. Renate Kimbrough, to do one of the first rat studies for the U.S. government on PCBs. Dr. Kimbrough found that rats fed large doses of PCBs had increased tumors in their livers. She was heavily involved in this work in the mid-1970s when she was at the Centers for Disease Control and Prevention and later at the EPA. Just as I had in 1975 with Dr. Selikoff, I wanted a recognized scientist with unassailable integrity and credentials to look at PCBs again. This time, in April 1992, we asked Dr. Kimbrough to take on the assignment.

Internally, our PCB efforts were led by Steve Ramsey, former head of the Justice Department's Environmental Enforcement, who now leads GE's environmental and safety operations. He and a GE scientist, Dr. Steve Hamilton, knew critics would still be skeptical of GE-funded research. They established an advisory panel to peer review the Kimbrough and other studies. The panel was made up of U.S. government and academic researchers led by the former head of the National Cancer Institute, Dr. Arthur Upton.

Kimbrough studied virtually everyone who ever worked at those two GE plants in Hudson Falls and Fort Edward between 1946 and 1977. Private investigators were hired to track down some of them through payroll records and old telephone directories. Death certificates were examined. Some 7,075 current and former employees were involved in the research.

In 1999, Dr. Kimbrough issued a striking report. The death rate due to all types of cancer for employees at our plants was at or significantly below the general and regional population rates.

As part of its review of the Kimbrough work before their final decision, the EPA asked an epidemiologist at the University of Southern California's Norris Comprehensive Cancer Center for his opinion. In a letter to the chief of the EPA's risk methods group, Dr. Thomas Mack had this to say: "I found the Kimbrough paper to be well designed, appropriately analyzed and fairly interpreted. The follow-up was complete . . . my bottom line is that the summary statements . . . in the paper are appropriate. I think it is appropriate to downgrade the priority given to PCBs."

We know about Dr. Mack's opinion only because we got it from EPA files after a Freedom of Information request. His final sentence is telling. *"I'm sure this has not been particularly useful for you, but it's the best I can do."*

I doubt this would have seen the light of day if we hadn't used the law to dig it out of the EPA.

Through this long, drawn-out controversy, GE has been portrayed as an uncaring big business that "dumped" PCBs from plants in Hudson Falls and Fort Edward, New York.

The truth is, we never "dumped" PCBs, and we never made them. Their use was dictated by fire and building codes because they solved a long-standing problem in electrical equipment. The prior insulating material caught fire and could explode. PCBs were viewed as a lifesaving chemical. New York State approved our discharge and issued permits to us for it.

What do our critics using PCBs as the foil say about us?

First, they say GE has more Superfund sites than any other company. (In 1980, Congress passed a law to address the cleanup of sites where wastes had been disposed in the past. This law was known as the Superfund Act.) The implication is that we did something wrong. We do have a large number of these sites, 85 to be exact. But the number has everything to do with our longevity and our size. GE was founded in 1892 and has had more factories in more towns than any other company in the world. Like most other companies, we disposed of our wastes legally, under government permits when required.

At the majority of the Superfund sites, GE has less than 5 percent of the liability for what was put there. The remaining liability is shared by dozens of other parties, including municipalities, other companies, and waste haulers. GE has taken its responsibility for these sites seriously. We've spent almost $1 billion in the last decade on their cleanup.

Criticizing us for having these sites is like criticizing someone for having gray hair. It says nothing about character and everything about age.

Another common complaint is that we're challenging the Superfund law so we can get off the hook for our cleanup obligations. Yes, we have challenged a portion of the law. Americans are used to getting their day in court. This is true for everything from traffic offenses to murder.

This isn't the case when the EPA issues a Superfund order. You really have only one choice under the law: Do what the agency tells you or else. Otherwise you face treble damages and daily fines. The law gives the EPA power to issue orders of unlimited scope. You get no hearing before being ordered to do the work. You get no hearing until many years later, and then only when the EPA chooses to tell you the work is done.

It's a shoot first, ask questions later law.

We believe that's wrong. I'm a chemical engineer and not a constitutional lawyer, but I can't understand why in God's name this makes any sense under our Constitution. It denies you the basic right of due process. The EPA is using this law in their dredging proposal.

Today, the EPA says the Hudson is safe for swimming, boating, wading, and use as a source of drinking water. Bald eagles and other wildlife are flourishing in the Hudson Valley. The government's proposal to dredge is based on a wild risk assessment:

If a person eats half a pound of fish every week for 40 years, the EPA contends that the person's risk of cancer may increase by one in 1,000. In other words, you've got to eat 52 meals a year for four decades before the increase might go up by one in a thousand. Why doesn't a rational mind come to the conclusion that that risk is practically lower than breathing?

Never mind that eating fish from the river has been banned for two decades or that PCB levels in the water and fish have fallen 90 percent since 1977. More than 20 studies—most completely independent of GE—show no link between PCBs and cancer. At the end of the day, what happens in rats does not happen in humans when both are exposed to PCBs. Levels in fish are now down to between three to eight parts per million. Two is the level the FDA says is safe for sale at the fish market.

Think about the magnitude of what the EPA's proposal would do. The agency proposes removing 8 billion pounds of sediment from the Hudson to get at probably 100,000 pounds of PCBs. It would take 24 hours of dredging a day, six days a week, for six months each year. Some 50 boats and barges would have to be in the river full-time, along with miles of pipelines to carry PCBs.

The EPA proposes building plants along the river to dry the

mud that would be carried away in tens of thousands of trucks or railcars. After the EPA gets the sediment out, they're proposing to add 2 billion pounds of sand and gravel back into the river. Divers would also have to replace 1 million aquatic plants destroyed by dredging.

After doing all this, dredging won't get PCBs out of the Hudson. It will cause resuspension of buried PCBs that will flow downriver.

Imagine if someone came along with a commercial proposition to dredge anything out of the Hudson River. Tear up the banks. Destroy the ecosystem. Knock the trees down to widen the roads through farmlands and backyards to remove whatever they were after.

It would be an environmental disaster.

Why would anyone rip up the Hudson? The EPA itself rejected dredging in 1984, saying it could be devastating to the ecosystem. Nothing has changed since then, except the politics—and PCB levels in fish have been reduced by 90 percent.

GE has spent more than $200 million on research, investigation, and cleanup. We've reduced the PCBs coming out of the bedrock under our old facilities from five pounds per day to three ounces. We think we now have the technology to reduce the daily seepage to zero. Source control coupled with the natural sedimentation in the river would reduce PCBs in fish to the same level as dredging might, without resuspension—and without destroying the river.

One of the puzzling things about the EPA's proposal is that it failed to analyze whether there were less destructive and less disruptive alternatives.

This isn't about money. We'll spend whatever it takes to do the job right.

To tell this story to the people in the Upper Hudson and explain why we oppose dredging, we've spent over $10 million on an information campaign. That caused a controversy as well. There was little argument over the information in the campaign. Activists think we should be quiet and do what we're told.

We made some progress in getting the facts out. Polls show that by more than three to one, the people in the Upper Hudson, from Washington to Dutchess Counties, are against the EPA dredging proposal. More than 60 Upper Hudson River local governments and organizations oppose dredging. The EPA's final decision should take into account the views of those most affected by their proposal.

Unfortunately, this issue is no longer about PCBs, human health, and science. This isn't about what's best for the Hudson River. It's about politics and punishing a successful company.

Do you for a minute believe that if we thought PCBs were harming anyone, I or my associates would be taking these positions? There's just no way!

Nothing is more important than a company's integrity. It is the first and most important value in any organization. It not only means that people must abide by the letter and spirit of the law, it also means doing the right thing and fighting for what you believe is right.

On PCBs, we've assured ourselves that they are not harmful to our employees or our neighbors. We've spent hundreds of millions using the best science to clean up our sites and the Hudson in the most ecologically sensitive way—and we will continue to invest whatever it takes.

I've seen a lot since that day I saw my mother crying over Franklin Roosevelt's death. Yes, I've become a skeptic—hopefully, not a cynic about government. Only a company with great integrity and the resources to fight for what's right can afford to take on the government.

Fortunately, we have both.

SECTION **IV**

GAME CHANGERS

I f you like business, you have to like GE.

   If you like ideas, you have to love GE.

   This is a place where ideas can flow freely from and through more than 20 separate businesses and more than 300,000 employees.

   Boundaryless behavior allows ideas to come from anywhere. We formalize our freewheeling style in a series of operating meetings that blend one into another. We can be doing a Session C review of managers in power systems and someone will come up with an idea on sourcing in Hungary.

   The next day we're in medical, bragging about what power has just done in Hungary. Before you know it, they have something new going in Eastern Europe. It's wild, sometimes humorous, and informal. The net effect is powerful. The best practices and the best people are always moving across the units and driving our businesses. In effect, boundaryless behavior has given us a "social architecture" that thrives on learning.

   In the 1990s, we pursued four major initiatives: Globalization, Services, Six Sigma, and E-Business.

   Every initiative started off with the seed of a smaller idea.

Once put into the operating system, it had the chance to grow. Our four have flourished. They've been a huge part of the accelerated growth we've seen in the past decade.

These are not "flavors of the month."

At GE, we defined an initiative as something that grabs everyone—large enough, broad enough, and generic enough to have a major impact on the company. An initiative is long lasting, and it changes the fundamental nature of the organization. Regardless of the source, I became the cheerleader. I followed up on all of them with a passion and a mania that often veered toward the lunatic fringe.

Initiatives come from anywhere and everywhere. Globalization grew out of Paolo Fresco's passion for it. Product services accelerated after a Crotonville class's recommendation to define our markets more broadly for faster growth. Six Sigma sprang out of an employee survey in 1995. While our employees thought our quality was okay, they believed it could be a lot better. And e-business came, arguably late, because it couldn't be ignored. We jumped in and got wet in a revolution we didn't understand. We trusted our operating system to teach us what it was all about.

To make the initiatives work, it took a passionate all-consuming commitment from the top. Beyond the passion, there was a lot of rigor. Not only did we put the best people on each initiative, we trained them, measured them, and reported their results. In the end, each initiative had to develop people and improve the bottom line.

The leaders of every business had to be the champion—and timid and rational advocacy wouldn't work. They made sure we got our A players to lead every initiative. We made sure the rewards—salary increases, stock option grants, and role-model recognition at company meetings—were highly visible.

The organization judges an initiative's importance by whom they see getting the leadership assignments. Nowhere was this more important to GE's success than in Six Sigma. If we didn't get the best and brightest, it could have been perceived as just another "quality program."

We pounded all our initiatives in January at Boca, at every quarterly CEC meeting, at the human resources reviews in April, the planning sessions in July, the officers meeting in October, and the operating plan meetings in November.

There was always a relentless drumbeat of follow-up.

We used the annual employee survey to find out how deep in the organization the initiatives were taking hold. We started anonymously polling 1,500 employees in 1995 and are including 16,000 today. We used the survey to help set our direction—and as a BS detector. The survey got right at questions about the initiatives—whether or not our messages were getting through.

When we launched Six Sigma in 1995, for example, we asked employees if they agreed or disagreed with the statement, "Actions taken by this business clearly show that quality is a top priority." Some 19 percent of our top 700 senior executives disagreed. In 2000, that dropped to 8 percent. In 1995, in our 3,000-person executive band population, a quarter disagreed. Five years later, that number was down to 9 percent.

Making initiatives successful is all about focus and passionate commitment. The drumbeat must be relentless. Every leadership action must demonstrate total commitment to the initiative.

The initiatives' impact showed up where it should have—in our operating results. Our top-line growth rate has doubled in the last five years, and our operating margins have increased from 14.4 percent in 1995 to 18.9 percent in 2000.

19

Globalization

GE has always been a global trading company.

In the late 1800s, Thomas Edison installed the 3,000-bulb electric lighting system at London's Holborn Viaduct. At the turn of the century, GE built the largest power plant in Japan. Some of the company's earliest CEOs traveled by boat for a month or two to look for business in Europe and Asia.

I had an early start in globalization.

Reuben Gutoff and I formed two joint ventures in plastics in the mid-1960s, one with Mitsui Petrochemical in Japan and the other with AKU, the chemical and fiber company in Holland. Mitsui and AKU were large chemical corporations, and our little project in specialty plastics turned out to be too small to get their attention. We had locked ourselves up in long-term agreements. We had to get out.

I'll never forget my final negotiations with Mitsui. Tom Fitzgerald, the sales head of plastics, and I were having lunch at the Okura Hotel in Tokyo with the Mitsui officials. We were sitting on the floor, with our shoes off. After a day or two of negotiations, I had drafted two letters of intent to significantly change our relationship. One copy spelled out a clear separation after a negligible payment. The other detailed Mitsui's staying in the deal and being diluted down.

At lunch, it was clear that Mitsui wanted out of the agreement as much as we did. I couldn't have been happier. I was expecting a negotiation. I immediately handed them the "staying-in-the-deal" document. It was only after looking at my copy that I recognized I had given them the wrong papers.

I blurted out, "Oh, my God, there's a typo."

I grabbed the document back and pulled out of my briefcase the letter of intent that would end the deal. They signed it, and we were free to look for a new partner in Japan. Tom must have told that story a thousand times to show what a dope his boss was.

We also got out of the AKU deal—without my screwing it up this time. AKU had built a pilot plant to produce PPO and had spent $20 million to $30 million on the project. Their principal interest in PPO was as a fiber. When the polymer turned out not to be useful for that purpose, they lost interest.

However, their vice chairman met with me at his office in Arnhem and wanted a couple of million dollars to end the venture in order to offset some of the losses they had incurred. I told him it would take me months to get through the GE bureaucracy, and even then I had no idea if I could get approval. I said I had the authority to spend up to $500,000, however, and I could give him the money on the spot. He accepted it, and we set up our own wholly owned company in Europe.

In Japan, we knew we needed distribution, and we wanted a relatively small partner. We looked at several and picked Nagase & Co., which at that time was principally a Kodak film distributor. I made the deal with the head of the Nagase family. We brought the product and technology to the partnership. They brought their knowledge of Japan's complex distribution market. Together we invested in local plants to compound plastics for the Japanese market. Today, it's the heart of our Asian plastics business. We used the same model for a deal we did for medical systems in the late

1970s with Shozo Yokogawa of Yokogawa, an instrumentation company.

Those relationships and the deals behind them have endured for more than 25 years and have thrived even as they have changed. GE may appear big, but it is made up of lots of small pieces. The success of our deals with Nagase and Yokogawa reinforced the idea that our most successful partnerships are with smaller companies that feel the project is critical to their operations. Whenever there was an issue to work out, our people could get to the top—and not have to work through a massive bureaucracy.

I remember being frustrated by how long the Japanese took to make a decision. But when they made one, you could bet your house on it. In over 35 years, almost every business relationship I had in Japan turned into an enduring personal friendship.

When I became CEO, I spent the first several years doing only an isolated deal or two outside the United States, visiting Europe and Asia once a year to review current operations. One of the early deals, a joint venture in 1986 with Fanuc of Japan, bore a large resemblance to the Yokogawa and Nagase partnerships. I had always admired Fanuc and its head, Dr. Seiuemon Inaba. They were the clear market leaders in numerical controls for machine tools, and we were in the process of trying to launch a factory automation effort. Selling the concept of a "factory of the future" was going nowhere for GE. We had slogans like "Automate, Emigrate, or Evaporate," but we didn't have much business. All we had was U.S. distribution and a couple of strong product niches.

I asked Chuck Pieper, who was head of GE Japan at the time, to visit with Dr. Inaba to see if there was any fit between our two companies. Chuck had several visits with Fanuc that set the stage for my meeting with Dr. Inaba in New York in November 1985.

We hit it off immediately. Our distribution and Fanuc's product technology would make a great marriage. A couple of sessions later, we struck a worldwide deal. At $200 million, it was the biggest international deal that we had done in the 1980s. Like

Nagase and Yokogawa, Fanuc and Dr. Inaba have been great partners and our 50/50 joint company has prospered. It saved our
"factory of the future" venture.

Truth is, I didn't put much focus on the global direction of the
company in the first half of the 1980s. I did eliminate a separate international sector and made the business CEOs clearly in charge of
their own global activities. The international sector had been
something of a hybrid between scorekeeper and helper.

I always believed there was no such thing as a global company:
Companies aren't global—businesses are. I've given that speech a
thousand times or more to make clear that the CEOs of each business were responsible for globalizing their businesses.

In the early 1980s, the only truly global businesses in GE were
plastics and medical systems. GE Capital had invested in only U.S.
assets. Our other businesses had global sales of one size or another; two—aircraft engines and power systems—were very
large. But these were primarily export businesses with facilities exclusively in the United States. In the 1970s, GE forged a joint venture with the French company Snecma on the aircraft engine that
would power the most popular commercial airplane ever, the Boeing 737.

It was Paolo Fresco who really got us going. In 1986, he was
named senior vice president of international, based in London and
placed on an equal footing with all the business leaders—but without operating responsibility. Paolo epitomized the global executive. Tall, handsome, charming, and urbane, Paolo was known
around the world. An Italian-born lawyer who joined GE in 1962,
he had long dominated the old international organization. As vice
president for Europe, the Middle East, and Africa, he also was one
of the best negotiators in the company.

Paolo became Mr. Globalization, the father of all our global
activity. He got up every morning thinking about expanding the
company outside our U.S. borders. At every meeting, he'd press
his colleagues for their global expansion plans. At times he was a

nuisance, always bugging the business CEOs for details on their international operations and prodding people to do more deals that would make us truly global. He was a relentless globe-trotter, comfortable in any time zone, always out of the country at least once a month.

For 15 years, he and I traveled the world together. We'd go out for one or two weeks three times a year. We had a ball together, and on most trips we took our wives with us. All four of us became as close as family. Fortunately, our wives became best friends. While we were building relationships and doing deals, they were out exploring the sights and cultures of the countries we visited.

If there was a breakthrough year for globalization, it might have been 1989. It began with a phone call from Lord Arnold Weinstock, chairman of General Electric Co. Ltd. In the United Kingdom. (GEC had the exact same name as ours, even though there was never a connection between our two companies. It wasn't until 2000 when they changed their name to Marconi that we were able to buy the full rights to the GE name.)

Weinstock called me because his company was being threatened with a hostile takeover and he wanted to see if we could help. Paolo, Dennis Dammerman, Ben Heineman, and I went to London to meet with GEC. The takeover attempt was front-page news, and business reporters followed our every move. As we got close to a deal, we broke and returned to our London offices while they mulled over our offer. We agreed that Weinstock would contact me using the code name of our vice chairman Ed Hood.

He called a couple of times and was told repeatedly by one of the office assistants that we were in meetings and would call him back. Weinstock finally reached Paolo's secretary, Lin. She knew Ed Hood but nevertheless came into the conference room and said, "I think there's a reporter on the line posing as Ed Hood. He has a strong British accent."

"Oh no," I said, "I forgot to tell anyone that Weinstock would be using Ed's name as his code."

It probably looked to Weinstock as though we were playing it cool.

Not that it helped. He was a cool customer himself, as shrewd, wily, and clever as anyone I ever met. In some ways, he was two different people. Outside the office, he was a great storyteller, charming and gracious. He had racehorses stabled with the Queen's thoroughbreds, had elegant homes filled with great art, and had a spectacular wife. He was a generous and entertaining host.

Inside his drab office, he was the original "green eyeshade accountant." GEC's headquarters in London reflected his tightfisted ways. The lighting was dim, the furniture sparse, and the corridors so narrow that you had to walk sideways to get by an open door.

The entrance to the bathroom was on a narrow landing in front of an open staircase. If you were waiting to enter, there was always a chance that someone coming out could knock you down two flights of stairs.

At his desk, sitting directly under a hanging lamp, Weinstock in his suspenders seemed a formidable figure. He often peered over his glasses, hunched over massive financial ledgers. He'd mark them up in colored pencils, circling any numbers that were below expectation.

Complex as he was, I found him fascinating on the whole.

Our negotiations eventually led to a series of joint ventures and acquisitions with GEC in April 1989 in medical systems, appliances, power systems, and electrical distribution. The agreements gave GE a good industrial business, a foothold in power that kept us in the European gas turbine business, and a 50 percent share of GEC's appliance business.

Later that same year, it was Paolo who helped to nail down our purchase of a majority interest in Tungsram, one of Hungary's largest and oldest businesses. We had been searching for a spot in Austria to build a lighting plant near the Hungarian border when we discovered that Tungsram might be for sale. Even under the Communists, the company had a great reputation and a lot of technology. It was the biggest lighting company outside of the big three: Philips, Siemens, and us.

Paolo went to Hungary with a small team and began to negotiate. After spending the day at the negotiating table, he'd call back from the Hilton Hotel in Budapest to fill me in on the details. It didn't take long for Paolo to notice some strange behavior during his negotiations. His counterparts seemed to begin reacting to things he had said privately to me on the telephone.

Paolo tipped me off that he believed the Hungarians were intercepting our conversations. So we began saying some crazy things to see if there would be a reaction at the table the next day. Sure enough, there was. So Paolo and I began using the telephone calls to set up the next day's negotiations. He'd tell me they were asking $300 million for a majority interest.

"Listen, tomorrow, if they want you to pay more than $100 million, I want you to walk out."

The next day, Paolo found them more realistic about the price. Whenever we had to make a secure phone call, a GE executive traveled by train across the border to Vienna or used the soundproof phone booth in the American embassy. Otherwise, we kept playing the game on the hotel phone. In the end, it didn't hurt.

We closed the deal, paying $150 million for 51 percent of Tungsram and buying the remaining piece five years later. Paolo closed the deal at midnight over a bottle of vodka with the Communists.

The next day, the Berlin Wall fell. Without knowing it, we had done the first big deal in the new Eastern Europe. Since Thomas Edison put us in light bulbs, lighting had been almost exclusively an American business. The Tungsram deal, coupled with our 1991 acquisition of a majority of Thorn lighting in the United Kingdom, made GE the No. 1 light bulb maker in the world, with over a 15 percent market share in Western Europe.

Another memorable global event of that year was my trip to India during the end of September 1989. Paolo dragged me there for the first time, and I instantly fell in love with the people. Paolo had built a great relationship there with K.P. Singh, a prominent Indian real estate entrepreneur.

K.P. Singh was a true ambassador for India. Tall, natty, and aristocratic, he was a perfect gentleman. He lined up four days of wall-to-wall business meetings and evening celebrations for us.

After a day of meetings with business and government leaders in Delhi, including Prime Minister Rajiv Gandhi, a night had been arranged we would never forget. He had everyone who was anyone at his compound for a huge party. Two bands played music while hundreds of people mingled among pools filled with flower petals and tables of food from every country around the world.

What a welcome!

We continued our business meetings for two more days. During the trip, we were scheduled to select a high-technology partner who could help develop the lower-end, low-cost products in medical systems. Chuck Pieper, who had initiated the earlier Japanese deal with Fanuc, had been promoted to head GE medical systems in Asia. He had narrowed it down to two finalists, whom he brought in to see us at a hotel in Delhi. Both were successful Indian entrepreneurs: One was flamboyant, while the other was reserved.

Paolo and I loved the first presentation from the more flamboyant guy, who excitedly presented his plans. The quiet one, Azim Premji, came in after him and gave a thoughtful presentation as to why his company, Wipro, was the right partner for GE. Chuck was convinced that Premji was the one for us. K.P., who sat in on all our meetings, was neutral. He thought both entrepreneurs were terrific.

After we left, Chuck made his case for Wipro in writing. Paolo and I agreed to back off and go with Chuck's 50/50 joint venture with Premji. The medical venture flourished, and Wipro went on to dramatically expand its software capabilities, becoming the poster child of India's high-tech industry. Premji was worth billions, becoming one of the world's richest businessmen.

For our final day in India, K.P. had arranged a visit to the Taj Mahal. The night before we flew to Jaipur. If we thought the first night in India was special, we hadn't seen anything yet.

K.P. was about to outdo himself. We were greeted at the hotel, the former palace of the Maharaja, by colorful riders on elephants and horses. The entire front lawn of the hotel was done up in fresh flowers in the form of the GE logo.

That evening in Jaipur, the Maharaja hosted a dinner at his palace. After dinner, just about the largest fireworks display I ever saw was put on in our honor. We walked up long, winding passageways to the roof, where we sat on huge pillows and beautiful old carpets.

This was "pinch me" stuff. This was literally the "royal treatment." They really wanted GE to love and invest in India—and were pulling out all the stops.

The next day, I was struck by the contrasts. Animals filled the dirt streets as our car wended its way to the Taj Mahal. The Taj exceeded my expectations in every way. It was a magnificent structure, glistening in the sun, which gave it an almost pinkish tint. Behind this beautiful creation, sitting across the river, was an enormous satellite communications dish—a picture of the old and the new in one glimpse.

The efforts of K.P. and his friends worked. They showed us an India and a people that we loved. We saw all kinds of opportunities there. After that trip, I became the champion for India.

At our annual officers meeting the next month, I portrayed the country as a great place to make a bet. I wanted to gamble on India because it had a strong legal system, a potential market, and an enormous number of people with great technical skills.

I saw India as a huge market, with a rapidly growing middle class of 100-plus million people out of an 800 million population. The Indian people were highly educated, they spoke English, and the country had lots of entrepreneurs trying to break the shackles of heavy government bureaucracy.

Highly developed from an intellectual standpoint, India was an underdeveloped country from an infrastructure perspective. I thought the bureaucracy would fix the infrastructure problems and loosen some of the red tape.

I was dead wrong. We tried to build lighting and appliance companies there. They went nowhere. Power generation has been a series of starts and stops. Financial services and plastics have had modest success. Only medical systems has flourished.

I was also dead right. The real benefit of India turned out to be its vast intellectual capability and the enthusiasm of its people. We found terrific scientific, engineering, and administrative talent that today serves almost every business at GE.

In the early 1990s, we kept pushing our global growth by acquisitions and alliances and by moving our best people into global assignments. In late 1991, we made two important moves. We appointed Jim McNerney, one of our best business CEOs, to a newly created position as president of GE Asia. Jim didn't go out there to run any businesses, but to promote the region and demonstrate to the business leaders the region's potential. His job was all about looking for deals, building business contacts, and being a champion for Asia. He was a helluva persuasive guy and had a huge impact.

Eight months after Jim's move to Asia, we sent Del Williamson from our power generation business in Schenectady, where he was head of sales and marketing, to Hong Kong as head of worldwide sales. Moving the center of gravity there was logical because no one was buying power plants in the United States. The business opportunities were in Asia. Psychologically, the impact on the organization of seeing a senior guy like Del managing the top line away from "Mother Schenectady" was enormous.

The symbolism of these moves shocked the system. Suddenly we heard people say: "They really mean it. Globalization is for real." The numbers would prove it. Our global sales went from

$9 billion in 1987 or 19 percent of total revenues when Paolo was named a senior VP, to $53 billion, or more than 40 percent of our total revenues today.

Another key part of our strategy was taking a contrarian view of globalizing. We focused most of our attention on areas of the world that were either in transition or out of favor. We thought the best risk-reward activities were there.

In the early to mid-1990s, when Europe was slumping, we saw many opportunities, particularly for financial services. In the mid-1990s, when Mexico devalued the peso and the economy was in turmoil, we made over 20 acquisitions and joint ventures and significantly increased our production base. In the late 1990s, our financial services business moved into Japan, which had long excluded foreign investment. These were opportunistic moves, but not in the traditional sense. We were there to build businesses for the long haul.

Our acquisitions of CGR in France, Tungsram in Hungary, and Nuovo Pignone in Italy in 1994 involved taking over either unprofitable or barely profitable operations that had been state run. They gave us new distribution or good technology that helped to globalize our medical, lighting, and power systems businesses.

GE Capital began its global expansion in the early 1990s, mainly in Europe, by acquiring insurance and finance companies. The activity picked up when Gary Wendt hired Christopher MacKenzie in London in 1994. With great support from Gary, Christopher spearheaded a massive European expansion. Gary led the way on a similar effort in Japan in the late 1990s. From 1994 until 2000, $89 billion of the $161 billion in assets bought by GE Capital were outside the United States. GE Capital Services took a while to globalize, but when they did, they really went after it.

There was no overnight success. It took at least a decade to make the Thomson medical deal work. The same was true of our acquisition of Tungsram. Yet, one of our most satisfying accomplishments was taking over three government-owned companies—CGR, Nuovo Pignone, and Communist-controlled Tungsram—and transforming them into highly energized organizations and profitable companies.

Some ideas didn't pan out. When we picked a business to crack the Chinese market, we started first with lighting. We thought that our typical global competitors would be the players in China. Instead, it turned out that almost every local mayor was putting up light bulb facilities. Today, there are more than 2,000 light bulb manufacturers in China.

Not all the global deals we tried to do got off the ground— and some experiences left a bitter taste. I can only think of one, maybe two times, when trust and integrity broke down. The worst example of that was in 1988, when Paolo and I went to Eindhoven in the Netherlands for a meeting with the CEO of Philips N.V. We had heard that he was interested in selling the company's appliance business. That deal would have given us a strong position in the European appliance market.

He had become CEO of Philips in the mid-1980s and had some bold ideas on how to change his company. Over a dinner discussion at Philips House, he told us that he wanted to sell his major appliance business, where Philips was the second largest European player, and would consider selling Philips's medical businesses. He wasn't even sure about staying in lighting—even though the Dutch company was our biggest competitor in light bulbs.

He liked semiconductors and consumer electronics.

After the dinner, we were driving to the airport in the rain when I turned to Fresco.

"Have you ever been in a room where you heard two totally different perspectives on the same businesses? We both can't be right. One of us is going to get our ass fired."

Our meeting led to the start of a negotiation for Philips's appliance business. The CEO arranged for his president to negotiate with Paolo. We agreed to a price and thought the deal was done, after spending weeks on due diligence. Then came the shock.

Only a day after they shook hands, the president came back with a big surprise: "Sorry, Paolo, we're going to go with Whirlpool."

I called the CEO. "This isn't fair," I said.

He agreed. "Send Paolo down here and we'll work it out this week."

On vacation in Cortina, Italy, at the time, Paolo left his wife and flew immediately to Eindhoven. He spent all of Thursday negotiating a new deal, agreeing to pay more for Philips's appliance business. By Friday noon, the details were all worked out. The Philips team told Paolo to go back to his hotel.

"We'll be over by four in the afternoon with the formal papers all typed so they can be signed," the president said. "We'll have a glass of champagne then."

When he showed up at Paolo's hotel about five, he threw the second bomb.

"I'm sorry. We're going with Whirlpool. They came back and beat your offer."

Paolo couldn't believe it. When he called me around midnight, I was shocked. Having Philips shake on a deal once and walk was bad enough. The second negotiation was beyond anything I'd seen in a top-level business deal.

The nice thing is that in 20-plus years as CEO and literally thousands of acquisitions, partnerships, and deals, this happened rarely—and only once as blatantly as that time in Eindhoven.

Like our other initiatives, the seed bloomed into a garden. We moved from thinking of globalization in terms of markets to thinking of it in terms of sourcing products and components—and finally tapping the intellectual capital of countries.

Take India. I was optimistic about the country's brainpower, but our use of it has far outpaced my wildest dreams. The scientific and technical talent in India to do software development, design work, and basic research is incredible. We opened a central $30 million R&D center in 2000, have gone to the second phase, and will more than triple our investment when it's complete in 2002. It will be the largest multidisciplinary research facility in GE worldwide, eventually employing more than 3,000 engineers and scientists. Today we have over 1,000, including 250 Ph.D.s.

India has a wealth of highly educated people who can do many different things very well. GE Capital moved its customer service centers to Delhi, and the results have been sensational. Our Indian global customer centers have had better quality, lower costs, better collection rates, and greater customer acceptance than our comparable operations in the United States and Europe. All the GE industrial businesses have followed GE Capital there. We took Peter Drucker's advice. We moved the GE "back rooms" in the United States to the "front room" in India.

We can hire a level of talent in India for customer service and collection work that would be impossible to attract in the United States. Customer call centers in the United States are plagued by heavy turnover. In India, these are sought-after jobs. Some contend that globalization hurts developing countries and their people. I see it differently. Globalization never looks better than when you see the bright faces of the people whose lives have been measurably improved for having these jobs.

In recent years, our globalization initiative has increasingly put a global face on the company as more local nationals take on leadership roles. In the early years of globalization, we had to use U.S. expatriates. They were critical to our successful start, but we were having trouble getting off this "crutch."

We accelerated the development of a global face for GE by forcing a rigorous reduction of U.S. expatriates. We got two benefits from measuring the monthly reduction of expatriates by business: First, more locals had to be promoted faster to key jobs. Second, in the first year of doing this, we reduced our expenses by over $200 million. When we have someone from the United States in Japan on a $150,000 salary, it costs the company over $500,000. I constantly reminded our business leaders, "Would you rather have three to four smart University of Tokyo graduates who know the country and the language, or a friend of yours from down the hall?"

Globalization took a big step forward with an exciting promotion that showed our efforts are paying off. Yoshiaki "Fuji" Fujimori, a 1975 Tokyo University graduate, joined us in business development in 1986. Fuji was promoted in May 2001 from head of medical systems Asia to president and CEO of GE Plastics in Pittsfield.

He is the first Japanese national to lead a global GE business—a long way from the plastics business I started in 40 years ago.

20

Growing Services

Like just about everything at GE, growing services was all about people.

With the exception of our medical business, most of the people making the heavy hardware in the company thought of services as the "after market"—supplying spare and replacement parts for the aircraft engines, locomotives, and power generation equipment we sold.

"After market"—the name itself puts it in the backseat.

In our big-equipment businesses, the engineers liked to spend their time on the newest, the fastest, and the most powerful. They didn't think much about the "after market." They weren't alone—our salespeople also focused primarily on the customers' new equipment needs.

We had been pushing services without great success. When Three Mile Island forced our nuclear business to stop building new reactors, they had to build a service company to survive. They did it and transformed the nature of their business, getting double-digit earnings growth in a virtually no-growth market.

Medical has always had a strong service focus. The primary buyers were the radiologists, and they were also the ongoing users of the equipment. From the first introduction of our CT scanner in 1976, we sold our machines under "the continuum" banner. That slogan was meant to show radiologists that a software upgrade would get them to the "next-generation model." They wouldn't have to throw away a million-dollar machine and start all over again. The continuum concept helped increase service revenues and equipment market share as customers got longer lives out of their investments.

John Trani, who became medical CEO in 1986, built on that early foundation. He was a strong leader with an obsession for making the numbers. John saw services as an even bigger opportunity. Medical systems was the first business to introduce long-term service contracts. It was also the only business doing remote diagnostics. Medical set up global facilities to give 24/7 remote diagnosis of their installed equipment.

Customers from anywhere in the world could get an answer and often a fix directly on-line from a technical rep in Paris, Tokyo, or Milwaukee, depending on the time zone. With an equal focus on service as original equipment, medical got results. Overall medical revenues grew 12-fold from 1980 to 2000. Services were a big part of the growth, going from 18 percent of total medical revenues in 1980 to 31 percent in 1990 and to 41 percent of their $7 billion-plus revenues in 2000.

Other than those two businesses, we weren't having much success. The Crotonville class that challenged us to redefine our markets in 1995 was a turning point. When other businesses defined their markets more broadly, the importance of services was self-evident.

At Boca in January 1996, I made the point that we had been a "new socket company to a fault." We might have scores of executives debating whether we'd sell 50 or 58 gas turbines or several hundred aircraft engines a year while "we routinely handle the service opportunities for an installed base of 10,000 existing turbines and 9,000 jet engines."

That had to change.

After the Crotonville class, we held a special Session C in November of 1995 to focus on services staffing. We made our first big unconventional organizational move in aircraft engines in January 1996. We created a new vice president of engine services and made the business a separate P&L center. We put a real change agent in the job, a true bull in the china shop, Bill Vareschi, who had been the chief financial officer of the aircraft engine business.

Bill was loud, opinionated, and tough-minded—just what I thought might make the initiative come alive. He hired Jeff Bornstein, a young finance star from the audit staff, who, like his boss, wasn't afraid to take a swing at anything in his way. Bill and Jeff spent most of 1996 putting all the services pieces together.

They had several building blocks to work with. We had engine service shops located around the world. We acquired a large shop in Wales from British Airways in 1991 as part of a deal to sell BA our new GE-90 engines. It was an unprofitable operation that primarily serviced and overhauled Rolls-Royce engines, and British Airways wanted out of it. This shop was our first significant foray into servicing other manufacturers' engines. In 1996, Bill, with Dennis Dammerman's help, acquired Celma, a former state-owned service shop in Brazil that had been privatized. It gave us the capability to service Pratt & Whitney engines. Two years later, we'd buy Varig's Brazilian service shop, which would give us the capability to service GE engines at lower cost.

In late 1996, the engine service business had $3 billion in revenues, up from $2.2 billion in 1994, and was on a good trajectory. However, the industry was starting to consolidate. In 1996, Greenwich Air Services in Miami had bought out Aviall, a jet engine overhaul operation. I asked Bill and others why we didn't buy them. In mid-February of 1997, Greenwich was at it again, announcing their plans to buy another services company, UNC.

I called Bill again and asked, "What the hell is going on?" This new acquisition made Greenwich a big player. I wanted a hard look at them. Ten days after Greenwich announced its deal, I had a videoconference with aircraft engines CEO Gene Murphy and Bill Vareschi to find out what it would take to buy Greenwich. Bill was digesting Celma and thought we had enough facilities and could grow the business on our own.

But the more I thought about it, the more frantic I became. I didn't want to take the chance that one of our competitors would buy Greenwich before us. I urged Gene and Bill to think about it overnight and arranged a follow-up videoconference the next day.

At this session, they agreed to take a shot at it. Vareschi, who had known Greenwich founder and CEO Gene Conese for some time, agreed to call him to set up a Sunday morning meeting for us. When I left the videoconference with Dennis Dammerman, I grabbed him by the arm and said, "We just have to get this thing." He was as enthusiastic as I was.

On March 2, I flew down to Miami and went with Bill Vareschi to meet Gene Conese at his home. He was a gregarious bear of a guy, a clever entrepreneur who had built his company from scratch. As we sat down over coffee in his dining room, it was obvious he was interested in selling. Though Gene didn't say it outright, I had the feeling that after he had put this service network together, he was thinking, "Where the hell have you guys been?"

That morning we talked about a deal, and with Greenwich stock trading at $23 per share, I made an offer to buy the company for $27 a share. Gene countered at $35, and as you can imagine, we ended up at $31 after a couple of hours. Over the week, our teams did the due diligence. Dennis showed up at midweek to keep things moving.

The next weekend, I went back down and we did the usual haggling on Friday and Saturday nights over last minute details. The deal came to $1.5 billion. When I called Conese shrewd, I wasn't just casually throwing out a line. Gene wanted to be sure he got GE stock for his equity. He did, and since the deal closed, the price of the stock has tripled. The deal really put us on the map in aircraft services, increasing revenues by 60 percent overnight.

With Greenwich, we now had a real business, with over $5 billion in revenues. Bill had to take the business to the next level. To do that, he had to upgrade the overall organization. More specifically, he had to get the engineering mind-set away from designing new engines to upgrading the installed base of engines. We moved one of the best design engineers in the business, Vic Simon, from his design job to head of engineering for services. We also gave Bill a young "high potential" manufacturing manager, Ted Torbeck from GE Transportation, as manufacturing manager for services and upgraded the position to corporate vice president.

Both moves reinforced the message that services were important. Services went from under 40 percent of total aircraft engine revenues in 1994 to over 60 percent in 2000.

We used this same model and had the same results in power systems and transportation. Now we needed to broaden our base.

To spread the learning, we launched a council in 1996, bringing to Fairfield on a quarterly basis all of GE's service leaders. Either Vice Chairman Paolo Fresco or I would be at every meeting. Once again, it became immediately obvious who was delivering and who wasn't—and the next session usually corrected that. Idea sharing was particularly helpful in stirring up interest in acquisitions and structuring long-term service agreements.

Acquisitions played a big role in service growth. From 1997 through 2000, medical systems acquired 40 service companies, power systems 31, and aircraft engines 17. Even transportation got into the acquisition game in 2000, paying $400 million for Harmon Industries, a Kansas City railway signaling and service company.

Three separate businesses—transportation, power, and aircraft—set up 50/50 joint ventures with Harris Corp., a high-tech aerospace company. It was another great example of idea sharing.

These information systems ventures let railroad companies know the location of a train or let a utility company learn where it was having grid problems. We've since amicably bought out Harris' 50 percent in 2001 in power and transportation.

We pounded the idea of more technology investment at every step of the operating system. The businesses delivered—in most cases tripling our investments in service technology R&D to $500 million annually by 2000.

Investing heavily in technology for services has changed the fundamentals of our service business. Long-term service agreements wouldn't be possible without these large investments in technology and our Six Sigma commitment. Taking on long-term agreements required sophisticated models to predict the reliability costs over 10 to 15 years. Since the business leaders have to eat any shortfalls if the equipment doesn't perform as predicted, these contracts also reinforced the push to allocate more dollars to services technology.

These technology investments have greatly increased our intimacy with customers. The service upgrades that we provide today allow our customers to get increased productivity and longer lives for their installed equipment.

Doing this, we've learned a lot.

Some of our earlier technological upgrades were too sophisticated. Payback times for customers were measured in three to five years instead of the one to two or less that they needed to justify their investment. We've fixed that and now focus on rapid customer payback solutions across every business, whether it's increasing the life of a jet engine, improving the power output of a utility plant, or increasing the throughput of patients for a CT machine. For example, Southwest Airlines in 2001 placed an order with us for 300 upgrade kits at $1 million each to increase the life and fuel efficiency of engines on several older versions of their Boeing 737s.

Nothing demonstrates the value of high technology in a hardware business better than a chart from our locomotive business (opposite). Locomotive units will drop from a 1999 peak of 905 to

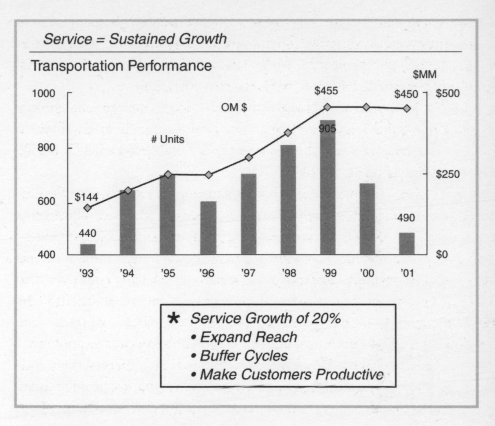

Service = Sustained Growth

Transportation Performance

490, their lowest level in eight years. Transportation shipped 440 locomotives, earning only $144 million of operating margin in 1993. This year, because of the growth of high-tech services, operating margin will be roughly equal to that of 1999 peak volume and three times the margin on approximately the same units shipped in 1993.

As always, the litmus test of how an initiative works is the numbers. Our product services business grew from $8 billion in 1995 to $19 billion in 2001 and should grow to $80 billion by 2010. Our long-term service backlog has grown tenfold, from $6 billion in 1995 to $62 billion in 2001.

Today, we're spending as much time insuring our installed "sockets" are increasingly productive—as we are on finding new "sockets."

21

Six Sigma and Beyond

In 20 years as CEO, I missed only one Corporate Executive Council (CEC) meeting. It was in June 1995, one of the most important meetings we ever had.

I had invited my friend and former colleague Larry Bossidy, then CEO of AlliedSignal, to come to Crotonville to talk about Six Sigma quality.

There was a good excuse for my not being there. I was home in bed, recovering from open-heart surgery.

After returning from India in late January, I couldn't stop feeling tired all the time. I thought I'd just caught some kind of bug that was making me feel lousy. I never took an afternoon nap in my life, but I started taking them on the couch in my office. I went to doctors all over New York, and I must have had every test ever invented. They never found anything.

My complaining continued—so much so that Jane went to my doctor, described the symptoms, and walked out with a prescription for nitroglycerin pills, just in case.

One Saturday night in late April, Jane and I went out with our friends the LoFriscos for dinner at Spazzi's in Fairfield. We ate a lot of pizza and consumed plenty of wine. Jane and I got home late and went straight upstairs. While brushing my teeth in the bathroom, I felt a bomb hit me in the chest. I'd had chest pains in the past, and with my family history of heart trouble, I'd imagined heart attacks at least 20 times before. But this was like nothing I had ever experienced.

This wasn't a little angina or a sore arm. This was the real thing. It felt like a massive rock sitting on my chest.

I yelled for Jane and she came into the bathroom and surprised me with the nitro pills. I slipped one under my tongue. Fairly quickly, I got some relief. Then my impatience took over. Instead of calling 911, I told Jane to get the car so we could drive straight to Bridgeport Hospital, where she served on the board of trustees. On the way, barreling up Route 25, I spotted a hospital sign and shouted for Jane to get off at the next exit.

It turned out not to be for Bridgeport Hospital, but rather St. Vincent's Medical Center in Bridgeport. When Jane sped through a red light, a cop stopped us. After we explained what was going on, he escorted us to the hospital, with flashing lights and siren.

When Jane pulled up to the emergency room at 1 A.M., I rushed out of the car, ran through a crowded waiting area, and jumped onto an empty gurney.

"I'm dying!" I yelled. "I'm dying!"

That got the nurses' attention—and they had me on intravenous nitro quickly. The pain subsided. Tests confirmed I had suffered a heart attack. On Tuesday, May 2, Dr. Robert Caserta did an angioplasty to open up my main artery. Bob was a sports nut, a UConn and Yankees fan. Since I went to UMass and was a Red Sox diehard, we had a lot to argue about. Shortly after the procedure, I was back in my hospital room when the rock landed on my chest again. The vein had closed. I was having another heart attack. As they rushed me down to the cardiac room for another procedure, a priest wanted to give me the last rites.

I watched on the monitor and saw Dr. Caserta having trouble

trying to reopen the vein. The surgeon was standing by to do the bypass that I dreaded.

"Don't give up!" I shouted. "Keep trying."

I was being a pain in the butt again, giving orders—but fortunately the doctor stayed with it. He got the vein open, and I didn't need the surgery at that time.

When I left the hospital in three or four days, I called a number of people for advice, including Henry Kissinger and Michael Eisner of Disney, who both had had bypass operations. Michael was encouraging, telling me that surgery was no big deal. Henry strongly pushed for having it done at Massachusetts General Hospital. So did Dr. Saul Milles, GE's medical director, who flew to Boston with the films of my angioplasty.

Saul was a saint and a wonderful doctor. For years, I had bugged him with my chest pains and perceived heart attacks. Saul had to put up with three of the world's biggest hypochondriacs: Larry Bossidy, Paolo Fresco, and me. All of us carried a pharmacy of pills wherever we went and were always ready to call the doctor at a moment's notice to complain about every ache and pain. Together, we probably have been more responsible for GE's increasing medical costs than a hundred other employees. For the last several years, Saul's task has fallen to our current medical director, Dr. Bob Galvin, and his partner, Dr. Ken Grossman.

On May 10, 1995, in the middle of a business meeting with Paolo and Bill Conaty in my family room at home, Saul arrived with not-so-good news. He told me the films confirmed that I'd need open-heart surgery. He made an appointment for me to go to Mass General the next day and have the operation a day later. The suddenness of it all was actually a break. With my family's history and my angina over the last 15 years, I had been dreading this moment, but I didn't have much time to think about it.

On Wednesday night, I called the kids and told them the news. On Thursday, I was in Boston with Saul and Jane to meet Dr. Cary Akins, who would do the surgery. Jane remembers more about that Thursday night than I do. As she tells the story, at one point at 4 A.M. in the hospital, I turned to her and said, "If something goes wrong, don't let them pull the plug. Even if they can't tell, I want you to know I'll be fighting like hell in here."

Nothing went wrong. In fact, everything went right. I was lucky to have a great surgeon. Cary performed a quintuple bypass in three hours. Since then, he and I have become very good friends. We see each other once or twice a year—outside the hospital. Bypass surgery knocks you for a loop at first. Every part of you hurts like hell. Fortunately, you feel a lot better every day. I returned to the office on July 5, and I was back on the golf course by the end of the month. In mid-August, I won my first three matches but lost in the 36-hole finals of the Sankaty Head Club Championship in Nantucket.

When I was home recuperating from the surgery, Larry Bossidy called and suggested that he withdraw from the CEC meeting in June. He was concerned it might look like he was coming back to GE with me on the sidelines. I appreciated his sensitivity and told him not to worry.

"Go give them everything you've got on Six Sigma."

I sensed we might be at an important moment. I knew Larry was the perfect person to help. For years as colleagues, neither of us had been fans of the quality movement. We both felt that the earlier quality programs were too heavy on slogans and light on results.

In the early 1990s, we flirted with a Deming program in our aircraft engine business. I didn't buy it as a companywide initiative because I thought it was too theoretical.

The rumblings within GE were unmistakable. In our April 1995 employee survey, quality emerged as a concern of many employees. The "New Larry" had become fervent about Six Sigma. He said for most companies the average was 35,000 defects per million operations. Getting to a Six Sigma quality level means that you have fewer than *3.4 defects* per million operations in a manufacturing or service process.

That's 99.99966 percent of perfection.

In industry, things generally go right about 97 times out of 100. That's between Three and Four Sigma. For example, quality like this means 5,000 incorrect surgical operations per week, 20,000 lost articles of mail per hour, and hundreds of thousands of wrong drug prescriptions filled per year. Not much fun to think about.

By all accounts, Larry made a great pitch to our troops. He demonstrated that Allied got real cost savings—not just "feel good" benefits. Our team loved what he said, and I received positive phone calls from several attendees.

I came back to work and concluded: Larry really loved Six Sigma, the team thought it was right, and I had the survey, which said quality was a problem at GE.

Once everything came together, I went nuts about Six Sigma and launched it.

We put two key guys on it. Gary Reiner, head of corporate initiatives, and Bob Nelson, my longtime financial analyst, ran a cost-benefit analysis. They showed that if GE was running at three to four Sigma, the cost-saving opportunity of raising this quality to Six Sigma was somewhere between $7 billion and $10 billion. This amounted to a huge number, 10 percent to 15 percent of sales.

With that opportunity, it wasn't rocket science for us to decide to take a big swing at Six Sigma.

As with each of our major initiatives, when we decided to go forward, we did so with a vengeance. The first thing we did was appoint Gary Reiner as permanent head of Six Sigma. With his clear thinking and relentless focus, he was the perfect bridge to transmit our passion into the program.

We then brought in Mikel Harry, a former Motorola manager who was running the Six Sigma Academy in Scottsdale, Arizona. If there is a Six Sigma zealot, Harry's the guy. We invited him to our annual officers meeting in Crotonville in October. I canceled our usual golf outing—a symbolic gesture if there ever was one—so that 170 of us could listen to Harry talk about his program.

For four solid hours, he jumped excitedly from one easel to

another, writing down all kinds of statistical formulas. I couldn't tell if he was a madman or a visionary. Most of the crowd, including me, didn't understand much of the statistical language.

Nonetheless, Harry's presentation succeeded in capturing our imagination. He had given us enough practical examples to show there was something to this. Most left the session that day somewhat frustrated with our lack of statistical comprehension but excited about the program's possibilities. The discipline from the approach was particularly appealing to the engineers in the room.

I sensed it was a lot more than statistics for engineers, but I didn't have any idea just how much more it would become. The big myth is that Six Sigma is about quality control and statistics. It is that—but it's a helluva lot more. Ultimately, it drives leadership to be better by providing tools to think through tough issues. At Six Sigma's core is an idea that can turn a company inside out, focusing the organization outward on the customer.

We rolled out the Six Sigma program at Boca in January 1996.

"We can wait no longer," I said. "Everyone in this room must lead the quality charge. There can be no spectators on this. What took Motorola ten years, we must do in five—not through shortcuts, but in learning from others."

I thought the short-range financial impact alone would justify the program. Longer-range, I thought it could be even bigger.

In my Boca close, I called Six Sigma the most ambitious undertaking the company had ever taken on. "Quality can truly change GE from one of the great companies to absolutely the greatest company in world business." (Once again, I was going over the top.)

We left Boca that year really psyched to make Six Sigma a big hit. We told the business CEOs to make their best people Six Sigma leaders. That meant taking our people off their existing jobs and giving them two-year project assignments to qualify them for what were called "Black Belts" in Six Sigma terminology.

The first four months of the assignment would be taken up with classroom training and application of the tools. Every assigned project had to tie into the business objectives and the bottom line. Black Belt projects sprang up in every business, improving call center response rates, increasing factory capacity, and reducing billing errors and inventories. A fundamental requirement in our Six Sigma program was that we measured it. We had a financial analyst certify the results of every project.

We also trained thousands as Six Sigma "Green Belts." Green Belts underwent a ten-day training period to learn Six Sigma concepts and enough tools to solve problems in their everyday work environment. They didn't leave their current jobs. Instead, they gained a methodology to improve everyday performance.

In the top management classes, which I called "Six Sigma for little folks," we did all kinds of experiments to capture the concept. We made paper airplanes, flung them across the room, and measured where they landed. I said to the Black Belt teacher that I hoped our employees weren't looking in the window to see us playing with paper airplanes. Watching them land all over the room was our introduction to variance.

As with every initiative, we backed it up with our rewards system. We changed our incentive compensation plan for the entire company so that 60 percent of the bonus was based on financials and 40 percent on Six Sigma results. In February, we focused our stock option grants on employees who were in Black Belt training. These were supposed to be our best.

When the request for option recommendations went out in February, the phone calls started coming in. A typical phone call went something like this:

"Jack, I don't have enough options. We didn't get enough for the business."

"What do you mean? You got enough options to make sure all the Black Belts were covered."

"Yeah, but we couldn't give options exclusively to our Black Belts. We had to take care of a lot of other people."

"Why? I thought the black belts were your best people. They're the ones that should be getting the options."

"Well . . . they aren't *all* our best," they'd say.

My reply was: "Get only your best people in the Six Sigma program and give them the options. We don't have any more to give you."

I always wanted the rewards systems to make sure we were getting the best people into every initiative. No one wants to give up their best talent on a full-time basis. They've got high targets to reach and need their best managers to make them. We got push-back on the Six Sigma initiative. At first, only a quarter or perhaps half of the Black Belt candidates were the best and brightest. They faked the rest.

One of the more notable experiences came in an S-I strategy review with GE Capital's commercial finance business headed by Mike Gaudino. This is a transaction business that deals mostly with non-investment grade companies. Finding a Six Sigma leader among these deal makers wasn't easy.

This became apparent at the S-I in 1996. We asked all the CEOs to bring in their Six Sigma leaders to show their progress on the initiative.

Mike had found someone to fill the job. Now he had to sit through and watch his guy give an "air ball" presentation. It was clear to everyone in the room that Six Sigma wasn't going any-where in this business. The standard joke was that the Six Sigma leader "decided to leave" before the elevator reached the ground floor at headquarters.

The next time, Mike wasn't going to take any chances. He put in one of his stars as a replacement. Steve Sargent took over and did a great job, later becoming GE Capital's Six Sigma leader. In 2000, he was promoted again to be CEO of our European equip-ment finance business. The S-I review process worked. Mike got a better quality program and five years later GE had a new CEO for one of its businesses.

We also used the stock option program for Black Belts to smoke out the weakest links. If this or any initiative was going to be successful, it had to start with the best. I became a fanatic about it, insisting that no one would be considered for a management job without at least Green Belt training by the end of 1998. Even with my constant cheerleading and a lot of pounding in Session Cs and everywhere else, it took us three years to get all the best people into Six Sigma.

At one review, the nuclear business gave us the name of a candidate, Mark Savoff, to head up the services side. Their recommendation didn't make his Six Sigma credentials clear. Bill Conaty, our human resources head, phoned out to California and said, "We'd like to have him come in and talk to us about his Six Sigma qualifications." Mark flew from San Jose to Fairfield and convinced us that he was deeply committed to Six Sigma.

He got the job and has since been promoted to run the total GE nuclear business.

Today the Six Sigma qualifications are made clear before anybody is recommended for anything.

In the first full year we trained 30,000 employees, spent about $200 million on the training—and got somewhere in the neighborhood of $150 million in savings.

We had some good early success stories. GE Capital, for instance, fielded about 300,000 calls a year from mortgage customers who had to use voice mail or call us back 24 percent of the time because our employees were busy or unavailable. A Six Sigma team found that one of our 42 branches had a near-perfect percentage of answered calls. The team analyzed its system, process flows, equipment, physical layout, and staffing and then cloned it to the other 41. Customers who once found us inaccessible nearly one quarter of the time now had a 99.9 percent chance of getting a GE person on the first try.

GE Plastics gave us another great example. Lexan polycarbonate had very high purity standards, but it didn't meet Sony's requirements for its new high-density CD-ROMs and music CDs. Two Asian suppliers were getting all the Sony business, and we were out in the cold. A Black Belt team solved the problems and designed a change in the production process that gave us the color and static qualities Sony demanded. We went from 3.8 Sigma to 5.7 Sigma and earned Sony's business.

In the first year, we used Six Sigma all over the company to attack costs, improve productivity, and fix broken processes. One business, admittedly an extreme, found that by using Six Sigma, it could increase the capacity of their factories, eliminating the need for any capacity investment for a decade.

The next phase was to use Six Sigma's statistical tools to fix and design new products. Nowhere did this prove to be more important than in power systems. In the mid-1990s, when demand for power plants was modest, we were having forced outages in our newly designed gas turbine power plants. Rotors were cracking due to high vibration. A third of the 37 operating units in the installed base had to be removed in 1995.

Using Six Sigma processes, we reduced the vibrations by 300 percent and fixed the problem in late 1996. Since then, with a fleet of more than 210 units today, we haven't had a single unplanned removal—better than Six Sigma. Solving this problem put us in the lead of the new technology gas turbine market just in time for the power surge that would come in the late 1990s. It gave GE the major share of the global market for new power plants.

In new product design, our medical systems business took the lead. The first major Six Sigma–designed product to hit the market was a new CT scanner called the LightSpeed, which came out in 1998. A chest scan that took a conventional scanner three minutes to perform took only 17 seconds with this new product. Even better, I got a letter from a radiologist who wrote that he was amazed that a $1 million machine could be taken out of a box, plugged into a wall, and it would work immediately. That was Six Sigma at its best. In the last three years, medical launched 22 new Six Sigma–designed products.

In 2001, 51 percent of medical's overall revenues will come from Six Sigma designs, and every new product that hits the market has it. Today, all our businesses are aiming to do this.

We went from 3,000 Six Sigma projects in 1996 to 6,000 in 1997, when we achieved $320 million in productivity gains and profits, more than double our original goal of $150 million. The benefits were showing up in our financial results. By 1998, we had generated $750 million in Six Sigma savings over and above our investment and would get $1.5 billion in savings the next year.

Our operating margins went from 14.8 percent in 1996 to 18.9 percent in 2000. Six Sigma was working.

We liked the results, but too often we were hearing that our customers weren't feeling the difference in quality. We thought the problem was that many of the products in the field had been in development for years before Six Sigma was started.

It took a trip to Spain to find a solution.

In June 1998, I was thinking of hiring a full-time vice president of Six Sigma, the first and only new staff job I created as CEO. I was visiting our new plastics facility in Cartagena, Spain, for a project review with Piet van Abeelen and his team. Piet was global manager of manufacturing for plastics and had demonstrated the power of Six Sigma in one of his factories in Bergen op Zoom on the coast of the Netherlands. Using Six Sigma, Piet and his team doubled Lexan output from 2,000 tons per week to 4,000 tons without adding significant investment. Piet had the best practical handle on just what Six Sigma could do and the skill to explain it in the simplest terms.

We were having lunch on the back porch of a hacienda on our Cartagena site. I asked Piet if he would be interested in coming to Fairfield to take a new staff job I was thinking about creating. I told

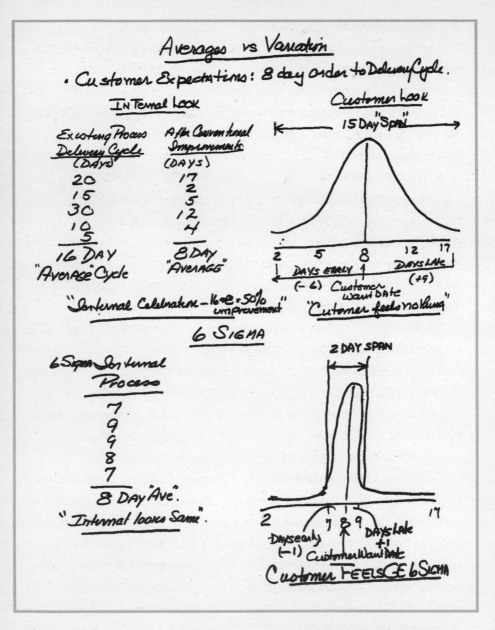

Piet he would have a very small group, two to three people, established to teach and transfer Six Sigma learning across the company. The teacher in him—and there is a lot of it—found the job appealing, despite the fact that he was currently running a huge global manufacturing operation with thousands of employees.

Fortunately, he signed on.

It was Piet who came up with the answer to why our customers weren't feeling our Six Sigma improvements. Piet's reason was simple: He got all of us to understand that Six Sigma was about one thing—variation! We had all studied it, including me, in the class with the paper airplanes. But we never saw it the way Piet laid it out. He made the connection between averages and variation. It was a breakthrough.

We got away from averages and focused on variation by tightening what we call "span." We wanted the customer to get what they wanted when they wanted it. Span measures the variance, from the exact date the customer wants the product, either days early or days late. Getting span to zero means the customers always get the products when they ask for them.

Internally, our problem was that we were measuring improvement based on an average—a figure that calculated only our manufacturing or services cycle without regard to the customer. If we reduced product delivery times from an average of 16 days to 8 days, for example, we saw it as a 50 percent improvement (see opposite).

Foolishly, we were celebrating.

Our customers, however, felt nothing—except variance and unpredictability. Some customers got their orders 9 days late, while others got them 6 days early. We used Six Sigma and a customer-oriented perspective involving span to guide us. That reduced the delivery span from 15 days to 2. Now customers really felt the improvement because orders arrived closer to their want dates.

Sounds simple—and it was—once we got it.

We were three years into Six Sigma before we "got" it. Span reduction was easy for everyone to understand and became a rallying cry at every level of the organization. It was just what we needed to take the complexity out of Six Sigma. Our plastics business reduced their span from 50 days to 5; aircraft engines from 80 days to 5, and mortgage insurance from 54 days to 1.

Now, our customers noticed!

Span also helped us focus on what we were measuring. In most cases, we were using promised dates of delivery made by a salesperson negotiated on both sides—with the customer and with the factory. What we weren't measuring was what customers really wanted and when they wanted it.

Today, we take it a step further. We measure span from our requested delivery date to our customers' first revenue: a CT scanner delivery cycle from the request date by the customer to the first scan of a patient; the turnaround time in jet engine service shops from the time it leaves the wing of an airplane to the time it takes to get back in the air; and power plant delivery cycles from the time of the order to the first generation of electricity.

Every order is tagged with the customer's start-up dates, and charts tracking the variation are put up in every facility. Visibility is clear to everyone. Using these measurements makes variation come alive. Customers see and feel what we do.

Six Sigma is a universal language. Variation and span are as understandable in Bangkok and Shanghai as they are in Cleveland and Louisville.

We expanded the initiative further by taking it directly to our customers in what we called "Six Sigma: At the customer, for the customer" (ACFC). This means taking GE Black Belts and Green Belts and putting them in customer shops to help them improve their performance.

When we have customer receptivity, it really works. In 2000, aircraft engines had 1,500 projects at over 50 airlines, helping customers earn $230 million in operating margin. Medical systems had close to 1,000 projects, creating over $100 million of operating margin for their hospital customers.

By aligning what we measure internally with our customers' needs, Six Sigma has given us better customer intimacy and trust.

*   *   *

We found out that Six Sigma isn't only for engineers. A common misperception made in quality programs is thinking that it's only for technical minds. It's for the best and brightest in any function.

Plant managers can use Six Sigma to reduce waste, improve product consistency, solve equipment problems, or create capacity.

Human resources managers need it to reduce the cycle time for hiring employees.

Regional sales managers can use it to improve forecast reliability, pricing strategies, or pricing variation.

For that matter, plumbers, car mechanics, and gardeners can use it to better understand their customers' needs and tailor their service offerings to meet customers' wants.

While it's worked in many functions at NBC, it hasn't improved our batting average in picking sit-coms.

I must admit I have trouble getting examples for lawyers and consultants. It's probably difficult for them to apply it because they make a living off of variance.

Overall, Six Sigma is changing the fundamental culture of the company and the way we develop people—especially our "high potentials." We've always had great functional training programs over the years, particularly in finance. But the diversity of the company has made it difficult to have a universal training program. Six Sigma gives us just the tool we need for generic management training since it applies as much in a customer service center as it does in a manufacturing environment.

In 2000, 15 percent of GE's executive band population were Black Belt trained. By 2003, that number should hit 40 percent. The high probability is that Jeff Immelt's successor will be a Six Sigma Black Belt.

At my Crotonville sessions in the last couple of years, I used to joke that the reason I was so slow on the uptake for e-business was that we were perfecting Six Sigma first.

"When I eventually write my book," I told the class, "I'll write that we knew we had to adopt the Six Sigma initiative at GE before we tackled e-business. E-business relied on speed and accurate fulfillment. Six Sigma gave us that."

The class would roar with laughter. They were younger and wiser and knew I had been slow to understand the impact of the Internet.

That transformation was next.

22

E-Business

The Internet revolution nearly passed me by—until Jane made me comfortable with it. She had been using the Net for years to keep up with friends. Many nights, I'd be going through my work papers while she would sit across from me, plugged in and typing away.

Jane started buying and selling stocks on-line in 1997, keeping track of her portfolio on the Internet. She was doing so well that I asked her to watch over mine. Wherever we went, Jane's laptop came along with us. Whenever she tried to convince me to use a laptop on my own, I resisted, thinking my inability to type hardly made it worth it.

"Jack," she protested, "you can teach a monkey to type."

In late 1998, however, I began to hear about people at work doing their Christmas shopping on-line. Finally, I took it seriously and developed my Boca remarks over the Christmas holidays around the importance of the Internet. Those were words that would get us going—but the Internet would really get into my blood three months later.

Jane and I were at a resort in Mexico in April of 1999 to celebrate our tenth wedding anniversary. This time, she wasn't any more romantic than I was in Barbados.

Jane was absorbed by her laptop. One afternoon she told me that people on-line were talking about the possibility of a GE stock split and my succession plan. She called me over to look at the GE message boards on Yahoo!, and I was taken in by what people were saying about the company.

"It's okay to look," Jane said, laughing. "But you can never answer."

She coaxed me into writing a few e-mails and took me through a few sites. As our vacation continued, I began to get the urge to go on-line to check the news and latest comments about GE. Once, I even skipped out on Jane at poolside, returned to our room, and flipped on the computer.

She walked in 20 minutes later, only to find me hunched over her laptop.

She knew I was hooked. It was Barbados all over again.

I came to the e-party late, but when it hit me—it hit me hard. I finally saw what impact this new technology could have on GE. I was not exactly sure what, when, and how—I only knew we had to dive in with a vengeance.

In the dot.com atmosphere of the late 1990s, everyone was quick to write off the big, old companies. Everything was focused on anyone starting a new Internet business. One thing I never fell for was the popular line "old versus new economy." People were only buying and selling goods over the Internet—just as they did a hundred years ago from a wagon. The only difference was the technology.

Yes, this new buying and selling was faster and more global, and it had profound ramifications on business. The big insight for us came when we realized creating business sites on the Internet was not Nobel Prize work. We saw this when transportation showed everyone how easily and inexpensively an auction site could be developed.

Once we knew digitizing was easy, it became obvious that big companies that got the message had little to be afraid of and, in fact, had nothing but upside.

I drew a chart that helped me understand the Internet and its implications for GE. At the time, the world was ga-ga over anything that had "dot.com" next to it. I used the chart all over the company and with the investment community. It generated a lot of conversation and was helpful to calm any employees who thought they might be playing yesterday's game. It also reassured investors that GE had a winning game plan.

In the dot.com model, expenses increase rapidly to cover the

costs of Internet development, brand advertising, and fulfillment. Losses increase in direct proportion to those expenses.
The breakeven point is uncertain and is almost always revenue
dependent.

In the "big-old-gets-it" category, the only extra expense is for
Internet development. The big company already has strong
brands and the systems to fulfill orders. Quickly, the cost savings
from Internet productivity kick in. There's a shorter time to break
even and a bigger, more certain payback, and the benefits are generally independent of revenue.

The chart captured GE's advantages over the dot.coms. We
didn't have to increase advertising. We had established brands. We
didn't have to create fulfillment organizations or build warehouses
to ship goods. Six Sigma was in place to improve our operations.
We could use digitization to focus on its main benefit—taking out
the low-value-added work in the guts of the company. Every
process can be improved and productivity increased. The efficien-
cies from this technology are enormous for big companies.

E-business allowed us to expand our markets and find new
customers. GE's supplier base became more global. Our size leveraged technology investments so that being big actually helped. For
me, the bottom line in the Internet world was: The productivity
and market share gains in the "old economy" companies dwarfed
the growth opportunities of the "new economy" models.

The skeptics, thinking that we couldn't find any more efficiency at GE, used to ask me if there was any juice left in the
lemon. The Net gave us a whole new lemon, a grapefruit, and perhaps even a watermelon—all on a platter.

We saw the Internet opportunity in three pieces: the buy, the
make, and the sell.

The "buy"—what we as a company purchase—was $50 bil-
lion of goods and services every year. Transferring some of this

activity to on-line auctions gave us access to more suppliers and lower costs. Even getting a sliver of this on-line would bring us significant savings.

Initially, we were hearing about savings of between 10 percent and 20 percent on nearly everything we bought. By the time it dropped to the bottom line, the savings turned out to be more in the 5 percent to 10 percent range. In many cases, new suppliers brought with them new costs—quality qualification costs, duties, taxes, shipping, and other charges. There were still enormous savings on the $6 billion we auctioned in 2000 and the $14 billion we expect to buy on-line in 2001.

For GE, the "make" improvements from digitization were the hidden jewel. Big companies have what I call "scud-works," massive backroom operations that generate mounds of paper. Digitization eliminates much of this and other tedious work, improving job quality for many. In 2000, we had $150 million of benefits. In 2001, we expect to save $1 billion from the "make" piece of digitization, even after $600 million of implementation costs.

On the sell side, the Net allowed us to improve service. We could fulfill faster. New and existing customers could get input on their shipments without multiple phone calls. This was the end of the expediter falsely reassuring a customer that the order was on the way. Combined with Six Sigma, the Internet could help us give our customers better service. We had $7 billion in on-line sales in 2000 and $14 billion to $15 billion in 2001.

Digitization took off once it got into our operating system. At our management meeting in Boca in January of 1999, I asked our business leaders to offer up their best thinking on e-business at the strategy sessions in June. In March, I invited the first of four outside e-business guests to the CEC: Joe Liemandt of Trilogy Systems, Lou Gerstner of IBM, Rich McGinn of Lucent Technologies, and John Chambers of Cisco.

It was Joe who scared the hell out of us with the dot.com threat. Lou brought us back to earth with his more practical views of the Net and the role of dot.coms. Rich described how the new technologies were in their infancy and laid out a vision of what the Internet could eventually become. John demonstrated that the biggest cost benefits would come from using the Internet to streamline our internal processes.

Joe Liemandt helped galvanize us. I had known him since he was a child in Pittsfield. His late father was my strategic planner during the early plastics days. Joe described, in no uncertain terms, that there were thousands of young kids out there just waiting to pick us off.

He told us, in effect, "You're big, fat, and dumb. You're sitting ducks."

His outrageous predictions were just what we needed to energize the place. We put together separate teams, in many cases housed in different buildings, to analyze potential Internet-based models that could do to us what Amazon.com was trying to do to bookselling.

With typical revolutionary fervor, we designated these units as "destroyyourbusiness.com" (DYB) teams. The goal of the DYB teams was to define a new business model for our existing businesses, without getting interference from those in the business who had been doing it "the old way."

The next chapter in my own education came on a business trip in the spring of 1999. I met the 36-year-old CEO of our consumer finance unit in London. He happened to mention during our business review that he had just met with his mentor.

I asked him, "Your mentor? Why aren't *you* mentoring the high potentials?"

"No, this is something different," he said. "I have a 23-year-old spending three to four hours a week teaching *me* how to use the Internet—I am the mentee!"

I immediately fell in love with the idea, particularly when a guy that young was using a mentor. The next day, I was giving a luncheon speech in Budapest to a group of Hungarian entrepreneurs. As usual, I thought I was imparting all kinds of wisdom. After the speech, several members of the audience rushed up to me with the obligatory "great speech" comment. Then they said, "You had one great thought that we'll all remember." I was quietly disappointed that my "eloquent remarks" had been reduced to one idea. They confirmed that the mentoring idea really hit a nerve.

When I returned home, I immediately asked our top 500 leaders to get Internet mentors, preferably under the age of 30. The mentors, many less than half our age, worked with us Neanderthal types for three to four or more hours a week. I had two. My formal mentor was Pam Wickham, who worked in GE's public relations department. She really loved the Internet and knew everything about it. She had been a key player in setting up the first GE Web site at plastics and later was promoted to headquarters.

My assistant, Rosanne, was my day-to-day savior. Every time I'd get stuck I'd yell out the door, "Ro, help!" She knew that it was time to come in and get me out of the trouble I had gotten myself into as I tried to be more advanced than my skills. She was always able to solve my problem.

In early 2000 we expanded the program to the top 3,000 managers in the company. It was a great way to turn the organization "upside down." We had bright, energetic young managers meeting with the top management in the organization. Yes, they were teaching them about the Internet. But through many casual conversations during these Internet learning sessions, managers were also discovering new talent and gaining a better understanding of what was really going on in the company.

We even recruited a "mentor" for the board. In October 1999, I asked Scott McNealy, CEO of Sun Microsystems, to become a director. We've used him to challenge all our thinking. He has, and in his outspoken way, Scott gave a great presentation that got everyone's attention at our 1999 officers meeting in Crotonville.

Scott has not only been a terrific, constructive critic, he's also become a golfing buddy. (At my age, his chances of winning are improving. Scott also has a great sense of humor. I got an e-mail announcing that he and his wife, Susan, are having their fourth baby. "I shouldn't be surprised," Scott wrote. "We've been playing hockey without the goalie.")

At GE, we were learning a lot, but there still was tremendous pressure on us to mimic the dot.com buy-and-sell model and jump into things that could be counterproductive. A good example was the third-party electronic exchanges. We, like others, almost forgot a cardinal rule of business: Never allow anyone to get between you and your customers or your suppliers. Those relationships take too long to develop and are too valuable to lose.

A good example of what we avoided was PlasticsNet, an on-line aggregator in the plastics business. It had no product other than what they could source, and were taking a cut of everything they sold—becoming a middleman at a time when the Net was supposed to get rid of people who stood between the maker and the buyer.

On our side, we had Polymerland.com. Gary Rogers, then CEO of plastics before being elected vice chairman in June of 2001, was on the leading edge of e-business in the company. Unlike PlasticsNet, he knew we had the product to sell and the information to sell it. At the time, Polymerland was doing less than $10,000 a week in on-line sales. Not much to speak of, but more than PlasticsNet was doing.

To build this business, plastics changed their incentive sales plans to encourage on-line sales and put full-time e-business specialists in the regions to get customers comfortable buying on-line. I became a fanatic about the plastics model, hounding the management team with phone calls and e-mails. I'd get their numbers daily. It was a great learning experience and lots of fun. Everyone got tired of hearing me talk about the plastics site and started swarming all over the Polymerland people.

The learning was spreading.

We originally thought plastics might reach $500 million in on-line sales in 1999. The business hit $1 billion. We underestimated the opportunity. We hadn't dreamed big enough because we had thought it was brain surgery. It wasn't. Today, Polymerland sells $50 million a week and will reach $2.5 billion in annual sales in 2001.

Plastics wasn't alone. In 2000, we did $7 billion in on-line sales across the company. While most of these revenues were from existing customers who moved on-line, we also gained new customers and increased share from existing customers.

Another folly of ours during the height of the dot.com frenzy was our desire to build sites—any sites. It was a reflection of our enthusiasm and energy, but by early 2000 it was getting out of hand. Our appliance business developed a fun new site called MixingSpoon.com. It was great: It had recipes, discussion boards, coupon downloads, shopping tips—everything a cook could need for the kitchen. Problem was, it didn't sell any appliances.

It became the poster child for what we called "dot.com dust"—sites that were created to look pretty but never had a financial reason for existing. We learned that if you couldn't monetize the screen—either directly with products or indirectly with better service—you shouldn't have built it.

Our DYB teams were quickly concluding that the Internet presented more opportunities than threats. We redefined their mission, and they became GYB, or "growyourbusiness.com" teams. They were no longer separated from the mainstream business. The digitization teams were integrated into the existing business models.

In June 1999, I sent out my first companywide e-mail (I know I was late). Within 48 hours, I got nearly 6,000 replies to a separate site we had set up. Employees from every business, in operations around the world, from factory workers to upper-level management, were e-mailing me back their thoughts, impressions, responses, complaints, concerns, and excitement. Everybody was getting into the game.

*   *   *

Our e-business initiative led to many new ways of doing business. Plastics put electronic sensors in the storage silos of some of its major customers. They automatically alert GE warehouses when material levels drop, triggering a new order via the Internet to replenish the product. GE Capital is using the Net to monitor the daily flow of cash in and out of a loan customer's income statement. The business knows instantly when the customer might be short, reducing the potential for losses. Most GE business leaders now have digital cockpits on their computer screens that update in real time all the important data to help them manage their businesses.

Every Friday, everyone in top management shared the buy, sell, and make numbers for GE's 22 largest businesses. The figures were a snapshot of what each business purchased on-line, how many auctions it ran, how much deflation occurred in the auction, and what the target for the year was or what it has increased to. By being so visible, these weekly numbers energized everyone to do more.

E-business is the only activity I've seen where targets set only 30 days earlier can look ridiculous 30 days later because the learning curve is so steep. We were always shocked when we looked back at what we *thought* we knew.

Another important lesson came from John Chambers of Cisco. He urged us to shut down the "parallel paths" of on-line and off-line work-flow processes. Until we did that, people would still rely on paper and wouldn't really use digitization to drive productivity. Within months of John's presentation, more than 150 GE managers were crawling all over Cisco. Everyone wanted to know what Cisco was doing to digitize work flow. Soon we were taking out printers and networking copiers, moving on-line all travel and expense reports, benefits information, and every internal financial report.

Everyone began to think digitally. Today it's not uncommon to have GE business leaders say that no paper is allowed in their office. It was a great mind-set shift for the entire organization.

That spring I sat and listened to an e-business review presentation from our mortgage insurance business. Their business leader outlined a strategy to remove from work flow what he called "touchpoints"—the steps of the approval process where paper had to be handled by an employee. If they could do it, they estimated that as much as 30 percent of their overhead costs would come out of the business.

It was the beginning of our "e-make" strategy. We figured out that work-flow digitization could create huge savings: $10 billion, or 30 percent of our total overhead expenses. The opportunity was staggering. We always fought to be more efficient. In digitization, we'd found the holy grail of overhead reduction.

Ultimately, e-business will improve many jobs. Take sales: Today, 30 percent to 35 percent of a salesperson's face time is spent with the customer. Salespeople spend too much time on administrating, expediting orders, arguing over receivables, and finding late shipments. The Internet can do all this more efficiently. We're increasing the face time salespeople have with customers, transforming their roles from order takers and expediters to true consultants.

In our medical systems business, it's now possible for doctors or radiologists in Denver to call up their home pages and compare their patients' throughput with thousands of others—unnamed—around the world. This relative performance data allows them to see how they compare with other hospitals. On-line, we have service offerings that can fix any shortfalls they see.

In our power systems business, it's possible for the chief engineers of local utilities to go to their home pages and compare the heat rate and fuel burn of their turbines with those of nearly 100 other unnamed utilities. With just another click, they can order service packages from us to get up to world-class performance levels.

E-business and GE's installed base are made for each other.

E-business became part of the DNA of the company because we eventually came to see it as a way to reinvent and transform GE.

As for me, I'm still struggling with my own computer.

"Hey, Ro, come help. I'm stuck!"

LOOKING BACK, LOOKING FORWARD

23

"Go Home, Mr. Welch"

We were flying to Brussels on Thursday, June 7, 2001, hoping to gain final approval from the European Commission for GE's $44 billion acquisition of Honeywell International. Honeywell chairman Mike Bonsignore and I had announced the deal eight long months earlier at NBC's *Saturday Night Live* studio in New York. Since then, thousands of people from both companies had worked feverishly to put the merger plans in place.

When Mike Smith, Honeywell's head of avionics, and I boarded the plane in New York, our team in Brussels had already taken an important step toward resolving issues raised by the European merger task force. Earlier in the week, we'd offered to divest about $425 million in Honeywell's aerospace sales—one of the larger divestitures proposed to secure approval of a merger by the European Commission.

Those concessions included the divestiture of Honeywell's new aircraft engine for regional jets and Honeywell's engine starters, whose customers included GE and our largest engine rivals, Rolls-Royce and Pratt & Whitney. We felt the concessions were meaningful and sufficient since antitrust officials in the United States and 11 other countries had already considered both divestitures unnecessary.

I had been surprised the night before we left when competition commissioner Mario Monti's office called, while I was in Boston speaking at a Harvard Business School class day, to cancel a face-to-face meeting scheduled for that Friday. This obviously wasn't a good sign.

Nevertheless, as we were flying toward Brussels, our team remained at the negotiating table, assessing the task force's reaction to what we had proposed. These negotiations were difficult because the task force asks you to keep coming up with solutions. In effect, you're negotiating against yourself.

Despite the obstacles, I was hoping to finish the negotiations and close the deal. On the plane, I was going through a briefing book with Mike Smith. In the likely event the commission would demand more than our earlier offer, Mike was helping me understand the strategic implications of each piece of his avionics business. I was trying to find some $30 million to $50 million "sweeteners" that might satisfy the demands of the commission.

It was a painful process. Mike and his team had built many of these businesses from scratch. As we were talking about possible product line divestitures, I felt like I was taking his children away. If some boss had sold a piece of my plastics business, it would have torn out a part of my stomach.

All of a sudden, I got a telephone call on the plane from Dennis Dammerman and Ben Heineman in Brussels. The task force was asking for *billions*—not millions—more in additional concessions.

Mike and I closed our briefing books. Tweaks weren't going to get this deal done.

The deal the media called the biggest industrial acquisition in history started off innocently enough.

On October 19, 2000, I was on the floor of the New York

Stock Exchange (NYSE) with an old friend. Azim Premji, the entrepreneur I met 11 years ago on my first trip to India, was in town to celebrate the listing of his company, Wipro, on the NYSE. I came along to help Azim get his new listing off to a fast start.

After Azim rang the closing bell at 4 P.M., we went on the exchange floor. A CNBC reporter interviewing Azim turned and stuck a microphone in my face. The journalist, Bob Pisani, asked what I thought of a breaking report that United Technologies might buy Honeywell.

"It's an interesting idea," I managed to say.

"What are you going to do about it?" he asked.

"We'll have to go back and think about it."

Fact is, I damn near fell on the floor. I looked up at the ticker and saw that Honeywell's stock was up nearly $10 a share. The news from Bob Pisani came as a complete surprise—and it really grabbed me.

We had looked at Honeywell earlier in the year. I thought it might be a good fit with GE. Honeywell's business was complementary to our own in three key areas—aircraft engines, industrial systems, and plastics. At the product level, there was no direct overlap. Honeywell, for example, is a leader in the small business jet engine field. GE is the leader in large jet engines. In total, the deal would add $25 billion in revenues and 120,000 employees to GE.

In early February of 2000, after our staff took a close look at the financial picture, no one liked it at the price we then thought would be necessary to acquire Honeywell. The stock was then trading in the $50 to $60 range.

Since February, however, a lot had changed. Larry Bossidy, who had merged AlliedSignal with Honeywell in late 1999 and become chairman, retired in April. The next quarter, Honeywell announced it wouldn't make its earnings estimates and the stock fell. The day before my visit to the exchange, Honeywell's shares were down to $36.

Overall, the company's weak quarter had driven its market value down to $35 billion, from over $50 billion in early 2000.

I left the exchange dying to know more. Before going to dinner that night, I started making telephone calls. I reached board member Si Cathcart and reminded him that we had looked at this deal before. At the current stock price, it looked attractive. I asked Dennis Dammerman to come to New York the next morning with a team to work on a possible acquisition.

We were in the middle of choosing my successor, so I called all three of the final candidates to bring them up to speed on what we might do. All of them wanted to go for it—especially Jim McNerney, CEO of our aircraft engines business.

In the past few weeks, in fact, McNerney and Dave Calhoun, his chief operating officer, had been working with a team of outside bankers, looking at a possible Honeywell deal. They were proposing we do the acquisition. I also knew that Lloyd Trotter, CEO of GE Industrial Systems, liked Honeywell's industrial business. Even before Honeywell's merger with AlliedSignal, Lloyd had looked at it favorably.

The next morning, on Friday, teams of GE people piled into a couple of helicopters in Fairfield loaded with data from the previous internal reviews and came to New York. I called Bill Harrison, chairman of Chase Manhattan, and asked if his vice chairman and head of investment banking, Geoff Boisi, would be available as an adviser. He was and soon rushed over to GE's offices in Rockefeller Center to go over the numbers with our team.

We brought Jim McNerney and Dave Calhoun into the discussion by videoconference. They believed the high-tech avionics piece of Honeywell fit perfectly with our aircraft engine business—with no overlap at all. Honeywell's small engine business put us into a market where we had no offerings to compete with either Rolls or Pratt. Lloyd Trotter's analysis on the industrial side showed the same thing—virtually no overlap with GE's products.

Toward the end of our videoconference, we concluded that we

could make a modest increase in the offer and make a more compelling case for Honeywell than UT. The United Technologies deal had greater product overlap and more potential for antitrust issues. We realized we had to act fast. We heard that the boards of both companies were meeting to give their final approval to the merger.

We had one advantage in making a counteroffer—the terms of the UT acquisition had been leaked. We knew what we were up against. UT planned to buy Honeywell using its stock. The transaction valued Honeywell at a little over $50 a share, or $40 billion in total.

I thought United Technologies was getting a good deal, and I knew we could offer more.

Dennis and I discussed the impact the deal might have on my retirement. I had planned to leave on April 30, 2001, five months after my 65th birthday. If we did the deal, I'd have to stay a little longer to see it through. I couldn't throw an acquisition like this on top of a guy in a brand-new job.

On the other hand, I couldn't sit on my hands and let the biggest deal in GE history go by. If we got Honeywell, I'd stay a while, but we wouldn't delay our decision on who would replace me. That person would be "chairman-elect" several months longer than originally planned.

Dennis agreed, as did the board members when I reached them by phone, that we should proceed with an offer.

Around 10:30 A.M., I called Honeywell's headquarters in Morristown, New Jersey, to speak with CEO Mike Bonsignore. He was already in executive session with his board, discussing the UT offer. Mike's administrative assistant didn't want to interrupt the board meeting.

Luckily, my executive assistant, Rosanne Badowski, knew Mike's assistant, who had been Larry Bossidy's backup administrative assistant. Ro called and convinced her it was urgent. She relayed my message that I would put out a press release immediately making an offer for Honeywell if she didn't break into the meeting.

Mike Bonsignore came to the phone and said the board was five minutes away from closing the deal.

"Don't," I said. "I want to make you a better offer."

I told Mike I'd jump in a helicopter and meet with him and his board in Morristown within an hour. He said that wouldn't be necessary. If we were serious, Mike added, he would need something in writing.

"No problem. I'll fax you something in a few minutes."

I scrawled the basic outline of our offer on a sheet of paper, and he had it in his hands ten minutes later by 11:20 A.M. I was proposing an exchange of one GE share for each Honeywell share.

"Mike, I really want to come to Morristown ASAP to clarify any and all issues on your mind," I wrote.

After my fax and further phone discussion, the Honeywell board recessed and put UT on hold. The UT board had already approved the deal and was waiting to hear from Honeywell. By getting Mike to postpone the decision, we opened the door to a negotiation.

After the market closed, United Technologies put out a statement saying it had ended merger talks and word began leaking that we were in the deal.

When I left the office Friday night, it looked like we were going to be able to do it. I went downtown to meet NBC news president Andy Lack, his wife, Betsy, and my wife, Jane, for dinner at Campagna, an Italian restaurant on 21st Street off of Park Avenue South. I had been unable to reach Jane during the day. I excitedly told her the news over the table that night.

She didn't take it well, but she understood. She was looking forward to my retirement in April. We had begun designing a new, smaller house in Fairfield, and only a week earlier I had signed the lease for an office in Shelton, Connecticut. We also were planning a ten-day vacation in Capri, Italy, for June. If we did the deal, it obviously meant our holiday plans might change.

* * *

The newspapers that morning reported that we were negotiating with Honeywell.

Saturday afternoon, Dennis Dammerman, Ben Heineman, and Keith Sherin, our new CFO, who had replaced Dammerman, and I met with Mike Bonsignore, Peter Kreindler, Honeywell general counsel, and Richard Wallman, their CFO, in New York. We gathered at the offices of Honeywell's law firm, Skadden, Arps, Slate, Meagher & Flom, in Times Square. After negotiating for a couple of hours over the price, we hit a standstill. Our offer—all in GE stock—was a tad under $45 billion, nearly $5 billion more than United Technologies had agreed to pay.

I offered one GE share for every share of Honeywell. Mike wanted 1.1 shares and wouldn't budge. We became unstuck when I agreed to go to 1.055 shares.

We shook hands and agreed to the deal.

After Mike reviewed it with his board, he asked me to confirm to them that I would stay on through the transition of the merger. I did.

I rushed back to our offices so our lawyers could work out the fine print. It was now 6:20 P.M. I celebrated the deal by riding the D train to Yankee Stadium later that night for the opening game of the World Series between the Yankees and the Mets.

I made it to the game on time.

On Sunday, the lawyers and investment bankers were working to finish up the terms. To an outsider, this might have looked like a deal that turned on a dime. In truth, over the last three years, we had looked at Honeywell. When AlliedSignal was still an independent company, Jim's aircraft team had studied the numbers. When Honeywell was on its own, Lloyd's industrial team had looked at it. Once Allied and Honeywell merged and the stock dropped, an opening occurred.

United Technologies' bid made our own offer appear spontaneous.

This felt a lot like the RCA deal. Here the strategic centerpiece was aircraft. Acquiring Honeywell would double the size of our aircraft business, giving us a broader range of engines and something we didn't have at all—the high-tech avionics, the brains of the aircraft.

The acquisition would also double our industrial businesses. It gave us some new product lines in chemicals and added nylon to our plastics business. Like the RCA deal, it also offered some niche businesses, like turbochargers, that we could use as chips going forward.

There was one notable difference. In the RCA deal, we paid 19 percent of GE's market value to get 14 percent of earnings. In Honeywell, we were paying 8 percent of our market value to get 16 percent of earnings. I felt we could do so much more with Honeywell's assets by doing what we've done with GE: pushing more aggressively into services, and adding Six Sigma and e-business initiatives to Honeywell's operations. We figured on $1.5 billion in savings from these initiatives and other productivity measures.

Moreover, we were doing the deal at a time of great strength. We'd finish the year 2000 with record earnings of $12.7 billion, up 19 percent and record revenues of $130 billion. We had enjoyed five straight years of double-digit growth on the top and bottom lines.

Throughout Sunday, working with Beth Comstock, head of public relations for GE, we fleshed out the details of how to disclose the news of the deal to both Wall Street analysts and the news media. Beth is a star. I found her at NBC, where she first headed up public relations for news and then served as PR head of the network under Bob Wright. She was by far the highest-ranked talent that came to GE from NBC.

As more details leaked, Beth fielded the rush of telephone calls from reporters on Sunday morning and made all the plans for the press conference to announce the deal. I knew the media would make a big deal out of my staying as CEO. I didn't want this to be a story about me hanging on to my job. The easiest thing in the world would have been to walk out with a drum roll. At one point, I suggested to Beth that at our press conference we show a slide of a guy holding on for dear life by his fingertips. I thought we might as well poke fun at that news angle. (It turned out we couldn't get the slide together quickly enough.)

In any event, we had all the papers signed late Sunday night.

The next morning, Mike Bonsignore and I had a quick breakfast together. Then we did four solid hours of media and analyst interviews. It started with a 9 A.M. press conference before a packed house in NBC studio 8H, where *Saturday Night Live* is broadcast. Mike and I sat on stage in directors' chairs, fielding the questions.

"I'd like you to meet my date for the last 72 hours."

"He's right," Mike said. "I've spent more time with Jack than I've been with my wife in the past 72 hours."

We laid out the rationale for the deal. I tried to lay to rest any notion that we did the acquisition so I could stay in the job longer.

"This is not a story of the old fool who can't leave his seat," I said. "Don't worry. I'm not going to do another $50 billion deal to hang around another six months."

When someone asked about getting approval from the regulatory agencies, I said there should be no problem at all. I predicted the deal would close sometime in February.

"This is the cleanest deal you'll ever see." (I still believe that, and so did just about everybody except the European Commission.)

That night, I was feeling pretty good about myself. The day had gone well, from our media interviews to our sessions with Wall Street analysts. It was a long day, so I stayed in New York rather than return home to Fairfield. While taking my contact lenses out, I scratched the cornea of one eye. I was in bed, trying to get to sleep, but the pain was overwhelming.

I called my doctor, who suggested that I immediately go to New York Hospital. As luck would have it, I got a taxi driver who couldn't speak English. He ended up taking me first to the wrong address. When I finally reached the hospital's emergency room after midnight, it was crammed with people. It took me two hours to get in to see a doctor, who relieved the pain quickly.

I went back out on First Avenue, trying to get a taxi. It took a little while to get one. I didn't hit the sack until after 3 A.M.

Talk about being brought up short. My escapade in the middle of the night brought me back to reality fast. In retrospect, it might have been a bad omen.

The last thing I ever expected was a long antitrust review by the European Commission. The commission's approval of the AlliedSignal and Honeywell merger in the last year gave me confidence that we wouldn't have a problem. Honeywell only had to make a few behavioral remedies and a minor—roughly $30 million—concession to Thales, a French electronics company, to get approval.

It's true the European Commission had derailed a big telecommunications merger between WorldCom and Sprint, along with a merger between Time Warner and EMI. Those deals had product overlaps.

The first inkling of trouble for us came in January. We began hearing that Thales was back again, lobbying the commission to press for all kinds of Honeywell divestitures.

I flew to Brussels on January 11 for a get-acquainted meeting with Commissioner Monti and his staff. John Vassallo, GE's liaison for the European Union, and our outside lawyers joined me for this session. I was asking the commission to give us what they called a "Phase 1" decision by March 6. If they didn't, a lengthy "Phase 2" proceeding would take us into July.

Commissioner Monti opened the meeting, making the point that the cooperation between the staffs was excellent and highly appreciated. After some discussion of the procedures, I emphasized the urgency for a Phase 1 approval, acknowledging that every company that shows up there does the same.

In this case, we had a strong reason to get Phase 1 approval. Honeywell and AlliedSignal had been together only a year and they hadn't been fully integrated. Any undue delay would further exacerbate their problems. I said I would do everything I could to be sure that we would respond quickly to commission concerns.

I told the commission I was hearing that some competitors were viewing the European review process as a way to extort a "goodie bag" of Honeywell assets. We knew their mouths were watering to get these businesses.

Commissioner Monti responded that our rivals wouldn't affect the deal.

"I assure you that extortionist aspects will remain outside this investigation," he said.

When I later asked if he would give the same weight to the comments of customers and competitors, Commissioner Monti and Enrique Gonzalez-Diaz, the head of the commission's merger case team, said both sources were important and necessary to the process.

Gonzalez-Diaz said competitors were a good source of factual information and he had to listen to their concerns. But, he added, I take these most often with a "pinch of salt." (I'd learn the full meaning of that phrase later.)

"Do any of you think I should be doing anything differently?" I asked. "I have not been personally through this type of process before."

"I think you are doing everything that is expected," Commissioner Monti replied. "We will be very frank and look for all ways to improve and to speed up the process. I guarantee that."

After the meeting, I had a private two-and-one-half-hour

lunch with Commissioner Monti. I found him gracious, smart, but somewhat formal.

We had a broad-ranging conversation, and I felt good chemistry between us. Nevertheless, he insisted that he call me Mr. Welch.

"Mr. Monti, please call me Jack," I said.

"I'll only call you Jack when the deal is over," he replied.

Nevertheless, I left our lunch optimistic about getting an early decision. However, by mid-February, we were getting bad vibes. It looked like the task force was going to launch a more extensive investigation of the deal, something that would take up to four more months. I decided to fly back to Brussels, hoping to prevent any further delay.

I left my home in Florida on a sunny Sunday afternoon, February 25, and flew straight to Brussels. We touched down early on Monday morning in a light snow. Ben Heineman and a team of lawyers came aboard for a strategy session before all of us drove over to the headquarters of the European Commission.

Right off the bat, Commissioner Monti read from notes and appeared to have made up his mind to push the deadline back to July.

I argued my case for an hour and thought I was making some progress. I built the argument around GE's European performance, its remarkable success energizing former state-owned companies, its strong European presence with 85,000 employees, and the lack of any overlap between Honeywell and GE. We offered nondivestiture remedies, like those made earlier by Honeywell-AlliedSignal, to address any problems.

Again, I emphasized the importance of a quick decision.

Commissioner Monti seemed moved by these arguments and suggested we go back to our hotel while he and his staff met to consider the points I had made. We got a call to return about 6:30

P.M. only to learn they hadn't changed their view and were going to Phase 2.

More troublesome, they raised some unusual objections to the deal that went far beyond traditional antitrust concerns. They wanted to study the "range effect" of combining GE's and Honeywell's overall presence in the aircraft industry.

I found Commissioner Monti pleasant, but I couldn't move him. It was disappointing, but I guess it could be expected. There was nothing in it for the commissoner to approve the deal quickly. Some of the loudest complaints were coming from his European constituents, particularly Rolls-Royce and Thales. And they weren't alone. Our U.S. competitors, among them United Technologies and Rockwell Collins, were also a loud part of a negative chorus.

I was still optimistic that it would work out. Despite the regulatory hurdles in getting the deal completed, thousands of people on both sides were working to make sure that all the major integration decisions would be made by the time we closed the deal.

We got some good news on May 2 when the U.S. Justice Department approved the deal—after we agreed to sell Honeywell's military helicopter engine business and open up our servicing business on small jet engines and auxiliary power units.

Six days later, the European Commission put out a 155-page statement of objections. It was similar to what they'd said to justify a Phase 2 look, but in much more detail.

The final stage in the Phase 2 process comprised two days of hearings in late May. This was where things really began to break down. The case team and the commissioner, after acting as investigator and prosecutor for several months, became the judge and the jury. They ended up making the decision on their own proposal.

The hearing itself is priceless.

The first day, we made the case that the commission's arguments were flawed. We had outside economists, customers, and our own legal team tearing down the commission's arguments. During the hearing, Enrique Gonzalez-Diaz, who would eventually make the recommendation to the commissioner, frequently walked in and out of the hearing—sometimes for more than 30 minutes.

The second day, the competitors showed up. There were a couple of noteworthy incidents here. United Technologies had to pull an affidavit that was factually incorrect. Rockwell Collins, which was spinning off Collins in an IPO, made a different case in front of the hearing officer than it was making to potential investors. During this session, Gonzalez-Diaz rarely left his seat.

After listening to our competitors all day, the hearing officer gave us a total of 15 minutes to rebut the charges and claims they made.

What a process—a hearing where the prosecutor also serves as judge!

After the hearing, as the commission's merger task force moved closer to a decision, I made what would be my last trip to Brussels on June 7. On the flight over with Honeywell's Mike Smith, I had gotten the bad news that the commission's demands were increasing. We arrived in Brussels at 8:30 P.M. and went immediately to the Conrad Hotel, where Honeywell and GE teams and outside lawyers were reviewing what they had learned that day.

We were also agreeing to what we would propose in our next meeting, scheduled for Friday morning, June 8. I worked with the teams until midnight to put together a mutually agreed upon submission that raised our offer threefold to $1.3 billion and included for the first time some critical avionics products.

I did not go to the Friday morning meeting with Mr. Monti because he felt the parties' positions were too far apart and suggested our staffs meet instead. The teams did meet, and Honeywell and GE put our new $1.3 billion proposal on the table.

I left Friday night and joined my wife for the weekend in Capri with Marlene and Paolo Freso. Paolo, my former partner and GE board member, who had become chairman of Fiat, was always a helpful adviser. I returned to Brussels Monday evening for dinner with the GE teams. Dennis told me of an earlier meeting that day with the task force to review the commission's unfavorable reaction to the GE/Honeywell $1.3 billion offer.

He also had a beaut of an anecdote to tell.

In the $1.3 billion offer we had made on the preceding Friday, we had added significant concessions, including some attractive avionics pieces. On Monday morning, a task force staff member asked our team why the offer excluded an obscure component made in a specific building on Honeywell's property in Redmond, Washington.

Dennis was shocked. No one on our side even knew what component they were talking about. Only a competitor with a detailed knowledge of Honeywell's business and the manufacturing site could possibly figure out that something as small as this was missing.

So much for Gonzalez-Diaz's "pinch of salt."

Our teams went back to the negotiating table on Tuesday morning, June 12, and increased our offer to $1.9 billion. Honeywell general counsel Peter Kreindler, who provided key guidance on our offers, made the principal presentation to the task force. He argued that adding Honeywell's best avionics to the package should satisfy any commission concern. The task force staff asked a lot of questions and appeared interested.

Later that Tuesday, Ben, Peter, and I agreed on the final GE/Honeywell offer. Peter wrote Ben a letter defining what dollar level and specific divestitures would satisfy our obligations under the merger agreement. It had been a struggle for us to go that far, but we felt we could still make the deal work at this level. The agreed $2.2 billion list of divestitures was what we would propose by June 14, the final deadline for submitting a proposal under the commission's rules.

Peter's letter gave us another $340 million "sweetener" that I could offer Commissioner Monti the next day in an effort to close the deal. That would bring us to the $2.2 billion of concessions.

Everyone suggested I go alone to that session on June 13, not knowing if I'd meet with Commissioner Monti by himself or with others.

I walked into Mr. Monti's office on rue de la Loi and was greeted by his assistant, who seemed surprised that I had shown up by myself.

"Where's your staff?" she asked.

"It's only me. I'm here to listen to the official response to our latest offer."

Mr. Monti came out and escorted me into his office. After a brief and cordial exchange, we entered a conference room filled with officials of the merger task force and their staff members.

After laying my briefcase on the table, I took a seat on one side of the table. Across from me sat eight to ten government officials. Besides Commissioner Monti, there was Enrique Gonzalez-Diaz, the head of the merger task force investigation team; Alexander Schaub, director general of competition; and Götz Drauz, director of the merger task force.

Commissioner Monti opened the meeting by reading a statement that thanked our team for its good efforts. He concluded his remarks by saying our proposal was inadequate and then continued reading a scripted series of demands. I took notes as Commissioner Monti suggested we divest one Honeywell business after another.

The divestitures he was suggesting added up to somewhere in the neighborhood of $5 billion to $6 billion and basically took any notion of a merger between GE and Honeywell off the table.

"Mr. Monti, I'm shocked and stunned by these demands," I said. "There's no way I could consider this. If that's your position, I'll go home tonight. I've got a book to write."

Across the table, Alexander Schaub, a heavyset, round-faced German, broke out laughing.

"That can be your last chapter, Mr. Welch," he said. " 'Go Home, Mr. Welch' is a perfect title."

The remark broke the tension in the room. Everyone had a good chuckle, but my heart sank.

There was a brief additional discussion about a full or partial sale of GE Capital Aviation Services (GECAS), our aircraft financing and leasing business, plus significant other divestitures. This went nowhere.

I had a second meeting with Mr. Monti that evening. This session lasted no longer than 20 minutes. I told him we had gone just about as far as we could go and Honeywell was in agreement. I told him we would submit our final offer the following day.

He nodded and I left.

The next day, June 14, we spoke briefly on the phone. I included the final Honeywell divestiture of $340 million that took our offer to $2.2 billion.

"I was embarrassed to bring it out last night because we were billions of dollars apart," I said. "But it will be in our final submission."

He thanked me for letting him know but showed no interest in the offer.

We went to our lawyers' offices where the teams from Honeywell and GE had gathered for weeks. We were all devastated. While I had only several meetings with the task force, both our teams had spent countless hours slugging it out with them.

The formal GE/Honeywell submission was sent late that day to the commission's offices, describing the full divestitures of $2.2 billion.

Prior to leaving Brussels, Commissioner Monti called to wish me well. He told me our dealings had been pleasant, and for the first time he called me "Jack." I thanked him and said goodbye to "Mario."

"Now that the deal is over," he said, "I can say to you, 'Goodbye, Jack.'"

"Well, good-bye, Mario."

* * *

At that moment, I couldn't believe that they'd pass up all these goodies. Along with our U.S. divestiture, it brought the total amount of concessions to about $2.5 billion—about 40 percent of the key aerospace product lines.

I hoped the merger task force would have to think twice about what was on the table.

The task force's decision got a lot of attention. Many newspapers and magazines were critical of the commission's rejection of our deal. Some politicians in Washington publicly attacked the decision and urged the commission to reconsider.

After public pressure began to build, we agreed with Honeywell to make one last try. So on Monday, June 25, Dennis, Ben, and I met in New York with Mike Bonsignore and Peter Kreindler. We agreed to offer to sell 19.9 percent of GECAS in a private placement to one or more third-party investors of GE's choice and to invite one independent director on the five-person GECAS board. We said we would never accept having our competitors as minority shareholders in GECAS. Mike and Peter agreed.

We discussed aerospace divestitures and agreed to couple the 19.9 percent GECAS sale with an offer to divest Honeywell properties with $1.1 billion of sales, half the $2.2 billion offer on June 14. Mike and Peter agreed this was the last step we needed to take.

The following morning, I called Mr. Monti and asked if he would see Mike Bonsignore and me in Brussels so that we could submit our latest proposal. He thought it was inappropriate to see us now, preferring that our European lawyers present the new proposal. I asked him to convey the same message to Mike Bonsignore. Mike and I said we were ready to go to Brussels if we got the signal from Commissioner Monti.

Our lawyers did as instructed, and Commissioner Monti got back to us quickly. On Thursday, June 28, in an afternoon

conference call with Mike and me, Mr. Monti called our last offer "insufficient." He said that if we had submitted it two
months earlier, it wouldn't have been enough.

"We tried to be responsive to what we were hearing, and after
all we put into it, this is obviously disappointing," I told him.

Mike Bonsignore echoed similar feelings.

Mike called me back about 5:30 P.M. and told me he was going
to send over a last request in the morning.

I suggested that we had given it everything we had and all
we'd do now is irritate the commission.

"Jack, I've got to give it one last desperate shot," he said.

The next morning, I received a new proposal from Honeywell. In
a two-page letter that Mike also released to the public, he asked me
to return to our June 14 proposal of $2.2 billion of divestitures.
But he also asked us to modify our GECAS proposal so that the
European Commission would have to approve the minority investor and independent board member. In short, in response to the
commission's position, Honeywell was proposing all the previous
divestitures plus an onerous GECAS concept.

In exchange, Mike proposed a revision of the merger agreement. He lowered the price for Honeywell, reducing the exchange
ratio from 1.055 shares of GE for every Honeywell share to 1.01
shares of GE for every Honeywell share.

It was unacceptable. Jeff Immelt, who had been involved in
every Honeywell decision since becoming chairman-elect in December, agreed with me and our vice chairmen that the proposal
didn't make sense. We all felt terrible for the people in both companies who had devoted months to the deal, working on the details
of the integration plans. But we couldn't go along with Honeywell's proposal.

I then called the GE board, explained our position, and got its approval to turn down Honeywell's proposed revision of the merger agreement. This was not a hard decision. The commission had destroyed the strategic reasons for doing the deal.

"What the commission is seeking cuts the heart out of the strategic rationale of our deal," I wrote in a letter to Mike. "The new deal you propose, in response to the commission, makes no sense for our shareowners, for the same strategic reasons."

The commission's rejection of the Honeywell acquisition was unfortunate for both partners. It made so much sense. All of us tried very hard to make the deal work.

For me, if this deal had come along in the middle of my career, it would have been another swing and miss. Coming at the very end, after I had postponed my retirement, the loss of GE's biggest deal seemed to loom larger.

It was never a personal battle between Commissioner Monti and myself. He and I always had cordial dealings and our teams made many efforts to overcome our differences. Unfortunately, we were operating under a set of rules that allowed the commission to function as both the opposing team and the umpire.

Once the merger task force struck at the strategic rationale for the deal, it wasn't in the interests of our shareowners.

This wasn't about me.

It was about them—and our employees are our largest shareowners.

Over the weekend, I was having cocktails at a postwedding reception on the porch of the Country Club of Fairfield, looking out over the golf course and Long Island Sound. This is a gorgeous piece of property, surrounded by water.

My friends were asking me what happened to the Honeywell deal. I pointed out to the grounds and said, "Just imagine if you bought this beautiful golf course and in order to close the purchase, the city officials demanded that holes two, three, four, five, and eight—the best holes along the water—must be given to another golf course in the area. And then they ask you to give up part of your own house."

Understanding that helped them understand my Brussels experience.

In today's highly regulated and litigious world—where corporations are easy targets—the dangers of unchecked bureaucracy are a constant thorn in the CEO's side. In our case, we've had two instances where we've been denied any kind of reasonable due process.

With the EPA's use of the Superfund law, the rule is you either do the cleanup they demand or face treble damages and a $27,500 a day penalty. Your right of appeal only kicks in after all the work is completed—years later.

That lack of due process is why we've challenged the constitutionality of this law in federal court.

With the European Commission's rejection of the Honeywell acquisition, again there was no viable review process. The bureaucrats can take the most extreme positions and not have any incentive to compromise. In the United States, antitrust authorities have to get a court order to stop a deal. Not in Europe. Companies should have the right to a fair and public hearing in a reasonable time by an impartial tribunal.

Only governments can tackle this inequity.

Going forward, companies must fight for the same rights as someone contesting a traffic ticket—their timely day in court.

24

What This CEO Thing Is All About

Being a CEO is the nuts! A whole jumble of thoughts come to mind: Over the top. Wild. Fun. Outrageous. Crazy. Passion. Perpetual motion. The give-and-take. Meetings into the night. Incredible friendships. Fine wine. Celebrations. Great golf courses. Big decisions in the real game. Crises and pressure. Lots of swings. A few home runs. The thrill of winning. The pain of losing.

It's as good as it gets! You get paid a lot, but the real payoff is in the fun.

Like any job, though, it has its pluses and minuses—but the good sure overwhelms the bad. The schedule is packed, with many hours blocked out a year in advance, yet every day manages to bring new crises that butcher your calendar. The days are crazy long, yet the hours race by because you're always fighting for more time. The job never leaves you no matter what you're doing—what's on your mind is always so absorbing.

There are all kinds of boring external functions, but none internally—well, at least not for me because I set the agenda. I was invited to a lot of black-tie dinners and industry association meetings. The best thing is, I didn't have to go. Some of the dinners are real special, like the White House State Dinners you wish your parents were alive to see. I got to meet lots of bright people I'd otherwise only read about, and I found most of them self-effacing and fun.

There's no such thing as a typical day. While I was working on this book in late May, I happened to have a day that was packed wall-to-wall, with meetings from 8:30 in the morning until 8:30 at night. The next day, Warner Books CEO Larry Kirshbaum was ragging me about why I hadn't gotten more done on the book.

"For chrissakes, Larry, there was no way I could do anything yesterday. I had a crazy day."

"What happened?" he asked.

When I told him, he insisted I put it in the book.

The day started at 8:30 A.M. with what we often call "Deal Day," when the GE Capital board met for its monthly session. This time we had a full plate to review, ranging from a bid for a bankrupt life insurance company in Japan with $5.5 billion in assets to a $500 million loan for a power plant in Mississippi. Denis Nayden, CEO of GE Capital, introduced the rationale for each deal before the business leaders and their teams came in to pitch.

GE treasurer Jim Bunt is responsible for analyzing the deals with the GE Capital teams. The day prior to the meeting, he circulated via e-mail a one-to-two-page summary of each deal along with his personal recommendation. A GE Capital board member for years, Jim has always been the resident cynic, a brilliant madman who manages to find humor—and hidden perils—in the numbers. In the fall of 2000, I made a deal to keep him a couple of extra years because his brains and total irreverence are an absolute treasure. I wanted our new CEO to have the benefit of his sharp and witty insights.

At this latest meeting, he gave Jeff Immelt and me a real zinger for leaking our approval of a deal before he had opined. He wrote derisively: "Since the chairman and chairman-elect per attributed statements reported by Reuters on Thursday May 17, 2001, appear to want this . . . if anyone has an objection at this point, please speak now or forever hold your peace."

It took us over 4 hours to go through 11 deals, 5 of them from outside the United States. Nine got approved. One $4 billion acquisition was sent back for a further look, while a $111 million deal to finance four office properties in New York City was killed. We've been burned in real estate cycles at least twice. With cranes going up all over New York, everyone was worried about a glut—except Bunt, who did like the deal's structure and conceded, "P.S. I know I'm at risk of 'Bunt, are you nuts?'"

It was one of the few times we didn't go with one of his recommendations.

When the meeting broke up, I grabbed a sandwich in the hall and brought it back into a conference room for a strategizing session on our pending acquisition of Honeywell. Dave Calhoun, CEO of our aircraft engine business, had flown in from Cincinnati, and several Honeywell guys had come in from Phoenix for the meeting.

We were in the midst of a hearing before the European Commission, which was studying the impact of the deal on competition. Although I had never felt there were any antitrust issues, we were anticipating having to give up some chips to the commission to get approval of the deal. We needed to know Honeywell's views on the strategic value of each piece.

The Honeywell meeting took two full hours, pushing back our next scheduled meeting from 1 P.M. until after 3 P.M. This next session was one I always looked forward to because it was all about people: a wrap-up of the Session C field visits over the previous six weeks. Human resources head Bill Conaty prepared the material for the five-hour meeting. Jeff Immelt took the lead here, and I tried with some success to restrain myself.

During our field visits, we often "discover" three or four stars in every business and excitedly think up new opportunities for them. When we finally get to this wrap-up meeting, we inevitably find that we've slotted each new "star" in at least three to five different jobs. So among other things, this session helps us sort through what we promised in the field and leads to an intense discussion about just which executives we'll shift from one business to another.

We went over the leadership succession plans in each of GE's businesses and discussed plans for executives ranked in the bottom 10 percent. Sometimes, the bottom 10 in one business are better than some of the people ranked in the middle of another business. This always creates a lot of heat.

This time, we reviewed the Honeywell integration, including the new organizations proposed for aircraft engines, industrial, and plastics. We spent an hour discussing which positions Honeywell executives would occupy in the postmerged company and who from GE were going to move. We selected the 35 or so managers for the 2001 top executive development course (EDC) from a nomination pool of about 50. This is a big deal, because in essence we're signaling to every one of our leaders of the future.

For many years, a key part of these sessions has been diversity. This year's detailed summaries showed that women and minorities in management have increased by over 70 percent since 1996. Over 30 percent of our 3,000-plus executive band employees are "diverse."

The number of diverse vice presidents was up to 25 percent in the last year and now represents 16 percent of GE VPs. That's not "Six Sigma" yet, but over $30 billion of GE revenues are now being managed by women and minority executives. Our pipeline is building rapidly. Our mentoring program is working.

In the last half hour of the meeting, we reviewed the two or three best practices in each initiative found during the field visits that Jeff would highlight at our CEC meeting in June.

The meeting didn't end until after 8 P.M., and the last thing I was thinking about was going back to the damn book.

Every day, of course, wasn't this hectic. There's no pat formula to this CEO thing. Everyone does it differently, and there's no right or wrong way to go about it. I certainly don't have a magic formula, but since I was presumptuous enough to write this book, I'll take a shot at sharing some of the ideas that worked for me. I hope some might be helpful. Pick and choose among them, or just toss them all.

Integrity

A freshman at a Fairfield University Business School forum recently asked me, "How can you be a good Catholic and a businessman at the same time?"

I answered emphatically, "I am."

The simple answer is: By maintaining integrity. Establishing it and never wavering from it supported everything I did through good and bad times. People may not have agreed with me on every issue—and I may not have been right all the time—but they always knew they were getting it straight and honest. It helped to build better relationships with customers, suppliers, analysts, competitors, and governments. It set the tone in the organization.

I never had two agendas. There was only one way—the straight way.

The Corporation and the Community

Everybody has a view about a corporation's role in society. I do, too.

I believe social responsibility begins with a strong, competitive company. Only a healthy enterprise can improve and enrich the lives of people and their communities.

When a company is strong, it not only pays taxes that provide for important services. It also builds world-class facilities that meet or exceed safety and environmental standards. Strong companies reinvest in their people and their facilities. Healthy companies provide good and secure jobs that give their employees the time, the spirit, and the resources to give back to their communities a thousand-fold.

Weak and struggling companies, on the other hand, are often community liabilities. They have little or no profits and pay few if any taxes. They're tempted to take shortcuts to save a buck—investing little in the development of their employees and workplaces. The constant threat of layoffs breeds insecurity and fear in employees whose worries about their own future affect their ability to volunteer time and money to help others.

I saw this first-hand in Pittsfield, Massachusetts, where I spent almost all of my first 17 years in GE. In Pittsfield, I saw two types of businesses—one healthy and one failing. We had a vibrant, growing plastics business. We were hiring great people and building new central laboratories. We had an engaged workforce that could give back to the community. Down the street, GE's transformer business had struggled, losing more and more money every year for over a decade. The business had become noncompetitive, and we had to close the plants in the 1980s. That money-losing business could provide no long-term help to the community.

The town of Pittsfield was angry when we had to shut down the transformer facilities. But this was never about GE or me liking plastics more than transformers, or liking one town more than another. This was all about the health of a business and the implications its sickness had on the community.

That's why a CEO's primary social responsibility is to assure the financial success of the company. Only a healthy, winning company has the resources and the capability to do the right thing.

Setting a Tone

The organization takes its cue from the person on top. I always told our business leaders their personal intensity determined their organization's intensity. How hard they worked and how many people they touched would be emulated thousands of times over. The CEO sets the tone. Every day, I tried to get into the skin of every person in the place. I wanted them to feel my presence.

When I traveled to remote locations—Europe, Asia, or wherever—the days were 16 hours long, allowing me to touch hundreds, if not thousands, of people. At Crotonville, I've led exchanges with more than 18,000 managers. At every human resources review, I met with the union leaders to understand their concerns so they could understand mine. I didn't want to be a picture in the annual report. I wanted to be someone whom everyone in GE knew.

Maximizing an Organization's Intellect

Getting every employee's mind into the game is a huge part of what the CEO job is all about. Taking everyone's best ideas and transferring them to others is the secret. There's nothing more important. I tried to be a sponge, absorbing and questioning every good idea. The first step is being open to the best of what everyone, everywhere, has to offer. The second is transferring that learning across the organization. Work-Out drove boundaryless behavior and developed the ideas. We rigorously evaluated everyone on this value to reinforce its importance. Connecting all the meetings ("operating system")—from HR to strategy—gave new ideas increased momentum and helped refine them. Crotonville helped share the learning and brought out the best in everyone.

Searching for a better way and eagerly sharing new knowledge has today become second nature at GE.

People First, Strategy Second

Getting the right people in the right jobs is a lot more important than developing a strategy. This truth applied to all kinds of businesses. I sat in rooms for years, looking at promising strategies that never delivered results. We had great plans for ultrasound, but we could never make them happen until we found the perfect person with ultrasound in his veins. We had service strategies in aircraft engines, power, and transportation for years. Service was always a second-class citizen until we put leaders in place who had the courage to "kick ass and break glass."

We learned the hard way that we could have the greatest strategies in the world. Without the right leaders developing and owning them, we'd get good-looking presentations and so-so results.

Informality

Bureaucracy strangles. Informality liberates. Creating an informal atmosphere is a competitive advantage. Bureaucracy can be the ultimate insulator. Informality isn't about first names, unassigned parking spaces, or casual clothing. It's so much deeper. It's about making sure everybody counts—and everybody knows they count. Titles don't matter. There aren't epaulets on shoulders, or stiffs in corner offices making all the calls—just a wide-open spirit where everyone feels they can let it rip. "Covering your ass" is ridiculed. Passion, chemistry, and idea flow from any level at any place are what matter. Everybody's welcome and expected to go at it.

Self-Confidence

Arrogance is a killer, and wearing ambition on one's sleeve can have the same effect. There is a fine line between arrogance and self-confidence. Legitimate self-confidence is a winner. The true test of self-confidence is the courage to be open—to welcome change and new ideas regardless of their source. Self-confident people aren't afraid to have their views challenged. They relish the intellectual combat that enriches ideas. They determine the ultimate openness of an organization and its ability to learn. How do you find them? By seeking out people who are comfortable in their own skin—people who like who they are and are never afraid to show it.

Don't ever compromise "being you" for any damn job in any institution.

Passion

Whenever I went to Crotonville and asked a class what qualities define an "A player," it always made me happiest to see the first hand go up and say, "Passion." For me, intensity covers a lot of sins. If there's one characteristic all winners share, it's that they care more than anyone else. No detail is too small to sweat or too large to dream. Over the years, I've always looked for this characteristic in the leaders we selected. It doesn't mean loud or flamboyant. It's something that comes from deep inside.

Great organizations can ignite passion.

Stretch

Stretch is reaching for more than what you thought possible. I've always used the annual budget process as the best example of stretch.

You know the drill. There's a business team in the field, working for a month on a presentation at headquarters, trying to develop the case for the minimum number they think they could "sell." The headquarters team comes to the same meeting armed to squeeze out the maximum. The field team comes with all kinds of charts on the weak economy, the tough competition, and says, "We can produce 10." The top management comes in that morning wanting 20.

The presentation usually takes place in a windowless room. No customers are present. You know what happens. After mountains of PowerPoint and hours of give-and-take, the budget is set at 15.

It's an enervating exercise in minimalization.

The field team flies back, high-fiving one another. They didn't have to give all they had to headquarters. Top management thinks it had a great day, ratcheting the objectives to new heights.

Why is this game played? Over the years, people everywhere have learned that if you made your number, you got a pat on the back or better, and if you missed your budget, you'd get a stick in the eye or worse.

Everyone plays by these rules.

In a stretch environment, the same field team is asked to come in with "operating plans" that reflect their dreams—the highest numbers they think they had a shot at: their "stretch." The discussion revolves around new directions and growth, energizing stuff.

The team leaves with everyone on both sides of the table having a pretty good understanding of what the business will do and what they'll try to do. An operating plan is put together reflecting that reality. The team knows they're going to be measured against the prior year and relative performance against competitors—not against a highly negotiated internal number. Their stretch target keeps them reaching.

We've never yet made a "stretch operating plan." Yet we've always done a helluva lot better than we ever thought we'd do—and more than Wall Street expected.

A stretch mentality isn't easy to get, and by no means does GE have it throughout the company. Sometimes we found cases where managers at lower levels took stretch numbers and called them budgets, punishing those who missed. I don't think it happens much anymore, but I wouldn't bet on it.

Nevertheless, we'll never stop "stretching."

Celebrations

Business has to be fun. For too many people, it's "just a job."

I always found celebrations were a great way to energize an organization. From my first days in plastics, I was always looking for ways to celebrate even the smallest victories.

At Crotonville, I'd often get frustrated by the answer to the simple question "Are you celebrating enough?" The students turned silent or would murmur, "No."

I loved to push back on this one.

"Don't look at me. I can't celebrate for you. We're not going to have a vice president of celebrations at GE. You have to consider yourself the manager of celebrations. You've got the authority. Go back and make it happen. You don't have to hand out a new Mercedes. It can be a keg of beer or a dinner for two.

"Your job is to make sure your team is having fun—while they're being productive."

Aligning Rewards with Measurements

You have to get this one right.

One time, I was surprised to see a great fourth quarter revenue line and no income to go with it. I asked, "What the hell happened here?"

"Well, we had a fourth quarter sales contest and everyone did a great job!"

"Where's the margin?"

"We didn't ask for margin."

That's the simplest example of a universal problem: What you measure is what you get—what you reward is what you get.

Static measurements get stale. Market conditions change, new businesses develop, new competitors show up. I always pounded home the question "Are we measuring and rewarding the specific behavior we want?"

By *not* aligning measurements and rewards, you often get what you're *not* looking for.

Differentiation Develops Great Organizations

No one likes to play God and rank people, especially the bottom 10 percent. Differentiation is as tough an issue as any manager faces. I thought it was my job to talk about it, to force it every day, to demand it from everyone. From my first days, I thought it was the key to building a great organization. For us, the vitality curve made differentiation work. We used it relentlessly to push leaders to continually upgrade their teams. Year after year, forcing managers to weed out their worst performers was the best antidote for bureaucracy. Our surveys showed the lower we went in the organization, the louder the concerns about our weakest performers. The lower-level executives, more than senior managers, bore the brunt of laggards.

Differentiation is hard. Anybody who finds it easy doesn't belong in the organization, and anyone who can't do it falls in the same category.

Owning the People

We always told our business leaders, "You own the businesses. You're renting the people." Bill Conaty and I felt we had personal responsibility for the top 750 managers. We looked after their development, their rewards, and their advancement. We ran the people factory to build great leaders.

Our business CEOs knew they would be rewarded for teeing up high potentials. Our boundaryless culture changed the game from hoarding your best people to sharing your best.

Of course, I'd sometimes hear a groan on the other end of the phone when I'd call a business leader and say, "Sorry, you just lost X."

Giving up the best is not a natural act. Within minutes, we'd be talking about the backup slate to fill the new hole we created. With our bench, the backups sometimes turned out better than the starters.

Appraisals All the Time

Appraisals to me were like breathing. In a meritocracy, nothing is more important. I was giving appraisals all the time—whether I handed out a stock option grant or gave a raise—or even when I'd bump into someone in the hallway.

I always wanted everyone to know where they stood. Every year, I'd send a handwritten note with the annual bonus to my direct reports. I'd write two to three pages, outlining what I was looking for in the coming year. I'd attach to it the prior year's letter, which I would mark up in red, to give continuity to the process.

These notes did a couple of things. I had the chance to reflect on each business and what I thought was important. My direct reports realized that there would be follow-up—and that I cared a lot. The process was time-consuming, and sometimes late on a Sunday night, I would wish I hadn't started it, but it was great discipline for me. (Examples of these notes to my successor, Jeff Immelt, over the last four years, are in the appendix. These are on the favorable side, especially compared to some others I wrote.)

Culture Counts

Kidder sure as hell taught me that. I saw it in the Honeywell/ AlliedSignal merger. A year after those two companies merged, factions were still arguing over whose culture would dominate. When DaimlerChrysler came together as a "merger of equals," it appeared to lead to confusion.

Setting the culture straight on day one minimizes this. The resisters have to go quickly.

An organization that truly believes in maximizing intellect can't have multiple cultures. During the Internet craze of the late 1990s, we had some people in an equity group at GE Capital who suddenly thought they were geniuses. They decided they should have a piece of the action in the companies where they invested GE money.

We told them to take a hike. In our shop, there's only one currency: GE stock with GE values.

Culture is the reason we passed up a couple of high-tech acquisitions in the late 1990s in California. I didn't want to pollute GE with some nutty stuff going on in the midst of the dot.com craze.

That doesn't mean that at GE people can't be individualists or can't get paid extravagantly for great performance. When it comes to personal style and pay, our culture will bend, but we won't break it.

Strategy

Business success is less a function of grandiose predictions than it is a result of being able to respond rapidly to real changes as they occur. That's why strategy has to be dynamic and anticipatory.

Bob Nelson, my longtime financial analyst and GE's resident history buff, exposed me to this thinking when he passed on an article about the Prussian general Helmut von Moltke. Von Moltke's beliefs brought us to a series of questions that were much more useful to me over the years than all the data crunching in strategic plans.

Five simple questions brought strategic thinking to life for me:

- What is the detailed global position of your business and that of your competitors: market shares, strengths by product line, and by region today?
- What actions have your competitors taken in the past two years that have changed the competitive landscape?
- What have you done in the last two years to alter that landscape?
- What are you most afraid your competitors might do in the next two years to change the landscape?
- What are you going to do in the next two years to leapfrog any of their moves?

Competitors

Two "truths" I've learned to challenge over time dealt with competition.

One old chestnut is, "We're losing market share because our competitors are crazy, and they're giving the product away." I heard that more than a hundred times in my career. Usually, it turned out to be BS. The real truth was that a competitor had a better cost position or a strategic rationale for what it did.

It took me a while to figure out that I should have been asking, "What was wrong with us, not them?"

The other beauty goes something like this: A team comes in with a proposal to leapfrog the current position of its leading competitor. The implicit assumption is the competition will be sleeping while we're developing the new product. Doesn't usually happen that way.

Take our effort to build the GE-90 aircraft engine. The engineers convinced me that if we developed this brand-new engine for Boeing's new short- to medium-range 777 jets, we'd meet their requirements for a 90,000-pound thrust engine. They said Pratt & Whitney and Rolls-Royce couldn't stretch their existing technology to get to 90,000. Didn't happen. Pratt and Rolls found ways to get their engines to deliver as much as 94,000 pounds of thrust.

Fortunately, the project had a happy ending. Our new engine was capable of getting to 115,000 pounds, which was what Boeing needed when it later came out with a long-range version of the 777. Our engine got us a major contract on these planes.

It was tough, but we tried like hell to look at every new product plan in the context of what the smartest competitor could do to trump us.

Never underestimate the other guy.

The Field

I never really felt headquarters was the place to be, and becoming CEO reinforced my point of view. From my first job as an officer in February 1972, I wanted to be out with the people who really made things happen. I'd spend at least a third of my time with the GE businesses. I have no idea how much time CEOs should spend in the field. I do know I fought every day to get my butt out of the office.

I always reminded myself: Headquarters doesn't make anything or sell anything. Banging around the field was my best shot at getting some idea about what was really going on.

Markets vs. Mind-Sets

Markets aren't mature. Sometimes minds are. Nowhere was that more truthful than our pursuit with almost religious fervor of a No. 1 or No. 2, fix, sell, or close strategy. Looking at the same businesses from a different share perspective changed our mind-set. When we asked each business to redefine its market so they could have no more than a 10 percent share, what had looked like mature markets became growth opportunities. Even a few field horses started looking like thoroughbreds. With the same portfolio of businesses, our revenue growth rate more than doubled in the last half of the 1990s.

Initiatives vs. Tactics

In 20 years, we really had only four initiatives—Globalization, Services, Six Sigma, and E-business.

Initiatives live forever. They create fundamental change in a company. They build on one another. Everything in the GE operating system reinforces them.

On the other hand, short-term tactical moves are needed to revitalize and energize a function or company. Here are three examples. We upgraded sourcing leadership and globalized suppliers. That saved millions. We reduced foreign service employees (FSE), by bringing U.S. expatriates home. That saved millions— by forcing the businesses to promote local nationals and put a global face on the company. We reduced internal travel, using the Internet. That saved millions—and addressed the work/life balance issue. Our people got fewer Frequent Flyer miles but stayed home and had better lives.

Understanding the difference between the fundamental and the quick fix helps an organization stay focused.

The Communicator

I was an outrageous champion of everything we did—from our early need to face reality and change the culture to our major initiatives that reshaped the company. Whenever I had an idea or message I wanted to drive into the organization, I could never say it enough. I repeated it over and over and over, at every meeting and review, for years, until I could almost gag on the words.

I always felt I had to be "over the top" to get hundreds of thousands of people behind an idea.

Looking at my handwritten notes for my Boca speeches over 21 years only reminded me of how many times I said the same things from different angles and with different emphasis. "Boundaryless" was a clumsy word I could barely get out of my mouth, and I butchered it a million times, but I never stopped saying it.

My behavior was often excessive and perhaps obsessive. I don't know if that's the only way, but it worked for me.

Employee Surveys

We used all kinds of ways to get employee feedback: Crotonville, Session Cs, vitality curves, and stock options. These tools forced management to deal with employees in a straightforward manner. Making employee surveys meaningful was a big breakthrough for us in 1994.

We didn't ask about the quality of cafeteria food or the benefit plans. We asked questions that got at fundamental issues around the theme: "Is the company you read about in the annual report, the company you work for?"

We didn't run the company by polling, but the candor of our employees in these anonymous on-line surveys really helped us put the right emphasis on the right initiatives. We showed the results not only to our employees, but also to our board members and to the security analysts. The analysts were shocked the first time I did it, but it put a helluva lot more beef behind the charts I was presenting.

Knowing—and confronting—what was on the minds of our employees was a key part of our success.

Upgrading a Function

Whenever I thought a corporate function wasn't as strong as it should have been, I would appoint myself the unofficial head of it. Take sourcing—the process of buying billions of parts, products, and services.

Sourcing was once a place to park people who hadn't quite made it in manufacturing. In the mid-1980s, when our purchasing costs weren't coming down fast enough, it was clear we needed to change things. I set up a council that brought the businesses' sourcing leaders to meet with me in Fairfield every quarter. Some of the business CEOs nearly died when they realized whom they were sending.

I usually saw the weak ones once.

We did the same thing with service leaders, Six Sigma leaders, and e-business advocates—anything that really mattered. Putting the councils together and bringing leaders to Fairfield to meet with me or a vice chairman helped surface the best and brightest from within our organization.

Once we had highly energized leaders in place, ideas flowed like water downhill to the rest of the company.

The Advertising Manager

Managing image and company reputation is one of the more obvious jobs of a CEO. I might have taken it to an extreme. For 20-plus years, I looked at thousands of storyboards for corporate and product ads. I never allowed one advertisement on the air that I didn't like.

We had great two-person advertising teams, led first by Len Vickers and then by Richard Costello. When Len set up a runoff among several agencies for a new GE slogan in 1978, BBDO won the business. Phil Dusenberry, BBDO's creative head, came up with "GE: We bring good things to life."

I loved it the moment I heard it. Sometimes I drove the agency and our guys nuts with my micromanaging of the process. I liked playing with the ads, had a strong point of view, and wanted to be proud of everything GE put on the air. I thought that Sunday morning TV news programs were the place to reach the country's thought leaders, and most of our ad spending went there. My micromanaging continued. Just months before my retirement, I was reviewing storyboards for TV ads for a new line of energy-efficient refrigerators.

Image mattered. I was convinced it was my job.

Managing Loose, Managing Tight

Knowing when to meddle and when to let go was a pure gut decision. Although I dove into the tube problem at medical systems, I had no involvement in the planning or pricing of our biggest breakthrough in cancer detection, a $2.7 million scanner.

A lot of this is pure instinct. I managed tight when I sensed I could make a difference. I managed loose when I knew I had little if anything to offer.

Consistency was not a requirement here. Sometimes being an undisciplined, unmade bed got the job done faster. You pick and you choose your opportunities to make a difference. I loved to go on the field when I thought I could play, and I loved cheering from the sidelines when I didn't think I belonged in the game.

Chart Maker

In December of 2000, I was probably the only 65-year-old guy still drawing business charts for analyst presentations. I've always thought that chart-making clarified my thinking better than anything else. Reducing a complex problem to a simple chart excited the hell out of me. For every analyst meeting, I'd sit for hours with my finance and investor relations teams, sketching out and tearing up chart after chart. I loved doing charts and got so much out of them. The crazy thing about it was that we always felt the last presentation was our "best one ever."

Investor Relations

Wall Street is a big part of the job. We changed who we put into investor relations. We always had good people, but the old model was a career-ending job for financial types. They were generally at headquarters, expected to respond passively to questions from analysts and investors.

The model changed in the late 1980s when we picked young high-potential financial managers with a marketing sense. Each one of them became the chief marketing officer for GE stock, constantly on the road visiting investors and selling the GE story. The job went from defensive linebacker to offensive halfback. All those who held the job got up every morning and felt they were measured by the price of GE stock. Already on a fast track because of their financial acumen, they used the job to improve their sales and presentation skills.

The position went from a dead-end assignment to one of the most sought after. It became a terrific training ground: Warren Jensen, the first of the new model in 1989, went on to become CFO of NBC, then Delta Airlines, and now Amazon.com; Mark Begor followed him, and he's now CFO of NBC; Jay Ireland was next, and he's now president of the NBC station group; and Mark Vachon has held the job for the past three years. He's been a great sport, agreeing to stay beyond the typical two-to-three-year run to give us continuity through the CEO transition.

Our entire IR team consists of two people. That's because our rising stars are supported by a fabulous constant, Joanna Morris, a graduate of our audit staff. Joanna, who always gets teased about training these stars, is married with two kids and wanted to settle down in Fairfield without heavy travel.

We need only two people to tell the GE story—fewer than we had 20 years ago—and now it's launching careers, not ending them.

Wallowing

"Let's wallow in this" was a phrase I often used. It meant getting people together, often spontaneously, to wrestle through a complex issue. The sole ticket for admission was know-how, not titles or positions. We wallowed in public relations problems, environmental issues, Boca agendas, and big M&A deals. The idea was to get fresh thinking without paper and memos, then sit on the conclusions for a night, wallowing some more. From wallowing came some of our best decisions.

It was all about breaking down the concept of hierarchy. Everyone knew they were equal partners at the table, where their ideas could be thrown out with informality and candor.

Your Back Room Is Somebody Else's Front Room

Peter Drucker gets credit for this one. We practiced it.

Don't own a cafeteria: Let a food company do it. Don't run a print shop: Let a printing company do that. It's understanding where your real value added is and putting your best people and resources behind that.

Back rooms by definition will never be able to attract *your best*. We converted ours into someone else's front room and insisted on getting *their best*. That worked for us so many times. This is what outsourcing is all about. It's also what many of our layoffs were about in the early 1980s as these jobs migrated elsewhere.

It always made me mad when some politicians and economists claimed that all the job creation in America was coming from small entrepreneurial companies. Much of that, in fact, was the conscious transfer of work out of big business.

Speed

At Crotonville, a frequent complaint even in my final days as CEO is that we weren't fast enough. I learned in a hundred ways that I rarely regretted acting but often regretted *not* acting fast enough. I could scarcely remember a time when I said, "I wish I'd taken six more months to study something before making a decision."

I think acting decisively on people, plants, and investments was one of the reasons I got out of the pile very early at GE. Yet 40 years later when I retired, one of my great regrets was that I didn't act fast enough on many occasions. When I asked myself, How many times should I have held off on a decision? versus How many times do I wish I'd made that move faster?, I inevitably found that the latter won almost every time.

Forget the Zeros

In a big company, what's small tends to get lost. As businesses and companies grow, their size can become an inhibitor rather than an enabler. The disadvantages of size—the difficult communications, the layers, and the lack of informality—all work against the creation of an energizing atmosphere.

The entrepreneurial benefits of being small—agility, speed, and ease of communication—are often lost in a big company. Plastics taught me the value of being small, of "feeling like you owned it." I came to the CEO job knowing that isolating small projects and keeping them out of the mainstream was the way to grow.

We've had many great successes by breaking these projects out—and focusing on them—as separate, smaller businesses in larger entities. We did this everywhere—Noryl in plastics, CT scanners and ultrasound in medical, and vendor financing and commercial finance in GE Capital. It didn't always work. But in every case one thing was clear: Breaking out businesses created people who were high-spirited, energized, and backed by the right resources.

The smaller ventures got high visibility and created heroes, celebrating both those who won and those who missed and driving home the value of taking risks.

We were aware of what size meant. The worst thing a company can do with size is to focus on "managing" it. Size either liberates or paralyzes. We tried every day to remember that the benefit of size was that it allowed us to take more swings.

Just some thoughts—things that worked for me, along with a lot of luck.

For the past twenty-four years, I have had a lucky charm—a brown leather briefcase—that has come with me everywhere. My assistant, Rosanne, has nicknamed it "Mr. Lucky." I won the briefcase in an Atlanta golf tournament in 1977, the year I first came to Fairfield. It has seen better days. It's battered and bruised, or, as Rosanne liked to say, "It's disgusting and looks diseased!"

I've done extremely well with Mr. Lucky. It's been good to me, and I never wanted to give it up. The only time it's been out of my sight is when Rosanne took it home for a night to stitch a torn seam back in place. It's not that I have never been superstitious. I just never wanted to push my luck.

The last day I left headquarters, Mr. Lucky came with me. As my friend Larry Bossidy always said about my briefcase, "It's Jack. He doesn't need a new one. That's the one he came with. That's the one he's going out with."

25

A Short Reflection
on Golf

Being CEO of GE was the greatest thrill of my life. If I had another preference, I would've loved to have been a professional golfer. Ever since I picked up the game as a caddy at the Kernwood Country Club in Salem, it's been one of the true passions of my life. My father, who got me started on the game, was right: Unlike the hockey or football I played as a kid, golf was a game I would have all my life.

It is a sport that combines what I love: people and competition. The most enduring friendships of my life have been formed on and around the golf course. Every golfer who's ever hit a solid tee shot or has sunk a 14-foot putt knows the seductive power of the game.

I was pretty much a self-taught player. I started when I was nine years old, playing with the other older caddies at Kernwood. With a bag filled with half a dozen taped-up clubs, I was lucky to shoot below 120. If I wanted more playing time beyond a few hours on Monday mornings—caddy time—I had to sneak onto the course.

In golf, everything seems to happen backward. I would have given my right arm for five good clubs back then. Now people send me free sets of the best clubs, and I've been lucky enough to play on some of the greatest courses in the world.

I guess I never lost my touch for caddying. In the summer of 2000, I found myself lugging a bag all over again—at the age of 64—for my seven-year-old grandson, Jack, in a junior tournament at Sankaty Head Golf Club in Nantucket.

Little Jack had a better swing than I had first time out. I grew up with a typical caddy's swing—flat, without much style, and with the wrong grip. I'd just sort of hockey the ball around. I never practiced much and just wanted to go out and play. I was co-captain of the team at Salem High and played as a freshman in college.

My golfing buddies joke that I take golfing tips from everyone I meet—players, caddies, a locker room attendant, even a waiter at a club. Every tip is worth a try. I'll get the latest ball, the newest driver—anything to get a little more distance. For professional advice, I'd go to Jerry Pittman, the former pro at Seminole, the great Florida course. I'd ask him, "How do I get ten more yards on my drive?"

"How old are you now?" he'd ask. "How old were you last year? Why don't you realize it?"

I don't want to recognize that, because I'm convinced I can get better.

That's always been the case. Golf is a game where you constantly seek the illusion of perfection. If you enjoy the give-and-take of a match—and I certainly do—the game is a real high.

I can't think of a more social sport. I've met some of the world's greatest human beings playing golf: Many became lifelong friends. John Kreiger at the Berkshire Hills Country Club in Pittsfield 40 years ago; Anthony "Lofie" LoFrisco and Carl Warren at Silver Spring Country Club in Ridgefield, Connecticut, 25 years ago; and Jacques Wullschleger at Sankaty Head 15 years ago.

At work, I've had a great foursome over the years in Chuck Chadwell and Dave Calhoun from aircraft engines and Bill

Meddaugh from GE Supply. We all play about the same and compete like hell—at least 36 and sometimes 54 holes a day. (Some years their bonus checks have had to be reduced for "unspecified reasons.")

Being CEO of GE gave me access to lots of interesting people on the golf course. The outings made not only for great mornings and afternoons, they made for great stories. I remember one match in Nantucket with Warren Buffett, Bill Gates, and my friend Frank Rooney, who had sold his wife's shoe company to Warren. Bill and I paired up against Warren and Frank.

We got to the end of the first hole and Warren sank a putt for par.

"Well," said Bill, "the match is over."

"What's this all about?" I asked, confused.

Bill explained that he and Warren have an ongoing bet. The first one who gets a par wins a dollar. If they get to the ninth hole without a par, the lowest score wins. Here I was, with two of the richest guys in the world, and they were betting a buck on the game.

For a second, I thought they were going to walk back to the clubhouse.

I had another funny incident that involved Frank Rooney, former chairman of Melville. For years, he's had a contract with Warren to work a day a week. I think he spends every one of those days playing golf. One day, I played with Frank and he shot 78, almost his age, and kicked my butt.

Afterward I sent Warren a note about the game and complained that his employees obviously weren't working hard enough.

Warren sent one back. "No Berkshire Hathaway employee can break 80, and I have no recollection of a Rooney on my payroll," he wrote.

Golf even got me a GE board member. About three years ago, *Golf Digest* put out a list of CEO golfers and ranked Scott McNealy of Sun Microsystems a No. 1. Somehow, I was right behind him. Scott soon sent me a challenge: "If I'm going to be No. 1, I want to be sure I'm No. 1. Jack, you name the place—anytime, anywhere, *mano a mano,* and we'll settle it once and for all."

I called him the moment I saw his message. We set a date, and Scott was generous enough to come to Nantucket that summer for a 36-hole match, which I won. Within two weeks, Scott sent me a trophy inscribed with the words *Welch Cup.* I beat him again at Augusta the following year over 36 holes to keep the trophy. Last year, he won an "abbreviated" 18-hole match, and the trophy is now in California. (It kills him that I call it "an abbreviated match.")

Only after beating him the first time did I invite Scott on the GE board. It was good timing—just as we were about to launch our e-business initiative.

I was lucky. Scott showed up as my game was getting better. Most of my years in golf, I'd just work the ball around the course, grinding through 18 holes, surviving only because of my good short game.

It wasn't until after I married Jane in 1989 that my game went to a different level. I was up to about a 10 handicap then, but in the process of teaching her the game, I made myself a whole lot better. At one point, I got down to a two or three handicap and won two club championships at Sankaty Head. Before meeting Jane, I'd get knocked out in the first or second round.

I wasn't aware of it, but when I began teaching her, for the first time in my life, I actually slowed myself down and analyzed my own swing. When I was telling Jane to take a longer back swing, I realized that I had to do the same myself. So I worked on getting it back farther, and I worked on learning how to finish. Until then, I never finished off my swing.

Now I keep saying to myself, Fred Couples, Fred Couples, Fred Couples, when I get ready to take a whack at the ball. I thought Couples had a great finish, and I always try to picture that swing in my head when I'm following through.

Teaching Jane helped me to break down each element and focus on the mechanics. By being more aware of the technical stuff,

I found that I stopped choking late in the round. I started to play better and began to like the game even more.

In 1992, I played 36 holes a day for 10 straight days at Sankaty Head before the tournament. I worked my handicap down to a 2 to win the championship.

Two years later, I managed to win again. It went right down to the wire in a final with my friend Jacques Wullschleger. He is a terrific golfer. For the past 16 years, we've played 40 to 50 rounds a year together. He can beat me 99 times out of 100. Fortunately for me, my one in 100 chance occurred in the 1994 club championship. I won in sudden death, dropping a 15-foot putt on the thirty-seventh hole for a birdie.

Jacques is someone very special. After losing to me, he spent days carving a wooden Sankaty lighthouse and gave it to me as a memento of the occasion.

The most celebrated game I've ever played was in the spring of 1998 at the Floridian, Wayne Huizenga's course in Florida. Matt Lauer, co-host of the *Today* show, knew golf pro Greg Norman and asked him to join us. It was a friendly match, and Greg was a great sport playing with a bunch of average players. Greg, just fooling around, shot 70, 2 under par. Matt had a 78.

I actually had a lower score than Greg—69 from the back tees versus his 70 from the pro tips. It was an exciting day for me. I think I told everyone in the world, faxing the scorecard to anyone I knew. At the Business Council meeting a week later, whenever anyone asked me about my golf game, I said, "Wait a minute," and pulled the scorecard out of my pocket.

Greg had a lot of fun with it himself. He signed my scorecard and allowed me to show off, even though it was only a casual game. I told him that by the time I got through telling this story, he will have played the ladies' tees and I will have played the tips. I might have been taking it a little too far, especially after my "victory" showed up in magazines and newspapers and even Don Imus began talking about it on the radio.

At one point, Greg called and asked jokingly, "Jack, have you told everybody in the world?"

"Have you found anyone I haven't told?" I said, laughing. "If so, send me their address."

26

"New Guy"

To keep him anonymous, "NG" is what we called him. It was our code for the "New Guy."

Keeping the choice of my successor a secret was the easy part. But that was the only easy thing about it. Making the pick was not only the most important decision of my career, it was the most difficult and agonizing one I ever had to make. It damn near drove me crazy, causing many sleepless nights.

For at least a year, it was often the first thing I thought about each morning and the last thing on my mind at night.

What made it so hard was that we had three sensational final candidates: Jeff Immelt, who led our medical systems business; Bob Nardelli, who ran power systems; and Jim McNerney in aircraft engines. All three exceeded every expectation we set for them. Their performance was off the charts.

Any one of the three could have run GE. Not only were they great leaders, they were my good friends—and I knew I had to disappoint two of them.

I knew it was going to be one of the hardest things I ever had to do.

The decision ended a long and obsessive process. Having gone through this myself 20 years ago, I knew what I liked and didn't like about it. If I had run a succession process a few years after getting the job, it probably would have been identical to what Reg did to pick me. His succession was thorough and thoughtful, and it got praise from the academics. Over 20 years, the company had changed so dramatically that I could do it a little differently.

From the business-centric model of years ago, GE had evolved into an informal and more tightly integrated organization, supported by strong values and rewards. The candidates were all products of this social architecture. They thrived on change and had self-confidence to spare. And our processes, from the quarterly CEC meetings to the day-long Session C reviews, brought us together much more often and in much greater depth.

I approached the whole process with these thoughts:

One, I wanted my successor to be GE's unquestioned leader. I was concerned about sticking him with disappointed guys who could screw up the spirit and values we worked so hard to create.

Two, I wanted to take the politics out of the process. Leadership transitions are an enormous distraction to organizations that need to focus outward, not inward. When I went through the last succession, things became highly political and divisive. Reg didn't intentionally cause the politics. It was the process. By bringing all the candidates to headquarters, he got a closer look at everyone in the race. Tough politics was a heavy price for that look.

Three, I wanted to be sure the board was deeply involved in the decision. Going forward, our directors needed to be united behind one person. I had that support in my critical early years. It was a godsend. The board's coaching and support during my "down periods"—when I was called Neutron Jack and when I struggled with our problems at Kidder, Peabody—was incredibly valuable to me.

And four, I wanted to pick someone young enough to be in the job for at least a decade. While a CEO can have an immediate impact, I always felt people should live with their decisions and especially with their mistakes. I certainly had. Someone with less time might be tempted to make some crazy moves to put his stamp on the company. I've seen too many examples of that. Some companies have run through five or six different CEOs during my years as chairman. I didn't want that to happen at GE.

That's what I was thinking about when we started on this road in the spring of 1994. I was 58 then, with seven years to go. I felt we needed that much time to make the right choice. Picking your successor is hard. Your bet is all about what's ahead, not what's behind. We needed to pick the person who could thrive in a change environment and take the company to the next level: 5, 10, even 20 years out.

When I appointed Bill Conaty our new senior VP for human resources in November 1993, I told him that our biggest job was to select the next CEO for the company. "The thing you and I will both live with for a long time is getting the right person in this job."

It was. Little did either of us know it would almost consume us.

A few months later, in the spring of 1994, the wallowing began. We always had our hit-by-a-truck succession plan: a short list of people who could take over if something happened to me. Now, for the first time, we looked beyond an emergency and cast a wider net, to get at those with the potential to take over in 2001.

Before jotting down names, Chuck Okosky, our VP for executive development, put together a list of the stuff an "ideal CEO" should have.

The specs were filled with skills and characteristics you'd want: integrity/values, experience, vision, leadership, edge, stature, fairness, and energy/balance/courage. Chuck's list included such attributes as having an "insatiable appetite for increasing knowledge" and demonstrating "courageous advocacy." I tossed in a couple of things I wanted, like being "comfortable operating under a microscope" and having the "stomach to play for high stakes."

The exercise wasn't very helpful. When you got down to it, Christ couldn't have filled the job we described.

By wallowing with our Session C books, Bill, Chuck, and I did come up with 23 candidates. The list included the obvious people in big senior vice president jobs and, for the first time, 16 high-potential long shots in a broader consensus field, including the three people who would ultimately become the final players. The youngest was 36, the oldest was 58, obviously one of the emergency candidates. The field included CEOs of several of our businesses as well as young vice presidents. These were the best prospects we had in 1994.

We mapped out developmental plans for each of the candidates, plotting promotions for everyone until the year 2000. We wanted to give the younger ones broader, deeper, and more global exposure in several businesses.

Bill and I made our first formal pitch on succession to the management development committee of the board in June 1994. We showed the directors the "ideal CEO" list, the names of all 23 candidates, with specific plans for the 16 high-potential long shots. From that moment on, all the key decisions in their careers were made with succession in mind.

Despite our best-laid plans, looking at the results today is sobering. Only nine of the 23 people on that first list are with GE today. One obviously is the new CEO, three are vice chairmen, and five run big GE businesses. Eleven left for various reasons, including seven who are now CEOs of other public companies. Three retired, including two as vice chairmen.

Over the years, we watched these guys like hawks. We kept throwing new tests in front of them. The eight who remained contenders by June 1998 had moved through 17 separate jobs. We moved Jim McNerney from his job as president of GE Asia-Pacific, where we had put him to demonstrate our commitment to globalization. Jim already had experience in manufacturing, information services, and financial services. He became CEO of our lighting business. Two years later, we moved him to be CEO of aircraft engines.

Bob Nardelli, who had worked in our appliances and lighting

businesses, was at the time CEO of transportation systems. He became the head of power systems.

Jeff Immelt had spent most of his career in plastics, got a taste of the tough competition in the appliance industry, and moved back to plastics. He became CEO of medical systems in 1997.

After our first board presentation in June 1994, we began formal board reviews on succession every June and December. I also gave real-time assessments every February, when I went through the incentive payouts to our top executives, and every September, when we discussed stock option grants.

To help the directors form judgments outside the boardroom, they played golf with the candidates every April at Augusta and got together every July for golf or tennis in Fairfield. We had an annual Christmas party with spouses. Before each event, my assistant, Rosanne, and I would work out the golf foursomes and the dinner seatings, making sure board members always got a chance to spend time with different candidates.

In 1996, I wanted the comp committee members of the board to take a closer look—without me being around. I asked Si Cathcart, the chairman, to take his committee to each of the businesses. Si has been a terrific friend, a great board member, and a personal counselor. He is wise and tough, was always eager to give me a tweak when I needed one and generous with an "atta boy" when he thought I deserved one.

Two directors, Si and G. G. Michelson, had been on the board when Reg named me chairman. For continuity, I wanted them and a third member, Frank Rhodes, who also was a committee member, to remain through the transition. All three had been scheduled to retire. I asked the board to waive their mandatory retirement dates so the company could benefit from their experience. G.G. and Frank were on Si's committee with Claudio Gonzalez, CEO of Kimberly-Clark's Mexico operation, and Andy Sigler, the retired chairman of Champion International.

They spent a day with each business leader and his team,

including dinner or a ball game at night. Nothing was staged by me. Early on, a few of the candidates called and asked, "Jack what's the drill?"

"This is your show," I replied. I wanted the board to see how each business leader handled things. Some gave elaborate presentations. Others had few papers. Some brought their entire staffs. Some did it with one or two associates. After each trip, Si would drop me a note with the committee's impressions.

Four years after the first list—after retirements, departures, and people who fell out—the original 23 had been narrowed to eight serious candidates. We were still playing around with that "ideal CEO" list, adding and dropping things, but it still had a Superman feel to it. Much more helpful to me was a list of eight basic objectives Bill, Chuck, and I put together in 1998:

1. Pick the strongest leader.
2. Look for the best complementary mix of corporate executive officer skills.
3. Retain all contenders through transition and into the next administration.
4. Minimize dysfunctional competition.
5. Create opportunities for up close and personal view of the contenders before the final decision.
6. Provide the necessary transition time given the company's breadth and complexity.
7. Anticipate back-fill requirements for concurrent selection announcements.
8. Keep options open as long as possible, consistent with the fourth and fifth objectives.

This was a wish list. But it was a pretty good one. We wouldn't meet all these objectives. I became convinced number three was unrealistic. We weren't going to retain all the candidates, and I had come to the conclusion we shouldn't. Four and five turned out to be in conflict with each other. Getting an "up close" view by bringing them to Fairfield would risk dysfunctional competition. The other objectives held up.

The most important lesson I took from my own succession was the need to take out all the internal politics. This may be hard to believe, but that's the way it turned out. After it was over, the finalists told me they saw it the same way.

Our values had become so important that if any one of the candidates played games, their colleagues would have thrown them out. Even when we settled on the final three by the end of 1998, and the media began cranking up the pressure, not one of them did anything to undermine the other. In fact, if anything, it was the opposite.

Keeping all three in the field in their current jobs—Bob in Schenectady, Jim in Cincinnati, and Jeff in Milwaukee—allowed each to focus on nothing but his business. Not politics. Not second-guessing the business their friends once ran. And not maneuvering in a new bureaucratic layer in the organization. The downside was obvious. I wouldn't get that one-on-one personal view of each candidate Reg gained when he brought us all to Fairfield.

I didn't need a close-up view. I had been hanging around with these three for years. But I did create opportunities for a better look, without bringing them to headquarters. In 1997, for instance, I put all three on the GE Capital board. After every monthly meeting, I had lunch with them. I tried to take any formality out of these Fairfield luncheons. We'd fool around, and I'd get to hear their opinions on the deals that GE Capital was proposing. This worked for a while, but as we grew closer to the end, it became too awkward for everyone. So we stopped doing it.

I did something else. It was a little like Reg's process but handled outside the office. I began having private dinners with each of the 11 major business CEOs in the spring of 1999. Over a meal, I asked them for their opinions about our businesses: what we ought to keep, which ones we should throw out, and who should make up the leadership team at the top. I asked them to pick three leaders, not wanting to force anyone into the box of picking one winner.

These sessions were helpful for putting a team together but didn't do much to pick a clear successor.

I repeated the process again in the spring of 2000. This time, I focused more on things outside their own businesses. I wanted to know their thoughts on our current union negotiations and environmental issues. I had a candid exchange about what they thought of one another. Again, no surprises. They all liked and respected one another. I also asked a lot of questions about our processes and values, what they liked about them and what they'd jettison.

One of the most important questions I asked three of them was probably the most challenging to answer: "If you weren't picked as CEO, would you leave?" Two of them, one more directly than the other, made it clear they would leave. One said he wanted the job, he loved the company and the people so much that he would stay to see how it played out. I discounted that because the headhunters would have been all over him. With the enormous visibility they all got, that turned out to be a pretty good assumption. By this time, I had made up my mind that it was unrealistic to think we could keep all of them.

From the start, I always saw the process as more than just naming a CEO. I also wanted to create a broader team, using the vice chairman positions to help the new guy. I didn't want disappointed candidates or those who wouldn't be able to work with my successor in these roles. I thought the perfect choices were Dennis Dammerman, then CEO of GE Capital, and Bob Wright at NBC. The two of them always came up as big players with everyone in my dinner conversations. Dennis was named a vice chairman in late 1997 and Bob in July 2000. Dennis was involved in the selection process almost from the beginning, while Bob played a role after becoming vice chairman.

As the media heated up in 2000, the uncertainty mounted. At my Crotonville sessions, classes began asking how I would keep all three at GE and who would replace each of them as business CEOs. The analysts on Wall Street were asking the same questions.

I've had plenty of ideas, good and bad, but I got a really good one during a weekend in June. It came in the shower. I often do some of my best thinking there. Because I was sure two of the three would leave, I decided to "lose" them on my terms.

Instead of waiting to name their replacements after one moved up or left, I decided to put their successors in right away. Bob, Jim, and Jeff might have five uncomfortable months left in their jobs, but new leaders in their businesses would be well trained and ready to go. Their organizations would know who the next boss was going to be, and that would lessen the rumors and gossip. I also thought it would reassure Wall Street.

During our Session Cs, every business leader has to name his or her successor. It's often a rote exercise. In April 2000, with the CEO decision pending in December, I wrote all of our business leaders and asked each of them to spend at least an hour this time discussing their replacements. Those discussions flushed out who the three candidates in particular liked and wanted.

On Monday morning, I excitedly told Bill and Dennis about my idea developed over the weekend. They were enthusiastic. We could now put people in new chief operating roles who we knew were compatible with the CEOs. Since the board was up to speed on all the people, it was easy to get the directors on the phone that week and take them through this new thinking. They liked it.

Now I had to explain this decision to Bob, Jeff, and Jim. I acknowledged that it might seem unfair. But I made the case that it was in the best interests of their employees and our shareowners.

Nonetheless, it came as a surprise to them.

"Well, are you telling me I'm either up or out?" asked one.

"Yeah, that's it. You threw the gauntlet down by telling me you were going to leave if it didn't work out. I'm saying, 'Okay, here's the guy who is going to replace you. Now you train him for six months.'"

"What finality!" he replied.

"Look, I know this is a little cruel because it seems so final. But I have to make this call."

None of them thought it was the greatest thing that ever happened, but they understood it really was in the company's best interests. If the people factory ever needed validation, we certainly got it in June of 2000. We were ready with three great people as new chief operating officers—all were 43 years old.

Dave Calhoun had been head of the audit staff, and then went through a series of CEO jobs in Plastics Asia, transportation, lighting, and then reinsurance. He is bright, fun, quick, an avid sportsman, and a strong relationship builder. Dave was perfect to be COO under Jim McNerney at aircraft engines.

I first met John Rice during a luncheon with young auditors in Schenectady. He had a great personality, an incisive mind, and I liked him instantly. I told him, "Get out of finance and get into operations." John did and went directly into appliance manufacturing. After a series of promotions, he eventually replaced Dave Calhoun first as CEO of GE Plastics Asia and then as CEO of GE Transportation. This experience made him a natural as COO under Bob Nardelli at power systems.

Joe Hogan worked in plastics in many global assignments, before becoming CEO of GE-Fanuc. Joe is 43 and looks about 15. He probably gets carded at every bar. He might look that way, but he's a mature manager, with terrific interpersonal and natural leadership skills. We had brought him into medical systems as head of e-business several months earlier to get ready for his next job as COO under Jeff Immelt.

Putting these three stars into these new jobs was a game-changing event. While 300,000 employees, including me, still didn't know who their chairman was going to be, the people in three of our biggest businesses knew exactly who their new CEOs would be.

Publicly, I said the changes were "a natural step in our leadership succession plan." I continued to turn away reporters who wanted to talk about these moves or anything else involving succession.

So did Bob, Jeff, and Jim. None of us wanted to help the media make a circus of it. If anything, though, I was naive to think I could hold off the press completely. After all, the first stories about my succession had cropped up as early as 1996. As we moved into September, two months before naming my successor, it seemed that all the media could focus on was the succession at GE.

In the space of three or four days, stories cropped up in *Business Week*, *The Wall Street Journal*, the *Financial Times*, and the *Sunday Times* of London. The articles not only named the front-runners, they also handicapped and profiled them, without any help from us.

When the stories broke, I was at the Olympics in Australia. Reading the faxed articles in my hotel room, I was surprised at how much attention our succession was getting. I also felt terrible about it, knowing how much more pressure it was putting on the three of them.

I sat at my laptop in the hotel room at one-thirty in the morning, typing e-mails to all three:

> Jeff, Jim, Bob—
> I'm sorry that you have to go through all of this press nonsense.
>
> I thought I could do it better than Reg by leaving everyone in the field. It turns out the press will make every succession into some sort of conflict. Thanks for being such great guys. The company's lucky that you've stayed with the process. Your great results and tremendous attitude in every way have made the process even more challenging for me as well. Thanks for truly being so special.

I meant every word of it. One response was typical of those I received:

> The bottom line, Jack, is that we're all pretty lucky to have been part of it all, and that feeling overwhelms any discomfort with the public scrutiny. Growth, challenge, and fun have made it all un-forgettable, no matter what happens to whom next. You're doing the right thing for GE, and I'm certain we all support the process. Your favorite contender.

The replies were typical of the quality of the people who made it this far—and that only made it harder for me. There were times I joked that I wished one of them would do something dumb or crazy. A scandal would have made the decision easier. When I reviewed the process again with the board, I took the directors through how hard it had become for me. Sam Nunn, the former U.S. senator from Georgia who had been on our board since 1997, had a great response.

"Jack," Sam said, "stop feeling sorry for yourself about pick-ing one of these guys. You've made them all famous. They are go-ing for the best job in America, and it's not clear which one of them is going to get it. That means they are all great. Putting them in this position, you've done more for their careers than ever would have happened if they remained hidden."

That was some consolation for me, but I knew that it didn't make things any easier for them. As those stories popped up, all three were at a Prudential Securities investment conference in Stowe, Vermont, having breakfast together. They were the focus of everyone in the room. A few days later, I bumped into John Blystone, who had been at the same conference. John left GE in 1996 to become CEO of SPX.

"You should really be proud," he told me. "Those guys joked and teased each other from the stage. They were totally supportive of each other. The shareholders sitting there saw the top of the company operating as one team. You have to feel very good about that." Ironically, John didn't know that he was among the 16 stars on our first list in 1994.

Truth is, I was so proud of all three. Every one is a little different here or there, but all of them are terrific human beings. All were running their businesses at record margins, at record market shares, and with the highest employee morale ever.

Bob had been given a business in 1995 that had power turbines failing all over the field. The business's net earnings had gone down for three straight years. He drove the technical fix for the turbines and then got the benefit of a shortage in power capacity that caused demand to skyrocket. He put terrific operating mechanisms in place to take advantage of that surge. He made dozens of global acquisitions.

He was taking the business from a base of $770 million in operating income in 1995 to $2.8 billion in 2000. Even more important, he was projecting net income growth of $1 billion every year, from 1999 to 2002. There are only a few companies in the world that make $1 billion after taxes, and Bob was on track to add an incremental $1 billion annually for the next three years in a row.

Jim was turning in great results, too. In the three years that he led our aircraft engine business, it contributed more profit to GE than any single unit in GE's top twenty businesses. He pushed the business's top-line growth to $10.8 billion in 2000 from $7.8 billion in 1997, while growing earnings 21 percent per year. He drove services to the point that they had become more than half of the business's total profits. And getting the GE-90 engine, the largest and most powerful jet engine, for Boeing's long-range 777 jet was a terrific strategic accomplishment.

Jeff had likewise taken our medical systems business to new levels. He came up with the concept of a global product company that will be a model for almost every business in the company, sourcing intellect, components, and finished products from every

corner of the world. He made numerous acquisitions and integrated them well. He was making medical as much an information
company as a hardware business.

In three years, he led the business to record profit and revenue,
growing sales from $3.9 billion in 1996 to $7.2 billion in 2000, also
increasing net income 21 percent per year. Jeff made us a much
stronger competitor in Europe, and took us to No. 1 in Asia. In addition, medical had brought out more new products using Six
Sigma technology than any business in the company.

It wasn't just their great performance that was making the decision so hard. I went way back with these three guys. They had
been in my classes at Crotonville. Long before they became business CEOs, I had spent hours and hours with them in all kinds of
reviews. I had promoted them and watched them grow, often
through very tough jobs, into incredibly self-confident executives.

I had first met Jeff while he was still an MBA student at the
Harvard Business School in 1982. When he picked GE over Morgan Stanley, a Morgan partner tried to talk him out of it.

"GE? Listen, if you come to work for Morgan Stanley, you're
going to be presenting to Jack Welch in the first six months. If you go
to GE, maybe, just maybe, you'll get a glimpse of him in your tenth
year." Thirty days after joining the company, Jeff was sitting around
a table with me and five others from our corporate marketing group.

Like so many strong executives, he went through his lumps—
and I was in his knickers during the worst of them. We had moved
him to appliances in 1989 to broaden his experience in a tough industry. It gave him more experience, a lot faster than we expected.
He got right in the middle of a massive recall when a compressor
failed on a new line of refrigerators. Jeff had 7,200 employees fixing 3 million compressors. I saw him up close in the monthly operating reviews we had during this crisis.

Another time I was all over Jeff was when he had a really
tough year at plastics in 1994. As general manager of GE's Plastics
Americas, he had agreed to a number of fixed-price contracts at

plastics and was caught between rising material costs and his commitments to our customers. He missed his net income number by $50 million. As Jeff tells the story, when he came to Boca in January 1995, he tried hard to avoid me. He was coming to dinner late and going to bed early. I finally caught up with him the last night, as he was rushing off to the elevator and his room.

I grabbed him by the shoulder and turned him around.

"Jeff, I'm your biggest fan, but you just had the worst year in the company. Just the worst year. I love you, and I know you can do better. But I'm going to take you out if you can't get it fixed."

"Look," he said, "if the results aren't where they should be, you won't have to fire me because I'm going to leave on my own."

Of course, he fixed it—and then just nailed every job he held after that.

There are similar stories I could tell about Bob or Jim. For me, this was an emotional decision. There was a lot of blood, sweat, family, and feelings to it.

I never had trouble making decisions. This one was different.

At the July 2000 board meeting, we spent three hours with the comp committee, wrestling with the pros and cons of each candidate. It was a wide-open meeting. Throughout the session, I was fighting not to make up my mind. I wanted to keep my options open until the very end. After the morning session, we had the usual golf outing with the CEOs of our businesses. I asked the committee to come back an hour early the next morning after they had a chance to sleep on our three-hour discussion.

It wasn't until a Sunday night, October 29, 2000, that I made my recommendation. We were in Greenville, South Carolina, for a board visit to a power turbine plant. This board trip had been scheduled a year in advance. It probably wasn't the smartest move I ever made. It would place more pressure on Bob Nardelli than he deserved, but I liked to show the board stuff that was hot. Thanks to Bob, nothing was hotter than power systems, and the next morning, he put on a great show.

After a weekend golf outing at Augusta with many of our current and former directors, a tradition that dates back at least to Reg's years, we flew to Greenville for dinner in a private room at the Poinsett Club, a beautiful old southern mansion.

That Sunday evening, there was a bit of a sideshow prior to our succession decision. As it happened, *60 Minutes* was to air a profile of me. Bob's team from power systems was there along with our board members, watching any one of several television screens in a dining room.

When the football game delayed *60 Minutes* by nearly half an hour, I got really nervous. My interviews with Lesley Stahl had gone well, but you never know what to expect. They had over 23 hours of tape for a 15-minute profile.

When you're that exposed, almost anything could happen. In fact, Lesley treated me very well. I was relieved to have it over.

After the dinner, our directors were driven to the nearby Hilton Hotel. We had reserved an upstairs conference room at the Hilton for a special board meeting. To insure privacy, GE security was stationed outside. The only non–board member there was Bill Conaty, who had worked the process with me from day one. Bob and his team went to their rooms or home.

Shortly after 10 P.M., I opened the session.

"We've come to a conclusion."

For the next 15 minutes or so, I told the board why I thought Jeff should be the new guy. He had done great things in our medical business that would be a model for the future of GE. I felt Jeff had the perfect blend of intelligence and edge and epitomized the trait that's so important to me—he was really confortable in his own skin. While it was obviously close, I thought he was the perfect selection.

Dennis Dammerman and Bob Wright had their say. Dennis recalled how he first interviewed Jeff at the Harvard Business School in 1982. He focused on his leadership skills and customer focus. Bob commented on his runway. Then, every member of the board weighed in, all in unanimous approval. At the end of the table, Frank Rhodes spoke eloquently about Jeff's capacity to learn and grow. In his mind, he said, Jeff had the intellectual bandwidth and was clearly the right choice.

It was one of the best meetings I had ever been in. Everyone wanted to say something. We had all been carrying the same burden. At least two directors raised the possibility of trying to keep at least one of the two other candidates. It killed them to lose so much talent.

"Are you sure you don't want to try to keep one?" asked one board member.

"I've been there," I said. "I know what it's like. Whoever becomes chairman of this company has to be filled with self-confidence and full of enthusiasm. I want him to feel bigger than life. I don't want him looking over his shoulder."

I then asked Bill Conaty, who had favored keeping one of the two, to share his views. Bill said that he had initially thought the experience and skills of the other candidates were so great that we should try to keep one of them, but he had reluctantly come my way.

In the end, all of us felt that the two who weren't picked deserved to run their own shows as CEOs.

I ended the meeting by saying, "We don't want to make a final decision now. Take three weeks to think about it. Call me with whatever concerns you might have." I told the board I'd call the committee members the Wednesday before Thanksgiving to go over the decision and ask for their final endorsement.

We ended our two-hour session in Greenville at midnight, as my assistant, Rosanne, came into the conference room and cleared away all the papers.

Only six days before the October meeting in Greenville, something happened that changed my own timetable for leaving the company. We announced our acquisition of Honeywell, and I agreed to stay in the job as CEO longer to oversee the integration instead of leaving in April as planned. The deal, our largest ever, triggered lots of media talk that it would impact our succession.

Inside, however, none of us thought the deal should change anything. It didn't—and I'd ultimately leave in early September 2001, four months later than the original plan we had created in 1994.

Over the next three weeks, I received phone calls from at least half a dozen of the directors, who all said favorable things about the decision and the process. They also were trying to buck me up. I was thrilled with the decision but still agonizing over telling Bob and Jim that they weren't going to get the job.

On Wednesday before Thanksgiving, I called the comp committee members and got their approval to recommend to the full board on Friday the appointment of Jeff as chairman-elect. By making the decision over the Thanksgiving holiday, we'd minimize the publicity of another round of succession stories. Most people expected us to announce our choice after the regular December 15 board meeting.

I called the full board after the market closed on Friday for the official vote at 5 P.M.

After the board unanimously and wholeheartedly approved Jeff as chairman-elect on November 24, I called him at 5:30 P.M. in South Carolina, where he and his family were spending the holiday.

"The board made a decision. It's great news for you. I'd like you come down to Palm Beach tomorrow. Bring your family, and we'll meet you at noon for lunch." I reviewed the carefully planned logistics.

Instead of using one of GE's corporate jets, we arranged a charter to pick up Jeff, his wife, Andy, and their daughter, Sarah, in Charleston at 10:30 A.M. To assure security, Jeff was listed as James Cathcart, Si's son, and the plane was booked in his name. Si also sent a car from his club to pick up the Immelts and bring them to my home. As a final precaution, the plane flew into Stewart Airport rather than West Palm, where GE's planes normally landed.

As the car pulled up, I was in the driveway, waiting to greet him and give him the great news. We went to lunch at Carmine's, an Italian restaurant in North Palm Beach. After lunch, Jane drove Jeff's wife and daughter to a condo I had in Eastpointe. Jeff came back with me to prepare for the Monday press conference in New York. Bill Conaty, who was in Florida for the weekend, came over to help. We went over the already drafted press release announcing the appointment, tossing out "NGs" for "New Guy" and putting in Jeff's name.

Dennis Dammerman, Bob Wright, and their wives flew down that night so all of us could congratulate Jeff over dinner at my house. We had a great night together. But I had a knot in my stomach, because only half of my job was done—the easy half.

I was dreading the next day when I had to tell Bob and Jim that they weren't getting the job.

On Sunday, I waited until 2 P.M. to make my calls. I had gotten the schedules of all three candidates through the end of the year, so I knew where to reach them.

Both Bob and Jim were home when I called.

"The board and I have made a call. I'd like to come out and review the decision and the rationale behind it."

I wasn't about to tell either candidate that he was not going to be CEO over the telephone. I owed each one the opportunity to look me in the eye as I told him the news. Yet I didn't want to falsely raise their hopes. I practiced these words at least ten times to get them right, even going through the routine with Jane before making the calls.

I reached the West Palm airport at 3 P.M. in the middle of a torrential downpour. The Thanksgiving holiday air traffic was compounded by severe thunderstorms that rocked the entire eastern half of the country. Many airports were closed, the planes grounded. When I told our pilots that we weren't going to Westchester Airport as planned, but rather to Cincinnati, they were shocked. They had to change all the flight plans in weather that made any departure doubtful.

The pilots said the bad weather would keep us grounded for at least a couple of hours, so I lay on a couch, thinking over what I had to say. I hated what I had to do. It was like having to pick one child over another. It seemed so unfair. They had all busted their butts for the company. They had never played unfair with me or with each other.

They had given 1,000 percent.

In this case, I had asked these three people to do *this,* and they all did *this,* and *this,* and then *this.* They had vastly exceeded our expectations. Now I had to give two of them the worst news of their careers—and I had nothing else to give them, other than encouragement that they would make great CEOs somewhere else.

The afternoon grew dark early. We left Palm Beach through black skies at 5:30 P.M. and arrived at Lunken Aviation in Cincinnati around 7 P.M. The place was soaked, dreary, and dark. It was a bone-chilling night. I walked across the tarmac through a light fog toward the barely lit private airport hangar. I felt really alone, carrying only my old leather briefcase.

No one was in sight. When I reached the door, Jim was already there. I greeted him, and we quickly went into a small meeting room.

"Obviously," I said, "this is going to be the toughest conversation of my life."

Jim's disappointment wrapped his face.

"I picked Jeff. If there's anyone to be mad at, be mad at me. Put my picture on the wall and throw darts at it. I can't even tell you why. It's my nose and my gut. We had three Gold Medal winners, and only one Gold Medal to give."

Jim joked about there being no recount. It was during the Florida presidential election mess. He couldn't have been more gracious.

"I want you to know I wanted the job, but I also want to tell you I think the process was fair because you played it straight, and you gave us every chance."

For the next 40 minutes, we had a good conversation. We talked about life, his dad, and his 18 years at GE. I told Jim that I had seen tremendous growth in him since our first meeting in 1982. I recalled how he'd been hired out of the consulting firm of McKinsey by one of my old Pittsfield associates, Greg Liemandt. From his first job in business development in our information services division to his last, he had done great things for us—none greater than his transformation of our aircraft engine business.

"Your last two years have been your best, and you're getting better every day. You're going to be a great CEO wherever you go."

I walked back to the plane, only to surprise our crew again.

"We're not going to Westchester. We need to fly to Albany now." They scrambled to make changes, and we flew through heavy clouds into a deserted airport in Albany around 9 P.M. It was still wet and cold. We arrived earlier than expected because of heavy tailwinds, and Bob wasn't there.

I actually felt relieved by his absence. It would be especially difficult to tell him he hadn't gotten the job. Of the three, I had known Bob the longest, meeting him as a GE plant manager in the late 1970s. His dad had worked a lifetime at GE, just as Jeff's father had.

When Bob quit GE to join the Case Corp. in 1988, he was one of the few executives I ever tried to persuade to stay. I couldn't talk him into staying, but he did come back three years later. Since then, I had watched and admired his operating performance. The numbers he was delivering were the best I had seen in my 40 years at the company and could well be the best operating performance of any business in GE history.

Bob showed up on time, ten minutes after I arrived. We sat together on a couch in the corner of a large empty lounge. Just the two of us.

I told him the news, and his disappointment was visible.

"What more could I have done?" he asked.

"Bob, you've done more than I ever would have dreamt. You've done a great job. Everyone loves you, and you're going to be a great CEO. But I can't answer this question for you. I can't give you satisfaction on it. You did everything and more that was ever asked. I believe Jeff is the right guy for this company going forward. There's only one person to blame here. It's me."

Bob and I had a long, probing discussion. I wasn't able to satisfy his need for more information. His great operating results made the decision hard for him to accept.

Again, I tried to soften his disappointment.

"Bob, you're going to be an all-star CEO. There's a big, lucky company out there waiting to get you."

We shook hands and hugged.

Back on the plane, I ordered a large vodka on ice and finally flew back to Westchester. I stared out the window that night, sipping my drink, caught in lots of conflicting emotions. I was relieved it was over. I was thrilled for Jeff and totally confident we had picked the best candidate. I felt really sad to disappoint two friends who had done so much for the company. I vowed to be their agent, to help them in any way I possibly could.

We had an exciting press conference on Monday. I couldn't have been more pleased with Jeff's performance. He demonstrated all the self-confidence and qualities that I knew he had. The only obvious mistake we made—and we both made it—was not checking on each other's wardrobe. We both showed up wearing blue shirts and blue blazers.

The media had some fun with that.

After it was over, I spent the next few days talking to my friends Gerry Roche at Heidrick & Struggles and Tom Neff at Spencer Stuart about the jobs Bob and Jim were considering. At one point, Tom was actually lobbying me to get one of the guys to go to his client, Lucent Technologies. I told Tom I didn't think it was a good idea.

Within 10 days, Jim was chosen to be CEO of 3M, and Bob was picked to be CEO of Home Depot. One of our directors, Ken Langone, had a strong hand in Bob's move because he had been an active player in the succession and couldn't wait to call

Bob and recruit him to Home Depot, where Ken was a founder and large shareholder.

Nothing said more about the GE values than when Jim and Bob and their wives joined Reg, Jeff, and me at our annual Christmas party at the Rainbow Room of the GE building. When I mentioned them during my remarks, our directors and executives gave them standing ovations.

No one clapped harder than I did.

I would really burst with pride a few weeks later in Boca. By that time, I was looking forward to Jeff's first presentation as the new chairman-elect. President-elect George W. Bush, however, had asked a number of CEOs, including me, to go to Austin to meet with him for an economic briefing. I gave a brief opening at Boca and then left our operating managers meeting for the first time in 33 years.

It was an unexpected but lucky break, because it gave Jeff the chance to do his own thing, without me sitting in the front row. When I returned that evening, a videotape of his presentation was waiting in my hotel room.

Seeing him take command of the company was exhilarating. Jeff was witty, smart, visionary, and incredibly powerful.

He was the CEO!

In my closing remarks at Boca, I told the crowd that I watched Jeff's opening on the TV screen in my room and felt as proud of him as a first-time father. His performance triggered one of my happiest memories: the day I walked into the lab on Plastics Avenue in Pittsfield 39 years earlier with a box of candy under my arm to celebrate the birth of my first child, Katherine.

At Boca, I was figuratively vying with Jeff's own dad, who had spent 38 years working in GE's aircraft engines business, to see whose chest could pop out the most.

I was sure the "New Guy" was the "Right Guy."

Epilogue

Almost 20 years ago, I stood behind a podium at the Pierre Hotel in New York and gave my vision to Wall Street analysts for what I wanted GE to become. As high as my expectations were on that day, I never imagined that the company and the people in it would be able to achieve so much.

We took a bureaucracy and we shook it. We created a world-class organization, whose excellence is accepted on every continent. I believe the GE I'm leaving is a true meritocracy, a place filled with involved and excited people, with good values and high integrity.

It's a company that lives for great ideas, a place where the people do get up every morning searching for a better way.

The journey has been a great one. Yet what GE became in 20 years is a small snapshot of a company's lifetime. We built on the 100 years that came before us. What excites me even more is what the organization might become in the next 20 years. I know that its future will be guided by a spectacular team that will take the company to greater things.

At times, the first ten years of my journey felt like war. We were changing ahead of the curve, and we took our lumps for it. There are no modest revolutions.

There are no modest transformations of organizations, either.

Contrary to reputation, I've often been too cautious. I waited too long to get rid of managers who weren't willing or able to face reality. I was hesitant with some acquisitions, slow to embrace the Internet, even timid about blowing up all the rituals and traditions of what once had been a bureaucracy.

Almost everything should and could have been done faster.

Nonetheless, GE has become an organization that relishes change, uses its size to take more risks and is focused outward on its customers—not itself. I've always believed that when the rate of change inside an institution becomes slower than the rate of change outside, the end is in sight.

The only question is when.

Learning to love change is an unnatural act in any century-old institution, but the GE I'm leaving does just that. Our passion to learn and share new ideas was facilitated by an operating system that allowed diverse businesses to grow faster and perform better than they would if they were on their own.

Great people, not great strategies, are what made it all work. We spent extraordinary time recruiting, training, developing, and rewarding the best. Our reach and our success would have been limited without the best people stretching to become better.

Globalization was one logical outcome of stretch. We've searched the globe for the best products and intellect. Our new Proteus radiology system from medical systems is a perfect example. The system, now being made in Beijing, is a product of an intercontinental supply chain that takes advantage of the best quality and lowest cost for every one of its 719 parts. The components are made in the United States, Canada, Mexico, North Africa, Morocco, Bangalore, Korea, Taiwan, and countries in western and eastern Europe. The scanner's generator is built in India, its suspension system is made in Mexico, and the tube mechanism is produced in the United States. Those parts and many other components are then shipped to Beijing for assembly.

Six Sigma ties all the pieces together.

*   *   *

Books like this are supposed to end with predictions . . .

Predictions are difficult.

When I became chairman, the conventional wisdom could be distilled in three "inevitable" trends. Oil was at $35 a barrel and going to $100—if you could get it. The Japanese manufacturing juggernaut was going to take over America. And inflation, at 20 percent, would be in double digits forever.

So much for predictions.

There clearly are forces, however, that will change the way many of us think about markets, organizations, and management.

The capitalist genie is almost out of the bottle in China. This country will have enormous influence in the new century. Chinese entrepreneurs are open to change like never before. China's leaders are managing their society as they unleash their economy.

For those of you sitting in conference rooms drawing pie charts of the competitive landscape, leave half the pie open for the Chinese. There are companies in China today you've never heard of that will emerge as competitive giants in the next decade, threatening your very existence.

China is a lot more than a market. It is rapidly becoming a massive competitor.

The country's increasing economic power will complicate relationships among Europe, the United States, and Japan. Trade tensions will increase. I don't know what form protectionism will take, but I do know the discussions over it will be long and heated.

Hierarchy is dead. The organization of the future will be virtually layerless and increasingly boundaryless, a series of information networks in which more electrons and fewer people will manage processes. Information will become transparent. No leader will be able to hoard the facts that once made the corner office so powerful.

Most of the information a manager will need to run a business will reside on a computer screen in a "digital cockpit." It will contain every piece of real-time data, with automatic alerts spotlighting the trends requiring immediate attention.

While information will be available as never before, it will always be human judgment that will make the organization go.

One evening just a few months before I left GE, I was in a store on Fifth Avenue in New York to buy a new sweater. When the salesman helping me went downstairs to find my size in the stockroom, the manager of the store came up to me.

"Mr. Welch," he said, "can I talk to you?"

He was a young African American who said he'd seen me being interviewed by Charlie Rose on television the night before. He said he had enjoyed my comments but wanted to ask me a follow-up question. During the Rose interview, I had noted how important it was for organizations to continually remove the bottom 10 percent of their employees.

The store manager brought me to a secluded section, under a staircase, where no one could hear us.

He explained that he had 20 people in his sales force.

"Mr. Welch," he asked, "do I really have to let two go?"

"You probably do, if you want the best sales staff on Fifth Avenue."

I had to laugh over the fact that I was hearing my words come back to me not from someone inside GE this time, but from the floor manager of a Fifth Avenue clothing store. I think he understood that if you want to become the best at what you do, it's hard—really hard.

It takes self-confidence, courage, and a willingness to take the heat when you make the tough calls.

*   *   *

On a lighter note, the hookup between Bob Nardelli and Ken Langone at Home Depot has sparked a lot of funny banter among all of us. Ken is a larger-than-life figure. He's big, loud, generous, opinionated, and smart—an ideal director. But I brought him on the GE board in 1999 because he knows everyone, absolutely everyone. I wanted Jeff to have in Ken what I had in Walter Wriston 20 years earlier, a cheerleader telling everyone that Jeff is going to be the best CEO in America.

It almost worked. A few weeks after Bob joined Home Depot, however, I heard Ken was going around New York bragging about the job Bob was doing. I called him on it.

"You caught me," he said, laughing, "from now on it'll be Jeff, Jeff, Jeff."

Only a few weeks later, *Fortune* reporter Patty Sellers called on another story and mentioned she had interviewed Langone for an upcoming article on Home Depot. I asked her what Ken said about Jeff. She replied that he was full of praise for Bob—but never mentioned Jeff.

I had a witness now. I called Ken and gave him hell.

"You SOB," I joked. "I heard that you're still selling Bob. You promised me it's Jeff, Jeff, Jeff!"

I know Ken justifiably has mixed emotions. As a founder of Home Depot and a director of GE, he gets to see two great CEOs. I just have to keep him "honest."

Before leaving GE in September 2001, I had many opportunities to say good-bye. One of the more memorable farewells was the last meeting of GE's 550 top leaders in Boca Raton in early January. After 33 years of attending these meetings—more than half my lifetime—this one would be the last.

I had taken over a very good company in 1981 that a lot of

people had made better. I believed my successor would take over a great company and make it much greater. That's what the chairman's job is all about.

I wanted to make sure that the message got through in my closing remarks. I jotted down my thoughts on a yellow legal pad, just as I always did. It took me two days to develop what I wanted to say. I didn't want to be maudlin or sentimental.

I wanted everyone to know that GE had to change more in the next two decades than it had in the past 20 years.

What I told them that morning could apply to any business. The message was simple: Forget what we've achieved together. Forget about yesterday.

"I got this job 20 years ago, and together we changed a lot," I said. "It has been a fun, wonderful journey filled with great memories and lasting friendships. For much of what we've done, forget it. Today's clippings wrap yesterday's fish.

"This will be a whole new ball game: Change, as you have never seen it, at speeds you've never seen. What fun for those who relish it. What fear for those who don't grasp it."

I ended by telling everyone to turn the organization upside down, shake it up, and go blow the roof off.

The speech got a warm reaction. The ending was emotional for me and for many of my longtime friends.

The custom at Boca is that on the last of the three nights, Joyce Hergenhan, my former head of public relations and now president of the GE Fund, announces the afternoon's golf and tennis scores.

It had been a windy and cold day on the course. Some actually quit after four holes because it was so cold. Joyce reported my score for the day and said, "I'm sure everyone here has a favorite Jack Welch story, but since I have the microphone, you're going to hear mine."

I thought—not another farewell.

"Thirteen years ago," she said, "I was in the hospital in New

Haven for major surgery. The day after the operation, I received a phone call from Jack saying he was coming to visit me. Instead of being thrilled, I told him I didn't want to see him because my hair was a mess.

"His response was pure Jack: 'I can't believe you. I'm coming to cheer you up, Joyce, not to jump into bed with you!' That kind of sums up Jack. There I was, thinking I was dying but worrying about my hair. Jack's humor, candor, and friendship very quickly brought me back to reality."

The 550 people in the ballroom roared, and my face turned a little red. What she said was certainly true. I guess it was something only the chairman of a really informal company, a corner grocery store, could ever say to an employee.

Jeff Immelt took over next as a bunch of waiters scrambled through the room with glasses filled with champagne. Jeff said some very nice things about me that night. He reflected on my remarks at the Pierre Hotel in 1981 when I told the analysts that my dream was to create a company where people could stretch beyond their limits. Jeff said he and everyone in the room had experienced things they'd never thought possible.

I was really touched by Jeff's remarks, especially when everyone stood and applauded. Jeff fought his way through the maze of tables toward me. We hugged each other, and I sat down, hoping everyone else would, too.

They wouldn't. I finally jumped on top of my chair, raised my glass, and toasted everyone in the room.

"Together, we've all done things we never imagined. We've all gone places we never thought we would see. We've all reached dreams we never thought possible. I came from a place just like most of you, and I got lucky thanks to all of your good work. Thanks for being so special. I love you all."

It was some night. I wish my mother could have been there.

Acknowledgments

At every moment of my life, I've been lucky to have people at my side whose support, encouragement, and love made all the difference in the world. They filled my journey with great fun and learning. They often made me look better than I am. Some of them, like my mother, are so obvious they are all through the text of the book and they hardly need to be mentioned here. There are many others, however, who didn't always fit into the story line and are barely mentioned. Dr. Jim Westwater, my thesis advisor at Illinois, was one of them. Yet if not for all of them, no one would have ever heard of this guy Jack Welch.

I've sometimes said that while I might not be the brightest bulb in the chandelier, over the years I've always thought I was pretty good at getting most of the bulbs to light up. I worry that it's not possible to give credit to all of them. So if I have forgotten anyone who played a role in my life, please accept my apologies. Even if my words of thanks seem short, my gratitude is long and deep.

I first need to thank my wife, Jane, for her patience and love. She's my best friend and confidante. Jane has been more than just understanding as I obsessed over this book. I want to thank my four terrific kids, Kathy, John, Anne, and Mark. I know it's not always easy to have Jack Welch as a dad, but they've always made it easy for me. They've given me eight fantastic grandchildren who have greatly enriched my life and will be an even more important part of it going forward.

I learned early on in my career that the key to getting a job done was having a super effective administrative assistant. I've had four of them: Eunice Hurley in plastics, Louise Koval in my group job, Helga Keller when I went to Fairfield and for my first seven years as CEO, and finally Rosanne Badowski. I wouldn't have been able to get through many of my days at GE without Rosanne. She has been an incredible supporter over the past 13 years. Rosanne's dedicated assistant, Sue Baye, has helped keep things together for the last 20 years.

I've had many good teachers in life, and I've tried to include all of them in the book. GE was around for 100 years before Jack Welch had any impact. I'm obviously in debt to the people who built the businesses we inherited. I'm indebted to Fred Borch, Reg Jones's predecessor, who had the courage to make me a vice president, and his entrepreneurial strategist, Jack McKitterick. Fred and Jack were adventurers. While everything they attempted didn't work out, a lot did. They were always swinging for the fences and loved trying new things.

When I think about GE and its past, it's impossible to give credit to everyone. There are a few names that often came up in my early years with GE. Their efforts would have a major impact on what would come later. Whit Ridgway promoted the globalization of our gas turbine business. Gerhard Neumann was the early driver of the jet engine business. "Ticker" Klock saw the promise in GE Capital. They and their associates helped to set the stage for the rest of us.

I want to thank everyone in Selkirk who made my first management job successful, from Billy Mack to Kevin Murray, who started out on day one and stayed over 30 years.

I'll never be able to thank Ted LeVino enough. As GE's former head of human resources, Ted saw the need for major change at GE, and his backing of me during the succession race was critical.

I've been fortunate to have had smart, helpful human resource partners in my day, Frank Doyle and Jack Peiffer preceded Bill Conaty. Frank was particularly helpful during the difficult years, when many were questioning our early restructuring moves.

None of them got enough ink in this book. Neither did Glen Hiner, who successfully ran our plastics business for years, or Gary Rogers, who was CEO of three major businesses: electrical distribution, appliances, and plastics. I was thrilled to see Jeff Immelt nominate Gary to the board as a vice chairman in 2001.

We've had many other great executives who left a mark on GE's businesses, including Dick Stonesifer and Larry Johnston in appliances, Jack Urquhart in power systems, Jim Rogers in motors, Uwe Wascher in plastics, and Carl Schlemmer in transportation. Carl convinced us to invest in locomotives when few favored the business. Transportation has become a training ground for top GE CEO talent.

I've already given credit in the book to Lloyd Trotter, the CEO of our industrial business, for his terrific operational performance, but I especially want to thank Lloyd for making GE better in so many other ways. His generosity of spirit makes him a role model for every GE employee. He founded and successfully drove GE's African-American Forum, which brings together the company's top management with diverse employees.

Over the years, we've had many terrific people who've created deep and lasting relationships with GE customers. They have always been critical but never more than in times of management transitions. They include, among others, Ed Bavaria and Chuck Chadwell in aircraft engines; Del Williamson in power systems; Jim DelMauro, Paul Mirabella, and Tom Dunham in medical systems; Dave Tucker in transportation; and Charlie Crew, Omer Murphy, and Herb Rammrath in plastics.

I've mentioned several GE board members in the book, but many others who weren't part of the book have been an important part of the story. I'd especially like to thank Sandy Warner, who always brought a valuable global economic perspective to every meeting,

Henry Henley, Charlie Dickey, Barbara Preiskel, Wayne Calloway, George Low, Bob Mercer, and Jim Cash, and some of my more recent partners, including Andrea Jung, Ann Fudge, and Shelly Lazarus.

From RCA, we not only got Gene Murphy, who later became a vice chairman. We also gained Rick Miller, who successfully put together GE and RCA's TV set manufacturing businesses; and John Rittenhouse, who did the same with the aerospace and defense businesses. We also got three great directors: Thornton "Brad" Bradshaw; General David Jones, former head of the joint chiefs of staff and a great American if there ever was one; and former U.S. attorney general William French Smith.

I want to mention three people who have run our pension trust and made all GE employees' retirements more secure: Ed Malone; Dale Frey, who dramatically expanded the scope of its activities; and the current head, John Myers. An example of how creative Dale and John were in their approach to the job is their investment in the Gulf & Western building in New York on 1 Central Park West. They took over the property in the mid-1990s in an uncertain real estate market, partnered with Donald Trump, and used the magic of his name and his marketing genius to turn the building into one of the most profitable hotel/condo developments in New York.

In addition to Peter Drucker, one other non-GE person who helped stimulate my thinking was Ram Charan. I loved batting ideas around with Ram. When Ram and I were discussing GE values and their importance, he coined the phrase "social architecture."

I'm especially grateful to Bill Lane, a guy who worked with me on the annual report letters every year. Bill took them as seriously as I did.

I've been very fortunate to have many special friends outside of my business associates. Two have been particularly close: Anthony LoFrisco and his wife, Eleanor, and Carl Warren and his wife, Donna. Along with my close business/social friends, the Frescos, Bossidys, Wrights, and Puccinis, they provided many laughs and wonderful company.

Everywhere I went, I had a great golf foursome that made my weekends so much fun. In my early days at the Berkshire Hills Country Club, they were Dave Dansereau, Pete Jones, and John Kreiger. At the Country Club of Pittsfield, they were Sel Atherton, Ernie Sagalyn, and Jim O'Brien. At Silver Spring Country Club, it was Carl Warren, Ron Weber, and Chuck Lokey. Finally, at the Country Club of Fairfield, there were five of us who rotated around: Ocie Adams, Tom Graham, Bill Gray, and Tom Kreitler.

I want to thank Bill Hutton and his wife, Joan. At age 94, Bill still comes to the office every day at Prudential Securities. He is the ultimate gentleman. Bill and Joan had been club champions at Sankaty Head years before, yet they took Jane under their wings when she couldn't hit the ball past the tee. Bill still calls my office every time GE stock hits a new high to let me know he's still rooting for us.

I want to thank Strat Sherman and Noel Tichy for writing the first book about me. Working with them helped to clarify a lot of my thinking. Noel also played a key role in the rejuvenation of Crotonville.

Writing a book is like nothing I've ever done before. It was a far greater challenge than I ever imagined. Thankfully, I received plenty of help from GE people in every business. Jeff Immelt and Dennis Dammerman were particularly helpful and offered valuable critiques and insights to the book. I'd also like to thank Bob Nelson, Brackett Denniston, Bill Conaty, Beth Comstock, and Joyce Hergenhan for editing portions of the manuscript. Pam Wickham and Katie Varner were helpful in researching important facts and figures.

I'm also grateful to Andy Lack of NBC for coming up with the title of the book. Bob Woodward of *The Washington Post* later gave Andy's notion a boost by suggesting a title along the same lines. With two successful journalists, independently coming to the same conclusion, it sounded like a good idea to me.

I've already thanked Reg Jones in this book in every way I know how for his unwavering support of me. But I also want to thank him for sharing his life and his view of his succession with my collaborator John Byrne during two long interviews.

No one from GE, however, put in more time or made a more valuable contribution to the book than Rosanne, my assistant. She gave up many weekends and worked late nights to greatly improve the book. She helped to untangle some of my more awkward sentences, made numerous suggestions, and caught a good number of errors along the way.

Several of my boyhood friends, especially Bill Cullen and George Ryan, also helped recall details of our days in Salem. John Kreiger, another old friend, was particularly helpful in recalling some of our Pittsfield days. I'd also like to thank my first wife, Carolyn, who was terrific to take time on several occasions to talk with John Byrne about our years together.

Bernadine Healy, head of the Red Cross, gave me the phrase "superficial congeniality" that I thought perfectly described the behavior of bureaucracies.

It was Mark McCormack whose semi-annual visits over several years convinced me to write the book. Mark Reiter, my agent with McCormack's IMG, helped me pick great publishers in the United States and around the world.

Finally, and most important, I'd like to thank my collaborator John Byrne. We easily spent over 1,000 hours together, going over every sentence, word, and comma. John also interviewed more than 50 people to help jog my memory. His low blood pressure and even temperament gave the team great stability. After 15 or 16 straight hours, when we were ready to drop, he'd demonstrate his curiosity and persistence by opening up his computer again to fix a troubled phrase or thought.

The Time Warner Trade Publishing team made a big difference. We chose Warner as our publisher because of the passion chairman Larry Kirshbaum and executive editor Rick Wolff immediately had for the project. We were right.

Larry delivered it—even over nights and weekends. We

couldn't keep him away, and he basically moved in with John and me. During one of those late-night sessions, I turned to Larry and said, "You know, every time I look at you it seems like I just came out of the womb and I'm seeing myself." I love Larry and his passion.

Rick was always into the book. We nicknamed him the "Trainmaster" because he was always bugging the three of us to meet our deadlines. Because the train was sometimes late, Harvey-Jane Kowal, executive managing editor, and Bob Castillo, managing editor, had to perform miracles to get the book out on time.

Again, I probably missed more than a few people who made this journey possible. I hope every one of you know how grateful I am to you.

Growing Fast In a Slow-Growth Economy

Where are we going?—What *will* General Electric be?—What is the strategy?

If I could, this would be the appropriate moment for me to withdraw from my pocket a sealed envelope containing the grand strategy for the General Electric Company over the next decade. But I can't, and I am not going to attempt, for the sake of intellectual neatness, to tie a bow around the many diverse initiatives of General Electric—initiatives as diverse as the allocation of $1.5 billion for new plastic plants—the acquisition of a CAD/CAM supplier like Calma—the acquisition of four software companies in the last four months—a $300 million commitment for a locomotive plant productivity upgrade and capacity expansion—a new microelectronics laboratory at the Research Center in Schenectady—investments in a microelectronics application center in Raleigh/Durham and a new factory automation laboratory in Charlottesville, Virginia.

It just doesn't make sense for neatness' sake to shoehorn these initiatives and scores of other individual business plans into an all-inclusive, all-GE, central strategy—one grand scheme.

What does relate and will enhance the many decentralized plans and initiatives of this Company isn't a central *strategy,* but a central *idea*—a simple core concept that will guide General Electric in the '80s and govern our diverse plans and strategies.

Presented to Financial Community Representatives, Hotel Pierre, New York City, December 8, 1981.

In trying to find a way to express these ideas and to share them with you, we found a powerful letter written by a Bendix planning manager to the editor of *Fortune* magazine. I want to share it with you because it captures, in words I find difficult to improve on, much of my own thinking about strategic planning for a company like General Electric. The letter reads like this:

"Through your excellent series on the current practice of strategic planning runs a common thread: the endless quest for a paint-by-numbers approach, which automatically gives answers. Yet that pursuit continually fails.

"Von Clausewitz summed up what it had all been about in his classic *On War*. Men could not reduce strategy to a formula. Detailed planning necessarily failed, due to the inevitable frictions encountered: chance events, imperfections in execution, and the independent will of the opposition. Instead, the human elements were paramount: leadership, morale, and the almost instinctive savvy of the best generals.

"The Prussian general staff, under the elder Von Moltke, perfected these concepts in practice. They did not expect a plan of operations to survive beyond the first contact with the enemy. They set only the broadest of objectives and emphasized seizing unforeseen opportunities as they arose . . . *Strategy was not a lengthy action plan. It was the evolution of a central idea through continually changing circumstances.*

"Business and war may differ in objectives and codes of conduct. But both involve facing the independent will of other parties. Any cookbook approach is powerless to cope with independent will, or with the unfolding situations of the real world."

Now let me tie this thinking—this notion of "strategy not being a lengthy action plan but the evolution of a central idea through continually changing circumstances"—to the management of the General Electric Company.

The real world, as we see the decade of the '80s, will be a time when inflation is clearly the number one enemy and most countries and most governments will fight that inflation with some form of tight money and fiscal responsibility medicine. The result—slower worldwide growth—slower growth than in any of the past three decades will clearly be the planning base for the '80s.

In this slower growth environment of the '80s, as companies—yes, as companies and countries fight for that reduced volume, fight their own unemployment problems, there will be no room for the mediocre supplier of products and services—the company in the middle of the pack. The winners in this slow-growth environment will be those who search out and participate in the real growth industries and insist upon being number one or number two in every business they are in—the number one or number two leanest, lowest-cost, worldwide producers of quality goods and services or those who have a clear technological edge, a clear advantage in a market niche.

The challenge for General Electric when we participate in these real growth industries, when we are number one or number two, is to ask ourselves—how big, how fast? Yes, how many resources—people and money—can we put behind the opportunity to ensure that we capitalize on this leadership position.

On the other hand, where we are not number one or number two, and don't have or can't see a route to a technological edge, we have got to ask ourselves Peter Drucker's very tough question: "If you weren't already in the business, would you enter it today?" And if the answer is no, face into that second difficult question: "What are you going to do about it?"

The managements and companies in the '80s that don't do this, that hang on to losers for whatever reason—tradition, sentiment, their own management weakness—won't be around in 1990. Think about the fact that in the high growth period between 1945 and 1970, almost one-half of the companies that would have been on a Fortune 500 roster disappeared either through acquisition, failure, or slipped quietly off the list due to lack of growth.

We believe this central idea—being number one or number two—more than an objective—a requirement—will give us a set of businesses which will be unique in the world business equation at the end of this decade.

Around this tangible central idea we will wrap these intangible central values—unifying dominant themes that, because of GE's common culture, will become second nature in the organization. One we've termed reality, a second we call quality/excellence, and third, the human element.

Let me try to describe what we mean by reality. It may sound simple, but getting any organization or group of people to see the world the way it is and not the way they wished it were or hoped it will be is not as easy as it sounds. We have to permeate every mind in this Company with an attitude, with an atmosphere that allows people—in fact, encourages people—to see things as they are, to deal with the way it is, not the way they wished it would be. Establishing throughout the organization this concept of reality is a prerequisite to executing the central idea—the necessity of being number one or number two in everything we do—or doing something about it.

When we talk about quality and excellence, we mean creating an atmosphere where every individual across the whole Company is striving to be proud of every product and service we provide. I think it really means all of us stretching beyond our limits, to be, in some cases, better than we ever thought we could be. I see it happening every day in almost every way all over this Company.

This excellence theme leads to our third and final value, what I can only call the human resource element where we have been creating, and will increasingly create, an atmosphere where people dare to try new things—where people feel assured in knowing that only the limits of their creativity and drive, their own standards of personal excellence, will be the ceiling on how far and how fast they move.

The net of these three values—reality, quality, the human element—what could be called soft values—will be a company not simply more high spirited, but more adaptable, more agile than companies that are a twentieth or even a fiftieth of our size. These values will permit us to maintain our common heritage, our common culture, but at the same time, to give ownership to those managers who are leading, operating, and building our stable of number one and number two businesses. We'll give them the resources to take head-on, in skirmish after skirmish, the marketplace competitors they come up against. Yes, give them all the benefits of a company the size of General Electric—financial, technological, and managerial—yet at the same time, provide them the freedom and flexibility that the owners of enterprises their size must have to win in the '80s.

General Electric is a set of diverse enterprises that has to be the envy of every single product line business in America, from oil to high technology. Most of them have been trying to become broader than they are, but most have difficulty finding the route. We are already there—a successful, widely diversified, highly profitable, industrial and financial enterprise. By any measure, we outperformed the GNP and

S&P 400 by a good margin in the '70s. We have the commitment and the potential to do better in the '80s. For those of you who like in some way to associate GE and the GNP, if anything, we will be a locomotive pulling the GNP, not a caboose following it.

I predict that you will come to see this Company from the same perspective—and I invite you to measure and judge us by how well we progress along the path I have tried to describe.

Thanks for listening. Now my associates will join me for your questions.

2001 Session C Agenda

1. **Business Leadership**
   - Forecast Business and Organization Drivers During the Next Year and Discuss Required Organization and Leadership Changes *(On Organization Charts, Highlight Those With Less Than Two Years in Role)*.
   - Evaluation of Direct Reports. Reference all EMS's from the e-EMS System for Performance/Promotability Discussion.
   - Utilize Format Provided for Relative Rankings *(20-70-10)* for all Officers and SEB's.
   - List Best Back-Ups for Each Direct Report Position *(Indicate 6σ Experience)*.
   - Use "Bar Chart" to Indicate Compensation Differentiation and "Bucket Chart" to Illustrate Hire/Attrition Dynamics.

2. **e-Business - Digitization**
   - CEO, CFO and Team to Review Digitization of Decision Support and How You Are Changing Your "Leadership Day."
   - Review your Vision/Actions of a Digitized Organization *(Fewer Layers, Front-Room/Back-Room Resources Redeployment, New Ideas)*. Provide Examples of Your "Leadership Cockpit."

3. **Quality - Customer Centricity**
   - CEO/Quality Leader Discussion re 6σ Organization Status and Vitality.
   - Provide 6σ "DNA" Summary of 2000 Promotions From MBB/BB Positions Into Operating Roles With Best/High Impact Examples. Discuss Future MBB/BB Pipeline.
   - Discuss Quality Training Programs and Describe Plans to Achieve and Maintain 100% Employee Six Sigma Certification.

4. **Globalization**
   - CEO/Sourcing/Manufacturing Leader Review Describing Organization/Leadership Moves to Accelerate Major Sourcing Initiatives Globally *(Intellect, Technology, Auctions etc)*.
   - Review Metrics and Structure of your Global Business *(Team Measurements, Global vs. Regional Dynamics, FSE and Localization Plans)*.

5. **Sales/Services - Technology**
   - CEO/Sales/Service/Technology Leader *(Service, Product)* Discussion regarding Performance and Effectiveness of the Leadership Team in Driving New Opportunities.
   - Describe Processes and Resources for Seamless Integration of Sales and Service Teams to Drive Growth.

6. **EB Talent**
   - Rank the Performance of EB Employees (20-70-10) with Promotability Overlay *(Format Attached)*. For Key Top Performers, Discuss Development Plans. For Least Effective, Planned Resolution.
   - Use "Bar Chart" to Indicate Compensation Differentiation and "Bucket Chart" to Illustrate Hire/Attrition Dynamics.

7. **Diversity**
   - 2000 Progress/2001 Plans (Including EB+ U.S. Diversity #'s) For All Populations.
   - Review Status and Results of Staff Mentoring and Plans to Increase Diverse EB and Above Population.
   - CEO/Affinity Group Leaders Review of 2001 Game Plans to Develop and Coach High Potentials.

8. **Pipeline Development**
   - High Potential Lists and Best Bets for Officer and SEB.
   - Nominations for EDC/BMC/Executive Assessments *(Include Name, Title, Band, Performance Rating, Diversity Status, Home Country)*.

9. **Honeywell Integration**
   - Detail Organization Opportunities and Key Talent.

10. **Appendix**
    - "Bucket Chart" Back-Up for Officers/SEB's/EB's *(#, Name, Diversity Status, Title, "From/To")*.
    - "Bar Chart" Back-Up *(Name, Ranking, Diversity Status, Title)*.

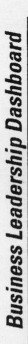

Business Leadership Dashboard

2001 Session C

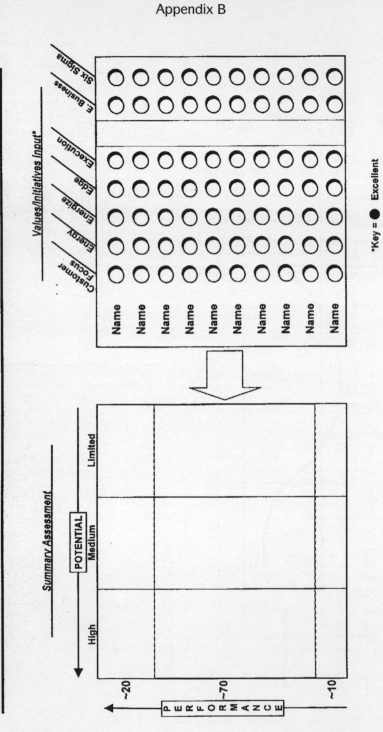

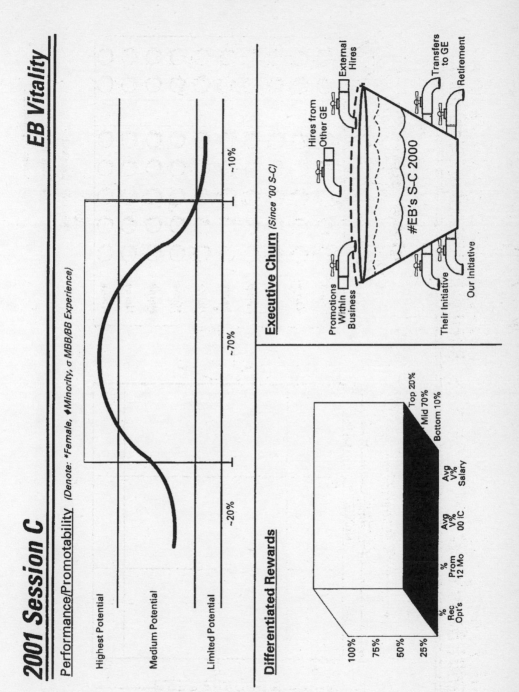

EB Vitality

2001 Session C

Performance/Promotability *(Denote: *Female, ♦Minority, σ MBB/BB Experience)*

Highest Potential

Medium Potential

Limited Potential

~20%   ~70%   ~10%

Executive Churn *(Since '00 S-C)*

External Hires

Hires from Other GE

Promotions Within Business

#EB's S-C 2000

Transfers to GE

Retirement

Their Initiative

Our Initiative

Differentiated Rewards

100%
75%
50%
25%

% Rec Opt's   % Prom 12 Mo   Avg V% 00 IC   Avg V% Salary

Top 20%
Mid 70%
Bottom 10%

John F. Welch
Chairman of the Board

General Electric Company
3135 Easton Turnpike, Fairfield, CT 06431

2/19/01

Dear Jeff,

Congratulations on everything --- Your year at Medical, your selection as CEO of the best Company in the world and the wonderful start you have in this new role. I knew you were really good ---- but you are even better than I could imagine.

Congratulations on the, $_____ --- it is just the beginning!

I look forward to cheering you on and will always be available when you feel it would be useful.

Very yours,

Jack

Dear Jeff,   2/13/00

    Congratulations on a sensational year. Your IC is $_____ up 41% over last year reflecting this. Attached are my comments on last year.

    For 2000, I think it is — — —

1.) More new products (DFSS)

2.) Better "operations" Cash, cost mgt. — — — Have to both grow & acquire — — — and get prepared for a rainy day. We can tighten up and really execute in 2000

3.) Make the Global Product Company a way of life — — Another year should really do this.

Jeff, Congratulations.   Jack

GE

John F. Welch
Chairman of the Board

General Electric Company
3135 Easton Turnpike, Fairfield, CT 06431

2/8/99

Dear Jeff,

Congratulations on sensational year! Your IC is $_____ up 42% reflecting this. My comments on last year's letter illustrate the wonderful results you had.

For '99.

1.) Integration is the name of the game. With Marquette, Elscint, and all the global service acquisite, this is the risk. If I were you, I would review progress on these formally at least once a month. Conclude later pt

Great job.

2.) Digital x-ray can change the whole game -- but ECK6 has to deliver as does the center. This game change after light speed can really open up the distance between ourselves & #2.

Wow! 2/29 will be Ed.

3.) I know you will make this once a huge deal. This is bigger than Med Systems for GE.

Yes

John F. Welch
Chairman of the Board

General Electric Company
3135 Easton Turnpike, Fairfield, CT 06431

2/8/99

Wonderful! 4.) Your customer GP focus on order to first image can be the company role model. Lightspeed touched a few --- this can touch them all.

You have it 5.) Ultrasound & Nuclear have gone from also-rans to real players. Be sure you use Session C to review their teams' capabilities --- Have the people matched the businesses growth?

Jeff, another great year. I like everything you are doing in every way. Call on me for anything. As I said last year, I want to help.

Best,

Jack

P.S. I'll be looking for your businesses' Internet ideas! --- New Distribution??

PPS. The "Global Product Company" is a huge deal. It will take enormous energy & decisiveness to make it happen.

GE

John F. Welch
Chairman of the Board

General Electric Company
3135 Easton Turnpike, Fairfield, CT 06431

2/16/98

Dear Jeff —

What a great year! Congratulation and your '97 IC of $_____ up 51% reflects my comments on the attached '97 letter.

As you look to '98 there are several things to focus on —

Appears to be going well!
1.) The ultrasound integration — We've never bought a silicon valley Co. and made it work. It must be nurtured by you personally + we can't lose external focus on the pieces.

You did it
2.) The initial take, success must be proliferated across full line.

Great!
3.) Europe must have another big Delta. We've had "fixes" before --- they just never lasted.

Lightspeed a huge hit!
4.) 60 must have another sensational business oriented year.

Wonderful job!
5.) The focus on services must continue and more acquisitions found. Differentiated pricing models must be developed to stop overall erosion from cro. A great opportunity

John F. Welch
Chairman of the Board

General Electric Company
3135 Easton Turnpike, Fairfield, CT 06431

2/16/98

Better 6.) I'd like to see us get L America and Mexico clarified organizatione. Mexico is a separate opportunity as is LA. They each need team.

Will see 7.) The Euro and Yr 2000 represent a chance for Larry first and you to set company role models. The Euro presents opportunities for harry to show we can get margin out of this change.

'99 is the year! 8.) Apollo is a huge deal — both as a product and the GE image. Push Lonnie on this and stay on him. The Mammo competitors will be hyping this.

Jeff — I loved the year you had and look for another spectacular one in 98. Your concise communications, willingness to learn & give were very special. I am available to play any role you want — just call on anything.
Have a great year.

Jack

OMM2001
Operating Managers Meeting

Business Agenda

**January 3-4, 2001
Operating Managers Meeting
Boca Raton, Florida**

January 3, 2001 – Day I

7:30	Opening Remarks	*Jack Welch*
	Financial Report	*Keith Sherin*
	Honeywell Update	*Dennis Dammerman*
	Integrity	*Ben Heineman*
	NBC Update	*Bob Wright*
	Break	

e-BUSINESS

Overview	*Jeff Immelt*

Make

Driving Productivity Through Digitization	*Denis Nayden* *John Rice* *Joe Hogan* *Dave Calhoun*
Break	

Sell

Changing Industry Structure	*Larry Johnston*
Growth Through Digitization	*Bill Meddaugh*

Buy

e-Sourcing Best Practices	*Lloyd Trotter*
e-Transactions	*Ted Torbeck*
Integration of Make Buy, Sell	*Rick Smith*

January 4, 2001 – Day II

7:30	Overview	*Jeff Immelt*

GLOBALIZATION

Global Best Practice Translations	*Gary Rogers*
Sourcing Intellect Globally	*Scott Donnelly*
Sourcing Services Globally	*Tiger VN Tyagarajan*
Global Sourcing and Digitization	*Marc Onetto*
Break	

SIX SIGMA

Overview	*Piet van Abeelen*
At the Customer	*David Joyce*
Price Management Using Span	*Charlene Begley*
Fulfillment Span	*Bill Driscoll*
Break	

SERVICES

The Installed Base Growth Opportunity	*George Oliver* *Ric Artigas* *Dennis Cooke* *Mike Neal*
Stretch Break	
Closing Remarks	*Jack Welch*

Index